Spiritual Narratives

THE SCHOMBURG LIBRARY OF
NINETEENTH-CENTURY BLACK WOMEN WRITERS

General Editor, Henry Louis Gates, Jr.

Titles are listed chronologically; collections that include works published over a span of years are listed according to the publication date of their initial work.

Spiritual Narratives

With an Introduction by
SUE E. HOUCHINS

New York   Oxford
OXFORD UNIVERSITY PRESS
1988

Oxford University Press

Oxford   New York   Toronto
Delhi   Bombay   Calcutta   Madras   Karachi
Petaling Jaya   Singapore   Hong Kong   Tokyo
Nairobi   Dar es Salaam   Cape Town
Melbourne   Auckland

and associated companies in
Beirut   Berlin   Ibadan   Nicosia

Library of Congress Cataloging-in-Publication Data

Spiritual narratives/introduction by Sue E. Houchins.
p.   cm.—(The Schomburg library of nineteenth-century black
women writers)
Contents: Productions of Mrs. Maria W. Stewart/presented to the
First African Baptist Church & Society—Religious experience and
journal of Mrs. Jarena Lee—A brand plucked from the fire/by
Mrs. Julia A. J. Foote—Twenty year's experience of a missionary/
by Virginia W. Broughton
1. Afro-American women—Biography.   2. Afro-American women—
Religion.   I. Houchins, Sue E.   II. Series.
BR1713.S65 1988   209'.22—dc19 [B]   87-31846

ISBN 0-19-505266-8
ISBN 0-19-505267-6 (set)

2 4 6 8 10 9 7 5 3 1

Printed in the United States of America
on acid-free paper

The
Schomburg Library
of
Nineteenth-Century
Black Women Writers
is
Dedicated
in Memory
of
PAULINE AUGUSTA COLEMAN GATES

1916–1987

PUBLISHER'S NOTE

FOREWORD
In Her Own Write

Henry Louis Gates, Jr.

One muffled strain in the Silent South, a jarring chord and a vague and uncomprehended cadenza has been and still is the Negro. And of that muffled chord, the one mute and voiceless note has been the sadly expectant Black Woman, ...

The "other side" has not been represented by one who "lives there." And not many can more sensibly realize and more accurately tell the weight and the fret of the "long dull pain" than the open-eyed but hitherto voiceless Black Woman of America.

. . . as our Caucasian barristers are not to blame if they cannot *quite* put themselves in the dark man's place, neither should the dark man be wholly expected fully and adequately to reproduce the exact Voice of the Black Woman.

—ANNA JULIA COOPER, *A Voice From the South* (1892)

The birth of the Afro-American literary tradition occurred in 1773, when Phillis Wheatley published a book of poetry. Despite the fact that her book garnered for her a remarkable amount of attention, Wheatley's journey to the printer had been a most arduous one. Sometime in 1772, a young African girl walked demurely into a room in Boston to undergo an oral examination, the results of which would determine the direction of her life and work. Perhaps she was shocked upon entering the appointed room. For there, perhaps gathered in a semicircle, sat eighteen of Boston's most notable citizens. Among them were John Erving, a prominent Boston merchant; the Reverend Charles Chauncy, pastor of the Tenth Congregational Church; and John Hancock, who would later gain fame for his signature on the Declaration of Independence. At the center of this group was His Excellency, Thomas Hutchinson, governor of Massachusetts, with Andrew Oliver, his lieutenant governor, close by his side.

Why had this august group been assembled? Why had it seen fit to summon this young African girl, scarcely eighteen years old, before it? This group of "the most respectable Characters in *Boston*," as it would later define itself, had assembled to question closely the African adolescent on the slender sheaf of poems that she claimed to have "written by herself." We can only speculate on the nature of the questions posed to the fledgling poet. Perhaps they asked her to identify and explain—for all to hear—exactly who were the Greek and Latin gods and poets alluded to so frequently in her work. Perhaps they asked her to conjugate a verb in Latin or even to translate randomly selected passages from the Latin, which she and her master, John Wheatley, claimed that she "had made some Progress in." Or perhaps they asked her to recite from memory key passages from the texts of John Milton and Alexander Pope, the two poets by whom the African claimed to be most directly influenced. We do not know.

We do know, however, that the African poet's responses were more than sufficient to prompt the eighteen august gentlemen to compose, sign, and publish a two-paragraph "Attestation," an open letter "To the Publick" that prefaces Phillis Wheatley's book and that reads in part:

> We whose Names are under-written, do assure the World, that the Poems specified in the following Page, were (as we

verily believe) written by Phillis, a young Negro Girl, who
was but a few Years since, brought an uncultivated Barbarian
from *Africa*, and has ever since been, and now is, under the
Disadvantage of serving as a Slave in a Family in this Town.
She has been examined by some of the best Judges, and is
thought qualified to write them.

So important was this document in securing a publisher for
Wheatley's poems that it forms the signal element in the
prefatory matter preceding her *Poems on Various Subjects, Religious and Moral,* published in London in 1773.

Without the published "Attestation," Wheatley's publisher
claimed, few would believe that an African could possibly
have written poetry all by herself. As the eighteen put the
matter clearly in their letter, "Numbers would be ready to
suspect they were not really the Writings of Phillis." Wheatley and her master, John Wheatley, had attempted to publish
a similar volume in 1772 in Boston, but Boston publishers
had been incredulous. One year later, "Attestation" in hand,
Phillis Wheatley and her master's son, Nathaniel Wheatley,
sailed for England, where they completed arrangements for
the publication of a volume of her poems with the aid of the
Countess of Huntington and the Earl of Dartmouth.

This curious anecdote, surely one of the oddest oral ex-
aminations on record, is only a tiny part of a larger, and
even more curious, episode in the Enlightenment. Since the
beginning of the sixteenth century, Europeans had wondered aloud whether or not the African "species of men," as
they were most commonly called, *could* ever create formal
literature, could ever master "the arts and sciences." If they
could, the argument ran, then the African variety of humanity was fundamentally related to the European variety. If not,
then it seemed clear that the African was destined by nature

to be a slave. This was the burden shouldered by Phillis Wheatley when she successfully defended herself and the authorship of her book against counterclaims and doubts.

Indeed, with her successful defense, Wheatley launched two traditions at once—the black American literary tradition *and* the black woman's literary tradition. If it is extraordinary that not just one but both of these traditions were founded simultaneously by a black woman—certainly an event unique in the history of literature—it is also ironic that this important fact of common, coterminous literary origins seems to have escaped most scholars.

That the progenitor of the black literary tradition was a woman means, in the most strictly literal sense, that all subsequent black writers have evolved in a matrilinear line of descent, and that each, consciously or unconsciously, has extended and revised a canon whose foundation was the poetry of a black woman. Early black writers seem to have been keenly aware of Wheatley's founding role, even if most of her white reviewers were more concerned with the implications of her race than her gender. Jupiter Hammon, for example, whose 1760 broadside "An Evening Thought. Salvation by Christ, With Penitential Cries" was the first individual poem published by a black American, acknowledged Wheatley's influence by selecting her as the subject of his second broadside, "An Address to Miss Phillis Wheatly [*sic*], Ethiopian Poetess, in Boston," which was published at Hartford in 1778. And George Moses Horton, the second Afro-American to publish a book of poetry in English (1829), brought out in 1838 an edition of his *Poems By A Slave* bound together with Wheatley's work. Indeed, for fifty-six years, between 1773 and 1829, when Horton published *The Hope of Liberty*, Wheatley was the *only* black person to have published a book of imaginative literature in English. So

central was this black woman's role in the shaping of the
Afro-American literary tradition that, as one historian has
maintained, the history of the reception of Phillis Wheatley's
poetry *is* the history of Afro-American literary criticism. Well
into the nineteenth century, Wheatley and the black literary
tradition were the same entity.

But Wheatley is not the only black woman writer who
stands as a pioneering figure in Afro-American literature.
Just as Wheatley gave birth to the genre of black poetry, Ann
Plato was the first Afro-American to publish a book of essays
(1841) and Harriet E. Wilson was the first black person to
publish a novel in the United States (1859).

Despite this pioneering role of black women in the tradition, however, many of their contributions before this century have been all but lost or unrecognized. As Hortense
Spillers observed as recently as 1983,

> With the exception of a handful of autobiographical narratives
> from the nineteenth century, the black woman's realities are
> virtually suppressed until the period of the Harlem Renais-
> sance and later. Essentially the black woman as artist, as
> intellectual spokesperson for her own cultural apprenticeship,
> has not existed before, for anyone. At the source of [their]
> own symbol-making task, [the community of black women
> writers] confronts, therefore, a tradition of work that is quite
> recent, its continuities, broken and sporadic.

Until now, it has been extraordinarily difficult to establish
the formal connections between early black women's writing
and that of the present, precisely because our knowledge of
their work has been broken and sporadic. Phillis Wheatley,
for example, while certainly the most reprinted and discussed
poet in the tradition, is also one of the least understood. Ann
Plato's seminal work, *Essays* (which includes biographies and
poems), has not been reprinted since it was published a cen-

tury and a half ago. And Harriet Wilson's *Our Nig,* her
compelling novel of a black woman's expanding consciousness in a racist Northern antebellum environment, never received even *one* review or comment at a time when virtually
all works written by black people were heralded by abolition-
ists as salient arguments against the existence of human slavery. Many of the books reprinted in this set experienced a
similar fate, the most dreadful fate for an author: that of
being ignored then relegated to the obscurity of the rare book
section of a university library. We can only wonder how
many other texts in the black woman's tradition have been
lost to this generation of readers or remain unclassified or
uncatalogued and, hence, unread.

This was not always so, however. Black women writers
dominated the final decade of the nineteenth century, perhaps
spurred to publish by an 1886 essay entitled "The Coming
American Novelist," which was published in *Lippincott's
Monthly Magazine* and written by "A Lady From Philadelphia." This pseudonymous essay argued that the "Great
American Novel" would be written by a black person. Her
argument is so curious that it deserves to be repeated:

> When we come to formulate our demands of the Coming
> American Novelist, we will agree that he must be native-
> born. His ancestors may come from where they will, but we
> must give him a birthplace and have the raising of him. Still,
> the longer his family has been here the better he will represent
> us. Suppose he should have no country but ours, no traditions
> but those he has learned here, no longings apart from us, no
> future except in our future—the orphan of the world, he
> finds with us his home. And with all this, suppose he refuses
> to be fused into that grand conglomerate we call the "Amer-
> ican type." With us, he is not of us. He is original, he has
> humor, he is tender, he is passive and fiery, he has been

taught what we call justice, and he has his own opinion about it. He has suffered everything a poet, a dramatist, a novelist need suffer before he comes to have his lips anointed. And with it all he is in one sense a spectator, a little out of the race. How would these conditions go towards forming an original development? In a word, suppose the coming novelist is of African origin? When one comes to consider the subject, there is no improbability in it. One thing is certain,—our great novel will not be written by the typical American.

An atypical American, indeed. Not only would the great American novel be written by an African-American, it would be written by an African-American *woman:*

Yet farther: I have used the generic masculine pronoun because it is convenient; but Fate keeps revenge in store. It was a woman who, taking the wrongs of the African as her theme, wrote the novel that awakened the world to their reality, and why should not the coming novelist be a woman as well as an African? She—the woman of that race—has some claims on Fate which are not yet paid up.

It is these claims on fate that we seek to pay by publishing The Schomburg Library of Nineteenth-Century Black Women Writers.

This theme would be repeated by several black women authors, most notably by Anna Julia Cooper, a prototypical black feminist whose 1892 *A Voice From the South* can be considered to be one of the original texts of the black feminist movement. It was Cooper who first analyzed the fallacy of referring to "the Black man" when speaking of black people and who argued that just as white men cannot speak through the consciousness of black men, neither can black *men* "fully and adequately . . . reproduce the exact Voice of the Black Woman." Gender and race, she argues, cannot be conflated, except in the instance of a black woman's voice, and it is this voice which must be uttered and to which we must listen. As Cooper puts the matter so compellingly:

> It is not the intelligent woman vs. the ignorant woman; nor the white woman vs. the black, the brown, and the red,—it is not even the cause of woman vs. man. Nay, 'tis woman's strongest vindication for speaking that *the world needs to hear her voice*. It would be subversive of every human interest that the cry of one-half the human family be stifled. Woman in stepping from the pedestal of statue-like inactivity in the domestic shrine, and daring to think and move and speak,— to undertake to help shape, mold, and direct the thought of her age, is merely completing the circle of the world's vision. Hers is every interest that has lacked an interpreter and a defender. Her cause is linked with that of every agony that has been dumb—every wrong that needs a voice.
>
> It is no fault of man's that he has not been able to see truth from her standpoint. It does credit both to his head and heart that no greater mistakes have been committed or even wrongs perpetrated while she sat making tatting and snipping paper flowers. Man's own innate chivalry and the mutual interdependence of their interests have insured his treating her cause, in the main at least, as his own. And he is pardonably surprised and even a little chagrined, perhaps, to find his legislation not considered "perfectly lovely" in every respect. But in any case his work is only impoverished by her remaining dumb. The world has had to limp along with the wobbling gait and one-sided hesitancy of a man with one eye. Suddenly the bandage is removed from the other eye and the whole body is filled with light. It sees a circle where before it saw a segment. The darkened eye restored, every member rejoices with it.

The myopic sight of the darkened eye can only be restored when the full range of the black woman's voice, with its own special timbres and shadings, remains mute no longer.

Similarly, Victoria Earle Matthews, an author of short stories and essays, and a cofounder in 1896 of the National Association of Colored Women, wrote in her stunning essay, "The Value of Race Literature" (1895), that "when the literature of our race is developed, it will of necessity be different in all essential points of greatness, true heroism and real Christianity from what we may at the present time, for convenience, call American literature." Matthews argued that this great tradition of Afro-American literature would be the textual outlet "for the unnaturally suppressed inner lives which our people have been compelled to lead." Once these "unnaturally suppressed inner lives" of black people are unveiled, no "grander diffusion of mental light" will shine more brightly, she concludes, than that of the articulate Afro-American woman:

> And now comes the question, What part shall we women play in the Race Literature of the future? . . . within the compass of one small journal ["Woman's Era"] we have struck out a new line of departure—a journal, a record of Race interests gathered from all parts of the United States, carefully selected, moistened, winnowed and garnered by the ablest intellects of educated colored women, shrinking at no lofty theme, shirking no serious duty, aiming at every possible excellence, and determined to do their part in the future uplifting of the race.
>
> If twenty women, by their concentrated efforts in one literary movement, can meet with such success as has engendered, planned out, and so successfully consummated this convention, what much more glorious results, what wider spread success, what grander diffusion of mental light will not come forth at the bidding of the enlarged hosts of women writers, already called into being by the stimulus of your efforts?
>
> And here let me speak one word for my journalistic sisters

who have already entered the broad arena of journalism. Before the "Woman's Era" had come into existence, no one except themselves can appreciate the bitter experience and sore disappointments under which they have at all times been compelled to pursue their chosen vocations.

If their brothers of the press have had their difficulties to contend with, I am here as a sister journalist to state, from the fullness of knowledge, that their task has been an easy one compared with that of the colored woman in journalism.

Woman's part in Race Literature, as in Race building, is the most important part and has been so in all ages. . . . All through the most remote epochs she has done her share in literature. . . .

One of the most important aspects of this set is the republication of the salient texts from 1890 to 1910, which literary historians could well call "The Black Woman's Era." In addition to Mary Helen Washington's definitive edition of Cooper's *A Voice From the South*, we have reprinted two novels by Amelia Johnson, Frances Harper's *Iola Leroy*, two novels by Emma Dunham Kelley, Alice Dunbar-Nelson's two impressive collections of short stories, and Pauline Hopkins's three serialized novels as well as her monumental novel, *Contending Forces*—all published between 1890 and 1910. Indeed, black women published more works of fiction in these two decades than black men had published in the previous half century. Nevertheless, this great achievement has been ignored.

Moreover, the writings of nineteenth-century Afro-American women in general have remained buried in obscurity, accessible only in research libraries or in overpriced and poorly edited reprints. Many of these books have never been reprinted at all; in some instances only one or two copies are extant. In these works of fiction, poetry, autobiography, biography, essays, and journalism resides the mind of the nineteenth-century Afro-American woman. Until these works are made readily available to teachers and their students, a significant segment of the black tradition will remain silent.

Oxford University Press, in collaboration with the Schomburg Center for Research in Black Culture, is publishing thirty volumes of these compelling works, each of which contains an introduction by an expert in the field. The set includes such rare texts as Johnson's *The Hazeley Family* and *Clarence and Corinne*, Plato's *Essays*, the most complete edition of Phillis Wheatley's poems and letters, Emma Dunham Kelley's pioneering novel *Megda*, several previously unpublished stories and a novel by Alice Dunbar-Nelson, and the first collected volumes of Pauline Hopkins's three serialized novels and Frances Harper's poetry. We also present four volumes of poetry by such women as Mary Eliza Tucker Lambert, Adah Menken, Josephine Heard, and Maggie Johnson. Numerous slave and spiritual narratives, a newly discovered novel—*Four Girls at Cottage City*—by Emma Dunham Kelley (-Hawkins), and the first American edition of *Wonderful Adventures of Mrs. Seacole in Many Lands* are also among the texts included.

In addition to resurrecting the works of black women authors, it is our hope that this set will facilitate the resurrection of the Afro-American woman's literary tradition itself by unearthing its nineteenth-century roots. In the works of Nella Larsen and Jessie Fauset, Zora Neale Hurston and Ann Petry, Lorraine Hansberry and Gwendolyn Brooks, Paule Marshall and Toni Cade Bambara, Audre Lorde and Rita Dove, Toni Morrison and Alice Walker, Gloria Naylor and Jamaica Kincaid, these roots have branched luxuriantly. The eighteenth- and nineteenth-century authors whose works are presented in this set founded and nurtured the black women's literary tradition, which must be revived, explicated, analyzed, and debated before we can understand more completely the formal shaping of this tradition within a tradition, a coded literary universe through which, regrettably, we are only just beginning to navigate our way. As Anna Cooper said nearly one hundred years ago, we have been blinded by the loss of sight in one eye and have therefore been unable to detect the full *shape* of the Afro-American literary tradition.

Literary works configure into a tradition not because of some mystical collective unconscious determined by the biology of race or gender, but because writers read other writers and *ground* their representations of experience in models of language provided largely by other writers to whom they feel akin. It is through this mode of literary revision, amply evident in the *texts* themselves—in formal echoes, recast metaphors, even in parody—that a "tradition" emerges and defines itself.

This is formal bonding, and it is only through formal bonding that we can know a literary tradition. The collective publication of these works by black women now, for the first time, makes it possible for scholars and critics, male and female, black and white, to *demonstrate* that black women writers read, and revised, other black women writers. To demonstrate this set of formal literary relations is to demonstrate that sexuality, race, and gender are both the condition and the basis of *tradition*—but tradition as found in discrete acts of language use.

A word is in order about the history of this set. For the past decade, I have taught a course, first at Yale and then at Cornell, entitled "Black Women and Their Fictions," a course that I inherited from Toni Morrison, who developed it in

the mid-1970s for Yale's Program in Afro-American Studies. Although the course was inspired by the remarkable accomplishments of black women novelists since 1970, I gradually extended its beginning date to the late nineteenth century,
studying Frances Harper's *Iola Leroy* and Anna Julia Cooper's *A Voice From the South*, both published in 1892. With
the discovery of Harriet E. Wilson's seminal novel, *Our Nig*
(1859), and Jean Yellin's authentication of Harriet Jacobs's
brilliant slave narrative, *Incidents in the Life of a Slave Girl*
(1861), a survey course spanning over a century and a quarter
emerged.

But the discovery of *Our Nig*, as well as the interest in
nineteenth-century black women's writing that this discovery
generated, convinced me that even the most curious and
diligent scholars knew very little of the extensive history
of the creative writings of Afro-American women before
1900. Indeed, most scholars of Afro-American literature
had never even read most of the books published by black
women, simply because these books—of poetry, novels, short
stories, essays, and autobiography—were mostly accessible only
in rare book sections of university libraries. For reasons un-
clear to me even today, few of these marvelous renderings of
the Afro-American woman's consciousness were reprinted in
the late 1960s and early 1970s, when so many other texts of
the Afro-American literary tradition were resurrected from
the dark and silent graveyard of the out-of-print and were
reissued in facsimile editions aimed at the hungry readership
for canonical texts in the nascent field of black studies.

So, with the help of several superb research assistants—
including David Curtis, Nicola Shilliam, Wendy Jones, Sam
Otter, Janadas Devan, Suvir Kaul, Cynthia Bond, Elizabeth
Alexander, and Adele Alexander—and with the expert advice

of scholars such as William Robinson, William Andrews, Mary Helen Washington, Maryemma Graham, Jean Yellin, Houston A. Baker, Jr., Richard Yarborough, Hazel Carby, Joan R. Sherman, Frances Foster, and William French, dozens of bibliographies were used to compile a list of books written or narrated by black women mostly before 1910. Without the assistance provided through this shared experience of scholarship, the scholar's true legacy, this project could not have been conceived. As the list grew, I was struck by how very many of these titles that I, for example, had never even heard of, let alone read, such as Ann Plato's *Essays*, Louisa Picquet's slave narrative, or Amelia Johnson's two novels, *Clarence and Corinne* and *The Hazeley Family*. Through our research with the Black Periodical Fiction and Poetry Project (funded by NEH and the Ford Foundation), I also realized that several novels by black women, including three works of fiction by Pauline Hopkins, had been serialized in black periodicals, but had never been collected and published as books. Nor had the several books of poetry published by black women, such as the prolific Frances E. W. Harper, been collected and edited. When I discovered still another "lost" novel by an Afro-American woman (*Four Girls at Cottage City*, published in 1898 by Emma Dunham Kelley-Hawkins), I decided to attempt to edit a collection of reprints of these works and to publish them as a "library" of black women's writings, in part so that I could read them myself.

Convincing university and trade publishers to undertake this project proved to be a difficult task. Despite the commercial success of *Our Nig* and of the several reprint series of women's works (such as Virago, the Beacon Black Women Writers Series, and Rutgers' American Women Writers Series), several presses rejected the project as "too large," "too limited," or as "commercially unviable." Only two publishers recognized the viability and the import of the project and, of these, Oxford's commitment to publish the titles simultaneously as a set made the press's offer irresistible.

While attempting to locate original copies of these exceedingly rare books, I discovered that most of the texts were housed at the Schomburg Center for Research in Black Culture, a branch of The New York Public Library, under the direction of Howard Dodson. Dodson's infectious enthusiasm for the project and his generous collaboration, as well as that of his stellar staff (especially Diana Lachatanere, Sharon Howard, Ellis Haizip, Richard Newman, and Betty Gubert), led to a joint publishing initiative that produced this set as part of the Schomburg's major fund-raising campaign. Without Dodson's foresight and generosity of spirit, the set would not have materialized. Without William P. Sisler's masterful editorship at Oxford and his staff's careful attention to detail, the set would have remained just another grand idea that tends to languish in a scholar's file cabinet.

I would also like to thank Dr. Michael Winston and Dr. Thomas C. Battle, Vice-President of Academic Affairs and the Director of the Moorland-Spingarn Research Center (respectively) at Howard University, for their unending encouragement, support, and collaboration in this project, and Esme E. Bhan at Howard for her meticulous research and bibliographical skills. In addition, I would like to acknowledge the aid of the staff at the libraries of Duke University, Cornell University (especially Tom Weissinger and Donald Eddy), the Boston Public Library, the Western Reserve Historical Society, the Library of Congress, and Yale University. Linda Robbins, Marion Osmun, Sarah Flanagan, and Gerard Case, all members of the staff at Oxford, were

extraordinarily effective at coordinating, editing, and producing the various segments of each text in the set. Candy
Ruck, Nina de Tar, and Phillis Molock expertly typed reams
of correspondence and manuscripts connected to the project.

I would also like to express my gratitude to my colleagues
who edited and introduced the individual titles in the set.
Without their attention to detail, their willingness to meet
strict deadlines, and their sheer enthusiasm for this project,
the set could not have been published. But finally and ulti-
mately, I would hope that the publication of the set would
help to generate even more scholarly interest in the black
women authors whose work is presented here. Struggling
against the seemingly insurmountable barriers of racism *and*
sexism, while often raising families and fulfilling full-time
professional obligations, these women managed nevertheless
to record their thoughts and feelings and to *testify* to all who
dare read them that the will to harness the power of collective
endurance and survival is the will to write.

The Schomburg Library of Nineteenth-Century Black
Women Writers is dedicated in memory of Pauline Augusta
Coleman Gates, who died in the spring of 1987. It was she
who inspired in me the love of learning and the love of literature. I have encountered in the books of this set no will
more determined, no courage more noble, no mind more
sublime, no self more celebratory of the achievements of all
Afro-American women, and indeed of life itself, than her
own.

A NOTE FROM
THE SCHOMBURG CENTER

Howard Dodson

The Schomburg Center for Research in Black Culture, The New York Public Library, is pleased to join with Dr. Henry Louis Gates and Oxford University Press in presenting The Schomburg Library of Nineteenth-Century Black Women Writers. This thirty-volume set includes the work of a generation of black women whose writing has only been available previously in rare book collections. The materials reprinted in twenty-four of the thirty volumes are drawn from the unique holdings of the Schomburg Center.

A research unit of The New York Public Library, the Schomburg Center has been in the forefront of those institutions dedicated to collecting, preserving, and providing access to the records of the black past. In the course of its two generations of acquisition and conservation activity, the Center has amassed collections totaling more than 5 million items. They include over 100,000 bound volumes, 85,000 reels and sets of microforms, 300 manuscript collections containing some 3.5 million items, 300,000 photographs and extensive holdings of prints, sound recordings, film and videotape, newspapers, artworks, artifacts, and other book and nonbook materials. Together they vividly document the history and cultural heritages of people of African descent worldwide.

Though established some sixty-two years ago, the Center's book collections date from the sixteenth century. Its oldest item, an Ethiopian Coptic Tunic, dates from the eighth or ninth century. Rare materials, however, are most available for the nineteenth-century African-American experience. It is from these holdings that the majority of the titles selected for inclusion in this set are drawn.

The nineteenth century was a formative period in African-American literary and cultural history. Prior to the Civil War, the majority of black Americans living in the United States were held in bondage. Law and practice forbade teaching them to read or write. Even after the war, many of the impediments to learning and literary productivity remained. Nevertheless, black men and women of the nineteenth century persevered in both areas. Moreover, more African-Americans than we yet realize turned their observations, feelings, social viewpoints, and creative impulses into published works. In time, this nineteenth-century printed record included poetry, short stories, histories, novels, autobiographies, social criticism, and theology, as well as economic and philosophical treatises. Unfortunately, much of this body of literature remained, until very recently, relatively inaccessible to twentieth-century scholars, teachers, creative artists, and others interested in black life. Prior to the late 1960s, most Americans (black as well as white) had never heard of these nineteenth-century authors, much less read their works.

The civil rights and black power movements created unprecedented interest in the thought, behavior, and achievements of black people. Publishers responded by revising traditional texts, introducing the American public to a new generation of African-American writers, publishing a variety of thematic anthologies, and reprinting a plethora of "classic texts" in African-American history, literature, and art. The reprints usually appeared as individual titles or in a series of bound volumes or microform formats.

The Schomburg Center, which has a long history of supporting publishing that deals with the history and culture of Africans in diaspora, became an active participant in many of the reprint revivals of the 1960s. Since hard copies of original printed works are the preferred formats for producing facsimile reproductions, publishers frequently turned to the Schomburg Center for copies of these original titles. In addition to providing such material, Schomburg Center staff members offered advice and consultation, wrote introductions, and occasionally entered into formal copublishing arrangements in some projects.

Most of the nineteenth-century titles reprinted during the 1960s, however, were by and about black men. A few black women were included in the longer series, but works by lesser known black women were generally overlooked. The Schomburg Library of Nineteenth-Century Black Women Writers is both a corrective to these previous omissions and an important contribution to Afro-American literary history in its own right. Through this collection of volumes, the thoughts, perspectives, and creative abilities of nineteenth-century African-American women, as captured in books and pamphlets published in large part before 1910, are again being made available to the general public. The Schomburg Center is pleased to be a part of this historic endeavor.

I would like to thank Professor Gates for initiating this project. Thanks are due both to him and Mr. William P. Sisler of Oxford University Press for giving the Schomburg Center an opportunity to play such a prominent role in the set. Thanks are also due to my colleagues at The New York Public Library and the Schomburg Center, especially Dr. Vartan Gregorian, Richard De Gennaro, Paul Fasana, Betsy

Pinover, Richard Newman, Diana Lachatanere, Glenderlyn Johnson, and Harold Anderson for their assistance and support. I can think of no better way of demonstrating than in this set the role the Schomburg Center plays in assuring that the black heritage will be available for future generations.

CONTENTS

INTRODUCTION

Sue E. Houchins

When Maria W. Stewart (1835), Jarena Lee (1836 and 1849),[1] Julia A. J. Foote (1879 and 1886),[2] and Virginia W. Broughton (1907) published their meditations and religious autobiographies—seized *author*ity—they laid claim to their rights as citizens and assumed places for themselves in the literary history of two beseiged *imperia in imperio*—the nation of women and the nation of Africans (blacks) within the patriarchal "empire" of the USA. These women were convinced—like Afro-American writers of the preceding seventy-five years, as well as female testifier-revivalists of the Second Awakening (1795–1830), women evangelists of the Holiness Movement (1835–1930s), and even prayerfully exhortative anchoresses and women mystical chroniclers from such far-removed times as the Middle Ages and the Counter-Reformation—that, in choosing the autobiographical genre to depict their religious conversion and consequent manumission from the bondage of sin, they had entered into a discourse that would produce both a comparable spiritual and a political metanoia in their "promiscuous"[3] reader-audience.

The goal of black autobiography had never been just an attempt at an "objective reconstruction of an individual's past or a public demonstration of the qualities of selfhood or a private meditation on the meaning of a life of struggle." It had also sought to be discursive by initiating a dialogue with those who doubted the very existence of black folks' souls—not to mention the possibility of their redemption[4]—to participate in what Henry Louis Gates, Jr., calls "the Discourse of the Black Other," that "complex intertextual Signifyin(g) relation" between eighteenth- and nineteenth-century European and American writers who doubted the humanity of blacks and their black interlocutor-authors.[5] For African-American female evangelical writers, the intertextual network of repetition and revision was further complicated by several factors. First, as blacks, they appealed to the same audiences as early male writers of the same race—that is, to both the aforementioned whites who doubted the capacity of Afro-Americans for learning, managing freedom responsibly, and indeed for religious salvation, and to disheartened blacks who had rejected conversion to Christianity and had not learned the value of living virtuously.[6] Second, as women, they addressed the entire patriarchy, black and white, like their revivalists sisters.[7] And third, as both black and female, they sought valorization for their arguments, like the black men and white women autobiographers who preceded them, from the same authenticating text, the Bible. In addition, the discursive autobiographical form was particularly suited to, and a logical extension of, these women's vocation to preach, teach, pray publicly, and testify. It retained the orality of both their homiletic exhortations—lively conflations of Biblical texts with personal accounts of how God's grace infused their spirits and worked in their *lives* to effect an "ontological transformation"—and their prayers, the "consecration of words," that "ontological necessity" which is the "act of self-purification"[8] by the making of one's *life* an oblation to God.

It is through its foundations in discursive prayer that the black woman's spiritual autobiography traces its relationship as "distant cousin . . . to the Puritan Narrative,"[9] which according to Jonathan Edwards, an eminent practitioner of the art, is composed in "solitary places" while engaged in "meditation, soliloquy, and *prayer*, and *converse* with God" (italics mine).[10] Further, despite their origins in Protestant religious literary genres, "these genuinely American forms," the Puritan and black spiritual narratives, as well as the more famous slave narratives they antedate,

> are the offspring of that hoary confession by the first philo-
> sophical black writer: Saint Augustine. In *The Confessions* we
> notice (and perceive also in the Slave and Puritan [and
> Spiritual] Narratives) a nearly Platonic movement from ig-
> norance to wisdom, nonbeing to being. No form . . . loses
> its *ancestry;* rather, these meanings accumulate in layers of
> tissue as the form evolves. (Johnson, p. 119)

And through this kinship with Augustine's work,[11] a literary genealogist can trace the lineage of early black women's self-writing to the writings of their visionary sister autobiographers who wrote during the Middle Ages and the Counter-Reformation—e.g., Christina of Markyate (twelfth century), Julian of Norwich (1342–c. 1420), Margery Kempe (c. 1373–1438), and Teresa of Avila (1515–1582). Even the allegedly unlettered Maria Stewart acknowledges her spiritual legacy from these women of long ago:

> In the 15th century, the general spirit of this period is
> worthy of observation. We might then have seen women
> preaching and mixing themselves in controversies. Women
> occupying the chairs of Philosophy and Justice; women ha-
> rangueing in Latin before the Pope; women writing in Greek
> and studying Hebrew; Nuns were Poetesses, and women of
> quality Divines; and young girls who studied Eloquence,
> would with the sweetest countenances, and most plaintive
> voices exhort the Pope and the Christian Princes. . . .
> Women in those days devoted their leisure hours to contem-
> plation and study.

The dictated texts of Christina of Markyate and Margery Kempe's lives and the book of contemplations or *Showings* by Julian of Norwich numbered among the earliest examples of the autobiographical form in English. These women sought to document in their self-writing their quests for perfection through mystical union and the concomitant rise to a sense of empowerment to claim a space in medieval society where, like the black women revivalists of subsequent centuries, they could "function as person[s] of authority," could resist the pressures of family and society, thereby rejecting the politics of gender, and could achieve legal and structural support from the church for their work as spiritual advisors, teachers, and occasional preachers.[12] For example, regardless of marital status, all these women were "virgins," if one uses the "ancient meaning" for the word; each was "she-who-is-unto-herself," a woman who defined herself "by choice, neither in relation to children nor to men, who was self-identified, who had chosen herself."[13] Christina of Markyate rejected the young nobleman to whom her parents betrothed her and embraced a life as a celibate anchoress; Dame Julian was also a celibate recluse. However, Margery Kempe, "the most controversial of the English mystics," was married to John Kempe and bore him fourteen children, but her search for sanctity led her to embark on pilgrimages alone, to seek permission to take the vow of marital chastity, and finally to live apart from her husband.[14]

By comparison, of the four religious black women autobiographers whose works are included in this volume, three (Stewart, Lee, and Foote) achieved release from the "escalating battle of wills over the propriety of . . . [a wife's] religious activism" (Andrews, *Sisters*, p. 18) through the death of their husbands, and one, Mrs. Broughton, simply defied her husband until he became reconciled to her vocation. When an irate Mr. Broughton inquired how long it would take before that evangelism "business would stop," his wife replied, "I belong to God first, and you next, so you two must settle it." Furthermore, in keeping with their status as "virgins," these black women evangelists placed themselves in even greater jeopardy of censure by forsaking their sick children to fulfill speaking obligations elsewhere. Upon returning home from a preaching tour, Jarena Lee "found all well; no harm had come to [her sick] child," so she took this for a sign that she should break up housekeeping, leave her children with friends, and forsake all to continue evangelizing. On the other hand, when Virginia Broughton decided to cancel a speaking obligation to tend to her ailing daughter, she "was made to see plainly that she could stay home and sit by the bedside of her children and have all the assistance that medical skill could render, and yet God could take her children to himself if he so willed it." As a result, after the death of that child, she missed no other speaking engagements.

Clearly, it was confidence in the privileged nature of their relationship with God, which the early mystics and the sanctified black women enjoyed, that freed both groups to reject the gender roles of their respective societies. The simplest definition of the mystical experience is an individual's recognition or consciousness of her union with the Divine and, through the Divine, with all of creation. The path toward mystical union is threefold. First, during a period of purification, the individual recalls her past life, reviews her autobiographical data—so to speak—attains profound self-knowledge, and is overcome with remorse. Second, along the mystic way, God enlightens her, reveals to her esoteric theological truths, sometimes bestows a gift of deeply erotic visions, which symbolize the depth of their shared mystical love, and promises her eternal salvation. And third, the mystic is profoundly affected and permanently transformed (sanctified) by the experience. For example, in Teresa of Avila's *Way of Perfection* and in *Showings'* Revelation XIII, which depicts Dame Julian's illuminative experience, the mystics "saw," were brought to understand the controversial principle of " 'godly will,' as it is found in all those [mystical] souls who are to form one soul with the heavenly host, and who have love for one another in Christ"; the "godly will" is present in all of those who achieve spiritual *perfection* as a result of transforming union and, thus, can never *will* evil, "but always good." [15]

This theological principle of "godly will" as expounded by Julian and her predecessor William of St. Thierry (whom John Wesley, cofounder of Methodism, studied during his time in Oxford) found expression three hundred years later in the Methodist spiritual doctrine of "sanctification." Both John and Charles Wesley and their followers during the Second Awakening and the Holiness Movement maintained that the soul "pilgrimaged" toward "Christian perfection" or evolved in accordance with a prescribed "order of salvation." After a prolonged period of self-doubt, each person was "graced" with the knowledge that her sins were forgiven and she was "justified" before God. Finally, through the inter-action of faith, hope, and most importantly, love, the soul was gifted with "a new birth"; the person was given the "assurance" that she was "on the way," and she received " 'sanctification'—the sharing in the divine nature, dwelling in God, attaining perfect love for God and [humanity], and entering into Christ's glorification. . . . Christian perfection [sanctification] was utter surrender and resignation to the will of God." So pervasive was the acceptance of the Wesleyan tenet of "sanctification" that all four black women spiritual autobiographers claimed to have experienced the assurance of "Christian perfection," though only two (Lee and Foote) professed to be Methodists (AME).

Some scholars have insisted on a difference between the two spiritual traditions represented by the medieval mystics and the black women revivalists of the nineteenth century and have characterized the former as contemplative and monastic and the latter as actively evangelical or missionary. However, both traditions share an "emphasis on the workings of the Spirit in the inner life, on the psychology of spiritual response, and on an intimate experience of Jesus."[16] In other words, at the core of both mystical traditions is the belief in the profound union of God with humanity, which is a reflection of that essential, central Christian teaching of the incarnation—the symbolic (and maybe historical) enfleshment of God in the person of Christ.

Therefore, the piety of all of the "sisters of the spirit"[17] (medieval and revivalist) was not only Pentecostal but also "Christocentric, a theology of love that found its supreme expression in the incarnation." This incarnational aspect of union allowed the mystic to recognize "the male sex of the historical Jesus [while] find[ing] the cohumanity by which she shared his human nature not in maleness, but in the capacity of suffering, a capacity beyond but not excluding sexuality" (McLaughlin, "Christian Past," p. 101). The effect of this profound identification was to prompt mystics to experiment with new ways of envisioning and naming their kinship with Christ. Theodora of Markyate changed her name to Christina. Maria Stewart occasionally apostrophizes the Deity, in gender-inclusive language, as "Parent," and the more *linguistically* radical Julian calls Jesus "Mother":

The human mother will suckle her child with her own milk, but our beloved Mother, Jesus, feeds us with himself, and with most tender courtesy, does it by means of the Blessed Sacrament, the precious food of true life. . . . The human mother may put her child tenderly to her breast, but our Mother Jesus simply leads us into his blessed breast through his open side, and there gives us a glimpse of the Godhead and heavenly joy, the inner certainty of eternal bliss. (Julian, p. 298)

The image of Mother Jesus ceases to startle when it is understood as one in a set of metaphors and symbols chosen by women as the appropriate vehicles to "express their relationship to the transcendent in language that reflected [some of their] dominant experiences" (McLaughlin, "Christian Past," p. 100). Therefore, it is fitting that the most prevalent image in women's mystical literature is the mystical marriage—e.g., in Christina of Markyate, Teresa of Avila, and in Julia Foote, who quotes Isaiah, "For thy Maker is thine husband."

In addition, if the doctrine of the incarnation and the possibility of its expression in the flesh of all humans through mystical union was one way Christians dignified the body as the temple of the Holy Spirit, and if these theological mysteries of enfleshment were symbolized in the figure of marriage, then it follows that this metaphor would eventually accrete erotic imagery to itself. Such was the case with Christina of Markyate, who envisioned a visitation of the Christ Child and conflated it with an appearance of Jesus as spouse/lover:

For in the guise of a small child, He came to the arms of his sorely tried spouse and remained with her the whole day, not only being felt but also seen. So the maiden took Him in her hands, gave thanks and pressed Him to her bosom. And with measurable delight she held Him at one moment to her virginal breast, at another she felt His presence within her flesh.[18]

Portions of the autobiographies of Lee and Foote verge on the erotic when the metaphor of nudity to express both vulnerability and innocence is coupled with the sensuous depiction of nakedness and ecstasy to create a dynamic tension. For example, in the following ambiguous passage, the audience of Jarena Lee must read, "That instant, it appeared to me as if a garment, which had entirely enveloped my whole person, even to my fingers' ends, split at the crown of my head, and was stripped away from me, passing like a shadow from my sight—when the glory of God seemed to cover me," against the statement two lines later, "Great was the ecstasy of my mind." One should compare the preceding text with a similar spiritual baptism passage by Julia Foote that reveals a certain sensuousness:

> My hand was given to Christ, who led me into the water and stripped me of my clothing, which at once vanished from sight. Christ then appeared to wash me, the water feeling quite warm. . . . When the washing was ended, the sweetest music I had ever heard greeted my ears. We walked to the shore, where an angel stood with a clean, white robe, which the Father at once put on me.

Images of the body abound and, indeed, are appropriate in texts dealing with incarnational theology, which asserts that "the Word was made flesh." That is to say, the *Logos,* the Word—not simply the utterance but the breath/the spirit of the Creator—not only is spoken/breathed into the world, but also the world is heard in return through the intercession of the incarnational, Christic being. The incarnation, then, is discursive like prayer, like autobiography. And one site of this discourse is woman's body—sometimes the sick body (Julian, Teresa, Lee, Foote, and Broughton), sometimes the involuntarily fasting body (Teresa, Lee, Foote, and Broughton), and sometimes the figural bosom and heart upon which God's angelic messenger wrote the text of Lee's and Foote's license to preach. If the critic allowed herself to indulge in the dubious tendency to "secularize," to "medicalize," and to "psychologize" sacred experience, she, in consultation with her colleague Caroline Walker Bynum, would diagnose these women mystics as hysterics who, according to Freud, "suffer[ed] mainly from [sinful] reminiscences"—from their autobiographies—and who wrote their herstories through their symptoms across their bodies.[19]

According to feminist theologian Nelle Morton, the entire argument for women's right to preach the Word, to testify about God out of their own experiences, and to read the Christ-story into and as their own personal story could only be advanced if the theologian examined and rethought the incarnation in the light of a "feminist-style hermeneutic" and only if she first confronted

> the woman herself—her flesh and blood self. Her body had to be dealt with before she would be allowed to preach or before the word could be heard from her as Word. "This is my body . . ." Whose body? Which body? What kind of voice is necessary to proclaim the word? What ear hears it? When is the word Word?[20]

Further, Morton reasons, those who envisioned *Logos* deified as male were those who saw religion and religious experience only in terms of hierarchy and who thus misinterpreted mysticism as possession and not as union. They reduced incarnational discourse to "a one-way relationship—that of *speak*-ing—and bypass[ed] the far more radical aspect of *hearing!* . . . The more divine act is *hearing to speech* rather than *speaking to hearing*. . . . The Transcendent One hears the human being to speech . . . and creates new personhood" (Morton, pp. 54–55).

The operating principle by which the reader decodes the feminist spiritual autobiographical project, then, is found in the word "discourse," for the mystical/incarnational experience about which the spiritual woman wrote and preached was discursive. Her autobiography was written as a dialogue (note the passages directly addressed to the audience), and it sought to imitate her exhortations, which were delivered in hopes of evoking conversions and other personal testimonies/ autobiographies from her congregations. Further, her autobiography was her prayer, for "prayer is not soliloquy. . . . [It is making] ourselves communicable to [God]. Prayer is an emanation of what is most precious in us toward [God]. . . . Prayer is an answer to God: 'Here am I. And this is the record of my days' " (Heschel, p. 10). Prayer is call and response, response and call, a sacred blues. The religious reader of the spiritual autobiographies understood them as prayer and prayer as autobiography. Readers therefore perceived Maria Stewart's *Productions*—a collection of homiletic meditations and prayers—as autobiography, for the devout needed only to call to mind a generic prayer:

> Holy One of Being hear my petition; hark unto me. You have known me from all eternity. You know my sins, and you are aware of my contrition. I place my life before You and ask that You transform it, that you give me courage to confront, to name, and to change the political injustices in this world [racism and sexism]. Empower me to stand in solidarity with all of Your people and, in particular, with those members of Your community who share a common heritage with me—all Blacks and all women.

Julia Foote and Jarena Lee recognized that worship was to be heard into selfhood by God, and thus "the Pentecost story reverses the going logic and puts hearing before speaking as the work of the spirit" (Morton, p. 128). So when, early in their spiritual lives, they encountered silence, they knew that this was not an instance of *deus absconditus* but of a God listening—waiting to hear their requests before speaking. For example, Lee heard a small holy voice say, "Ask for sanctification," as though the Divine was prompting, "Girl, tell me what you want." Obviously, once a woman was bold enough to demand and to receive assurance of her sanctification from God, her courage was boundless, and she was empowered to believe that her story was significant enough to repeat across the land as well as to defy and to combat the political forces of slavery (racism, in general) and sexism.

The motif of travel and journey is an integral part of the Stewart, Lee, Foote, and Broughton autobiographies for a number of reasons. First, in modeling their lives after the apostles, these women took seriously Christ's command to go empty-handed into the world to spread the Gospel. Second, as women and as blacks, they professed the naive faith that their stories, texts from which they discovered their "relation to the divine, to one another, and to the self,"[21] were part of the great *true* story—myth, which metaphorizes as the quest journey the human search for meaning in life "through multiple layers of spiritual evolution" (Andrews, *Free Story*, p. 7). And finally, these women inherited "the sense of otherness, or the sense of the other that has arisen out of the black [and female] experience" and that is "present when . . . black communities contemplate the meaning of America as a free society." To be free in America would mean the society would "indeed have to become a radically different

one, *an-other* place," "*an-other space.*"[22] As such, these itin-
erant black women preachers whose autobiographies occasionally read like travelogues—or in the case of Maria Stewart,
a mournful adieu upon embarkation—were living out on the
geographical landscape the metaphor of their psychic and
spiritual journey, were literalizing the quest for a locus of
freedom, a place—a "de-sexed" pulpit that "can no longer be
labeled as the phallic symbol in the sanctuary with the Book
on top" (Morton, p. 49)—from which to speak and to be
heard. Since few such places existed then or exist now, they
had to content themselves, as we must content ourselves now,
with the knowledge that the "journey [itself] is home"
(Morton, pp. xvii, xviii).

NOTES

1. The 1836 edition of *Religious Experience and Journal of Mrs.
Jarena Lee* was recently reissued in a volume entitled *Sisters of the
Spirit*, which was edited by William L. Andrews (Bloomington,
Ind.: Indiana University Press, 1986). This collection *(Spiritual
Narratives)* uses the later 1849 text, which Andrews says "reads
very much like a log of distances traveled" (p. 23). It is my
contention that the travelbook quality of the autobiography empha-
sizes the theme of the woman preacher's literal search for a locus
from which to speak.
2. The 1879 edition of *A Brand Plucked from the Fire* was also
published in *Sisters of the Spirit*.
3. Dorothy Sterling, ed., *We Are Your Sisters* (New York: W.
W. Norton and Company, 1984), p. 154. Maria Stewart's speech
delivered "in Boston's Franklin Hall on September 21, 1832, was
the first public lecture by an American woman" to a mixed (promiscuous) audience—men and women, black and white. All of these

black women evangelists speak about their occasional mixed audiences, and since this introduction argues that the autobiographies in this collection are imitations, written extensions of these women's sermons, testimonies, and exhortations, the mixed audience implies that the texts were produced for a mixed readership.

4. William L. Andrews, *To Tell a Free Story* (Urbana and Chicago: University of Chicago Press, 1986), p. 17.

5. Henry Louis Gates, Jr., *Figures in Black* (New York: Oxford University Press, 1987) p. 49.

6. Andrews notes that spiritual autobiographies by males antedated "fugitive slave narratives by almost fifty years." The religious writings of "James Gronnisaw (1770), John Marrant (1785), and George White (1810) gave the twin themes of the Afro-American 'pregeneric myth'—knowledge and freedom—their earliest narrative form." *Sisters of the Spirit,* p. 1. In Maria Stewart's *Productions,* the author declares her discipleship of David Walker.

7. Nancy Hardesty, Lucille Sider Dayton, and Donald W. Dayton,"Women in the Holiness Movement: Feminism in the Evangelical Tradition," in Reuther and McLaughlin, eds., *Women of Spirit* (New York: Simon and Schuster, 1979), pp. 226–54. Jarena Lee mentioned Mrs. Mary Fletcher as a precedent for women preachers. Fletcher's "life story became must reading in nineteenth-century American Holiness circles" (p. 228). Contemporary with Stewart, Lee, and Foote was the famous black woman evangelical preacher, Amanda Berry Smith. Martha Tomhave Blauvelt, "Women and Revivalism," in Reuther and Keller, eds., *Women and Religion in America, Volume 1: The Nineteenth Century* (New York: Harper and Row, 1982), pp. 1–45.

8. Abraham Joshua Heschel, *Man's Quest for God* (New York: Charles Scribner's Sons, 1954), pp. xii, xiii.

9. Charles Johnson, *Oxherding Tale* (New York: Grove Press, Inc., 1984), pp. 118–19.

10. Jonathan Edwards, *Personal Narrative,* in George McMichael, ed., *Anthology of American Literature,* vol. 1 (New York: Macmillan, 1974), p. 228.

11. David A. Fleming, S. M., ed., *The Fire and the Cloud* (New York: Paulist Press, 1978), pp. 53–54.

12. Eleanor L. McLaughlin, "Women Power and the Pursuit of Holiness in Medieval Christianity," in Reuther and McLaughlin, *Women of Spirit*, pp. 100–130; and Eleanor L. McLaughlin, "The Christian Past: Does it Hold a Future for Women?" in Christ and Plaskow, eds., *Womanspirit Rising* (San Francisco: 1979), pp. 93–106.

13. Adrienne Rich, *Of Woman Born* (New York: Bantam Books, 1981), p. 253.

14. Maureen Fries, "Margery Kempe," in Paul Szarmach, ed., *An Introduction to the Medieval Mystics of Europe* (Albany: State University of New York, 1984), p. 217.

15. Julian of Norwich, *Showings* (New York: Paulist Press, 1978), pp. 241–42.

16. Frank Whaling, intro. and ed., *John and Charles Wesley* (New York: Paulist Press, 1981), pp. 45–51. David Lyle Jeffrey, ed., *A Burning and a Shining Light* (Grand Rapids: William B. Erdman Publishing Company, 1987), pp. 24–25. Much has been made of the difference between the monastic meditative spirituality and the active missionary mystic, between spiritual quest and social quest. However, this author believes these are false dichotomies because anyone familiar with the history of the monastic mystics, who were bound by a vow of stability, is aware of how often they left their cloisters to dabble in church and secular politics and to evangelize. Teresa of Avila, Catherine of Siena, and John of the Cross were just three of many. In addition, Carol Christ maintains that the social quest is dependent upon spiritual quest. The two are interwoven. Carol Christ, *Diving Deep and Surfacing* (Boston: Beacon Press, 1980), pp. 8, 11–12.

17. Obviously, this is a reference to Andrews' book and to the Pentecostal nature of the Holiness Movement. An emphasis on the spirit does not invalidate the incarnational aspect of their mysticism. One must remember that Christ sends the Pentecostal spirit.

18. Charles H. Talbot, trans. and ed., *The Life of Christina of*

Markyate: A Twelfth Century Recluse (Oxford: Clarendon Press, 1959), p. 119.

19. Caroline Walker Bynum, *Holy Feast and Holy Fast: The Religious Significance of Food to Medieval Women* (Berkeley: University of California Press, 1987), pp. 194–207; Charles Bernheimer and Claire Kahane, eds., *In Dora's Case: Freud—Hysteria—Feminism* (New York: Columbia University Press, 1985), pp. 1–32; and Jane Gallop, "Keys to Dora," in Bernheimer and Kahane, pp. 200–220.

20. Nelle Morton, *The Journey Is Home* (Boston: Beacon Press, 1985), pp. 40–55. I want to pay tribute to Nelle Morton, my mentor, who died during the writing of this introduction.

21. Lynda Sexson, *Ordinarily Sacred* (New York: Crossroad, 1982), p. 26.

22. Charles H. Long, *Significations: Signs, Symbols, and Images in the Interpretation of Religion* (Philadelphia: Fortress Press, 1986), p. 153.

PRODUCTIONS

OF

MRS. MARIA W. STEWART.

PRODUCTIONS

OF

MRS. MARIA W. STEWART,

PRESENTED TO THE

FIRST AFRICAN BAPTIST CHURCH & SOCIETY,

Of the City of Boston.

BOSTON:
PUBLISHED BY FRIENDS OF FREEDOM AND VIRTUE.
. . . .
1835.

RELIGION

AND THE

PURE PRINCIPLES OF MORALITY,

THE SURE FOUNDATION ON WHICH WE MUST BUILD.

INTRODUCTION.

FEELING a deep solemnity of soul, in view of our wretched and degraded situation, and sensible of the gross ignorance that prevails among us, I have thought proper thus publicly to express my sentiments before you. I hope my friends will not scrutinize these pages with too severe an eye, as I have not calculated to display either elegance or taste in their composition, but have merely written the meditations of my heart as far as my imagination led; and have presented them before you, in order to arouse you to exertion, and to enforce upon your minds the great necessity of turning your attention to knowledge and improvement.

I was born in Hartford, Connecticut, in 1803; was left an orphan at five years of age; was bound out in a clergyman's family; had the seeds of piety and virtue early sown in my mind; but was deprived of the advantages of education, though my soul thirsted for knowledge. Left them at 15 years of age; attended Sabbath Schools until I was 20; in 1826, was married to James W. Steward; was left a widow in 1829; was, as I humbly hope and trust, brought to the knowledge of the truth, as it is in Jesus, in 1830; in 1831, made a public profession of my faith in Christ.

From the moment I experienced the change, I felt a strong desire, with the help and assistance of God, to devote the remainder of my days to piety and virtue, and now possess that spirit of independence, that, were I called upon, I would willingly sacrifice my life for the cause of God and my brethren.

All the nations of the earth are crying out for Liberty and Equality. Away, away with tyranny and oppression! And shall Afric's sons be silent any longer? Far be it from me to recommend to you, either to kill, burn, or destroy. But I would strongly recommend to you, to improve your talents; let not one lie buried in the earth. Show forth your powers of mind. Prove to the world, that

> Though black your skins as shades of night,
> Your hearts are pure, your souls are white.

This is the land of freedom. The press is at liberty. Every man has a right to express his opinion. Many think, because your skins are tinged with a sable hue, that you are an inferior race of beings; but God does not consider you as such. He hath formed and fashioned you in his own glorious image, and hath bestowed upon you reason and strong powers of intellect. He hath made you to have dominion over the beasts of the field, the fowls of the air, and the fish of the sea. He hath crowned you with glory and honor; hath made you but a little lower than the angels; and, according to the Constitution of these United States, he hath made all men free and equal. Then why should one worm say to another, "Keep you down there, while I sit up yonder; for I am better than thou?" It is not the color of the skin that makes the man, but it is the principles formed within the soul.

Many will suffer for pleading the cause of oppressed Africa, and I shall glory in being one of her martyrs; for I am firmly persuaded, that the God in whom I trust is able to protect me from the rage and malice of mine enemies, and from them that will rise up against me; and if there is no other way for me to escape, he is able to take me to himself, as he did the most noble, fearless, and undaunted David Walker.

NEVER WILL VIRTUE, KNOWLEDGE, AND TRUE POLITENESS BEGIN TO FLOW, TILL THE PURE PRINCIPLES OF RELIGION AND MORALITY ARE PUT INTO FORCE.

MY RESPECTED FRIENDS,

I feel almost unable to address you; almost incompetent to perform the task; and, at times, I have felt ready to exclaim, O that my head were waters, and mine eyes a fountain of tears, that I might weep day and night, for the transgressions of the daughters of my people. Truly, my heart's desire and prayer is, that Ethiopia might stretch forth her hands unto

1*.

God. But we have a great work to do. Never,
no, never will the chains of slavery and ignorance burst, till we become united as one, and
cultivate among ourselves the pure principles of
piety, morality and virtue. I am sensible of my
ignorance ; but such knowledge as God has
given to me, I impart to you. I am sensible of
former prejudices; but it is high time for prejudices and animosities to cease from among us.
I am sensible of exposing myself to calumny
and reproach; but shall I, for fear of feeble
man who shall die, hold my peace? shall I for
fear of scoffs and frowns, refrain my tongue?
Ah, no ! I speak as one that must give an account at the awful bar of God ; I speak as a
dying mortal, to dying mortals. O, ye daughters of Africa, awake! awake! arise! no longer sleep nor slumber, but distinguish yourselves. Show forth to the world that ye are endowed with noble and exalted faculties. O, ye
daughters of Africa ! what have ye done to im-
mortalize your names beyond the grave? what
examples have ye set before the rising generation? what foundation have ye laid for generations yet unborn? where are our union and
love? and where is our sympathy, that weeps at
another's wo, and hides the faults we see? And
our daughters, where are they? blushing in innocence and virtue? And our sons, do they bid
fair to become crowns of glory to our hoary
heads? Where is the parent who is conscious
of having faithfully discharged his duty, and at
the last awful day of account, shall be able to
say, here, Lord, is thy poor, unworthy servant,

and the children thou hast given me? And
where are the children that will arise, and call
them blessed? Alas, O God! forgive me if I
speak amiss; the minds of our tender babes are
tainted as soon as they are born; they go astray,
as it were, from the womb. Where is the
maiden who will blush at vulgarity? and where
is the youth who has written upon his manly
brow a thirst for knowledge; whose ambitious
mind soars above trifles, and longs for the time
to come, when he shall redress the wrongs of his
father, and plead the cause of his brethren?
Did the daughters of our land possess a deli-
cacy of manners, combined with gentleness and
dignity; did their pure minds hold vice in abhorrence and contempt, did they frown when
their ears were polluted with its vile accents,
would not their influence become powerful?
would not our brethren fall in love with their
virtues? Their souls would become fired with
a holy zeal for freedom's cause. They would
become ambitious to distinguish themselves.
They would become proud to display their talents. Able advocates would arise in our defence. Knowledge would begin to flow, and
the chains of slavery and ignorance would melt
like wax before the flames. I am but a feeble
instrument. I am but as one particle of the
small dust of the earth. You may frown or
smile. After I am dead, perhaps before, God
will surely raise up those who will more powerfully and eloquently plead the cause of virtue
and the pure principles of morality than I am
able to do. O virtue! how sacred is thy name!

how pure are thy principles! Who can find a virtuous woman? for her price is far above rubies. Blessed is the man who shall call her his wife; yea, happy is the child who shall call her mother. O, woman, woman, would thou only strive to excel in merit and virtue; would thou only store thy mind with useful knowledge, great would be thine influence. Do you say, you are too far advanced in life now to begin? You are not too far advanced to instil these principles into the minds of your tender infants. Let them by no means be neglected. Discharge your duty faithfully, in every point of view: leave the event with God. So shall your skirts become clear of their blood.

When I consider how little improvement has been made the last eight years; the apparent cold and indifferent state of the children of God; how few have been hopefully brought to the knowledge of the truth as it is in Jesus; that our young men and maidens are fainting and drooping, as it were, by the way-side, for the want of knowledge; when I see how few care to distinguish themselves either in religious or moral improvement, and when I see the greater part of our community following the vain bubbles of life with so much eagerness, which will only prove to them like the serpent's sting upon the bed of death, I really think we are in as wretched and miserable a state as was the house of Israel in the days of Jeremiah.

I suppose many of my friends will say, "Religion is all your theme," I hope my conduct will ever prove me to be what I profess, a true

follower of Christ; and it is the religion of
Jesus alone, that will constitute your happiness
here, and support you in a dying hour. O, then,
do not trifle with God and your own souls any
longer. Do not presume to offer him the very
dregs of your lives; but now, whilst you are
blooming in health and vigor, consecrate the
remnant of your days to him. Do you wish to
become useful in your day and generation? Do
you wish to promote the welfare and happiness
of your friends, as far as your circle extends?
Have you one desire to become truly great? O,
then, become truly pious, and God will endow
you with wisdom and knowledge from on high.

> Come, turn to God, who did thee make,
> And at his presence fear and quake ;
> Remember him now in thy youth,
> And let thy soul take hold of truth.
>
> The devil and his ways defy,
> Believe him not, he doth but lie ;
> His ways seem sweet : but youth, beware !
> He for thy soul hath laid a snare.

Religion is pure; it is ever new; it is beautiful; it is all that is worth living for; it is worth
dying for: O, could I but see the church built
up in the most holy faith ; could I but see men
spiritually minded, walking in the fear of God,
not given to filthy lucre, not holding religion in
one hand and the world in the other, but diligent in business, fervent in spirit, serving the
Lord, standing upon the walls of Zion, crying
to passers by, "Ho, every one that thirsteth,
come ye to the waters, and he that hath no
money ; yea, come and buy wine and milk with-

out money and without price ; Turn ye, turn ye,
for why will ye die ?" Could I but see mothers
in Israel, chaste, keepers at home, not busy
bodies, meddlers in other men's matters, whose
adorning is of the inward man, possessing a
meek and quiet spirit, whose sons were like
olive-plants, and whose daughters were as pol-
ished corner-stones ; could I but see young men
and maidens turning their feet from impious
ways, rather choosing to suffer affliction with
the people of God than to enjoy the pleasures
of sin for a season ; could I but see the rising
youth blushing in artless innocence, then could
I say, now, Lord, let thine unworthy handmaiden
depart in peace, for I have seen the desire of
mine eyes, and am satisfied.

PRAYER.

O, Lord God, the watchmen of Zion have
cried peace, peace, when there was no peace ;
they have been, as it were, blind leaders of the
blind. Wherefore hast thou so long withheld
from us the divine influences of thy Holy Spirit ?
Wherefore hast thou hardened our hearts and
blinded our eyes ? It is because we have honored thee with our lips, when our hearts were
far from thee. We have polluted thy Sabbaths,
and even our most holy things have been solemn
mockery to thee. We have regarded iniquity
in our hearts, therefore thou wilt not hear. Return again unto us, O Lord God, we beseech
thee, and pardon this the iniquity of thy servants. Cause thy face to shine upon us, and
we shall be saved. O visit us with thy salva-

tion. Raise up sons and daughters unto Abraham, and grant that there might come a mighty
shaking of dry bones among us, and a great in-
gathering of souls. Quicken thy professing
children. Grant that the young may be constrained to believe that there is a reality in religion, and a beauty in the fear of the Lord.
Have mercy on the benighted sons and daughters of Africa. Grant that we may soon become so distinguished for our moral and religious
improvements, that the nations of the earth may
take knowledge of us; and grant that our cries
may come up before thy throne like holy incense.
Grant that every daughter of Africa may consecrate her sons to thee from the birth. And do
thou, Lord, bestow upon them wise and understanding hearts. Clothe us with humility of soul,
and give us a becoming dignity of manners :
may we imitate the character of the meek and
lowly Jesus; and do thou grant that Ethiopia
may soon stretch forth her hands unto thee.
And now, Lord, be pleased to grant that Satan's
kingdom may be destroyed; that the kingdom
of our Lord Jesus Christ may be built up; that
all nations, and kindreds, and tongues, and people might be brought to the knowledge of the
truth, as it is in Jesus, and we at last meet
around thy throne, and join in celebrating thy
praises.

I have been taking a survey of the American
people in my own mind, and I see them thriving
in arts, and sciences, and in polite literature.

Their highest aim is to excel in political, moral
and religious improvement. They early consecrate their children to God, and their youth indeed are blushing in artless innocence; they
wipe the tears from the orphan's eyes, and they
cause the widow's heart to sing for joy! and
their poorest ones, who have the least wish to
excel, they promote! And those that have but
one talent, they encourage. But how very few
are there among them that bestow one thought
upon the benighted sons and daughters of Africa,
who have enriched the soils of America with
their tears and blood : few to promote their
cause, none to encourage their talents. Under
these circumstances, do not let our hearts be
any longer discouraged; it is no use to murmur
nor to repine; but let us promote ourselves and
improve our own talents. And I am rejoiced
to reflect that there are many able and talented
ones among us, whose names might be recorded
on the bright annals of fame. But, " I can't,"
is a great barrier in the way. I hope it will soon
be removed, and " I will," resume its place.

Righteousness exalteth a nation, but sin is a
reproach to any people. Why is it, my friends,
that our minds have been blinded by ignorance,
to the present moment? 'Tis on account of sin.
Why is it that our church is involved in so much
difficulty? It is on account of sin. Why is it
that God has cut down, upon our right hand and
upon our left, the most learned and intelligent
of our men? O, shall I say, is it on account of
sin! Why is it that thick darkness is mantled
upon every brow, and we, as it were, look sadly

upon one another? It is on account of sin. O, then, let us bow before the Lord our God, with all our hearts, and humble our very souls in the dust before him ; sprinkling, as it were, ashes upon our heads, and awake to righteousness and sin not. The arm of the Lord is not shortened, that it cannot save; neither is his ear heavy, that it cannot hear ; but it is your iniquities that have separated you from me, saith the Lord. Return, O ye backsliding children, and I will return unto you, and ye shall be my people, and I will be your God.

O, ye mothers, what a responsibility rests on you! You have souls committed to your charge, and God will require a strict account of you. It is you that must create in the minds of your little girls and boys a thirst for knowledge, the love of virtue, the abhorrence of vice, and the cultivation of a pure heart. The seeds thus sown will grow with their growing years; and the love of virtue thus early formed in the soul will protect their inexperienced feet from many dangers. O, do not say, you cannot make any thing of your children ; but say, with the help and assistance of God, we will try. Do not indulge them in their little stubborn ways; for a child left to himself, bringeth his mother to shame. Spare not, for their crying ; thou shalt beat them with a rod, and they shall not die ; and thou shalt save their souls from hell. When you correct them, do it in the fear of God, and for their own good. They will not thank you for your false and foolish indulgence ; they will rise up, as it were, and curse you in this world, and, in the world to come, condemn you. It is no use to say, you can't do this, or, you can't do that; you will not tell your Maker so, when you meet him at the great day of account. And you must be careful that you set an example worthy of following, for you they will imitate. There are many instances, even among us now, where parents have discharged their duty faithfully, and their children now reflect honor upon their gray hairs.

Perhaps you will say, that many parents have set pure examples at home, and they have not followed them. True, our expectations are often blasted; but let not this dishearten you. If they have faithfully discharged their duty, even after they are dead, their works may live; their prodigal children may then return to God, and become heirs of salvation; if not, their children cannot rise and condemn them at the awful bar of God.

Perhaps you will say, that you cannot send them to high schools and academies. You can have them taught in the first rudiments of useful knowledge, and then you can have private teachers, who will instruct them in the higher branches; and their intelligence will become greater than ours, and their children will attain to higher advantages, and *their* children still higher; and then, though we are dead, our works shall live : though we are mouldering, our names shall not be forgotten.

Finally, my heart's desire and prayer to God is, that there might come a thorough reformation among us. Our minds have too long grovelled in ignorance and sin. Come, let us incline our ears to wisdom, and apply our hearts to understanding; promote her, and she shall exalt thee; she shall bring thee to honor when thou dost embrace her. An ornament of grace shall she be to thy head, and a crown of glory shall she deliver to thee. Take fast hold of instruction; let her not go; keep her, for she is thy life. Come, let us turn unto the Lord our God, with all our heart and soul,·and put away every unclean and unholy thing from among us, and walk before the Lord our God, with a perfect heart, all the days of our lives: then we shall be a people with whom God shall delight to dwell; yea, we shall be that happy people whose God is the Lord.

I am of a strong opinion, that the day on which we unite, heart and soul, and turn our attention to knowledge and improvement, that day the hissing and reproach among the nations of the earth against us will cease. And even those who now point at us with the finger of scorn, will aid and befriend us. It is of no use, for us to sit with our hands folded, hanging our heads like bulrushes, lamenting our wretched condition; but let us make a mighty effort, and arise; and if no one will promote or respect us, let us promote and respect ourselves.

The American ladies have the honor conferred on them, that by prudence and economy in their domestic concerns, and their unwearied attention in forming the minds and manners of their children, they laid the foundation of their becoming what they now are. The good women

of Wethersfield, Conn. toiled in the blazing
sun, year after year, weeding onions, then sold
the seed and procured money enough to erect
them a house of worship; and shall we not imitate their examples, as far as they are worthy
of imitation? Why cannot we do something to
distinguish ourselves, and contribute some of
our hard earnings that would reflect honor upon
our memories, and cause our children to arise
and call us blessed? Shall it any longer be
said of the daughters of Africa, they have no
ambition, they have no force? By no means.
Let every female heart become united, and let
us raise a fund ourselves; and at the end of one
year and a half, we might be able to lay the
corner-stone for the building of a High School,
that the higher branches of knowledge might
be enjoyed by us; and God would raise us up,
and enough to aid us in our laudable designs.
Let each one strive to excel in good house-
wifery, knowing that prudence and economy
are the road to wealth. Let us not say, we
know this, or, we we know that, and practise
nothing; but let us practise what we do know.

How long shall the fair daughters of Africa
be compelled to bury their minds and talents
beneath a load of iron pots and kettles? Until
union, knowledge and love begin to flow among
us. How long shall a mean set of men flatter
us with their smiles, and enrich themselves with
our hard earnings; their wives' fingers spark-
ling with rings, and they themselves laughing
at our folly? Until we begin to promote and
patronize each other. Shall we be a by-word

among the nations any longer? Shall they laugh us to scorn forever? Do you ask, what can we do? Unite and build a store of your own, if you cannot procure a license. Fill one side with dry goods, and the other with groceries. Do you ask, where is the money? We have spent more than enough for nonsense, to do what building we should want. We have never had an opportunity of displaying our talents; therefore the world thinks we know nothing. And we have been possessed of by far too mean and cowardly a disposition, though I highly disapprove of an insolent or impertinent one. Do you ask the disposition I would have you possess? Possess the spirit of independence. The Americans do, and why should not you? Possess the spirit of men, bold and enterprising, fearless and undaunted. Sue for your rights and privileges. Know the reason that you cannot attain them. Weary them with your importunities. You can but die, if you make the attempt; and we shall certainly die if you do not. The Americans have practised nothing but head-work these 200 years, and we have done their drudgery. And is it not high time for us to imitate their examples, and practise head-work too, and keep what we have got, and get what we can? We need never to think that any body is going to feel interested for us, if we do not feel interested for ourselves. That day we, as a people, hearken unto the voice of the Lord our God, and walk in his ways and ordinances, and become distinguished for our ease, elegance and grace, combined with other virtues, that day the Lord will raise us up, and enough to aid and befriend us, and we shall begin to flourish.

Did every gentleman in America realize, as one, that they had got to become bondmen, and their wives, their sons, and their daughters, servants forever, to Great Britain, their very joints would become loosened, and tremblingly would smite one against another; their countenance would be filled with horror, every nerve and muscle would be forced into action, their souls would recoil at the very thought, their hearts would die within them, and death would be far more preferable. Then why have not Afric's sons a right to feel the same? Are not their wives, their sons, and their daughters, as dear to them as those of the white man's? Certainly, God has not deprived them of the divine influences of his Holy Spirit, which is the greatest of all blessings, if they ask him. Then why should man any longer deprive his fellow-man of equal rights and privileges? Oh, America, America, foul and indelible is thy stain! Dark and dismal is the cloud that hangs over thee, for thy cruel wrongs and injuries to the fallen sons of Africa. The blood of her murdered ones cries to heaven for vengeance against thee. Thou art almost become drunken with the blood of her slain; thou hast enriched thyself through her toils and labors; and now thou refuseth to make even a small return. And thou hast caused the daughters of Africa to commit whordoms and fornications; but upon thee be their curse.

O, ye great and mighty men of America, ye
rich and powerful ones, many of you will call
for the rocks and mountains to fall upon you,
and to hide you from the wrath of the Lamb,
and from him that sitteth upon the throne;
whilst many of the sable-skinned Africans you
now despise, will shine in the kingdom of heaven
as the stars forever and ever.   Charity begins
at home, and those that provide not for their
own, are worse than infidels.   We know that
you are raising contributions to aid the gallant
Poles ; we know that you have befriended
Greece and Ireland ; and you have rejoiced with
France, for her heroic deeds of valor.   You
have acknowledged all the nations of the earth,
except Hayti; and you may publish, as far as
the East is from the West, that you have two
millions of negroes, who aspire no higher than
to bow at your feet, and to court your smiles.
You may kill, tyrannize, and oppress as much
as you choose, until our cry shall come up before the throne of God; for I am firmly persuaded, that he will not suffer you to quell the
proud, fearless and undaunted spirits of the
Africans forever ; for in his own time, he is
able to plead our cause against you, and to pour
out upon you the ten plagues of Egypt.   We
will not come out against you with swords and
staves, as against a thief; but we will tell you
that our souls are fired with the same love of
liberty and independence with which your souls
are fired.   We will tell you that too much of
your blood flows in our veins, and too much of
your color in our skins, for us not to possess

your spirits. We will tell you, that it is our gold that clothes you in fine linen and purple, and causes you to fare sumptuously every day; and it is the blood of our fathers, and the tears of our brethren that have enriched your soils. AND WE CLAIM OUR RIGHTS. We will tell you, that we are not afraid of them that kill the body, and after that can do no more; but we will tell you whom we do fear. We fear Him who is able, after he hath killed, to destroy both soul and body in hell forever. Then, my brethren, sheath your swords, and calm your angry passions. Stand still, and know that the Lord he is God. Vengeance is his, and he will repay. It is a long lane that has no turn. America has risen to her meridian. When you begin to thrive, she will begin to fall. God hath raised you up a Walker and a Garrison. Though Walker sleeps, yet he lives, and his name shall be had in everlasting remembrance. I, even I, who am but a child, inexperienced to many of you, am a living witness to testify unto you this day, that I have seen the wicked in great power, spreading himself like a green bay tree, and lo, he passed away; yea, I diligently sought him, but he could not be found; and it is God alone that has inspired my heart to feel for Afric's woes. Then fret not yourselves because of evil doers. Fret not yourselves because of the men who bring wicked devices to pass; for they shall be cut down as the grass, and wither as the green herb. Trust in the Lord, and do good; so shalt thou dwell in the land, and verily thou shalt be fed. Encourage the noble-hearted

Garrison. Prove to the world that you are neither ourang-outangs, nor a species of mere animals, but that you possess the same powers of intellect as those of the proud-boasting American.

I am sensible, my brethren and friends, that many of you have been deprived of advantages, kept in utter ignorance, and that your minds are now darkened; and if any of you have attempted to aspire after high and noble enterprises, you have met with so much opposition that your souls have become discouraged. For this very cause, a few of us have ventured to expose our lives in your behalf, to plead your cause against the great; and it will be of no use, unless you feel for yourselves and your little ones, and exhibit the spirits of men. Oh, then, turn your attention to knowledge and improvement; for knowledge is power. And God is able to fill you with wisdom and understanding, and to dispel your fears. Arm yourselves with the weapons of prayer. Put your trust in the living God. Persevere strictly in the paths of virtue. Let nothing be lacking on your part; and, in God's own time, and his time is certainly the best, he will surely deliver you with a mighty hand and with an outstretched arm.

I have never taken one step, my friends, with a design to raise myself in your esteem, or to gain applause. But what I have done, has been done with an eye single to the glory of God, and to promote the good of souls. I have neither kindred nor friends. I stand alone in your midst, exposed to the fiery darts of the devil, and to the assaults of wicked men. But though

all the powers of earth and hell were to com-
bine against me, though all nature should sink
into decay, still would I trust in the Lord, and
joy in the God of my salvation. For I am fully
persuaded, that he will bring me off conqueror,
yea, more than conqueror, through him who
hath loved me and given himself for me.

Boston, October, 1831.

HYMN.

God is a spirit, just and wise,
    He knows our inmost minds ;
In vain to heaven we raise our cries,
    And leave our souls behind.

Nothing but truth before his throne,
    With honor can appear ;
The painted hypocrites are known
    By the disguise they wear.

Their lifted eyes salute the skies,
    Their bended knees the ground ;
But God abhors the sacrifice,
    Where not the heart is found.

Lord, search my heart, and try my reins,
    And make my soul sincere ;
So shall I stand before thy throne,
    And find acceptance there.

                             WATTS.

MEDITATIONS.

INTRODUCTION.

Tell me no more of earthly toys,
Of sensual mirth and carnal joys,
For these are trifling things.

ONCE more I am about to make a feeble effort, in presenting the meditations of my heart before my friends and the public. I am sensible that my writings show forth the want of knowledge, and that they are scarce worthy of a perusal. But as I have said before, I say again, such knowledge as God giveth to me, I impart to you.

The author has, as it were, upon the one hand, basked in the sunshine of prosperity; and, on the other, she has drunk deep in the cup of sorrow.

Never did I realize, till I was forced to, that it was from God I derived every earthly blessing, and that it was God who had a right to take them away. I found it almost impossible to say "Thy will be done." It is now one year since Christ first spoke peace to my troubled soul. Soon after I presented myself before the Lord in the holy ordinance of baptism, my soul became filled with holy meditations and sublime ideas; and my ardent wish and desire have ever been, that I might become a humble instrument in the hands of God, of winning some poor souls to Christ. Though I am sensible that Paul may plant, and Apollos water, but that God alone giveth the increase, through Christ strengthening me I can do all things; without him I can do nothing.

It appears to me that because sin abounds, the love of many has waxed cold ; and I cannot believe that God would have so long withheld the divine influences of his Holy Spirit from this people, had the professing followers of Christ more faithfully defended the cause of their blessed Lord and Master ; for he has said that he will be inquired of by the house of Israel, to do those things for them that they need. I have borrowed much of my language from the holy Bible. During the years of childhood and youth, it was the book that I mostly studied ; and now, while my hands are toiling for their daily sustenance, my heart is most generally meditating upon its divine truths. I am more and more convinced that the cause of Christ will never be built up, Satan's kingdom will never be destroyed, the chains of slavery and ignorance will never burst, and morality and virtue will never flourish, till pure and holy examples are set home, and the professing followers of Christ arise and shine forth, and prove to the world that there is a reality in religion, and a beauty in the fear of the Lord.

MEDITATION I.

MY FRIENDS,

I have been sorely troubled in my mind; and why? It is because I have seen that many, who have professed the name of Christ, are not careful to discharge their duty faithfully to their dying fellow immortals around them. I have been considering that it will be but a poor excuse for me to say, when I appear at the awful bar of God, that the reason I neglected my duty was because I was fearful that this one would frown upon me, and that one would smile. Religion has become too unfashionable and too unpopular, even among the professing followers of Christ. O, how will they feel in that day to see their skirts filled with the blood of souls? Will not their eye-balls start from their sockets, to see sinners who have stumbled into hell over them? and will not their hearts be rent in twain, to hear them in anguish condemn them? "If thou warn not the wicked man to flee from his ways, and he die in his sins, his blood will I require at thy hand, saith the Lord of hosts." O, the value of time! O, the worth of immortal souls! The harvest indeed is plenteous, but the laborers are few. Pray ye, therefore, to the Lord of the harvest, that he would send forth faithful laborers into his vineyard.

My respected friends, I have indeed found that the Christian's life is a life of warfare; for

3

the spirit wars against the flesh, and the flesh against the spirit; and I am forced to cry out with St. Paul, from time to time, " O, wretched man that I am! who shall deliver me from this body of sin and death? for the good that I would do, that I do not; and the evil that I would not do, that I do."

MEDITATION II.

How pleased and blest was I,
To hear the people cry,
　　Come, let us seek our God to-day;
Yes, with a cheerful zeal,
We'll haste to Zion's hill,
　　And there our vows and honors pay.

How amiable are thy tabernacles, O Lord of hosts, and the place where thine honor dwelleth! Truly I can say with the Psalmist, that I had rather be a door-keeper in the house of my God, than to dwell in the tents of wickedness. What a sublimity dwells among the assemblies of thy saints! Truly thine abodes of worship are none other than the very gates of heaven. The sun has risen gloriously upon the earth. O, that its rays might shine into this benighted soul of mine. Soon I shall be laid in the silent tomb, or beneath the sod; and the places that know me now, will know me no more for ever. Then, O my soul, improve thy Sabbaths, and waste not their precious hours. Grant that what I hear this day, O God, may not be as water spilt upon the ground, which cannot be gathered up; but may it be as good seed sown in the heart, springing up unto life eternal.

I have just returned from church. The discourse made a deep and solemn impression on my mind. O, may what I have heard prove a rich and lasting blessing to my soul. Disrobe me, O God, of every impure and unholy affection, and make my soul a fit temple for thee to dwell in.

PRAYER.

O thou King eternal, immortal, invisible, and only wise God, before whom angels bow and seraphs veil their faces, crying, holy, holy, holy, is the Lord God Almighty. True and righteous are thy ways, thou King of saints. Help me, thy poor unworthy creature, humbly to prostrate myself before thee, and implore that mercy which my sins have justly forfeited. O God, I know that I am not worthy of a place at thy footstool; but to whom shall I go but unto thee? Thou alone hast the words of eternal life. Send me not away without a blessing, I beseech thee; but enable me to wrestle like Jacob, and to prevail like Israel. Be graciously pleased, O God, to pardon all that thou hast seen amiss in me this day, and enable me to live more to thine honor and glory for the time to come. Bless the church to which I belong, and grant that when thou makest up thy jewels, not one soul shall be found missing. Bless him in whom thou hast set over us as a watchman in Zion. Let not his soul be discouraged. May he not fail to declare the whole counsel of God, whether sinners will hear or forbear. And now, Lord, what wait I for? My hope is in thee. Do more for me than I can possibly ask or think, and finally receive me to thyself.

MEDITATION III.

My friends, I have been brought to consider that it is because the Lord he is God, that I have not been consumed. It is because that his tender compassion fails not, that I am not now in hell lifting up my eyes in torments, where the worm dieth not, and where the fire is not quenched. And I cannot help but exclaim, glory to God that I am yet a prisoner of hope. I rejoice that I have been formed a rational and accountable creature, and that ever I was born to be born again. I rejoice that the Lord God omnipotent reigneth, and that he searches the hearts and tries the reins of the children of men. When I sin, I feel that I have an advocate with the Father, even Jesus Christ the righteous, who was in all points tempted like unto ourselves, yet without sin. He knows what sore temptations mean, for he has felt the same; and with his supporting grace, I am determined to resist the lusts of the world, the flesh and the devil, and to fight the good fight of faith, and win the crown and by my Father's side sit down. Choose ye this day, therefore, whom ye will serve; but as for me, I am determined to serve the Lord.

MEDITATION IV.

Afflicted saints to Christ draw near,
The Saviour's gracious promise hear;
His gracious words declare to thee,
That as thy days, thy strength shall be.

Why art thou cast down, O my soul, and why art thou disquieted within me? Hope thou in God; for I shall yet praise him. Have just returned from church-meeting. Did not perceive that Christian spirit of fellowship which ought to exist. Is there an Achan among us, O God, who has done the accursed thing? or is there a Jonah among us, who has refused to obey thy will? If not, why hast thou so long hid thy face from us? for we are consumed by thine anger, and by thy wrath are we troubled. Return again unto us, O Lord God, we beseech thee, and open the eyes of our understanding, that we may see wherein we have sinned against thee. O God, we have robbed thee, in not presenting thee the first offering of our hearts. O turn away from us thy fierce anger, and pardon this our iniquity, and lift upon us more the light of thy reconciled countenance, and the joy of thy salvation. Have met with an earthly disappointment. Am somewhat disheartened.—Naked came I forth from my mother's womb, and naked shall I return thither. The Lord gave, and the Lord hath taken away ; blessed be the name of the Lord. O my soul, labor not for the meat that perisheth, but for that which endureth unto life eternal. Lord, thou hast chastened me sore ; but though thou hast caused me to fall, thou hast not utterly taken from me thy loving kindness; but thou hast dealt in tender mercy and compassion with me. I adore thee, praise thee, and bless thee Parent of mercies, for thy patience and forbearance with me ; for hadst thou left me to myself, where would my mad career have ended? Parent of mercies, give me calm submission to thy holy will, in all things; for thou hast said, that as thy day is, so shall thy strength be.

PRAYER.

Our Father, which art in heaven, hallowed be thy name. Thy kingdom come. Thy will be done. Enable me to say from my heart, Thy will be done, O God. The heaven is thy throne, and the earth is thy footstool; neither may any say unto thee, what doest thou? But thou art the high and lofty One that inhabiteth eternity, yet will thou condescend to look upon him that is of a humble, a broken, and a contrite heart. As such, enable me, O God, to bow before thee at this time, under a deep sense of my guilt and unworthiness. It was my sins that caused thee to arise in thy wrath against me. Be pleased, O God, to blot them from thy book, and remember them no more for ever. Bless the church to which I belong. Thine arm is not shortened that it cannot save, neither is thine ear heavy that it cannot hear; but it is our sins that have separated thee from us. Purge us from all our dross; hide thy face from our iniquities, and speak peace to our troubled souls. Bless thy servant, our pastor; let not his soul be discouraged, but may an angel appear unto him, strengthening him. Bless all the benighted sons and daughters of Africa, especially my unconverted friends. Send them not away from thy presence into that lake that burneth with fire and brimstone, but magnify the riches of thy grace in plucking their souls as brands from the burning; and though I may long sleep in death before thou wilt perform this work, yet grant that in the resurrection morn we may all awake in thy likeness, and our souls be bound in the sure bundle of eternal life.

MEDITATION V.

I have been contemplating that if we live pure and virtuous lives here, when we come upon the bed of death, we shall be enabled to lean our head upon the bosom of Jesus, and to breathe our souls out sweetly there. He will safely carry us through the dark valley and the shadow of death, and angels will convey us to heaven. There we shall sit down with Abraham, and Isaac, and Jacob, and with the spirits of just men made perfect. There the Lord God will wipe away tears from all our faces, and we shall join with the hundred and forty-four thousand, in singing the song of Moses and the Lamb:

> Worthy the Lamb that died, they cry,
>   To be exalted thus!
> Worthy the Lamb, our lips reply,
>   For he was slain for us!

My Christian friends, let us examine ourselves, and pray for peace of conscience, joy in the Holy Ghost, increase of grace, and persever-ance there unto the end.

MEDITATION VI.

Before we proceed any farther, permit me to ask you, my Christian friends, in the name of the Lord Jesus Christ, what progress are you making in the divine life? Are you bringing forth the fruits of righteousness, and proving to the world, by your own conduct, that there is a reality in religion, and a beauty in the fear of the Lord? Are you letting your light so shine before men, that they may see your good works, and glorify your Father which is in heaven? Christ has said, that he is more willing to give his Holy Spirit to them that ask him, than earthly parents are to bestow good gifts upon their children; and that if two or three shall ask any thing in his name, believing that he is able to perform, it shall be done for them of their Father which is in heaven; and certainly the fervent effectual prayer of the righteous availeth much. O, then, shall precious and immortal souls perish through our neglect? Shall they stumble into hell over us, and rise up in judgment and condemn us? Is it not to be feared that many who profess the name of Jesus, at the present day, are too much like the whited sepulchres, which indeed appear beautiful without, but inwardly are full of all manner of uncleanness? Do not many love the praise of man more than the praise of God? Have we not all been unprofitable servants? And is it not to be feared, that at the great and terrible day of the Lord, he will arise and shut the door? and many will stand without, and begin to knock, and say, Lord, Lord, open unto us; but he will say, I know not from whence ye are: depart from me, ye workers of iniquity. And soon the summons will go forth against you, my unconverted friends; cut them down, for why cumber they the ground? Christ has been seeking fruit of you these many years, and lo, he hath found none. O, how can you go on, year after year,

and month after month, sinning against a holy
and a righteous God, who is constantly shower-
ing down the choicest of his blessings upon you?
O, how can you see your friends dropping into
the eternal world, and yet feel no concern for
your never dying souls? Will not the terrors of
death alarm you, nor the calls and invitations of
mercy persuade you? Come, now, saith the
Lord, and let us reason together; though your
own sins have been as scarlet, they shall be
made as wool, and though they have been red
like crimson, they shall become whiter than
snow. O, my friends, believe me or not, I have
felt at times to exclaim with Moses, O Lord
God, this people have sinned a great sin; but
now if thou wilt forgive them, blot me I pray
thee from thy book. And the Lord said, him
that sinneth against me, him will I blot from
my book.

MEDITATION VII.

At his presence nature shakes,
  Earth affrighted hastes to flee;
Solid mountains melt like wax,
  What will then become of thee?

O, my unconverted friends, where will you
hide yourselves in the great and terrible day of
the Lord? Where will you secrete yourselves,
from the presence of the Almighty? If you
ascend into heaven, he is there; if you make
your bed in hell, he is there. If you take the
wings of the morning, and fly to the uttermost
parts of the earth, even there shall he find you,
and his right hand shall search you out. Be not

deceived; God is not mocked, If the righteous are scarcely saved, where will the sinner and the ungodly appear. Now consider this, ye that forget God, lest he tare you in pieces, and there be none to deliver rou.

> Where are now their haughty looks ?
> O, their horror and despair,
> When they see the open books,
> And the dreadful sentence hear!

O, friends, it is painful to tell you the truth, but you had better hear it now before it is eternally too late. Oh then, fly to the Saviour before the door of mercy is for ever shut against you. Repent and believe in the Lord Jesus Christ, and thou shalt be saved.

PRAYER.

O Lord God, Paul may plant, and Appollos water, but thou alone givest the increase. We are sensible that without thee we can do nothing. Vain are all our efforts without thy blessing. But, O Lord God, thou hast the hearts of all thy creatures in hand ; and thou canst turn them whithersoever thou wilt. Strip the hearts of this people from their idols, we humbly beseech thee. Take off their eyes from beholding vanity. Thou canst glorify thyself in making them the monuments of thy mercy ; and thou canst glorify thyself in making them the monuments of thy wrath. Glorify thyself in making them the monuments of thy victorious grace. Open their eyes that they may see that their feet stand upon slippery places, and that fiery billows roll beneath them. And, O Lord God, wilt thou in an especial manner have mercy on our unconverted brethren. Soften their proud and rebellious hearts, and be not angry with them forever. O, Jesus of Nazareth, hast thou not died that they might live? Hast thou not become poor, that they might become rich? Is not thy blood sufficient to atone? Wherefore, O Lord God, hast thou hardened their hearts, and blinded their eyes? Wherefore hast thou so long withheld from them the divine influences of thy holy Spirit? Open their eyes that they may see that they are going down to hell, as fast as the wheels of time can carry them. O, stop them in their mad career! Grant that a grievous cry might be heard among thy professing children, in behalf of perishing souls; and may it be like the cry of the Egyptians in the night that thou didst slay their first-born. And not only for ourselves do we pray, but for all nations, kindreds, tongues and people. Grant that an innumerable host, which no man can number, may be gathered in from the four winds of heaven; and when the last trumpet shall sound, grant that we may be caught up into the clouds of the air, and our ear saluted with the joyful sound, 'Well done, thou good and faithful servant; thou hast been faithful over a few things, I will make thee ruler over many things; enter thou into the joy of thy Lord.

MEDITATION VIII.

Is there no balm in Gilead, and is there no physician there? Yes, there is balm in Gilead and there is a physician there. And O, my soul thou hast found that physician, and he hath applied his healing medicines to thy bleeding heart, and hath cured thee of thy wounds. Come, then, all ye mourning souls to this physician ; he alone can heal your maladies. Are you poor ? He is inexhaustibly rich and benevolent, and will heal you without money and without price. Is your case a desperate one ? Are you full of wounds, and bruises, and putrefying sores ?— Come just as you are. Look steadfastly to him, believe in his skill, and you shall be made whole.

Another year is past and gone forever. Have been deeply impressed on account of past sins and ingratitude. But methinks I hear a voice which says,— Blessed are they that mourn, for they shall be comforted. Methinks I hear a voice which says, — Daughter, be of good cheer; thy sins be forgiven thee. Consoling thought ! O, thou compassionate Redeemer, was it love that induced thee to leave the realms of bliss, and take upon thee the form of a servant, and descend into this lower world, to die for fallen man? Infinite love ! Amazing condescension ! A mystery indeed, that the angels desire to look into. Even eternity will be too short for blood-washed millions to celebrate thy praises.

PRAYER.

O, thou sin-forgiving God, they that are whole need not a physician, but they that are sick. Lord, I am sick, and full of diseases. If thou wilt, thou canst make me clean. Though my sins have been as scarlet, thou canst make them as wool ; and though they be red like crimson, thou canst make them whiter than snow. Were it not that there is a sufficiency in thy blood to atone for the vilest, the view of my past sins and transgressions would sink me in despair. But thou hast said, him that cometh to thee, thou wilt in no wise cast out. Lord, I come, pleading alone the merits of my Redeemer; not only for myself do I plead, but for the whole race of mankind; especially for the benighted sons and daughters of Africa. Do thou loose their bonds, and let the oppressed go free. Bless thy churches throughout the world. Clothe thy ministers with salvation, and cause thy saints to shout for joy. Grant that the time may soon come, that all may know thee from the rising of the sun unto the going down thereof. In an especial manner wilt thou look down upon the church to which I belong. Fire our souls with a holy zeal for thy cause, and let us not rest at ease in Zion, whilst souls are perishing for the lack of knowledge. Wilt thou increase her number of such, and such only, as shall be saved. Bless our pastor with a double portion of thy Spirit. Encourage his heart, and strengthen him in the inward man, and may he see the work of the Lord prosper in his hands. And now, Lord, what wait I for? Dispel every gloomy fear that pervades my mind, and enable me to hope in thy mercy, and to thee will I ascribe praises everlasting.

MEDITATION IX.

I have been impressed in my mind, my unconverted friends, with the awful idea that God is about to execute upon us the fierceness of his

4

anger, and to pour forth heavy judgments upon this people. And why? Because your sins have reached unto heaven, and your iniquities unto the clouds. God has been calling you these many years to repentance, by his loving kindness and tender mercies; and Christ has been knocking at the door of your hearts for admittance, until his locks have become wet with the dews of heaven. Nay, even more; he hath chastened you with the rod of his wrath, and hath deprived you of your kindred and friends; he hath sent death and pestilence among you, and many have become widows, and their children fatherless; and still you go on unconcerned as though all were well, saying with proud Pharaoh, 'Who is the Lord, that we should obey him?' You have closed your eyes against the light; you have stopped your ears against the truth; and you have hardened your hearts against the calls and invitations of mercy; and I am fearful that the queen of the south will arise in judgment against this generation, and condemn it—for she came from the uttermost parts of the earth to hear of the wisdom of Solomon—and behold a greater than Solomon is here. I am fearful that the men of Nineveh will rise in judgment against this generation, and condemn it; for they repented at the preaching of Jonah; and behold a greater than Jonah is here. O, you that sit under the gospel's joyful sound, from Sabbath to Sabbath, and you that neglect the means of grace, who know your Lord's will, and obey it not! O, you that are exalted to heaven in point of privileges, shall be thrust down to hell; for if the mighty works that have been done in you had been done in Tyre and Sidon, it would have remained unto this day. Wherefore I beseech you, in the name of the Lord Jesus Christ, to repent and quickly put away from among you the evil of your doings, and turn unto the Lord your God with weeping, with mourning, and with fasting. It may be he will repent himself of the evil that he hath determined against you: lest if ye continue to rebel against the word of the Lord, he will arise in his wrath and say,—Because I have called, and ye have refused; I have stretched out my hand, and no man regarded; I will laugh at your calamities, and mock when your fear cometh; when your fear cometh as a whirlwind, and distress and anguish shall come upon you; then shall ye call, and I will not answer; ye shall seek me early, but ye shall not find me. And O, my Christian friends, you who have been the professed followers of Christ from ten to twenty years, bear with my plainness of speech, I beseech you, and permit me to ask you in the name of the Lord Jesus Christ, where are the fruits of righteousness that you have brought forth? Where are the souls that have been converted to God through your instrumentality? Where are the men that will give glory to God on account of your good works? Where are those among you that will boldly vindicate the cause of Jesus and him crucified? They that turn many to righteousness shall shine in the kingdom of heaven as the stars forever and ever; while the slothful and negligent shall be bound hand and foot, and cast in outer darkness, where there are weeping and wailing and gnashing of teeth. O, my Christian friends, if we are ever so happy as just to enter within the gates of the holy city—if it were possible, I say—we should mourn throughout the boundless ages of eternity, for having done so little to promote the cause of Christ and the good of souls.

> Broad is the road that leads to death,
>   And thousands walk together there;
> But wisdom shows a narrow path,
>   With here and there a traveller.

Yes. Glory be to God in the highest, there is here and there a faithful one, who is travelling towards Mount Zion, the city of our God.

MEDITATION X.

> The God who built the sky,
>   Hath said, and cannot lie,
> 'Impenitence must die,
>   And be damned.'

'What shall it profit a man if he gain the whole world, and lose his own soul?' dropt from the dying lips of the companion of my youth. O God, was not my conscience stung with remorse and horror, was not my soul torn with anguish, and did not my heart bleed when the summons came : "He must die, and not live." Die! Oh, must he die! Must we part to meet no more! And oh, must I be left, forlorn and unprotected! Spare his life, O God, if consistent with thy will, was my cry; if not, make me to say, Thy will be done. O, my soul, thou hast watched the sick bed of one who was near to thee, even the half of thyself; thou hast heard his

dying groans, and seen his restless head turn
from side to side, in quest of ease; and his dim
eye hath he turned upon thee, and implored thee
for relief. Alas, what could I do! Friends,
what were they but miserable comforters! And
he had no God to look to! Heart-rending scene!
who can describe it! O, my soul, thou hast
wiped the sweat of death from off his cold forehead, and his eyes hast thou seen glazed in
death, and those eyes were fixed upon thee!
And thine arm supported his expiring form, till
the spirit ascended to God who gave it. O, my
soul, forget not that awful scene; forget not that
awful moment. Come, all ye that pass by, and
see if there is any sorrow like unto my sorrow.
And what gratification will it be to you, my
friends, to think that you have been able to be
decked in fine linen and purple, and to fare
sumptuously every day, if you are not decked
in the pure robes of Christ's righteousness?
And friends, what are they in that awful moment, if the eternal God is not your friend and
portion? Could many of our departed friends
but speak, they would say, fools you may live,
but fools you cannot die. Do not as I have
done, but improve your precious hours; take
care of your immortal souls. But you have the
word of God to guide you. Search the Scriptures, for in them ye have eternal life. You
have the ministers of the gospel to counsel you,
to point you to the Lamb of God, which taketh
away the sins of the world. Hear ye them. If
you will not hearken to them, such are the hardness and obduracy of your hearts, that you would

not believe, though one arose from the dead, and told you of all the joys of heaven, or the terrors of hell.

PRAYER.

O, Lord God, when I consider thy heavens, the work of thy fingers, the sun, moon and stars, what is man that thou art mindful of him, or the son of man, that thou shouldst visit him? Thou didst at first create man after thine image, pure and upright; but man, by his disobedience, fell from that holy and happy state, and hath involved all his posterity in guilt and ruin. Thine awful sentence was just: "Dust thou art, and unto dust thou shalt return." Help me to realize that thou art a consuming fire to those that obey thee not, and that thou art arrayed in terrible majesty. Thou chargest thine angels with folly, and the heavens are not clean in thy sight; how much more filthy and abominable must be man, who drinketh in iniquity like water? Thou canst not look upon the least sin but with abhorrence, and thou wilt by no means clear the guilty. But though thy name alone is so terrible, yet Mercy stands pleading at thy bar, saying, Father, I have died: behold my hands and my side! Spare them a little longer, and have mercy upon the souls that thou hast made. O God, help me to realize that "man that is born of a woman is of few days, and full of trouble: he cometh forth as a flower, and is cut down; yea, man giveth up the ghost, and where is he?" And help me to realize that it is with great tribulation that we enter through the gates into the

holy city.   Once more I beseech thee to hear
the cry of thy children in behalf of the unconverted.   O God, this great work is thine ; thou
alone canst perform it.   My church and pastor
I recommend to thee ; it is all that I can do ;
and that thou wouldst supply them with all needful blessings is the prayer of thine unworthy
handmaiden.

MEDITATION XI.

" Not every one that saith, Lord, Lord, shall
enter into the kingdom of heaven, but he that
doeth the will of my Father which is in heaven.
Many will say unto me in that day, Lord, Lord,
have we not prophesied in thy name, and in thy
name cast out devils, and in thy name done
many wonderful works ? And then will I profess unto them, I never knew you.   Depart from
me, ye workers of iniquity.   Blessed is he that
doeth the will of my Father, that he may have
right to the tree of life, and may enter through
the gates into the holy city.   For the kingdom
of heaven is like unto a man, which sowed good
seed in his field ; but whilst men slept, the enemy came, and sowed tares among the wheat.
The servant saith unto him, sir, didst not thou
sow good seed in thy field ? from whence then
hath it tares ? He saith unto him, an enemy
hath done this : let both grow together until the
harvest ; and in time of harvest I will say to the
reapers, bind the tares in bundles to burn them."
Many who profess the name of Jesus, are not
careful to walk according to their profession ;
and thereby prove themselves a stumbling-block

and a rock of offence in the way of sinners;
but when the mighty angel shall descend from
heaven, and step one foot upon the earth, and
the other upon the sea, and swear by him that
liveth for ever and ever, that time shall be no
longer ; when the last trumpet shall sound,
" Awake, ye dead, and come to judgment ;"
when the world shall be on fire, and the elements shall pass away with a great noise, and
the heavens shall be rolled together as a scroll ;
when death and hell, and the sea shall deliver
up the dead that are in them, and all nations,
kindreds, tongues, and people, shall be arrayed
before the awful bar of God, and the books shall
be opened ; then, then, if we have not the pure
and undefiled religion of Jesus, wo, wo, wo, will
be unto us. Better for us that we had never
been born ; better for us that a mill-stone were
hanged about our necks, and that we were cast
into the depths of the sea.

MEDITATION XII.

Come, welcome death, the end of fears,
    I am prepared to die ;
I trust my soul will straight ascend,
    Up to the Lord on high.

Alas! and am I born to die ? O, my soul,
wilt thou ere long take thy flight to realms of
endless bliss, or to the shades of darkest night,
and leave this frail tenement ? Will these eyes
be closed, a lump of cold and lifeless clay ?
these lips cease to speak, and this heart cease
to beat ? these hands and feet become inactive,
cold, and stiff, and this form of mine become

food for worms, and turn to dust! Alas, alas, how mournful is the thought! but, pale messenger, I fear thee not, with all thy grim and ghastly terrors, for my Redeemer lives. He lives, and he is able to disarm thee of thy sting, and no one is able to pluck me out of my Redeemer's hand. He will safely carry me through the dark valley and the shadow of death, and angels will convey me to heaven. Then while my body lies mouldering here, my soul shall rest from all her sorrows, and shall chant the praises of my Redeemer, till the last trumpet shall sound; then shall my sleeping dust awake, and my soul and body be reunited and fly with transport to meet my Saviour, when he shall come with ten thousand of his saints and angels, to take vengeance on his enemies.

> The trumpet sounds,
> Hell trembles,
> Heaven rejoices;
> Lift up you heads, ye saints, with cheerful voices
> No more shall atheist mock his long delay.
> His vengeance sleeps no more.
> Behold the day!
> His guards are nigh;
> Tempest and fire attend him down the sky.

> When God appears,
> All nations shall adore him;
> Whilst sinners tremble,
> Saints rejoice before him.

PRAYER.

Almighty God, it is the glorious hope of a blessed immortality beyond the grave, that supports thy children through this vale of tears. Forever blessed be thy name, that thou hast implanted this hope in my bosom. If thou hast indeed plucked my soul as a brand from the burning, it is not because thou hast seen any worth in me ; but it is because of thy distinguishing mercy, for mercy is thy darling attribute, and thou delightest in mercy, and art not willing that any should perish, but that all should come to the knowledge of the truth as it is in Jesus. Clothe my soul with humility as with a garment. Grant that I may bring forth the fruits of a meek and quiet spirit. Enable me to adorn the doctrines of God my Saviour, by a well regulated life and conversation. May I become holy, even as thou art holy, and pure, even as thou art pure. Bless all my friends and benefactors : those who have given me a cup of cold water in thy name, the Lord reward them. Forgive all my enemies. May I love them that hate me, and pray for them that despitefully use and persecute me. Preserve me from slanderous tongues, O God, and let not my good be evil spoken of. Let not a repining thought enter my heart, nor a murmuring sigh heave from my bosom. But may I cheerfully bear with all the trials of life. Clothe me with the pure robes of Christ's righteousness, that when he shall come in flaming fire to judge the world, I may appear before him with joy and not with grief ; and not only for myself do I ask these blessings, but for all the sons and daughters of Adam, as thou art no respecter of persons, and as all distinctions wither in the grave. Grant all prejudices and animosities may cease from among men. May we all reallize that promotion cometh not from the East nor from the West, but that it is God that putteth up one and setteth down another. May the rich be rich in faith and good works towards our Lord Jesus Christ, and may the poor have an inheritance among the saints in light, a crown incorruptible that fadeth not away, eternal in the heavens. And now what wait we for ? Be pleased to grant that we may at last join with all the Israel of God, in celebrating thy praises.

MEDITATION XIII.

The widow and the fatherless,
Seek for his aid in sharp distress;
In him the poor and helpless find
A God just as a father kind.

'Leave thy faththerless children, I will preserve them alive :' and, Lord, thou hast preserved me alive. Whilst thousands as good by nature, and better by practice, have gone to silence, thine eye hath watched the helpless years of my infancy and youth, and thou hast preserved me from thousands of temptations to which I have been exposed. And let thy widows trust in me; Lord, in thee I have trusted, let me never be confounded.

'Thou shalt by no means afflict any fatherless child : if thou afflict them, and they cry at all unto me, I will surely hear their cry.' Lord, when mine enemies multiplied themselves against me, then I cried unto thee in my trouble, and thou didst deliver me from all my distresses. Thou didst behold from thy holy habitation, that I was wrongfully persecuted, and that there was none to help. Then was thine anger kindled, and thy wrath waxed hot against mine adversaries, and thine own arm saved me, and thine own right arm wrought salvation. Thou didst vindicate my cause in the presence of mine enemies, and didst bring forth my righteousness to light as the noon-day. "Let all those be ashamed that wrongfully persecute my soul; that say unto me, ha, ha, where is thy God?"

Bless the Lord, O my soul, and all that is within me, bless his holy name. Come, magnify the Lord, with me, and let us exalt his name together. I cried unto him in my trouble, and he delivered me from all my distresses. Come, all ye that have breath, and I will tell you what great things the Lord hath done for my soul: how he hath delivered my feet from the miry clay and the horrible pit, and hath put a new song in my mouth, even praise unto our God. What shall I render unto the Lord for all his benefits? I will take the cup of salvation, and will pay my vows before him in the presence of all his people. I will consecrate my soul and body, and all the powers of my mind, to his service, from this time henceforth, yea, even for ever more: for his mercies are more to me than the hairs of my head, or the sands upon the sea shore. Trust not in an arm of flesh; for vain is the help of man. Come, all ye poor and needy, ye widows and fatherless, trust in the Lord; he is your help and your shield; for whom he loveth, he chasteneth, even as a father the son in whom he delighteth; neither doth he willingly afflict nor grieve the children of men. Although the fig-tree shall not blossom, neither shall fruit be in the vine, yet will I rejoice in the Lord, I will joy in the God of my salvation.

PRAYER.

O Lord God, as the heavens are high above the earth, so are thy ways above our ways, and thy thoughts above our thoughts. For wise and holy purposes best known to thyself, thou hast seen fit to deprive me of all earthly relatives; but when my father and mother forsook me, then thou didst take me up. I desire to thank thee, that I am this day a living witness to testify that thou art a God, that will ever vindicate the cause of the poor and needy, and that thou hast always proved thyself to be a friend and father to me. O, continue thy loving kindness even unto the end; and when health and strength begin to decay, and I, as it were, draw nigh unto the grave, O then afford me thy heart-cheering presence, and enable me to rely entirely upon thee. Never leave me nor forsake me, but have mercy upon me for thy great name's sake. And not for myself alone do I ask these blessings, but for all the poor and needy, all widows and fatherless children, and for the stranger in distress; and may they call upon thee in such a manner as to be convinced that thou art a prayer-hearing and prayer-answering God; and thine shall be the praise, forever. Amen.

> Prayer is the Christian's vital breath,
> The Christian's native air;
> His watch-word at the gate of death,
> He enters heaven with prayer.

MEDITATION XIV.

> If there's an idol in my heart,
> Whate'er that idol be:
> Help me to tear it from thy throne,
> And worship only thee.

"And he gave them their request, but he sent leanness into their souls." O, my soul, has not the voice of thy weeping ascended up before the throne of God? Hast thou not almost offended the majesty of heaven, with thy murmurings? Hast thou not wept like the rebellious Israelites for the onions and for the garlics that were in Egypt? And hast thou not rejected the Lord, from reigning king over thee? O, my soul, are not thine affections prone to wander from the fountain of living waters, and to place themselves upon broken cisterns, that can hold no water? Parent of mercies, rivet this heart alone upon thyself. Help me truly to say, whom have I in heaven but thee? and there is none upon the earth that I desire beside thee. O, my soul, cast off from thee every darling sin, however dear, even to the plucking out of a right eye, or the cutting off a right hand. Soon this mortal will put on immortality, and this corruption incorruption, and these eyes will open upon eternal scenes; then, O my soul, what gratification will it be to thee, that all the desires of thine heart were given thee. As death leaves me, so judgment will find me. O, my soul, vain and trifling will then appear thy disappointments. Cleanse thou me, O God, from secret faults. O, my Father, strip this poor unworthy worm of thine from every impure and unholy desire; from all self-righteousness, pride and hypocrisy; from slander and deceit. Hast thou not a blessing for me? Bless me, even me, O my Father! Bless me when I go out, and when I come in; when I lie down, and when I rise up. Put underneath me thine everlasting arms, and keep me from all evil. Sooner extinguish the lamp of life, than leave me to bring a reproach upon thy cause, or wound the hearts of thy children. Hold me in the hollow of thine hand, or I shall fall. Lord, save me, or I perish. Mind filled with gloomy doubts and fears; feel at times as though I should fear to die. Death is truly the king of terrors. O, my Saviour, take from me this awful fear, I humbly beseech thee! and when I come upon the bed of sickness, do thou be graciously pleased to manifest thyself unto me, and enable me to lean my head upon thy bosom. Let guardian angels watch around my pillow; and when I behold my weeping friends, may I say to them with a cheerful smile, weep not for me, but weep for yourselves and for your children. And when pain and anguish shall distort these features, may I calmly say, did Jesus thus suffer, and shall I repine? O Death where is thy sting? O Grave, where is thy victory? May this poor unworthy worm

of thine be clothed with the breast plate of righteousness, and girded with the helmet of salvation.
May the testimony of Jesus be within her, his seal
engraved upon her forehead, and her name written
in the Lamb's book of life. May she overcome the
temptations of the wicked one, and wash her robes
white in the blood of the Lamb; and do thou present
her faultless before thy Father's throne, without
spot, or wrinkle, or any such thing; and when thou
shalt call me to go, may I arise, having my lamps
trimmed and burning, not having a wish or a desire
to stay, but to depart and dwell with thee, which is
far better. Blessed is that servant whom his Lord,
when he cometh, shall find watching.

LECTURE,

DELIVERED AT THE FRANKLIN HALL,

Boston, Sept. 21, 1832.

Why sit ye here and die? If we say we will go
to a foreign land, the famine and the pestilence are
there, and there we shall die. If we sit here, we
shall die. Come let us plead our cause before the
whites: if they save us alive, we shall live—and if
they kill us, we shall but die.

Methinks I heard a spiritual interrogation—'Who
shall go forward, and take off the reproach that is
cast upon the people of color? Shall it be a woman?' And my heart made this reply—'If it is
thy will, be it even so, Lord Jesus!'

I have heard much respecting the horrors of
slavery; but may Heaven forbid that the generality
of my color throughout these United States should
experience any more of its horrors than to be a servant of servants, or hewers of wood and drawers of
water! Tell us no more of southern slavery; for
with few exceptions, although I may be very erroneous in my opinion, yet I consider our condition

but little better than that. Yet, after all, methinks there are no chains so galling as the chains of igno-rance—no fetters so binding as those that bind the soul, and exclude it from the vast field of useful and scientific knowledge. O, had I received the advan-tages of early education, my ideas would, ere now, have expanded far and wide ; but, alas ! I possess nothing but moral capability—no teachings but the teachings of the Holy Spirit.

I have asked several individuals of my sex, who transact business for themselves, if providing our girls were to give them the most satisfactory refer-ences, they would not be willing to grant them an equal opportunity with others ? Their reply has been—for their own part, they had no objection ; but as it was not the custom, were they to take them into their employ, they would be in danger of los-ing the public patronage.

And such is the powerful force of prejudice. Let our girls possess what amiable qualities of soul they may ; let their characters be fair and spotless as in-nocence itself ; let their natural taste and ingenuity be what they may ; it is impossible for scarce an in-dividual of them to rise above the condition of ser-vants. Ah ! why is this cruel and unfeeling distinc-tion ? Is it merely because God has made our com-plexion to vary ? If it be, O shame to soft, relent-ing humanity ! "Tell it not in Gath ! publish it not in the streets of Askelon !" Yet, after all, methinks were the American free people of color to turn their attention more assiduously to moral worth and intel-lectual improvement, this would be the result : preju-dice would gradually diminish, and the whites would be compelled to say, unloose those fetters !

> Though black their skins as shades of night,
> Their hearts are pure, their souls are white.

Few white persons of either sex, who are calcu-lated for any thing else, are willing to spend their lives and bury their talents in performing mean, servile labor. And such is the horrible idea that I entertain respecting a life of servitude, that if I conceived of there being no possibility of my rising above the condition of a servant, I would gladly hail death as a welcome messenger. O, horrible idea, indeed! to possess noble souls aspiring after high and honorable acquirements, yet confined by the chains of ignorance and poverty to lives of continual drudgery and toil. Neither do I know of any who have enriched themselves by spending their lives as house-domestics, washing windows, shaking carpets, brushing boots, or tending upon gentlemen's tables. I can but die for expressing my sentiments; and I am as willing to die by the sword as the pestilence; for I am a true born American; your blood flows in my veins, and your spirit fires my breast.

I observed a piece in the Liberator a few months since, stating that the colonizationists had published a work respecting us, asserting that we were lazy and idle. I confute them on that point. Take us generally as a people, we are neither lazy nor idle; and considering how little we have to excite or stimulate us, I am almost astonished that there are so many industrious and ambitious ones to be found; although I acknowledge, with extreme sorrow, that there are some who never were and never will be serviceable to society. And have you not a similar class among yourselves?

Again. It was asserted that we were "a ragged set, crying for liberty." I reply to it, the whites have so long and so loudly proclaimed the theme of equal rights and privileges, that our souls have caught the flame also, ragged as we are. As far as our merit deserves, we feel a common desire to rise above the condition of servants and drudges. I have learnt, by bitter experience, that continual hard labor deadens the energies of the soul, and benumbs the faculties of the mind; the ideas become confined, the mind barren, and, like the scorching sands of Arabia, produces nothing; or, like the uncultivated soil, brings forth thorns and thistles.

Again, continual hard labor irritates our tempers and sours our dispositions; the whole system becomes worn out with toil and fatigue; nature herself becomes almost exhausted, and we care but little whether we live or die. It is true, that the free people of color throughout these United States are neither bought nor sold, nor under the lash of the cruel driver; many obtain a comfortable support; but few, if any, have an opportunity of becoming rich and independent; and the employments we most pursue are as unprofitable to us as the spider's web or the floating bubbles that vanish into air. As servants, we are respected; but let us presume to aspire any higher, our employer regards us no longer. And were it not that the King eternal has declared that Ethiopia shall stretch forth her hands unto God, I should indeed despair.

I do not consider it derogatory, my friends, for persons to live out to service. There are many whose inclination leads them to aspire no higher; and I would highly commend the performance of almost any thing for an honest livelihood; but where constitutional strength is wanting, labor of this kind, in its mildest form, is painful. And doubtless many are the prayers that have ascended to Heaven from Afric's daughters for strength to perform their work. Oh, many are the tears that have been shed for the want of that strength! Most of our color have dragged out a miserable existence of servitude from the cradle to the grave. And what literary acquirements can be made, or useful knowledge derived, from either maps, books or charts, by those who continually drudge from Monday morning until Sunday noon? O, ye fairer sisters, whose hands are never soiled, whose nerves and muscles are never strained, go learn by experience! Had we had the opportunity that you have had, to improve our moral and mental faculties, what would have hindered our intellects from being as bright, and our manners from being as dignified as yours? Had it been our lot to have been nursed in the lap of affluence and ease, and to have basked beneath the smiles and sunshine of fortune, should we not have naturally supposed that we were never made to toil? And why are not our forms as delicate, and our constitutions as slender, as yours? Is not the workmanship as curious and complete? Have pity upon us, have pity upon us, O ye who have hearts to feel for other's woes; for the hand of God has touched us. Owing to the disadvantages under which we labor, there are many flowers among us that are

> "———born to bloom unseen,
> And waste their fragrance on the desert air."

My beloved brethren, as Christ has died in vain for those who will not accept of offered mercy, so will it be vain for the advocates of freedom to spend their breath in our behalf, unless with united hearts and souls you make some mighty efforts to raise your sons and daughters from the horrible state of servitude and degradation in which they are placed. It is upon you that woman depends; she can do but little besides using her influence; and it is for her sake and yours that I have come forward and made myself a hissing and a reproach among the people; for I am also one of the wretched and miserable daughters of the descendants of fallen Africa. Do you ask, why are you wretched and miserable? I reply, look at many of the most worthy and interesting of us doomed to spend our lives in gentlemen's kitchens. Look at our young men, smart, active and energetic, with souls filled with ambitious fire; if they look forward, alas! what are their prospects? They can be nothing but the humblest laborers, on account of their dark complexions; hence many of them lose their ambition, and become worthless. Look at our middle-aged men, clad in their rusty plaids and coats; in winter, every

cent they earn goes to buy their wood and pay
their rents ; their poor wives also toil beyond their
strength, to help support their families. Look at our
aged sires, whose heads are whitened with the frosts
of seventy winters, with their old wood-saws on
their backs. Alas, what keeps us so? Prejudice,
ignorance and poverty. But ah ! methinks our oppression is soon to come to an end ; yea, before the
Majesty of heaven, our groans and cries have reached the ears of the Lord of Sabaoth. As the prayers
and tears of Christians will avail the finally impenitent nothing ; neither will the prayers and tears of
the friends of humanity avail us any thing, unless
we possess a spirit of virtuous emulation within our
breasts. Did the pilgrims, when they first landed
on these shores, quietly compose themselves, and
say, "the Britons have all the money and all the
power, and we must continue their servants forever ?" Did they sluggishly sigh and say, " our lot
is hard, the Indians own the soil, and we cannot cultivate it ?" No ; they first made powerful efforts to
raise themselves, and then God raised up those illustrious patriots, WASHINGTON and LAFAYETTE, to
assist and defend them. And, my brethren, have
you made a powerful effort ? Have you prayed
the Legislature for mercy's sake to grant you all
the rigths and privileges of free citizens, that your
daughters may rise to that degree of respectabilty
which true merit deserves, and your sons above the
servile situations which most of them fill ?

AN ADDRESS,

DELIVERED BEFORE THE AFRIC-AMERICAN FEMALE
INTELLIGENCE SOCIETY, OF BOSTON.

THE frowns of the world shall never discourage
me, nor its smiles flatter me ; for with the help of
God, I am resolved to withstand the fiery darts of
the devil, and the assaults of wicked men. The

righteous are as bold as a lion, but the wicked fleeth when no man pursueth. I fear neither men nor devils; for the God in whom I trust is able to deliver me from the rage and malice of my enemies, and from them that rise up against me. The only motive that has prompted me to raise my voice in your behalf, my friends, is because I have discovered that religion is held in low repute among some of us; and purely to promote the cause of Christ, and the good of souls, in the hope that others more experienced, more able and talented than myself, might go forward and do likewise. I expect to render a strict, a solemn, and an awful account to God for the motives that have prompted me to exertion, and for those with which I shall address you this evening.

What I have to say, concerns the whole of us as Christians and as a people; and if you will be so kind as give me a hearing this once, you shall receive the incense of a grateful heart.

The day is coming, my friends, and I rejoice in that day, when the secrets of all hearts shall be manifested before saints and angels, men and devils. It will be a great day of joy and rejoicing to the humble followers of Christ, but a day of terror and dismay to hypocrites and unbelievers. Of that day and hour knoweth no man, no, not even the angels 'n heaven, but the Father only. The dead that are n Christ shall be raised first. Blessed is he that shall have a part in the first resurrection. Ah, methinks I hear the finally impenitent crying, "Rocks and mountains! fall upon us, and hide us from the wrath of the Lamb, and from him that sitteth upon the throne!"

> High on a cloud our God shall come,
>   Bright thrones prepare his way;
> Thunder and darkness, fire and storm,
>   Lead on the dreadful day.

Christ shall descend in the clouds of heaven, surrounded by ten thousand of his saints and angels, and it shall be very tempestuous round about him; and before him shall be gathered all nations, and kindred, and tongues, and people; and every knee shall bow, and every tongue confess; they also that pierced him shall look upon him, and mourn. Then shall the King separate the righteous from the wicked, as a shepherd divideth the sheep from the goats, and shall place the righteous on his right hand, and the wicked upon his left. Then, says Christ, shall be weeping, and wailing, and gnashing of teeth, when ye shall see Abraham and the prophets, sitting in the kingdom of heaven, and ye yourselves thrust out. Then shall the righteous shine forth in the kingdom of their Father as the sun. He that hath ears to hear, let him hear. The poor despised followers of Christ will not then regret their sufferings here; they shall be carried by angels into Abraham's bosom, and shall be comforted; and the Lord God shall wipe away their tears. You will then be convinced before assembled multitudes, whether they strove to promote the cause of Christ, or whether they sought for gain or applause. "Strive to enter in at the strait gate; for many, I say unto you, shall seek to enter in, and shall not be able. For except your righteousness shall exceed the righteousness of the Scribes and Pharisees, ye shall in no wise enter into the kingdom of heaven."

Ah, methinks I see this people lying in wickedness; and as the Lord liveth, and as your souls live, were it not for the few righteous that are to be found among us, we should become as Sodom, and like unto Gomorrah. Christians have too long slumbered and slept; sinners stumbled into hell, and still are stumbling, for the want of Christian exertion; and the devil is going about like a roaring lion, seeking whom he may devour. And I make bold to say, that many who profess the name of Christ at the present day, live so widely different from what becometh the Gospel of our Lord Jesus Christ, that they cannot and they dare not reason to the world upon righteousness and judgment to come.

Be not offended because I tell you the truth; for I believe that God has fired my soul with a holy zeal for his cause. It was God alone who inspired my heart to publish the meditations thereof; and it was done with pure motives of love to your souls, in the hope that Christians might examine themselves, and sinners become pricked in their hearts. It is the word of God, though men and devils may oppose it. It is the word of God; and little did I think that any of the professed followers of Christ would have frowned upon me, and discouraged and hindered its progress.

Ah, my friends, I am speaking as one who expects to give account at the bar of God; I am speaking as a dying mortal to dying mortals. I fear there are many who have named the name of Jesus at the present day, that strain at a gnat and swallow a camel; they neither enter into the kingdom of heaven themselves, nor suffer others to enter in. They would pull the motes out of their brother's eye, when they have a beam in their own eye. And were our blessed Lord and Saviour, Jesus Christ, upon the earth, I believe he would say of many that are called by his name, "O, ye hypocrites, ye generation of vipers, how can you escape the damnation of hell." I have enlisted in the holy warfare, and Jesus is my captain; and the Lord's battle I mean to fight, until my voice expire in death. I expect to be hated of all men, and persecuted even unto death, for righteousness and the truth's sake.

A few remarks upon moral subjects, and I close. I am a strong advocate for the cause of God, and for the cause of freedom. I am not your enemy, but a friend both to you and to your children. Suffer me, then, to express my sentiments but this once, however severe they may appear to be, and then hereafter let me sink into oblivion, and let my name die in forgetfulness.

Had the ministers of the gospel shunned the very appearance of evil; had they faithfully discharged their duty, whether we would have heard them or not; we should have been a very different people from what we now are; but they have kept the truth as it were, hid from our eyes, and have cried, "Peace! Peace! when there was no peace; they have plastered us up with untempered mortar, and have been as it were blind leaders of the blind.

It appears to me that there are no people under the heavens, so unkind and so unfeeling towards their own, as are the descendants of fallen Africa. I have been something of a traveller in my day; and the general cry among the people is, "Our own color are our greatest opposers;" and even the whites say that we are greater enemies towards each other, than they are towards us. Shall we be a hissing and a reproach among the nations of the earth any longer! Shall they laugh us to scorn forever? We might become a highly respectable people; respectable we now consider ourselves, but we might become a highly distinguished and intelligent people. And how? In convincing the world, by our own efforts, however feeble, that nothing is wanting on our part but opportunity. Without these efforts, we shall never be a people, nor our descendants after us.

But God has said, that Ethiopia shall stretch forth her hands unto him. True, but God uses means to bring about his purposes; and unless the rising generation manifest a different temper and disposition towards each other from what we have manifested, the generation following will never be an enlightened people. We this day are considered as one of the most degraded races upon the face of the earth. It is useless for us any longer to sit with our hands folded, reproaching the whites; for that will never elevate us. All the nations of the earth have distinguished themselves, and have shown forth a noble and a gallant spirit. Look at the suffering Greeks!

Their proud souls revolted at the idea of serving a tyrannical nation, who were no better than themselves, and perhaps not so good. They made a mighty effort and arose; their souls were knit together in the holy bonds of love and union; they were united, and came off victorious. Look at the French in the late revolution! no traitors among them, to expose their plans to the crowned heads of Europe! "Liberty or Death!" was their cry. And the Haytians, though they have not been acknowledged as a nation, yet their firmness of character, and independence of spirit have been greatly admired, and high applauded. Look at the Poles, a feeble people! They rose against three hundred thousand mighty men of Russia; and though they did not gain the conquest, yet they obtained the name of gallant Poles. And even the wild Indians of the forest are more united than ourselves. Insult one of them, and you insult a thousand. They also have contended for their rights and privileges, and are held in higher repute than we are.

And why is it, my friends, that we are despised above all the nations upon the earth? Is it merely because our skins are tinged with a sable hue? No, nor will I ever believe that it is. What then is it; Oh, it is because that we and our fathers have dealt treacherously one with another, and because many of us now possess that envious and malicious disposition, that we had rather die than see each other rise an inch above a beggar. No gentle methods are used to promote love and friendship among us, but much is done to destroy it. Shall we be a hissing and a reproach among the nations of the earth any longer? Shall they laugh us to scorn forever?

Ingratitude is one of the worst passions that reigns in the human breast; it is this that cuts the tender fibres of the soul; for it is impossible for us to love those who are ungrateful towards us. "Behold," says that wise man, Soloman, counting one by one,

" a man have I found in a thousand, but a woman among all those have I not found."

I have sometimes thought, that God had almost departed from among us. And why ? Because Christ has said, if we say we love the Father, and hate our brother, we are liars, and the truth is not in us ; and certainly if we were the true followers of Christ, I think we could not show such a disposition towards each other as we do: for God is all love.

A lady of high distinction among us, observed to me, that I might never expect your homage. God forbid ! I ask it not. But I beseech you to deal with gentleness and godly sincerity towards me ; and there is not one of you, my dear friends, who has given me a cup of cold water in the name of the Lord, or soothed the sorrows of my wounded heart, but God will bless, not only you, but your children for it. Cruel indeed, are those that indulge such an opinion respecting me as that.

Finally, I have exerted myself both for your temporal and eternal welfare, as far as I am able ; and my soul has been so discouraged within me, that I have almost been induced to exclaim, " Would to God that my tongue hereafter might cleave to the roof of my mouth, and become silent forever !" and then I have felt that the Christian has no time to be idle, and I must be active, knowing that the night of death cometh, in which no man can work; and my mind has become raised to such an extent, that I will willingly die for the cause that I have espoused ; for I cannot die in a more glorious cause than in the defence of God and his laws.

O woman, woman ! upon you I call ; for upon your exertions almost entirely depends whether the rising generation shall be any thing more than we have been or not. O woman, woman ! your example is powerful, your influence great ; it extends over your husbands and over your children, and throughout the circle of your acquaintance. Then let me exhort you to cultivate among yourselves a spirit of Christian love and unity, having charity one for another, without which all our goodness is as sounding brass, and as a tinkling cymbal. And O, my God, I beseech thee to grant that the nations of the earth may hiss at us no longer! O suffer them not to laugh us to scorn forever!

AN ADDRESS,

DELIVERED AT THE AFRICAN MASONIC HALL,
Boston, Feb. 27, 1833.

African rights and liberty is a subject that ought to fire the breast of every free man of color in these United States, and excite in his bosom a lively, deep, decided and heart-felt interest. When I cast my eyes on the long list of illustrious names that are enrolled on the bright annals of fame among the whites, I turn my eyes within, and ask my thoughts, "Where are the names of *our* illustrious ones?" It must certainly have been for the want of energy on the part of the free people of color, that they have been long willing to bear the yoke of oppression. It must have been the want of ambition and force that has given the whites occasion to say, that our natural abilities are not as good, and our capacities by nature inferior to theirs. They boldly assert, that, did we possess a natural independence of soul, and feel a love for liberty within our breasts, some one of our sable race, long before this, would have testified it, notwithstanding the disadvantages under which we labor. We have made ourselves appear altogether unqualified to speak in our own defence, and are therefore looked upon as objects of pity and commiseration. We have been imposed upon, insulted and derided on every side; and now, if we complain, it is considered as the height of impertinence. We have suffered ourselves to be considered as dastards, cowards, mean, faint-hearted wretches;

and on this account, (not because of our complexion,) many despise us, and would gladly spurn us from their presence.

These things have fired my soul with a holy indignation, and compelled me thus to come forward, and endeavor to turn their attention to knowledge and improvement; for knowledge is power. I would ask, is it blindness of mind, or stupidity of soul, or the want of education, that has caused our men who are 60 or 70 years of age, never to let their voices be heard, nor their hands be raised in behalf of their color? Or has it been for the fear of offending the whites? If it has, O ye fearful ones, throw off your fearfulness, and come forth in the name of the Lord, and in the strength of the God of Justice, and make yourselves useful and active members in society; for they admire a noble and patriotic spirit in others; and should they not admire it in us? If you are men, convince them that you possess the spirit of men; and as your day, so shall your strength be. Have the sons of Africa no souls? feel they no ambitious desires? shall the chains of ignorance forever confine them? shall the insipid appellation of "clever negroes," or "good creatures," any longer content them? Where can we find among ourselves the man of science, or a philosopher, or an able statesman, or a counsellor at law? Show me our fearless and brave, our noble and gallant ones. Where are our lecturers on natural history, and our critics in useful knowledge? There may be a few such men among us, but they are rare. It is true, our fathers bled and died in the revolutionary war, and others fought bravely under the command of Jackson, in defence of liberty. But where is the man that has distinguished himself in these modern days by acting wholly in the defence of African rights and liberty? There was one, although he sleeps, his memory lives.

I am sensible that there are many highly intelligent gentlemen of color in these United States, in the force of whose arguments, doubtless, I should discover my inferiority; but if they are blest with wit and talent, friends and fortune, why have they not made themselves men of eminence, by striving to take all the reproach that is cast upon the people of color, and in endeavoring to alleviate the woes of their brethren in bondage? Talk, without effort, is nothing; you are abundantly capable, gentlemen, of making yourselves men of distinction; and this gross neglect, on your part, causes my blood to boil within me. Here is the grand cause which hinders the rise and progress of the people of color. It is their want of laudable ambition and requisite courage.

Individuals have been distinguished according to their genius and talents, ever since the first formation of man, and will continue to be while the world stands. The different grades rise to honor and respectability as their merits may deserve. History informs us that we sprung from one of the most learned nations of the whole earth; from the seat, if not the parent of science; yes, poor, despised Africa was once the resort of sages and legislators of other nations, was esteemed the school for learning, and the most illustrious men in Greece flocked thither for instruction. But it was our gross sins and abominations that provoked the Almighty to frown thus heavily upon us, and give our glory unto others. Sin and prodigality have caused the downfall of nations, kings and emperors; and were it not that God in wrath remembers mercy, we might indeed despair; but a promise is left us; "Ethiopia shall again stretch forth her hands unto God."

But it is of no use for us to boast that we sprung from this learned and enlightened nation, for this day a thick mist of moral gloom hangs over millions of our race. Our condition as a people has been low for hundreds of years, and it will continue to be so, unless, by true piety and virtue, we strive to regain that which we have lost. White Americans, by their prudence, economy and exertions, have sprung up and become one of the most flourishing nations in the world, distinguished for their knowledge of the arts and sciences, for their polite literature. While our minds are vacant, and starving for want of knowledge, theirs are filled to overflowing. Most of our color have been taught to stand in fear of the white man, from their earliest infancy, to work as soon as they could walk, and call "master," before they scarce could lisp the name of *mother.* Continual fear and laborious servitude have in some degree lessened in us that natural force and energy which belong to man; or else, in defiance of opposition, our men, before this, would have nobly and boldly contended for their rights. But give the man of color an equal opportunity with the white from the cradle to manhood, and from manhood to the grave, and you would discover the dignified statesman, the man of science, and the philosopher. But there is no such opportunity for the sons of Africa, and I fear that our powerful ones are fully determined that there never shall be. Forbid, ye Powers on high, that it should any longer be said that our men possess no force. O ye sons of Africa, when will your voices be heard in our legislative halls, in defiance of your enemies, contending for equal rights and liberty? How can you, when you reflect from what you have fallen, refrain from crying mightily unto God, to turn away from us the fierceness of his anger, and remember our transgressions against us no more forever. But a God of infinite purity will not regard the prayers of those who hold religion in one hand, and prejudice, sin and pollution in the other; he will not regard the prayers of self-righteousness and hypocrisy. Is it possible, I exclaim, that for the want of knowledge, we have labored for hundreds of years to support others, and been content to receive what they chose to give us in return? Cast your eyes about, look as far as you can see ; all, all is owned by the lordly white, except here and there a lowly dwelling which the man of color, midst deprivations, fraud and opposition, has been scarce able to procure. Like king Solomon, who put neither nail nor hammer to the temple, yet received the praise ; so also have the white Americans gained themselves a name, like the names of the great men that are in the earth, while in reality we have been their principal foundation and support. We have pursued the shadow, they have obtained the substance; we have performed the labor, they have received the profits ; we have planted the vines, they have eaten the fruits of them.

I would implore our men, and especially our rising youth, to flee from the gambling board and the dance-hall ; for we are poor, and have no money to throw away. I do not consider dancing as criminal in itself, but it is astonishing to me that our young men are so blind to their own interest and the future welfare of their children, as to spend their hard earnings for this frivolous amusement; for it has been carried on among us to such an unbecoming extent, that it has became absolutely disgusting. " Faithful are the wounds of a friend, but the kisses of an enemy are deceitful." Had those men among us, who have had an opportunity, turned their attention as assiduously to mental and moral improvement as they have to gambling and dancing, I might have remained quietly at home, and they stood contending in my place. These polite accomplishments will never enrol your names on the bright annals of fame, who admire the belle void of intellectual knowledge, or applaud the dandy that talks largely on politics, without striving to assist his fellow in the revolution, when the nerves and muscles of every other man forced him into the field of action. You have a right to rejoice, and to let your hearts cheer you in the days of your youth ; yet remember that for all these things, God will bring you into judgment. Then, O ye sons of Africa, turn your mind from these perishable objects, and contend for the cause of God and the rights of man. Form yourselves into temperance societies. There are temperate men among you; then why will you any longer neglect to strive, by your example, to suppress vice in all its abhorrent forms? You have been told repeatedly of the glorious results arising from temperance, and can you bear to see the whites arising in honor and respectability, without endeavoring to grasp after that honor and respectability also?

But I forbear. Let our money, instead of being thrown away as heretofore, be appropriated for schools and seminaries of learning for our children and youth. We ought to follow the example of the whites in this respect. Nothing would raise our respectability, add to our peace and happiness, and reflect so much honor upon us, as to be ourselves the promoters of temperance, and the supporters, as far as we are able, of useful and scientific knowledge. The rays of light and knowledge have been hid from our view; we have been taught to consider ourselves as scarce superior to the brute creation; and have performed the most laborious part of American drudgery. Had we as a people received one half the early advantages the whites have received, I would defy the government of these United States to deprive us any longer of our rights.

I am informed that the agent of the Colonization Society has recently formed an association of young men, for the purpose of influencing those of us to go to Liberia who may feel disposed. The colonizationists are blind to their own interest, for should the nations of the earth make war with America, they would find their forces much weakened by our absence; or should we remain here, can our "brave soldiers," and "fellow-citizens," as they were termed in time of calamity, condescend to defend the rights of the whites, and be again deprived of their

own, or sent to Liberia in return ? Or, if the colonizationists are real friends to Africa, let them expend
the money which they collect, in erecting a college
to educate her injured sons in this land of gospel
light and liberty ; for it would be most thankfully
received on our part, and convince us of the truth
of their professions, and save time, expense and
anxiety. Let them place before us noble objects,
worthy of pursuit, and see if we prove ourselves to
be those unambitious negroes they term us. But
ah ! methinks their hearts are so frozen towards us,
they had rather their money should be sunk in the
ocean than to administer it to our relief ; and I fear,
if they dared, like Pharaoh, king of Egypt, they
would order every male child among us to be drowned. But the most high God is still as able to subdue the lofty pride of these white Americans, as He
was the heart of that ancient rebel. They say,
though we are looked upon as *things*, yet we sprang
from a scientific people. Had our men the requisite
force and energy, they would soon convince them
by their efforts both in public and private, that they
were men, or things in the shape of men. Well
may the colonizationists laugh us to scorn for our
negligence ; well may they cry, "Shame to the
sons of Africa." As the burden of the Israelites
was too great for Moses to bear, so also is our burden too great for our noble advocate to bear. You
must feel interested, my brethren, in what he un-
dertakes, and hold up his hands by your good works,
or in spite of himself, his soul will become discouraged, and his heart will die within him ; for he
has, as it were, the strong bulls of Bashan to contend with.

It is of no use for us to wait any longer for a
generation of well educated men to arise. We have
slumbered and slept too long already ; the day is far
spent ; the night of death approaches ; and you have
sound sense and good judgment sufficient to begin
with, if you feel disposed to make a right use of it.

Let every man of color throughout the United States, who possesses the spirit and principles of a man, sign a petition to Congress, to abolish slavery in the District of Columbia, and grant you the rights and privileges of common free citizens; for if you had had faith as a grain of mustard seed, long before this the mountains of prejudice might have been removed. We are all sensible that the Anti-Slavery Society has taken hold of the arm of our whole population, in order to raise them out of the mire. Now all we have to do is, by a spirit of virtuous ambition to strive to raise ourselves; and I am happy to have it in my power thus publicly to say, that the colored inhabitants of this city, in some respects, are beginning to improve. Had the free people of color in these United States nobly and boldly contended for their rights, and showed a natural genius and talent, although not so brilliant as some; had they held up, encouraged and patronized each other, nothing could have hindered us from being a thriving and flourishing people. There has been a fault among us. The reason why our distinguished men have not made themselves more influential is, because they fear that the strong current of oppostion through which they must pass, would cause their downfall and prove their overthrow. And what gives rise to this opposition? Envy. And what has it amounted to? Nothing. And who are the cause of it? Our whited sepulchres, who want to be great, and don't know how; who love to be called of men 'Rabbi, Rabbi, who put on false sanctity, and humble themselves to their brethren, for the sake of acquiring the highest place in the synagogue, and the uppermost seats at the feast. You, dearly beloved, who are the genuine followers of our Lord Jesus Christ, the salt of the earth and the light of the world, are not so culpable. As I told you, in the very first of my writing, I tell you again, I am but as a drop in the bucket—as one particle of the small dust of the earth. God will surely raise up those among us who will plead the cause of virtue, and the pure principles of morality, more eloquently than I am able to do.

It appears to me that America has become like the great city of Babylon, for she has boasted in her heart,—'I sit a queen, and am no widow, and shall see no sorrow ? She is indeed a seller of slaves and the souls of men ; she has made the Africans drunk with the wine of her fornication ; she has put them completely beneath her feet, and she means to keep them there ; her right hand supports the reins of government, and her left hand the wheel of power, and she is determined not to let go her grasp. But many powerful sons and daughters of Africa will shortly arise, who will put down vice and immorality among us, and declare by Him that sitteth upon the throne, that they will have their rights ; and if refused,'I am afraid they will spread horror and devastation around. I believe that the oppresion of injured Africa has come up before the Majesty of Heaven ; and when our cries shall have reached the ears of the Most High, it will be a tremendous day for the people of this land ; for strong is the arm of the Lord God Almighty.

Life has almost lost its charms for me ; death has lost its sting and the grave its terrors ; and at times I have a strong desire to depart and dwell with Christ, which is far better. Let me entreat my white brethren to awake and save our sons from dissipation, and our daughters from ruin. Lend the hand of assistance to feeble merit, plead the cause of virtue among our sable race ; so shall our curses upon you be turned into blessings ; and though you should endeavor to drive us from these shores, still we will cling to you the more firmly ; nor will we attempt to rise above you : we will presume to be called your equals only.

The unfriendly whites first drove the native American from his much loved home. Then they stole our fathers from their peaceful and quiet dwellings, and brought them hither, and made bond-men and bond-women of them and their little ones; they have obliged our brethren to labor, kept them in utter ignorance, nourished them in vice, and raised them in degradation; and now that we have enriched their soil, and filled their coffers, they say that we are not capable of becoming like white men, and that we never can rise to respectability in this country. They would drive us to a strange land. But before I go, the bayonet shall pierce me through. African rights and liberty is a subject that ought to fire the breast of every free man of color in these United States, and excite in his bosom a lively, deep, decided and heart-felt interest.

MRS. STEWART'S

FAREWELL ADDRESS TO HER FRIENDS IN THE CITY
OF BOSTON.

Delivered September 21, 1833.

"Is this vile world a friend to grace,
    To help me on to God?"

AH no! for it is with great tribulation that any shall enter through the gates into the holy city.

MY RESPECTED FRIENDS,

You have heard me observe that the shortness of time, the certainty of death, and the instability of all things here, induce me to turn my thoughts from earth to heaven. Borne down with a heavy load of sin and shame, my conscience filled with remorse; considering the throne of God forever guiltless, and my own eternal condemnation as just, I was at last brought to accept of salvation as a free gift, in and through the merits of a crucified Redeemer. Here I was brought to see,

"'Tis not by works of righteousness
    That our own hands have done,
But we are saved by grace alone,
    Abounding through the Son."

After these convictions, in imagination I found myself sitting at the feet of Jesus, clothed in my right mind. For I before had been like a ship tossed to and fro, in a storm at sea. Then was I glad when I realized the dangers I had escaped; and then I consecrated my soul and body, and all the powers of my mind to his service, from that time, henceforth; yea, even for evermore, amen.

I found that religion was full of benevolence; I found there was joy and peace in believing, and I felt as though I was commanded to come out from the world and be separate; to go forward and be baptized. Methought I heard a spiritual interrogation, are you able to drink of that cup that I have drank of? and to be baptized with the baptism that I have been baptized with? And my heart made this reply: Yea, Lord, I am able. Yet amid these bright hopes, I was filled with apprehensive fears, lest they were false. I found that sin still lurked within; it was hard for me to renounce all for Christ, when I saw my earthly prospects blasted. O, how bitter was that cup. Yet I drank it to its very dregs. It was hard for me to say, thy will be done; yet I was made to bend and kiss the rod. I was at last made willing to be any thing or nothing, for my Redeemer's sake. Like many, I was anxious to retain the world in one hand, and religion in the other. "Ye cannot serve God and mammon," sounded in my ear, and with giant-strength, I cut off my right hand, as it were, and plucked out my right eye, and cast them from me, thinking it better to enter life halt and maimed, rather than having two hands or eyes to be cast into hell. Thus ended these mighty conflicts, and I received this heart-cheering promise, "That neither death, nor life, nor principalities, nor powers, nor things present, nor things to come, should be able to separate me from the love of Christ Jesus, our Lord."

And truly, I can say with St. Paul, that at my conversion, I came to the people in the fulness of the gospel of grace. Having spent a few months in the city of ———, previous, I saw the flourishing condition of their churches, and the progress they were making in their Sabbath Schools. I visited their Bible Classes, and heard of the union that existed in their Female Associations. On my arrival here, not finding scarce an individual who felt interested in these subjects, and but few of the whites, except Mr. Garrison, and his friend Mr. Knapp; and hearing that those gentlemen had observed that female influence was powerful, my soul became fired with a holy zeal for your cause; every nerve and muscle in me was engaged in your behalf. I felt that I had a great work to perform; and was in haste to make a profession of my faith in Christ, that I might be about my Father's business. Soon after I made this profession, the Spirit of God came before me, and I spake before many. When going home, reflecting on what I had said, I felt ashamed, and knew not where I should hide myself. A something said within my breast, "press forward, I will be with thee." And my heart made this reply, Lord, if thou wilt be with me, then will I speak for thee so long as I live. And thus far I have every reason to believe that it is the divine influence of the Holy Spirit operating upon my heart that could possibly induce me to make the feeble and unworthy efforts that I have.

But to begin my subject: "Ye have heard that it hath been said, whoso is angry with his brother without a cause, shall be in danger of the judgment; and whoso shall say to his brother, Raca, shall be in danger of the council. But whosoever shall say, thou fool, shall be in danger of hell-fire." For several years my heart was in continual sorrow. And I believe that the Almighty beheld from his holy habitation, the affliction wherewith I was afflicted, and heard the false misrepresentations wherewith I was misrepresented, and there was none to help. Then I cried unto the Lord in my troubles. And thus for wise and holy purposes, best known to himself, he has raised me in the midst of my enemies, to vindicate my wrongs before this people; and to reprove them for sin, as I have reasoned to them of righteousness and judgment to come. "For as the heavens are higher than the earth, so are his ways above our ways, and his thoughts above our thoughts." I believe, that for wise and holy purposes, best known to himself, he hath unloosed my tongue and put his word into my mouth, in order to confound and put all those to shame that have rose up against me. For he hath clothed my face with steel, and lined my forehead with brass. He hath put his testimony within me, and engraven his seal on my forhead. And with these weapons I have indeed set the fiends of earth and hell at defiance.

What if I am a woman; is not the God of ancient times the God of these modern days? Did he not raise up Deborah, to be a mother, and a judge in Israel? Did not queen Esther save the lives of the Jews? And Mary Magdalene first declare the resurrection of Christ from the dead? Come, said the woman of Samaria, and see a man that hath told me all things that ever I did, is not this the Christ? St. Paul declared that it was a shame for a woman to speak in public, yet our great High Priest and Advocate did not condemn the woman for a more notorious offence than this; neither will he condemn this worthless worm. The bruised reed he will not break, and the smoking flax he will not quench, till he send forth judgment unto victory. Did St. Paul but know of our wrongs and deprivations, I presume he would make no objections to our pleading in public for our rights. Again; holy women ministered unto Christ and the apostles; and women of refinement in all ages, more or less, have had a voice in moral, religious and political subjects. Again; why the Almighty hath imparted unto me the power of speaking thus, I cannot tell. "And Jesus lifted up his voice and said, I thank thee, O Father, Lord of heaven and earth, that thou hast hid these things from the wise and prudent, and hast revealed them unto babes: even so, Father, for so it seemed good in thy sight."

But to convince you of the high opinion that was formed of the capacity and ability of woman, by the ancients, I would refer you to "Sketches of the Fair Sex." Read to the 51st page, and you will find that several of the Northern nations imagined that women could look into futurity, and that they had about them, an inconceivable something, approaching to divinity. Perhaps that idea was only the effect of the sagacity common to the sex, and the advantages which their natural address gave them over rough and simple warriors. Perhaps, also, those barbarians, surprised at the influence which beauty has over force, were led to ascribe to the supernatural attraction, a charm which they could not comprehend. A belief, however, that the Deity more readily communicates himself to women, has at one time or other, prevailed in every quarter of the earth; not only among the Germans and the Britons, but all the people of Scandinavia were possessed of it. Among the Greeks, women delivered the Oracles; the respect the Romans paid to the Sybils, is well known. The Jews had their prophetesses. The prediction of the Egyptian women obtained much credit at Rome, even under the Emperors. And in the most barbarous nations, all things that have the appearance of being supernatural, the mysteries of religion, the secrets of physic, and the rites of magic, were in the possession of women.

If such women as are here described have once existed, be no longer astonished then, my brethren and friends, that God at this eventful period should raise up your own females to strive, by their example both in public and private, to assist those who are endeavoring to stop the strong current of prejudice that flows so profusely against us at present. No longer ridicule their efforts, it will be counted for sin. For God makes use of feeble means sometimes, to bring about his most exalted purposes.

In the 15th century, the general spirit of this period is worthy of observation. We might then have seen women preaching and mixing themselves in controversies. Women occupying the chairs of Philosophy and Justice ; women harangueing in Latin before the Pope; women writing in Greek, and studying in Hebrew ; Nuns were Poetesses, and women of quality Divines ; and young girls who had studied Eloquence, would with the sweetest countenances, and the most plaintive voices, pathetically exhort the Pope and the Christian Princes, to declare war against the Turks. Women in those days devoted their leisure hours to contemplation and study. The religious spirit which has animated women in all ages, showed itself at this time. It has made them, by turns, martyrs, apostles, warriors, and concluded in making them divines and scholars.

Why cannot a religious spirit animate us now? Why cannot we become divines and scholars? Although learning is somewhat requisite, yet recollect that those great apostles, Peter and James, were ignorant and unlearned. They were taken from the fishing boat, and made fishers of men.

In the 13th century, a young lady of Bologne, devoted herself to the study of the Latin language, and of the Laws. At the age of twenty-three she pronounced a funeral oration in Latin, in the great church of Bologne. And to be admitted as an orator, she had neither need of indulgence on account of her youth or of her sex. At the age of twenty-six, she took the degree of Doctor of Laws, and began publicly to expound the Institutions of Justinian. At the age of thirty, her great reputation raised her to a chair, where she taught the law to a prodigious concourse of scholars from all nations. She joined the charms and accomplishments of a woman to all the knowledge of a man. And such was the power of her eloquence, that her beauty was only admired when her tongue was silent.'

What if such women as are here described should rise among our sable race? And it is not impossible. For it is not the color of the skin that makes the man or the woman, but the principle formed in the soul. Brilliant wit will shine, come from whence it will; and genius and talent will not hide the brightness of its lustre.

But, to return to my subject; the mighty work of reformation has begun among this people. The dark clouds of ignorance are dispersing. The light of science is bursting forth. Knowledge is beginning to flow, nor will its moral influence be extinguished till its refulgent rays have spread over us from East to West, and from North to South. Thus far is this mighty work begun, but not as yet accomplished. Christians must awake from their slumbers. Religion must flourish among them before the church will be built up in its purity, or immorality be suppressed.

Yet, notwithstanding your prospects are thus fair and bright, I am about to leave you, perhaps, never more to return. For I find it is no use for me as an individual to try to make myself useful among my color in this city. It was contempt for my moral and religious opinions in private that drove me thus before a public. Had experience more plainly shown me that it was the nature of man to crush his fellow, I should not have thought it so hard. Wherefore, my respected friends, let us no longer talk of prejudice, till prejudice becomes extinct at home. Let us no longer talk of opposition, till we cease to oppose our own. For while these evils exist, to talk is like giving breath to the air, and labor to the wind. Though wealth is far more highly prized than humble merit, yet none of these things move me. Having God for my friend and portion, what have I to fear? Promotion cometh neither from the East or West, and as long as it is the will of God, I rejoice that I am as I am; for man in his best estate, is altogether vanity. Men of eminence have mostly risen from obscurity; nor will I, although a female of a darker hue, and far more obscure than they, bend my head or hang my harp upon willows; for though poor, I will virtuous prove. And if it is the will of my heavenly Father to reduce me to penury and want, I am ready to say, amen, even so be it. "The foxes have holes, and the birds of the air have nests, but the Son of man hath not where to lay his head."

During the short period of my Christian warfare, I have indeed had to contend against the fiery darts of the devil. And was it not that the righteous are kept by the mighty power of God through faith unto salvation, long before this I should have proved to be like the seed by the way-side. For it has actually appeared to me at different periods, as though the powers of earth and hell had combined against me, to prove my overthrow. Yet amidst their dire attempts, I have found the Almighty to be "a friend that sticketh closer than a brother." He never will forsake the soul that leans on him; though he chastens and corrects, it is for the soul's best interest. "And as a Father pitieth his children, so the Lord pitieth them that fear him."

But some of you have said, "do not talk so much about religion, the people do not wish to hear you. We know these things, tell us something we do not know." If you know these things, my dear friends, and have performed them, far happier, and more prosperous would you now have been. "He that knoweth his Lord's will and obeyeth it not, shall be beaten with many stripes." Sensible of this, I have, regardless of the frowns and scoffs of a guilty world, plead up religion, and the pure principles of morality among you. Religion is the most glorious theme that mortals can converse upon. The older it grows the more new beauties it displays. Earth, with its brilliant attractions, appears mean and sordid when compared to it. It is that fountain that has no end, and those that drink thereof shall never thirst; for it is, indeed, a well of water springing up in the soul unto everlasting life.

Again, those ideas of greatness which are held forth to us, are vain delusions, are airy visions which we shall never realize. All that man can say or do can never elevate us, it is a work that must be effected between God and ourselves. And, how? by dropping all political discussions in our behalf, for these, in my opinion, sow the seed of discord, and strengthen the cord of prejudice. A spirit of animosity is already risen, and unless it is quenched, a fire will burst forth and devour us, and our young will be slain by the sword. It is the sovereign will of God that our condition should be thus and so. "For he hath formed one vessel for honor, and another for dishonor." And shall the clay say to him that formed it, why hast thou formed me thus? It is high time for us to drop political discussions, and when our day of deliverance comes, God will provide a way for us to escape, and fight his own battles.

Finally, my brethren, let us follow after godliness, and the things which make for peace. Cultivate your own minds and morals; real merit will elevate you. Pure religion will burst your fetters. Turn your attention to industry. Strive to please your employers. Lay up what you earn. And remember, that in the grave distinction withers, and the high and low are alike renowned.

But I draw to a conclusion. Long will the kind sympathy of some much loved friend, be written on the tablet of my memory, especially those kind individuals who have stood by me like pitying angels, and befriended me when in the midst of difficulty; many blessings rest on them. Gratitude is all the tribute I can offer. A rich reward awaits them.

To my unconverted friends, one and all, I would say, shortly this frail tenement of mine will be dissolved and lie mouldering in ruins. O, solemn thought! Yet why should I revolt, for it is the glorious hope of a blessed immortality, beyond the grave, that has supported me thus far through this vale of tears. Who among you will strive to meet me at the right hand of Christ. For the great day of retribution is fast approaching, and who shall be able to abide his coming? You are forming characters for eternity. As you live so you will die; as death leaves you, so judgment will find you. Then shall we receive the glorious welcome, "Come, ye blessed of my Father, inherit the kingdom prepared for you from before the foundation of the world." Or, hear the heart-rending sentence, "Depart ye cursed into everlasting fire prepared for the devil and his angels." When thrice ten thousand years have rolled away, eternity will be but just begun. Your ideas will but just begin to expand. O, eternity, who can unfathom thine end, or comprehend thy beginning.

Dearly beloved: I have made myself contemptible in the eyes of many, that I might win some. But it has been like labor in vain. "Paul may plant, and Apollos water, but God alone giveth the increase."

To my brethren and sisters in the church, I would say, be ye clothed with the breast-plate of righteousness, having your loins girt about with truth, prepared to meet the Bridegroom at his coming; for blessed are those servants that are found watching.

Farewell. In a few short years from now, we shall meet in those upper regions where parting will be no more. There we shall sing and shout, and shout and sing, and make heaven's high arches ring. There we shall range in rich pastures, and partake of those living streams that never dry. O, blissful thought! Hatred and contention shall cease, and we shall join with redeemed millions in ascribing glory and honor, and riches, and power and blessing to the Lamb that was slain, and to Him that sitteth upon the throne. Nor eye hath seen, nor ear heard, neither hath it entered into the heart of man to conceive of the joys that are prepared for them that love God. Thus far has my life been almost a life of complete disappointment. God has tried me as by fire. Well was I aware that if I contended boldly for his cause, I must suffer. Yet, I chose rather to suffer affliction with his people, than to enjoy the pleasures of sin for a season. And I believe that the glorious declaration was about to be made applicable to me, that was made to God's ancient covenant people by the prophet, Comfort ye, comfort ye, my people : say unto her that her warfare is accomplished, and that her iniquities are pardoned. I believe that a rich reward awaits me, if not in this world, in the world to come. O, blessed reflection. The bitterness of my soul has departed from those who endeavored to discourage and hinder me in my Christian progress ; and I can now forgive my enemies, bless those who have hated me, and cheerfully pray for those who have despitefully used and persecuted me.

Fare you well, farewell.

MARIA S. STEWART.

New York, April 14, 1834.

THE NEGRO'S COMPLAINT.

FORC'D from home and all its pleasures,
  Afric's coast I left forlorn ;
To increase a stranger's treasures,
  O'er the raging billows borne.
Men from England* bought and sold me,
  Paid my price in paltry gold ;
But though slave they have enroll'd me,
  Minds are never to be sold.

Still in thought as free as ever,
  What are England's rights, (I ask ;)
Me from my delights to sever,
  Me to torture, me to task ?
Fleecy locks and black complexion,
  Cannot forfeit Nature's claim ;
Skins may differ, but affection
  Dwells in white and black the same.

Why did all-creating Nature,
  Make the plant for which we toil ?
Sighs must fan it, tears must water,
  Sweat of ours must dress the soil.
Think, ye masters iron-hearted,
  Lolling at your jovial boards :
Think how many backs have smarted
  For the sweets your cane affords.

Is there, as ye sometimes tell us,
  Is there ONE who reigns on high ?
Has HE bid you buy and sell us,
  Speaking from His throne, the sky ?
Ask Him if your knotted scourges,
  Fetters, blood-extorting screws,
Are the means which duty urges,
  Agents of his will to use ?

---

*ENGLAND had 800,000 Slaves, and she has made them FREE ! AMERICA has 2,250,000 ! and she HOLDS THEM FAST ! ! !

Hark! He answers—wild tornadoes,
  Strewing yonder sea with wrecks:
Wasting towns, plantations, meadows,
  Are the voice with which He speaks.
He, foreseeing what vexation
  Afric's sons would undergo,
Fix'd their tyrant's habitation
  Where his whirlwind answers—" No!"

By our blood in Afric wasted,
  Ere our necks receiv'd the chain;
By the miseries which we tasted,
  Crossing in your barks the main.
By our sufferings, since ye brought us
  To the man-degrading mart;
All sustain'd with patience, taught us
  Only by a broken heart.

Deem our nation brutes no longer,
  Till some reason ye shall find
Worthier to regard, and stronger
  Than the *color* of our kind!
Slaves of gold! whose sordid dealings
  Tarnish all your boasted powers;
Prove that *ye* have human feelings,
  Ere ye proudly question ours!

☞ For Sale at the Office of the Massachusetts Anti-Slavery Society, No. 46, Washington Street, Boston, by B. C. Bacon, Agent and Secretary; and by David Ruggles, No. 67, Lespenard Street, New York City.

RELIGIOUS EXPERIENCE

JOURNAL

From life by A.Hoffy.   Printed by P.S.Duval.

MRS JARENA LEE.

Preacher of the A. M. E. Church.

Aged 60 years on the 11th day of the 2nd month 1844.

Philada 1844

RELIGIOUS EXPERIENCE

AND

JOURNAL

OF

MRS. JARENA LEE,

GIVING

AN ACCOUNT OF HER CALL TO PREACH THE GOSPEL.

———o0o———

Revised and corrected from the Original Manuscript, written by herself.

PHILADELPHIA:

Printed and Published for the Author.

1849.

RELIGIOUS EXPERIENCE AND JOURNAL

OF

MRS. JARENA LEE,

—◆—

"And it shall come to pass .... that I will pour out my Spirit upon all flesh;
and your sons, and your *daughters* shall prophecy."—*Joel* ii. 28.

I was born February 11th, 1783, at Cape May, State of New Jersey.
At the age of seven years I was parted from my parents, and went
to live as a servant maid, with a Mr. Sharp, at the distance of about
sixty miles from the place of my birth.

My parents being wholly ignorant of the knowledge of God, had
not therefore instructed me in any degree in this great matter. Not
long after the commencement of my attendance on this lady, she had
bid me do something respecting my work, which in a little while
after she asked me if I had done, when I replied, Yes—but this was
not true.

At this awful point, in my early history, the Spirit of God moved
in power through my conscience, and told me I was a wretched sinner. On this account so great was the impression, and so strong were
the feelings of guilt, that I promised in my heart that I would not tell
another lie.

But notwithstanding this promise my heart grew harder, after a
while, yet the Spirit of the Lord never entirely forsook me, but continued mercifully striving with me, until his gracious power converted
my soul.

The manner of this great accomplishment, was as follows: In the
year 1804, it so happened that I went with others to hear a missionary of the Presbyterian order preach. It was an afternoon meeting,
but few were there, the place was a school room; but the preacher
was solemn, and in his countenance the earnestness of his master's
business appeared equally strong, as though he were about to speak
to a multitude.

At the reading of the Psalms, a ray of renewed conviction darted
into my soul. These were the words, composing the first verse of
the Psalms for the service:

"Lord, I am vile. conceived in sin,
Born unholy and unclean.
Sprung from man, whose guilty fall
Corrupts the race, and taints us all."

This description of my condition struck me to the heart, and made me to feel in some measure, the weight of my sins, and sinful nature. But not knowing how to run immediately to the Lord for help, I was driven of Satan, in the course of a few days, and tempted to destroy myself.

There was a brook about a quarter of a mile from the house, in which there was a deep hole, where the water whirled about among the rocks; to this place it was suggested, I must go and drown myself.

At the time I had a book in my hand; it was on a Sabbath morning, about ten o'clock; to this place I resorted, where on coming to the water I sat down on the bank, and on my looking into it, it was suggested that drowning would be an easy death. It seemed as if some one was speaking to me, saying put your head under, it will not distress you. But by some means, of which I can give no account, my thoughts were taken entirely from this purpose, when I went from the place to the house again. It was the unseen arm of God which saved me from self-murder.

But notwithstanding this escape from death, my mind was not at rest—but so great was the labor of my spirit and the fearful oppressions of a judgment to come, that I was reduced as one extremely ill,. on which account a physician was called to attend me, from which illness I recovered in about three months.

But as yet I had not found Him of whom Moses and the prophets did write, being extremely ignorant: there being no one to instruct me in the way of life and salvation as yet. After my recovery, I left the lady, who, during my sickness, was exceedingly kind, and went to Philadelphia. From this place I soon went a few miles into the country, where I resided in the family of a Roman Catholic. But my anxiety still continued respecting my poor soul, on which account I used to watch my opportunity to read in the Bible; and this lady observing this, took the Bible from me and hid it, giving me a novel in its stead—which when I perceived, I refused to read.

Soon after this I again went to the city of Philadelphia, and commenced going to the English Church, the pastor of which was an Englishman, by the name of P. Moore, one of the number who at first preached Methodism in America, in the city of New York.

But while sitting under the ministration of this man, which was about three months, and at the last time, it appeared that there was a wall between me and a communion with that people, which was higher than I could possibly see over, and seemed to make this impression upon my mind, *this is not the people for you.*

But on returning home at noon I inquired of the head cook of the house respecting the rules of the Methodists, as I knew she belonged to that society, who told me what they were; on which account I replied, that I should not be able to abide by such strict rules not even one year—however, I told her that I would go with her and hear what they had to say.

The man who was to speak in the afternoon of that day, was the Rev. Richard Allen, since bishop of the African Episcopal Methodists in America. During the labors of this man that afternoon, I had come to the conclusion, that this is the people to which my heart unites, and it so happened, that as soon as the service closed he invited such as felt a desire to flee the wrath to come, to unite on trial with them—I embraced the opportunity. Three weeks from that day, my soul was gloriously converted to God, under preaching, at the very outset of the sermon. The text was barely pronounced, which was 'I perceive thy heart is not right in the sight of God," when there appeared to *my* view, in the centre of the heart, *one* sin; and this was *malice* against one particular individual, who had strove deeply to injure me, which I resented. At this discovery I said, *Lord* I forgive *every* creature. That instant, it appeared to me as if a garment, which had entirely enveloped my whole person, even to my fingers' ends, split at the crown of my head, and was stripped away from me, passing like a shadow from my sight—when the glory of God seemed to cover me in its stead.

That moment, though hundreds were present, I did leap to my feet and declare that God, for Christ's sake, had pardoned the sins of my soul. Great was the ecstacy of my mind, for I felt that not only the sin of *malice* was pardoned, but all other sins were swept away together. That day was the first when my heart had believed, and my tongue had made confession unto salvation—the first words uttered, a part of that song, which shall fill eternity with its sound, was *glory to God*. For a few moments I had power to exhort sinners, and to tell of the wonders and of the goodness of Him who had clothed me with *His* salvation. During this the minister was silent, until my soul felt its duty had been performed, when he declared another witness of the power of Christ to forgive sins on earth, was manifest in my conversion.

From the day on which I first went to the Methodist Church, until the hour of my deliverance, I was strangely buffeted by that enemy of all righteousness—the devil.

I was naturally of a lively turn of disposition; and during the space of time from my first awakening until I knew my peace was made with God, I rejoiced in the vanities of this life, and then again sunk back into sorrow.

For four years I had continued in this way, frequently laboring under the awful apprehension, that I could never be happy in this life. This persuasion was greatly strengthened during the three weeks, which was the last of Satan's power over me, in this peculiar manner, on which account I had come to the conclusion that I had better be dead than alive. Here I was again tempted to destroy my life by drowning; but suddenly this mode was changed—and while in the dusk of the evening, as I was walking to and fro in the yard of the house, I was beset to hang myself with a cord suspended from the wall enclosing the secluded spot.

But no sooner was the intention resolved on in my mind, than an awful dread came over me, when I ran into the house; still the tempter pursued me. There was standing a vessel of water—into this I was strangly impressed to plunge my head, so as to extinguish the life which God had given me. Had I done this, I have been always of the opinion, that I should have been unable to have released myself; although the vessel was scarcely large enough to hold a gallon of water. Of me may it not be said, as written by Isaiah, (chap. 65, verses 1, 2.) "I am sought of them that asked not for me; I am found of them that sought me not." Glory be to God for his redeeming power, which saved me from the violence of my own hands, from the malice of Satan, and from eternal death; for had I have killed myself, a great ransom could not have delivered me; for it is written —"No murderer hath eternal life abiding in him." How appropriately can I sing—

"Jesus sought me when a stranger,
　Wandering from the fold of God;
He to rescue me from danger,
　Interposed his precious blood "

But notwithstanding the terror which seized upon me, when about to end my life, I had no view of the precipice on the edge of which I was tottering, until it was over, and my eyes were opened. Then the awful gulf of hell seemed to be open beneath me, covered only, as it were, by a spider's web, on which I stood. I seemed to hear the howling of the damned, to see the smoke of the bottomless pit, and to hear the rattling of those chains, which hold the impenitent under clouds of darkness to the judgment of the great day.

I trembled like Belshazzar, and cried out in the horror of my spirit, "God be merciful to me a sinner." That night I formed a resolution to pray; which, when resolved upon, there appeared, sitting in one corner of the room, Satan, in the form of a monstrous dog, and in a rage, as if in pursuit, his tongue protruding from his mouth to a great length, and his eyes looked like two balls of fire; it soon, however, vanished out of my sight. From this state of terror and dismay, I was happily delivered under the preaching of the Gospel as before related.

This view which I was permitted to have of Satan, in the form of a dog, is evidence, which corroborates in my estimation, the Bible account of a hell of fire, which burneth with brimstone, called in Scripture the bottomless pit; the place where all liars, who repent not, shall have their portion; as also the Sabbath breaker, the adulterer, the fornicator, with the fearful, the abominable, and the unbelieving, this shall be the portion of their cup.

This language is too strong and expressive to be applied to any state of suffering in *time*. Were it to be thus applied, the reality could no where be found in human life; the consequence would be, that *this* scripture would be found a false testimony. But when made to apply to an endless state of perdition, in eternity, beyond the bounds of human life, then this language is found not to exceed our views of a state of eternal damnation.

During the latter part of my state of conviction, I can now apply to my case, as it then was, the beautiful words of the poet:

"The more I strove against its power,
I felt its weight and guilt the more;
'Till late I heard my Saviour say,
Come hither soul, I am the way."

This I found to be true, to the joy of my disconsolate and despairing heart, in the hour of my conversion to God.

During this state of mind, while sitting near the fire one evening, after I had heard Rev. Richard Allen, as before related, a view of my distressed condition so affected my heart, that I could not refrain from weeping and crying aloud; which caused the lady with whom I then lived, to inquire, with surprise, what ailed me; to which I answered, that I knew not what ailed me. She replied that I ought to pray. I arose from where I was sitting, being in an agony, and weeping convulsively, requested her to pray for me; but at the very moment when she would have done so, some person wrapped heavily at the door for admittance; it was but a person of the house, but this occurrence was sufficient to interrupt us in our intentions; and I believe to this day, I should then have found salvation to my soul. This interruption was, doubtless, also the work of Satan.

Although at this time, when my conviction was so great, yet I knew not that Jesus Christ was the Son of God, the second person in the adorable Trinity. I knew him not in the pardon of my sins, yet I felt a consciousness that if I died without pardon, that my lot must inevitably be damnation. If I would pray—I knew not how. I could form no connexion of ideas into words; but I knew the Lord's prayer; this I uttered with a loud voice, and with all my might and strength. I was the most ignorant creature in the world; I did not even know that Christ had died for the sins of the world, and to save sinners. Every circumstance, however, was so directed as still to continue and increase the sorrows of my heart, which I now know to have been a Godly sorrow which wrought repentance, which is not to repented of. Even the falling of the dead leaves from the forests, and the dried spires of the mown grass, showed me that I too must die in like manner. But my case was awfully different from that of the grass of the field, or the wide spread decay of a thousand forests, as I felt within me a living principle, an immortal spirit, which cannot die, and must forever either enjoy the smiles of its Creator, or feel the pangs of ceaseless damnation.

But the Lord led me on; being gracious, he took pity on my ignorance; he heard my wailings, which had entered into the ear of the Lord of Sabaoth. Circumstances so transpired that I soon came to a knowledge of the being and character of the Son of God, of whom I knew nothing.

My strength had left me. I had become feverish and sickly through the violence of my feelings, on which account I left my place of service to spend a week with a colored physician, who was a member of the Methodist society, and also to spend this week in going to places where prayer and supplication was statedly made for such as me.

Through this means I had learned much, so as to be able in some degree to comprehend the spiritual meaning of the text, which the minister took on the Sabbath morning, as before related, which was "I perceive thy heart is not right in the sightof God."—Acts, chap. 8, verse 21.

This text, as already related, became the power of God unto salvation to me, because I believed. I was baptized according to the direction of our Lord, who said, as he was about to ascend from the mount, to his disciples, "Go ye into all the world and preach my gospel to every creature, he that believeth and is baptized shall be saved."

I have now passed through the account of my conviction, and also of my conversion to God: and shall next speak of the blessings of sanctification.

A time, after I had received forgiveness, flowed sweetly on; day and night my joy was full, no temptation was permitted to molest me. I could say continually with the psalmist, that "God had separated my sins from me as far as the east is from the west." I was ready continually to cry,

"Come all the world, come sinner thou,
All things in Christ are ready now."

I continued in this happy state of mind for almost three months, when a certain colored man, by name William Scott, came to pay me a religious visit. He had been for many years a faithful follower of the Lamb; and he had also taken much time in visiting the sick and distressed of our color, and understood well the great things belonging to a man of full stature in Christ Jesus.

In the course of our conversation, he inquired if the Lord had jus-

tified my soul. I answered yes. He then asked me if he had sanc-
tified me. I answered no ; and that I did not know what that was.
He then undertook to instruct me further in the knowledge of the
Lord respecting this blessing.

He told me the progress of the soul from a state of darkness, or
of nature, was three-fold ; or consisted in three degrees, as follows :
First, conviction for sin. Second, justification from sin. Third, the
entire sanctification of the soul to God. I thought this description
was beautiful, and immediately believed in it. He then inquired if I
would promise to pray for this in my secret devotions. I told him
yes. Very soon I began to call upon the Lord to show me all that
was in my heart, which was not according to his will. Now there
appeared to be a new struggle commencing in my soul, not accompanied with fear, guilt, and bitter distress, as while under my first
conviction for sin, but a laboring of the mind to know more of the
right way of the Lord. I began now to feel that my heart was not
clean in his sight; that there yet remained the roots of bitterness,
which if not destroyed, would ere long sprout up from these roots, and
overwhelm me in a new growth of the brambles and brushwood of
sin.

By the increasing light of the Spirit, I had found there yet remained
the root of pride, anger, self-will, with many evils, the result of fallen
nature. I now became alarmed at this discovery, and began to fear
that I had been deceived in my experience. I was now greatly
alarmed, lest I should fall away from what I knew I had enjoyed ;
and to guard against this I prayed almost incessantly, without acting
faith on the power and promises of God to keep me from falling. I
had not yet learned how to war against temptation of this kind. Satan
well knew that if he could succeed in making me disbelieve my conversion, that he would catch me either on the ground of complete
despair, or on the ground of infidelity. For if all I had passed through
was to go for nothing, and was but a fiction, the mere ravings of a
disordered mind, that I would naturally be led to believe that there
is nothing in religion at all.

From this snare I was mercifully preserved, and led to believe that
there was yet a greater work than that of pardon to be wrought in me.
I retired to a secret place, (after having sought this blessing, as well
as I could, for nearly three months, from the time brother Scott had
instructed me respecting it,) for prayer, about four o'clock in the afternoon. I had struggled long and hard, but found not the desire of my
heart. When I rose from my knees, there seemed a voice speaking
to me, as I yet stood in a leaning posture—"Ask for sanctification."
When to my surprise, I recollected that I had not even thought of it
in my whole prayer. It would seem Satan had hidden the very object
from my mind, for which I had purposely kneeled to pray. But when

this voice whispered in my heart, saying, "Pray for sanctification," I again bowed in the same place, at the same time, and said "Lord *sanctify* my soul for Christ's sake." That very instant, as if lightning had darted through me, I sprang to my feet, and cried, "The Lord has sanctified my soul!" There was none to hear this but the angels who stood around to witness my joy—and Satan, whose malice raged the more. That Satan was there, I knew; for no sooner had I cried out "The Lord has sanctified my soul," than there seemed another voice behind me, saying "No, it is too great a work to be done." But another spirit said "Bow down for the witness—I received it—*thou art sanctified!*" The first I knew of myself after that, I was standing in the yard with my hands spread out, and looking with my face toward heaven.

I now ran into the house and told them what had happened to me, when, as it were. a new rush of the same ecstacy came upon me, and caused me to feel as if I were in an ocean of light and bliss.

During this, I stood perfectly still, the tears rolling in a flood from my eyes. So great was the joy, that it is past description. There is no language that can describe it, except that which was heard by St. Paul, when he was caught up to third heaven, and heard words which it was not lawful to utter.

MY CALL TO PREACH THE GOSPEL.

Between four and five years after my sanctification, on a certain time, an impressive silence fell upon me, and I stood as if some one was about to speak to me, yet I had no such thought in my heart.— But to my utter surprise there seemed to sound a voice which I thought I distinctly heard, and most certainly understand, which said to me, "Go preach the Gospel!" I immediately replied aloud, "No one will believe me." Again I listened, and again the same voice seemed to say—"Preach the Gospel; I will put words in your mouth, and will turn your enemies to become your friends."

At first I supposed that Satan had spoken to me, for I had read that he could transform himself into an angel of light for the purpose of deception. Immediately I went into a secret place, and called upon the Lord to know if he had called me to preach, and whether I was deceived or not; when there appeared to my view the form and figure of a pulpit, with a Bible lying thereon, the back of which was presented to me as plainly as if it had been a literal fact.

In consequence of this, my mind became so exercised, that during the night following, I took a text and preached in my sleep. I thought there stood before me a great multitude, while I expounded to them the things of religion. So violent were my exertions and so loud were my exclamations, that I awoke from the sound of my own voice, which also awoke the family of the house where I resided. Two days after I went to see the preacher in charge of the African Society, who was the Rev. Richard Allen, the same before named in these pages, to tell him that I felt it my duty to preach the gospel But as I drew near the street in which his house was, which was in the city of Philadelphia, my courage began to fail me; so terrible did the cross appear, it seemed that I should not be able to bear it. Previous to my setting out to go to see him, so agitated was my mind, that my appetite for my daily food failed me entirely. Several times on my way there, I turned back again; but as often I felt my strength again renewed, and I soon found that the nearer I approached to the house of the minister, the less was my fear. Accordingly, as soon as I came to the door, my fears subsided, the cross was removed, all things appeared pleasant—I was tranquil.

I now told him, that the Lord had revealed it to me, that must preach the gospel. He replied, by asking, in what sphere I wished to move in? I said, among the Methodists. He then replied, that a Mrs. Cook, a Methodist lady, had also some time before requested the same privilege; who, it was believed, had done much good in the way of exhortation, and holding prayer meetings; and who had been permitted to do so by the verbal license of the preacher in charge at the time. But as to women preaching, he said that our Discipline knew nothing at all about it—that it did not call for women preachers. This I was glad to hear, because it removed the fear of the cross—but no sooner did this feeling cross my mind, than I found that a love of souls had in a measure departed from me ; that holy energy which burned within me, as a fire, began to be smothered. This I soon perceived.

O how careful ought we to be, lest through our by-laws of church government and discipline, we bring into disrepute even the word of life. For as unseemly as it may appear now-a-days for a woman to preach, it should be remembered that nothing is impossible with God. And why should it be thought impossible, heterodox, or improper for a woman to preach? seeing the Saviour died for the woman as well as for the man.

If the man may preach, because the Saviour died for him, why not the woman? seeing he died for her also. Is he not a whole Saviour, instead of a half one? as those who hold it wrong for a woman to preach, would seem to make it appear.

Did not Mary *first* preach the risen Saviour, and is not the doctrine of the resurrection the very climax of Christianity—hangs not all our hope on this, as argued by St. Paul ? Then did not Mary, a woman, preach the gospel ? for she preached the resurrection of the crucified Son of God.

But some will say that Mary did not expound the Scripture, therefore, she did not preach, in the proper sense of the term. To this I reply, it may be that the term *preach* in those primitive times, did not mean exactly what it is now *made* to mean ; perhaps it was a great deal more simple then, than it is now—if it were not, the unlearned fishermen could not have preached the gospel at all, as they had no learning.

To this it may be replied, by those who are determined not to believe that it is right for a woman to preach, that the disciples, though they were fishermen and ignorant of letters too, were inspired so to do. To which I would reply, that though they were inspired, yet that inspiration did not save them from showing their ignorance of letters, and of man's wisdom ; this the multitude soon found out, by listening to the remarks of the envious Jewish priests. If then, to preach the gospel, by the gift of heaven, comes by inspiration solely, is God straitened : must he take the man exclusively ? May he not, did he not, and can he not inspire a female to preach the simple story of the birth, life, death, and resurrection of our Lord, and accompany it too with power to the sinner's heart. As for me, I am fully persuaded that the Lord called me to labor according to what I have received, in his vineyard. If he has not, how could he consistently bear testimony in favor of my poor labors, in awakening and converting sinners?

In my wanderings up and down among men, preaching according to my ability, I have frequently found families who told me that they had not for several years been to a meeting, and yet, while listening to hear what God would say by his poor female instrument, have believed with trembling—tears rolling down their cheeks, the signs of contrition and repentance towards God. I firmly believe that I have sown seed, in the name of the Lord, which shall appear with its increase at the great day of accounts, when Christ shall come to make up his jewels.

At a certain time, I was beset with the idea, that soon or late I should fall from grace and lose my soul at last. I was frequently called to the throne of grace about this matter, but found no relief ; the temptation pursued me still. Being more and more afflicted with it, till at a certain time, when the spirit strongly impressed it on my mind to enter into my closet and carry my case once more to the Lord ; the Lord enabled me to draw nigh to him, and to his mercy seat, at this time, in an extraordinary manner ; for while I wrestled with him for the victory over this disposition to doubt whether I should persevere, there appeared a form of fire, about the size of a man's hand, as I was on my knees ; at the same moment there appeared to the eye of faith a man robed in a white garment, from the shoulders down to the feet ; from him a voice proceeded, saying : "Thou shalt never return from the cross." Since that time I have never doubted, but believe that God will keep me until the day of redemption. Now I could adopt the very language of St. Paul, and say, that nothing could have separated me from the love of God, which is in Christ Jesus. Since that time, 1807, until the present, 1833, I have not even doubted the power and goodness of God to keep me from falling, through the sanctification of the spirit and belief of the truth.

MY MARRIAGE.

In the year 1811, I changed my situation in life, having married Mr. Joseph Lee, pastor of a Society at Snow Hill, about six miles from the city of Philadelphia. It became necessary therefore for me to remove. This was a great trial at first, as I knew no person at Snow Hill, except my husband, and to leave my associates in the society, and especially those who composed the *band* of which I was one. None but those who have been in sweet fellowship with such as really love God, and have together drank bliss and happiness from the same fountain, can tell how dear such company is, and how hard it is to part from them.

At Snow Hill, as was feared, I never found that agreement and closeness in communion and fellowship, that I had in Philadelphia, among my young companions, nor ought I to have expected it. The manners and customs at this place were somewhat different, on which account I became discontented in the course of a year, and began to importune my husband to remove to the city. But this plan did not suit him, as he was the Pastor of the Society, he could not bring his mind to leave them. This afflicted me a little. But the Lord showed me in a dream what his will was concerning this matter.

I dreamed that as I was walking on the summit of a beautiful hill, that I saw near me a flock of sheep, fair and white, as if but newly washed; when there came walking toward me a man of a grave and dignified countenance, dressed entirely in white, as it were in a robe, and looking at me, said emphatically, "Joseph Lee must take care of these sheep, or the wolf will come and devour them." When I awoke I was convinced of my error, and immediately, with a glad heart, yielded to the right spirit in the Lord. This also greatly strengthened my faith in his care over them, for fear the wolf should by some means take any of them away. The following verse was beautifully suited to our condition, as well as to all the little flocks of God scattered up and down this land :

"Us into Thy protec'ion take,
　And gather wi'h Thine arm;
Unless the fold we first forsake,
　The wolf can never harm."

After this, I fell into a state of general debility, and in an ill state of health, so much so, that I could not sit up; but a desire to warn sinners to flee the wrath to come, burned vehemently in my heart, when the Lord would send sinners into the house to see me. Such opportunities I embraced to press home on their consciences the things of eternity, and so effectual was the word of exhortation made through the Spirit, that I have seen them fall to the floor crying aloud for mercy.

From this sickness I did not expect to recover, and there was but one thing which bound me to earth, and this was, that I had not as yet preached the gospel to the fallen sons and daughters of Adam's race, to the satisfaction of my mind. I wished to go from one end of the earth to the other, crying, Behold, behold the lamb! To this end I earnestly prayed the Lord to raise me up, if consistent with his will. He condescended to hear my prayer, and to give me a token in a dream, that in due time I should recover my health. The dream was as follows: I thought I saw the sun rise in the morning, and ascend to an altitude of about half an hour high, and then become obscured by a dense black cloud, which continued to hide its rays for about one-third part of the day, and then it burst forth again with renewed splendor.

This dream I interpreted to signify my early life, my conversion to God, and this sickness, which was a great affliction, as it hindered me, and I feared would forever hinder me from preaching the gospel, was signified by the cloud; and the bursting forth of the sun, again, was the recovery of my health, and being permitted to preach.

I went to the throne of grace on this subject, where the Lord made this impressive reply in my heart, while on my knees: "Ye shall be restored to thy health again, and worship God in full purpose of heart."

This manifestation was so impressive, that I could but hide my face as if some one was gazing upon me, to think of the great goodness of the Almighty God to my poor soul and body. From that very time I began to gain strength of body and mind, glory to God in the highest, until my health was fully recovered.

For six years from this time I continued to receive from above, such baptisms of the Spirit as mortality could scarcely bear. About that time I was called to suffer in my family, by death—five, in the course of about six years, fell by his hand; my husband being one of the number, which was the greatest affliction of all.

I was now left alone in the world, with two infant children, one of the age of about two years, the other six months, with no other dependence than the promise of Him who hath said—I will be the widow's God, and a father to the fatherless. Accordingly, he raised me up friends, whose liberality comforted and solaced me in my state of widowhood and sorrows, I could sing with the greatest propriety the words of the poet.

> " He helps the stranger in distress,
> The widow and the fatherless,
> And grants the prisoner sweet release."

I can say even now, with the Psalmist, "Once I was young, but now I am old, yet I have never seen the righteous forsaken, nor his seed begging bread." I have ever been fed by his bounty, clothed by his mercy, comforted and healed when sick, succored when tempted, and every where upheld by his hand.

THE SUBJECT OF MY CALL TO PREACH RENEWED.

It was now eight years since I had made applicaion to be permitted to preach the gospel, during which time I had only been allowed to exhort, and even this privilege but seldom. This subject now was renewed afresh in my mind; it was as a fire shut up in my bones. About thirteen months passed on, while under this renewed impression. During this time, I had solicited of the Rev. Bishop, Richard Allen, who at this time had become Bishop of the African Episcopal Methodists in America, to be permitted the liberty of holding prayer meetings in my own hired house, and of exhorting as I found liberty, which was granted me. By this means, my mind was relieved, as the house soon filled when the hour appointed for prayer had arrived.

I cannot but relate in this place, before I proceed further with the above subject, the singular conversion of a very wicked young man. He was a colored man, who had generally attended our meetings, but not for any good purpose; but rather to disturb and to ridicule our denomination. He openly and uniformly declared that he neither believed in religion, nor wanted any thing to do with it. He was of a Gallio disposition, and took the lead among the young people of color. But after a while he fell sick, and lay about three months in a state of ill health; his disease was a consumption. Toward the close of his days, his sister who was a member of the society, came and desired me to go and see her brother, as she had no hopes of his recovery, perhaps the Lord might break into his mind. I went alone, and found him very low. I soon commenced to inquire respecting his state of feeling, and how he found his mind· His answer was, " O tolerable well," with an air of great indfference. I asked him if I should pray for him. He answered in a sluggish and careless manner, "O yes, if you have time." I then sung a hymn, kneeled down and prayed for him, and then went my way.

Three days after this, I went again to visit the young man. At this time there went with me two of the sisters in Christ. We found the Rev. Mr. Cornish, of our denomination, laboring with him. But he said he received but little satisfaction from him. Pretty soon, however, brother Cornish took his leave ; when myself, with the other two sisters, one of which was an elderly woman named Jane Hutt, the other was younger, both colored, commenced conversing with him, respecting his eternal interest, and of his hopes of a happy eternity, if any he had. He said but little; we then kneeled down together and besought the Lord in his behalf, praying that if mercy were not clear gone for ever, to shed a ray of softening grace upon the hardness of his heart. He appeared now to be somewhat more tender, and we thought we could perceive some tokens of conviction, as he wished us to visit him again, in a tone of voice not quite as indifferent as he had hitherto manifested.

But two days had elapsed after this visit, when his sister came to me in haste, saying, that she believed her brother was then dying, and that he had *sent* for me. I immediately called on Jane Hutt, who was still among us as a mother in Israel, to go with me. When we arrived there, we found him sitting up in bed, very restless and uneasy, but he soon laid down again. He now wished me to come to him, by the side of his bed. I asked him how he was. He said, Very ill; and added, " Pray for me, quick ?" We now perceived his time in this world to be short. I took up the hymn-book, and opened to a hymn suitable to his case, and commenced to sing, but there seemed to be a *horror* in the room—a darkness of a mental kind, which was felt by us all; there being five persons, except the sick young man and his nurse. We had sung but one verse, when they all gave over singing, on account of this uneartlhy sensation, but myself. I continued to sing on alone, but in a dull and heavy manner, though looking up to God all the while for help. Suddenly I felt a spring of energy awake in my heart, when darkness gave way in some degree. It was but a glimmer from above. When the hymn was finished, we all kneeled down to pray for him. While calling on the name of the Lord, to have mercy on his soul, and to grant him repentance unto life, it came suddenly into my mind never to rise from my knees until God should hear prayer in his behalf, until he should convert and save his soul.

Now, while I thus continued importuning heaven, as I felt I was led, a ray of light, more abundant, broke forth among us. There appeared to my view, though my eyes were closed, the Saviour in full stature, nailed to the cross, just over the head of the young man, against the ceiling of the room. I cried out, brother look up, the Saviour is come, he will pardon you, your sins he will forgive. My sorrow for the soul of the young man was gone ; I could no longer pray—joy and rapture made it impossible. We rose up from our knees, when lo, his eyes were gazing with ecstacy upwards; over his face there was an expression of joy; his lips were clothed in a sweet and holy smile; but no sound came from his tongue; it was heard in its stillness of bliss; full of hope and immortality. Thus, as I held him by the hand, his happy and purified soul soared away, without a sigh or a groan, to its eternal rest.

I now closed his eyes, straightened out his limbs, and left him to be dressed for the grave. But as for me, I was filled with the power of the Holy Ghost—the very room seemed filled with glory. His sister and al lthat were in the room rejoiced, nothing doubting but he had entered into Paradise; and I believe I shall see him at the last and great day, safe on the shores of salvation.

But to return to the subject of my call to preach. Soon after this, as above related, the Rev. Richard Williams was to preach at Bethel Church, where I with others were assembled. He entered the pulpit, gave out the hymn, which was sung, and then addressed the throne of grace; took his text, passed through the exordium, and commenced to expound it. The text he took is in Jonah, 2d chap. 9th verse,—" Salvation is of the Lord." But as he proceeded to explain, he seemed to have lost the spirit; when in the same instant, I sprang, as by altogether supernatural impulse, to my feet, when I was aided from above to give an exhortation on the very text which my brother Williams had taken.

I told them I was like Jonah; for it had been then nearly eight years since the Lord had called me to preach his gospel to the fallen sons and daughters of Adam's race, but that I had lingered like him, and delayed to go at the bidding of the Lord, and warn those who are as deeply guilty as were the people of Ninevah.

During the exhortation, God made manifest his power in a manner sufficient to show the world that I was called to labor according to my ability, and the grace given unto me, in the vineyard of the good husbandman.

I now sat down, scarcely knowing what I had done, being frightened. I imagined, that for this indecorum, as I feared it might be called, I should be expelled from the church. But instead of this, the Bishop rose up in the assembly, and related that I had called upon him eight years before, asking to be permitted to preach, and that he had put me off; but that he now as much believed that I was called to that work, as any of the preachers present. These remarks greatly strengthened me, so that my fears of having given an offence, and made myself liable as an offender, subsided, giving place to a sweet serenity, a holy joy of a peculiar kind, untasted in my bosom until then.

The next Sabbath day, while sitting under the word of the gospel, I felt moved to attempt to speak to the people in a public manner, but I could not bring my mind to attempt it in the church. I said, Lord, anywhere but here. Accordingly, there was a house not far off which was pointed out to me; to this I went. It was the house of a sister belonging to the same society with myself. Her name was Anderson. I told her I had come to hold a meeting in her house, if she would call in her neighbors. With this request she immediately complied. My congregation consisted of but five persons. I commenced by reading and singing a hymn; when I arose I found my hand resting on the Bible, which I had not noticed till that moment. It now occurred to me to take a text. I opened the Scripture, as it happened, at the 141st Psalm, fixing my eye on the third verse, which reads : "Set a watch, O Lord, before my mouth, keep the door of my lips." My sermon, such as it was, applied wholly to myself, and added an exhortation. Two of my congregation wept much, as the fruit of my labor this time. In closing, I said to the few, that if any one would open a door, I would hold a meeting the next sixth-day evening : wnen one answered that her house was at my service. Accordingly I went, and God made manifest his power among the people. Some wept, while others shouted for joy. One whole seat of females, by the power of God, as the rushing of a wind, were all bowed to the floor, at once, and screamed out. Also a sick man and woman in one house, the Lord convicted them both; one lived, and the other died. God wrought a judgment—some were well at night, and died in the morning. At this place I continued to hold meetings about six months. During that time I kept house with my little son, who was very sickly. About this time I had a call to preach at a place about thirty miles distant, among the Methodists, with whom I remained one week, and during the whole time, not a thought of my little son came into my mind; it was hid from me, lest I should have been diverted from the work I had to do, to look after my son. Here by the instrumentality of a poor coloured woman, the Lord poured forth his spirit among the people. Though, as I was told, there were lawyers, doctors, und magistrates present, to hear me speak, yet there was mourning and crying among sinners, for the Lord scattered fire among them of his own kindling. The Lord gave his hand-maiden power to speak for his great name, for he arrested the hearts of the people, and caused a shaking amongst the multitude, for God was in the midst.

I now returned home, found all well; no harm had come to my child, although I left it very sick. Friends had taken care of it which was of the Lord. I now began to think seriously of breaking up housekeeping, and forsaking all to preach the everlasting Gospel. I felt a strong desire to return to the place of my nativity, at Cape May, after an absence of about fourteen years. To this place, where the heaviest cross was to be met with, the Lord sent me, as Saul of Tarsus was sent to Jerusalem, to preach the same gospel which he had neglected and despised before his conversion. I went by water, and on my passage was much distressed by sea sickness, so much so that I expected to have died, but such was not the will of the Lord respecting me. After I had disembarked, I proceeded on as opportunities offered, toward where my mother lived. When within ten miles of that place, I appointed an evening meeting. There were a goodly number came out to hear. The Lord was pleased to give me light and liberty among the people. After meeting, there came an elderly lady to me and said, she believed the Lord had sent me among them; she then appointed me another meeting there two weeks from that night. The next day I hastened forward to the place of my mother. who was happy to see me, and the happiness was mutual between us. With her I left my poor sickly boy, while I departed to do my Master's will. In this neighborhood I had an uncle, who was a Methodist, and who gladly threw open his door for meetings to be held there. At the first meeting which I held at my uncle's house, there was, with others who had come from curiosity to hear the woman preacher, an old man, who was a Deist, and who said he did not believe the coloured people had any souls—he was sure they had none. He took a seat very near where I was standing, and boldly tried to look me out of countenance. But as I labored on in the best manner I was able, looking to God all the while, though it seemed to me I had but little liberty, yet there went an arrow from the bent bow of the gospel, and fastened in his till then obdurate heart. After I had done speaking, he went out, and called the people around him, said that my preaching might seem a small thing, yet he believed I had the worth of souls at heart. This language was different from what it was a little time before, as he now seemed to admit that coloured people had souls, as it was to these I was chiefly speaking; and unless they had souls, whose good I had in view, his remark must have been without meaning. He now came into the house, and in the most friendly manner shook hands with me, saying, he hoped God had spared him to some good purpose. This man was a great slave holder, and had been very cruel; thinking nothing of knocking down a slave with a fence stake, or whatever might come to hand. From this time it was said of him that he became greatly altered in his ways for the better. At that time he was about seventy years old, his head as white as snow; but whether he became a converted man or not, I never heard.

The week following, I had an invitation to hold a meeting at the Court House of the County, when I spoke from the 53d chap. of Isaiah, 3d verse. It was a solemn time, and the Lord attended the word ; I had life and liberty, though there were people there of various denominations. Here again I saw the aged slaveholder, who notwith¶

standing his age, walked about three miles to hear me. This day I spoke twice, and walked six miles to the place appointed. There was a magistrate present, who showed his friendship, by saying in a friendly manner, that he had heard of me: he handed me a hymn-book, pointing to a hymn which he had selected. When the meeting was over, he invited me to preach in a schoolhouse in his neighborhood, about three miles distant from where I then was. During this meetng one backslider was reclaimed. This day I walked six miles, and preached twice to large congregations, both in the morning and evening. The Lord was with me, glory be to his holy name. I next went six miles and held a meeting in a coloured friund's house, at eleven o'clock in the morning, and preached to a well behaved congregation of both coloured and white. After service I again walked back, which was in all twelve miles in the same day. This was on Sabbath, or as I sometimes call it, seventh day ; for after my conversion I preferred the plain language of the Friends. On the fourth day, after this, in compliance with an invitation received by note, from the same magistrate who had heard me at the above place I preached to a large congregatiou, where we had a precious time : much weeping was heard among the people. The same gentleman, now at the close of the meeting, gave out another appointment at the same place, that day week. Here again I had liberty, there was a move among the people. Ten years from that time, in the neighborhood of Cape May, I held a prayer meeting in a school house, which was then the regular place of preaching for the Episcopal Methodists, after service, there came a white lady, of great distinction, a member of the Methodist Society, and told me that at the same school house ten years before, under my preaching, the Lord first awakened her She rejoiced much to see me, and invited me home with her, where I staid till the next day. This was bread cast upon the water, seen after many days.

From this place I next went to Dennis Creek meeting house, where at the invitation or an elder, I spoke to a large congregation of various and conflicting sentiments, when a wonderful shock of God's power was felt, shown everywhere by groans, by sighs, and loud and happy amens. I felt as if aided from above. My tongue was cut ,loose, the stammerer spoke freely ; the love of God, and of his service, burned with a vehement flame within me—his name was glorified among the people.

I had my little son with me, and was very much straitened for money—and not having means to procure my passage home, I opened a School, and taught eleven scholars, for the purpose of raising a small sum. For many weeks I knew not what to do about returning home, when the Lord came to my assistance as I was rambling in the fields meditating upon his goodness, and made known to me that I might go to the city of Philadelphia, for which place I soon embarked with a very kind captain. We had a perilous passage—a dreadful storm arose, and before leaving the Delaware bay, we had a narrow escape from being run down by a large ship. But the good Lord held us in the hollow of his hand, and in the afternoon of Nov. 12, 1821, we arrived at the city.

Here I held meetings in the dwelling house of sister Lydia Anderson, and for about three months had as many appointments as I could attend. We had many precious seasons together, and the Lord was with his little praying band, convincing and converting sinners to the truth. I continued in the city until spring, when I felt it impressed upon my mind to travel, and walked fourteen miles in company with a sister to meet with some ministers, there to assemble, from Philadelphia. Satan tempted me while on the way, telling me that I was a fool for walking so far, as I would not be permitted to preach. But I pursued my journey, with the determination to set down and worship with them. When I arrived, a goodly number of people had assembled, and no preacher. They waited the time to commence the exercises, and then called upon me. I took the 3d chapter John, 14th verse for my text. I had life and liberty, and the Lord was in the camp with a shout. Another meeting was appointed three miles from there, when I spoke from Psalms cxxxvii, 1, 2, 3, 4. My master was with me, and made manifest his power. In the County House, also, we held a meeting, and had a sweet waiting upon the Lord. I spoke from Hebrews ii, 3, when the Lord gave me peculiar liberty. At a dwelling house one night I spoke from John vii, 46, when six souls fell to the floor crying for mercy. We had a blessed outpouring of the spirit among us—the God of Jacob was in our midst—and the shout of heaven-born souls was like music to our ears.

About the month of February my little son James, then in his sixth year, gave evidence of having religious inclinations. Once he got up in a chair, with a hymn book in his hand, and with quite a ministerial jesture, gave out a hymn. I felt the spirit move me to sing with him. A worthy sister was in the room, who I asked to pray for him. I invoked the Lord to answer and seal this prayer in the courts of heaven. I believed He would and did, and while yet on our knees I was filled with the fulness of God, and the answer came. I cried out in the joy of my heart—"The dead is alive"—and ran down stairs to inform a neighbor. Tears ran down the cheeks of my now happy boy, and great was our rejoicing together. He had been the subject of many prayers, and often had I thought I would rather follow him to his grave than to see him grow up an open and profane sinner like many children I had seen. And here let me say, the promise of the Lord is, "ask and ye shall receive." Dear parents; pray for your children in childhood—carry them in the arms of faith to the mercy seat, and there present them an offering to the Lord. I can say from my own experience, the Lord will hear prayer. I had given James the Bible as Haman gave Samuel to God in his youth, and by his gracious favor he was received. For the further encouragement of fathers and mothers to engage in this blessed work, let me refer them to Ecclesiastes xi, 6: "In the morning sow thy seed, and in the evening withhold not thy hand, for thou knowest not whether shall prosper either this or that, or whether they both shall be alike good."

"Sow it in the youthful mind,
  Can you have a fairer field?
Be it but in faith consigned.
  Harvest, doubtless, it shall yield,
Fruits of early piety,
  All that God delights to see."

In November I journeyed for Trenton, N. J. At Burlington I spoke to the people on the Sabbath, and had a good time among them, and on Monday the 12th, in a School house. Sister Mary Owan, who had laid aside all the cares of the world, went with me. We had no means of travelling but on foot, but the Lord regarded us, and by some means put it into the heart of a stranger, to convey us to the Trenton bridge. We fell in with the elder of the circuit, who spoke to me in a cold and formal manner, and as though he thought my capacity was not equal to his. We went into the sister's house, where we expected to stay, and waited a long while with our hats and cloaks on, before the invitation to lodge there was given. In the morning I had thought to visit Newhope, but remained to discharge my duty in visiting the sick and afflicted three or four days in the neighborhood. I was invited to a prayer meeting, and was called upon by a brother to speak. I improved the offer, and made some remarks from Kings xviii, 21. One of the preachers invited me to preach for them on sixth day evening, which I complied with before an attentive congregation, when God followed the word with much power, and great was our joy. On the 17th I spoke in the morning at 11 o'clock. I felt my weakness and deficiency for the work, and thought "who is able for these things," and desired to get away from the task. My text was Timothy vi, 2-7. The Lord again cut loose the stammering tongue, and opened the Scriptures to my mind, so that, glory to God's dear name, we had a most melting, sin-killing, and soul-reviving time. In the afternoon I assisted in leading a class, when we found the Lord faithful and true—and on the same evening I spoke from Hebrews ii, 3.

The next day, sister Mary Owan and myself set out for Newhope, where we arrived, after walking sixteen miles, at about six o'clock in the evening. Though tedious, it was a pleasant walk to view the high mountain and towering hills, and the beauty and variety of nature around us, which powerfully impressed my mind with the greatness and wisdom of my Maker. At this place I stopt at the house of the gentleman with whose wife's mother I was brought up, and by whom we were agreeably received. The next evening we called upon brother Butler, where I addressed a small company, and God, through his words, quickened some. The next night I spoke in an Academy to a goodly number of people, from John iii, 14. Here I found some very ill-behaved persons, who talked roughly, and said among other things, "I was not a woman, but a man dressed in female clothes." I labored one week among them, and went next to Lambertsville, where we experienced kindness from the people, and had a happy time and parted in tears.

I now returned to Philadelphia, where I stayed a short time, and went to Salem, West Jersey. I met with many troubles on my journey, especially from the elder, who like many others, was averse to a woman's preaching. And here let me tell that elder, if he has not gone to heaven, that I have heard that as far back as Adam Clarke's time, his objections to female preaching were met by the answer— "If an ass reproved Balaam, and a barn-door fowl reproved Peter, why should not a woman reprove sin?" I do not introduce this for its complimentary classification of women with donkeys and fowls, but to give the reply of a poor woman, who had once been a slave. To the first companion she said—"May be a speaking woman is like an ass—but I can tell you one thing, the ass seen the angel when Balaam didn't."

Notwithstanding the opposition, we had a prosperous time at Salem. I had some good congregations, and sinners were cut to the heart. After speaking in the meeting house, two women came up into the pulpit, and falling upon my neck cried out "What shall I do to be saved?" One said she had disobeyed God, and he had taken her children from her—he had called often after her, but she did not hearken. I pointed her to the all-atoning blood of Christ, which is sufficient to cleanse from all sin, and left her, after prayer, to his mercy. From this place I walked twenty-one miles, and preached with difficulty to a stiff-necked and rebellious people, who I soon left without any animosity for their treatment. They might have respected my message, if not the poor weak servant who brought it to them with so much labor.

"If they persecute you in one city, flee into another," was the advice I had resolved to take, and I hastened to Greenwich, where I had a lively congregation, had unusual life and liberty in speaking, and the power of God was there. We also had a solemn time in the meeting house on Sabbath day morning, and in a dwelling house in the evening; a large company assembled, when the spirit was with us, and we had a mighty shaking among the dry bones.

On second day morning, I took stage and rode seven miles to Woodstown, and there I spoke to a respectable congregation of white and colored, in a school house. I was desired to speak in the colored meeting house, but the minister could not reconcile his mind to a woman preacher—he could not unite in fellowship with me even to shaking hands as christians ought. I had visited that place before, when God made manifest his power "through the foolishness of preaching," and owned the poor old woman. One of the brothers appointed a meeting in his own house, and after much persuasion this minister came also. I did not feel much like preaching, but spoke from Acts viii, 35. I felt my inability, and was led to complain of weakness—but God directed the arrow to the hearts of the guilty—and my friend the minister got happy, and often shouted "Amen," and "as it is, sister." We had a wonderful display of the spirit of God among us, and we found it good to be there. There is nothing too hard for the Lord to do. I committed the meeting into the hands of the elder, who afterwards invited me to preach in the meeting house. He had said he did not believe that ever a soul was converted under the preaching of a woman—but while I was laboring in his place, conviction seized a woman, who fell to the floor crying for mercy. This meeting held till 12 or 1 o'clock. O how precious is the sound of Jesus' name ! I never felt a doubt at this time of my acceptance with God, but rested my soul on his every promise. The elder shook hands, and we parted.

Nov. 22, 1822, I returned to Philadelphia, and attended meetings in and out of the city. God was still my help, and I preached and formed a class, and tried to be useful. The oppositions I met with, however, were numerous—so much so, that I was tempted to withdraw from the Methodist Church, lest some might go into ruin by their persecutions of me—but this was allowed only to try my faithfulness to God. At times I was pressed down like a cart beneath its shafts—my life seemed as at the point of the sword—my heart was sore and pained me in my body. But the Lord knows how to deliver the godly out of temptation, and to reserve the unjust till the day of judgment to be punished. While relating the feelings of my mind to a sister who called to see me, joy sprang up in my bosom that I was not overcome by the adversary, and I was overwhelmed with the love of God and souls. I embraced the sister in my arms, and we had a melting time together. Oh how comforting it is to have the spirit of God bearing witness with our spirits that we are his children in such dark hours !

When Satan appears to stop up our path,
And fill us with fears, we triumph by faith ;
He cannot take from us, (tho' oft he has tried,)
The soul cheering promise the Lord will provide.
He tells us we're weak, our hope is in vain,
The good that we seek we ne'er shall obtain ;
But when such suggestions our graces have tried,
This answers all questions, the Lord will provide.

I felt a greater love for the people than ever. It appeared to me that they erred through ignorance of my desire to do them good; and my prayer was that nothing but love might appear in my ways, and actuate my heart. Religion is love—God is love. But it was nothing less than the Divine power that brought me through, for it appeared that the hosts of darkness were arrayed against me to destroy my peace and lead me away from the throne of love.

June 24, I left the city of Philadelphia to travel in Delaware State. I went with captain Ryal, a kind gentleman, who took me to his house in Wilmington, and himself and lady both treated me well. The first night of my arrival; I preached in the stone Methodist meeting house. I tried, in my weak way, to interest the assembly from the 2d chapter of Hebrews, 3d verse—"How shall we escape, if we neglect so great salvation." God was there, as we had the most delightful evidence—and many had their eyes opened to see there was no escape from the second death while out of Christ, and cried unto God for his saving grace. I would that all who have not embraced the salvation offered in the gospel, might examine the question candidly and seriously, ere the realities of the other world break up their fancied security.

In July I spoke in a School house to a large congregation, from Numbers xxix, 17. Here we had a sweet foretaste of heaven—full measure, and running over—shouting and rejoicing—while the poor errand-bearer of a free gospel was assisted from on high. I wish my reader had been there to share with us the joyous heavenly feast. On the 15th of July I gave an exhortation in the meeting house again to a listening multitude—deep and solemn were the convictions of many, and good, I trust, was done.

The next place I visited was Newcastle. The meeting house could not be obtained, and two young gentleman interested themselves to get the Court house, but the Trustees objected, wishing to know why the Methodists did not open their Church. The reason was "I was not licensed," they said. My two friends waited on me to speak in the Market house, where I attended at early candlelight, and had the pleasure of addressing a few plain truths to a crowded but respectful congregation, from John vii, 46—"Never man spake like this man." On Sunday the same young gentlemen invited me to give another discourse, to which I consented, before a large gathering of all descriptions.

From here I proceeded to Christine, where we worshipped in a dwelling house, and I must say was well treated by some of my colored friends. I then returned to Wilmington, where in a few days I had a message to return again to C. My friends said I should have the Meeting house, for which Squire Luden interested himself, and the appointment was published. When the people met at the proper time, the doors remained locked. Amid cries of "shame" we left the Church steps—but a private house was opened a short distance up the road, and though disappointed in obtaining egress to a Church, the Lord did not disappoint his people, for we were fed with the bread of life, and had a happy time. Mr. and Mrs. Lewelen took me to their house, and treated me, not as one of their hired servants, but as a companion, for which I shall ever feel grateful. Mr. Smith, a doctor, also invited me to call upon them—he was a Presbyterian, but we prayed and conversed together about Jesus and his love, and parted without meddling with each others creeds. Oh, I long to see the day when Christians will meet on one common platform—Jesus of Nazareth—and cease their bickerings and contentions about non-essentials —when "our Church" shall be less debated, but "our Jesus" shall be all in all.

Another family gave me the invitation to attend a prayer meeting. It was like a "little heaven below." From here I walked about four miles that evening, accompanied by the house maid of Mrs. Ford, a Presbyterian, who said she knew her mistress would be glad to see me. Mrs. F. gave me a welcome—said she felt interested in my speaking, and sent a note to a Methodist lady, who replied that my labor would be acceptable, no doubt, in her Church that afternoon. When I came in, the elder was in the pulpit. He gave us a good sermon. After preaching, this lady spoke of me to the elder; in consequence, he invited me to his pulpit, saying "he was willing that every one should do good." My text was Hebrew ii, 3. Though weak in body, the good Master filled my mouth and gave me liberty among strangers, and seldom have I spent so happy a Sabbath. Mrs. F. had a colored woman in her family one hundred and ten years of age, with whom I conversed about religion—how Christ had died to redeem us, and the way of salvation, and the poor old lady said "she wished she could hear me every day." I also called upon another, one hundred and sixteen years old, who was blind. We talked together about Jesus—she had a strong and abiding evidence of her new birth, and in a few weeks went home to heaven. Here she was long deprived of the light of the sun, and the privilege of reading God's blessed word; but there her eyes are unsealed, and the Sun of righteousness has risen with healing in his wings.

> There glory beams on all the plains,
>   Which sight to her is given—
> There music rolls in sweetest strains,
> And spotless beauty ever reigns,
>   And all is love in heaven.

I left Mrs. Ford's and walked about three miles to St. George, with a recommend to a Mrs. Sutton, a noble-minded lady of the Presbyterian order, where I was generously treated. Here I preached in the

School house to a respectable company—had considerable weeping and a profitable waiting upon the Lord. I accepted an invitation from a gentleman to preach in a Methodist Church three miles distant—found there a loving people, and was highly gratified at the order and decorum manifested while I addressed them. Mrs. Smith took me home with her, who I found to be a christian both in sentiment and action. By invitation, I went next to Port Penn, and spoke with freedom, being assisted of the Lord, to a full house, and had a glorious feast of the Spirit. The next night found me at Canton Bride, to which place I had walked—spoke in a School house, from Math. xxii, 41—"What think ye of Christ?" The presence of the Lord overshadowed us—believers rejoiced—some were awakened to believe well of my Master, and I trust are on their way to glory. In Fieldsborough, also, we had gracious meetings.

At Smyrna I met brother C. W. Cannon, who made application for the Friend's Meeting house for me, where the Lord blessed us abundantly. We attended a Camp-meeting of the old connexion, and got greatly refreshed for the King's service. I rode ten miles and delivered a message from the Lord to a waiting audience—the Master assisted, and seven individuals, white and colored, prostrated themselves for prayer. Next day I rode to Middletown—spoke in a School house to a white congregation from Isaiah lxiii, 1, and a good time it was. In the morning at 11 o'clock, I addressed a Methodist Society, and in the afternoon at 3 o'clock, spoke under a tree in the grave yard, by the road side, to a large audience. Squire Maxwell's lady, who was present, invited me home to tea with herself and nieces, and a Quaker lady showed her benevolence by putting into my hand enough to help me on my journey. The Lord is good—what shall I do to make it known? I rode seven miles that night, and gave an exhortation after the minister had preached, and felt happier than a King.

I now travelled to Cecil county, Md., and the first evening spoke to a large congregation. The pastor afterwards baptized some adult persons—and we all experienced the cleansing and purifying power. We had a baptism within and without. I was next sent for by the servant of a white gentleman, to hold a meeting in his house in the evening. He invited the neighbors, colored and white, when I spoke according to the ability God gave me. It was pleasant to my poor soul to be there—Jesus was in our midst—and we gave glory to God. Yes, glory—glory be to God in the highest. "God forbid that I should glory, save in the cross of our Lord Jesus Christ." I boast not myself. Paul may plant and Apollos water, but God giveth the increase. I tried also to preach three times at a place 14 miles from here—had good meetings—backsliders were reclaimed and sinners convicted of sin, who I left in the hands of God, with the hope of meeting and recognizing again "when we arrive at home." * * * * *

Returned back to Middletown. The next day the preacher of the circuit conveyed me to his place of appointment at Elkton. We had a wonderful outpouring of the spirit. At Frenchtown I spoke at 11 o'clock, where I realized my nothingness, but, God's name he praised, he helped me in the duty. Went again to Middletown, and from there to Canton's Bridge, and talked to the people as best I could. Seven miles from this place I found, by the direction of a kind Providence, my own sister, who had been separated from me some thirty-three years. We were young when last we met, with less of the cares of life than now. Each heart then was buoyant with mildly hopes and pleasures—and little did we expect at parting that thirty-three years would pass over us, with its changes and vicissitudes, ere we should see each other's face. Both were much altered in appearance, but we knew each other, and talked over the dealings of the Lord with us, retracing our wanderings in the world and "the days when life was young."

"Our days of childhood quickly pass,
    And soon our happiest years are run—
As the pure dew that gems the grass
    Is dried beneath the summer sun.
There's such deceit—such guile in men,
Who would not be a child again ?"

During this visit I had three meetings in different directions in gentlemen's houses, and a prayer meeting at my brother's, who did not enjoy religion. My good old friend Mr. Lorton happened to be there, who told the people that he had been to my house—that he knew Mr. Lee (my husband) intimately, and that he had often preached for him while pastor of the Church at Snow Hill, N. J.

I next attended and preached several times at a camp meetinng; which continued five days. We had pentecostal showers—sinners were pricked to the heart, and cried mightily to God for succor from impending judgment, and I verily believe the Lord was well pleased at our weak endeavors to serve him in the tented grove. The elder in charge, on the last day of the camp, appointed a meeting for me in a dwelling house. Spoke from Acts ii, 41   The truth fastened in the hearts of two young women, who, after I was seated, came and fell down at my side, and cried for God to have mercy on them—we prayed and wrestled with the Lord, and both were made happy in believing, and are alive in the faith of the gospel. The next morning a brother preacher took me to St. Georgetown. From there I took stage to Wilmington, and called on my friend Captain Rial, in whose family I spent two days and nights. Went to Philadelphia to attend a camp-meeting. Returned again to W—, where I was taken sick with typhus fever, and was in the doctor's hands for some days—but the Lord rebuked the disease, gave me my usual health again, and I returned back to Philadelphia.

The Bishop gave me an invitation to speak in Bethel Church; but here my heart fluttered with fear at the commencement, in a manner known but to those who feel their unworthiness in addressing new and large assemblies. My text was in Isaiah x. 10, 11. Previous to dismission, the Bishop gave me another appointment in Wesley Church for first day morning, where I labored to encourage believers, from Ephesians ii, 19. The comforter was with us—we were sprinkled as with clear water from above—the hands of those that were hanging down were lifted up, and we truly had a refreshing season. Glory to God for the manifestation of His Spirit. "Now therefore ye are no more strangers and foreigners, but fellow-citizens with the saints, and of the household of God."

On the ensuing Thursday night, in Union Church, I had the opportunity of speaking a word for my Saviour again, and recommenced the impenitent to see to it that they took the advice of my text, in Rev. iii, 18. The Lord searched the heart as he did Jerusalem with a lighted candle, and there was a moving of the Spirit among the people.

From Philadelphia I travelled on foot thirty miles to Downingtown, and gave ten sermons while there; and remember the cold day in December I walked sixteen miles from the above place to brother Wells', where I staid one week, and labored both among colored and white. They had one class there. Three miles further, I talked on Lord's day to an apparently hardened people, and next night preached in a School-house, after a ride of ten miles. The call of the Lord was for me now to go to West Chester, N. Y., where I remained a little period with brother Thomas Henry and brother Miller; preached in a School-house and in the Wesleyan Methodist Meeting-house. When prepared to go home, a request was sent me to preach in the Court-house of the county, to which I rode ten miles, and addressed the citizens on two evenings. The Lord strengthened his feeble instrument in the effort to win souls to Christ, for which my heart at this time was heavily burthened. Next morning I left for Westhaven, where I visited a School of boys and girls, and was much pleased to see them engaged and improving in their studies. How great the difference now, thought I, for the mental and moral culture of the young than when I was a child!

In the month of June, 1823, I went on from Philadelphia to New York with Bishop Allen and several Elders, (including our present Rev. Bishop Brown,) to attend the New York Annual Conference of our denomination, where I spent three months of my time. We arrived about nine o'clock in the evening. As we left the boat, a person fell into the dock, and notwithstanding the effort made to save and find him, he was seen no more. 'In the midst of life we are in death.' On the 4th of June I spoke in the Asbury Church, from Psalms c, 33.

I think I never witnessed such a shouting and rejoicing time. The Church had then but recently adopted the African M. E. discipline. On the 5th I brought my master's message to the Bethel Church— Text Isaiah lviii, 1. "Cry aloud, spare not; lift up thy voice like a trumpet, and show my people their transgressions, and the house of Jacob their sins." The spirit of God came upon me; I spoke without fear of man, and seemed willing even there to be offered up; the preachers shouted and prayed, and it was a time long to be remembered.

June 6. Spoke in the Church in High Street, Brooklyn, from Jer. ix, 1—"Oh that my head were waters, and mine eyes a fountain of tears, that I might weep day and night for the slain of the daughter of my people." In these days I felt it my duty to travel up and down in the world, and promulgate the gospel of Christ, especially among my own people, though I often desired to be released from the great task. The Lord had promised to be with me, and my trust was in his strong arm.

> Renouncing every worldly thing,
> Safe 'neath the shadow of thy wing,
> My sweetest thought henceforth shall be
> That all I want I find in thee,
> In thee, my God, in Thee.

I left my friend in Brooklyn, and went to Flushing, L. I. Here we had quite a revival feeling, and two joined society. Visited Jamaica and Jericho; spoke in brother B's dwelling, in the church, and under a tree. Went to White Plains to the camp-meeting; the Lord was with us indeed; believers were revived, backsliders reclaimed, and sinners converted. Returned and spent a little time in Brooklyn, where I addressed the people from Rev. iii, 18, and John iii, 15.

July 22. Spoke in Asbury Church from Acts xiii, 41—"Behold ye despisers, and wonder and perish." I pointed out the portion of the hypocrite, the liar, the Sabbath-breaker, and all who do wickedly and die in their sins; they shall be to the judgment bar of Jehovah, and before an assembled universe hear their awful sentence, "Depart from me, ye cursed, into everlasting fire, prepared for the devil and his angels," while the righteous shall be received "into life eternal." On the 28th I went to Dutch Hill, L. I., and spoke before a congregation of white and colored, in a barn, as there was no other suitable place. I felt happy when I thought of my dear Redeemer, who was born in a stable and cradled in a manger, and we had a precious season. Brother Croker, of Brooklyn, and father Thompson were with me, at whose feet I desired rather to sit and learn, they being experienced "workmen that needed not to be ashamed." But the Lord sends by whom he will.

The next Sabbath I weakly attempted to address my friends in

New York again. Took the words in Math. xxviii, 13, for my text—"Say ye, his disciples came by night, and stole him away while we slept." The place was greatly crowded, and many came who could not get in. A class met here, to which the preacher invited all who desired to remain, and thirty persons tarried. He called upon me to lead, but He who led Israel over the Red Sea assisted, and it was a gracious time with us. Some who remained from curiosity were made, like Belshazzar, to tremble and weep, while the spirit strove powerfully with them. One experienced religion and joined society. I expect in the resurrection morning to meet many who were in that little company, in my Father's house, where we shall strike hands no more to part; where our song of redemption shall be raised to God and the Lamb forever. Dear reader, if you have not, I charge you to make your peace with God while time and opportunity is given, and be one of that number who shall take part and lot in the first resurrection. Though I may never see you in the flesh, I leave on this page my solemn entreaty that you delay not to obtain the pardoning favor of God; that you leave not the momentous subject of religion to a sick bed or dying hour, but NOW, even now, seek the Lord with full purpose of heart, and he will be found of thee. "If any man sin, he has advocate with the Father, Jesus Christ the righteous."

> "Oh that the world might taste and see
> The riches of his grace;
> The arms of love that compass me,
> Would all mankind embrace."

I visited a woman who was laying sick upon her death-bed. She told me "she had once enjoyed religion, but the enemy had cheated her out of it." She knew that she must die in a very little while, and could not get well, and her agony of soul, in view of its unprepared state for a judgment to come, awoke every feeling of sympathy within me. Oh! how loud such a scene calls upon us to be "faithful unto death"—then shall we "receive a crown of life.' Also visited Mrs. Miller, who once "tasted that the Lord was good," but had ceased now to follow him. She had been a Methodist for many years—got her feelings injured through some untoward circumstance—had fallen from grace, and now was sick. A good sister accompanied me? we conversed with Mrs. M., sung an appropriate hymn, and my friend supplicated the throne of grace in her behalf. She had frequently felt the need of a returning Saviour, and during prayer her heart became melted into tenderness. She cried aloud for mercy, wrestled like Jacob for the witness, and the Lord, faithful and true, "healed her backslidings," and we left her happy in his father. Praise the Lord for his matchless grace. I entertained no doubt of her well-grounded hope; and on seeing such a display of God's power, I was lost in wonder, love and praise. Let the backslider hear and take courage,

Let all who are out of Christ hear the invitation—"Repent ye and be converted, for God hath called all men everywhere to repent."

"Without reserve give Christ your heart,
Let him his righteousness impart—
Then all things else he'll freely give,
With him you all things shall receive."

With a serene and tranquil mind I now returned to Philadelphia. The Bishop was pleased to give me an appointment at Bethel Church, but a spirit of opposition arose among the people against the propriety of female preaching. My faith was tried—yet I felt my call to labor for souls none the less. "Shall the servant be above his Master?" The ministers of Jesus must expect persecution, if they would be faithful witnesses against sin and sinners—but shall they, "awed by a mortal's form, conceal the word of God?" Thou God knowest my heart, and that thy glory is all I have in view. Shall I cease from sounding the alarm to an ungodly world, when the vengeance of offended heaven is about to be poured out, because my way is sometimes beset with scoffers, or those who lose sight of the great Object, and stop on the road to glory to contend about non-essentials? Rather let the messengers of God go on—let them not be hindered by the fashions and customs of a gainsaying and mis-loving generation, but with the crown in view, which shall deck the brow of those only who are "faithful unto death"—let them "cry aloud and spare not." Who regarded the warnings of Noah? who believed in his report? Who among the antidiluvians, that witnessed the preparations of this righteous man to save himself and family from a deluge of waters, believed him any thing else than a fanatic, deluded, and beside himself? Let the servants of Christ gird on the armor, and "listen to the Captain's voice: "Lo I am with you always, even unto the end." With the promise of my Lord impressed upon my mind, I remained at home only a week, and walked twenty-one miles to Lumbertown, and preached in the Old Methodist Church and our African Church. Brother Joshua Edely was then a deacon there, and held a quarterly meeting soon after my reaching the place. He also appointed a love-feast in the morning, when the love that true believers enjoy at such scenes made the place akin to heaven. While here I spoke as the Spirit taught me from Solomon's Songs. It was a happy meeting—refreshing to the thirsty soul—and we had a shout of the king in the camp. I shall never forget the kindness I received here from dear sister G. B. May the blessings of heaven be hers in this and the world to come.

I travelled seven miles from the above place to Snow Hill on Sabbath morning, where I was to preach in the Church of which I was a member; and although much afflicted in body, I strove, by the grace of God, to perform the duty. This was once the charge of JOSEPH

LEE. In this desk my lamented husband had often stood up before me, proclaiming the "acceptable year of the Lord"—here he labored with zeal and spent his strength to induce sinners to be "reconciled to God"—here his toils ended. And could it be, that a poor unworthy being like myself should be called to address his former congregation, and should stand in the same pulpit! The thought made me tremble. My heart sighed when memory brought back the image, and the reminiscences of other days crowded upon me. But why, my heart, dost thou sigh? He has ceased from his labor, and I here see his works do follow. It will be enough, if these, the people of his care, press on and gain the kingdom. It will be enough, if, on the final day, "for which all other days were made," we pass through the gates into the city, and live again together where death cannot enter, and separations are unknown. Cease then, my tears—a little while, my fluttering heart! and the turf that covers my companion, perchance, may cover thee—a little while, my soul! if faithful, and the widow's God will call thee from this valley of tears and sorrows to rest in the mansions the Saviour has gone to prepare for his people. "Good what God gives—just what he takes away."

My mind was next exercised to visited Trenton, N. J. I spoke for the people there, but soon had felt the cross so heavy. Perhaps it was occasioned through grieving over the past, and my feelings of loneliness in the world. A sister wished me to go with her to Bridgeport—where I found brother Orwin, then elder over that church. He gave me an appointment. We had a full house, and God's power was manifest among the people, and I returned to the elder's house rejoicing. The following day I walked fourteen miles to a meeting, where also we were greatly favored with the presence of God. Soon after this, I thought of going home to Philadelphia. I got about three miles on foot, when an apparent voice said " f thou goest home thou wilt die." I paused for a moment, and not comprehending what it meant, pursued my journey. Again I was startled by something like a tapping on my shoulder, but, on turning round, I found myself alone, which two circumstances created a singular feeling I could not understand. I thought of Balaam when met by the angel in the way. I was taken sick and it seemed I should die in the road. I said I will go back, and walked about four miles to Bridgeport. Told a good sister my exercise, who was moved with sympathy, and got brandy and bathed me. On Wednesday night I spoke to the people at Trenton Bridge, and notwithstanding the opposition I had met with from brother Samuel R——, then on the circuit, the Lord supported the "woman preacher" and my soul was cheered. On Thursday I walked fourteen miles, when the friends applied to the elder to let me talk for them, but his prejudices also, against women preaching were very strong, and tried hard to disaffect the minds of the people. The dear man has since gone to stand before that God who knows the secrets of all hearts—and where, I earnestly pray, he may find some who have been saved by grace through the instrumentality of female preaching.

> "Then here, O God, thy work fulfil;
> And from thy mercy's throne
> O grant me strength to do thy will,
> And to resist my own."

Norristown, Bucks county, January 6, 1824. Brother Morris conveyed me here at his own expense, and made application for places for me to speak. Addressed a large congregation on the fourth day after my introduction into the place, in the court-house, from Isaiah liiii. 1,—"Who hath believed our report ? and to whom is the arm of the Lord revealed ?" I felt embarrassed in the commencement, but the Spirit came, and "helped our infirmities"—good attention, and some weeping. On the 18th I spoke in the academy—it was a solemn time, and the people came out in numbers to hear. I then walked four miles to brother Morris's—spoke twice in the school-house, and once in a dwelling house.

On the 14th April, I went with Bishop Allen and several elders to Baltimore, on their way to attend Conference ; at the end of which the Bishop gave me permission to express a few thoughts for my Lord. On leaving the city of B., I travelled about 100 miles to Eastern Shore, Maryland. Brother Bailey was then laboring on that circuit, who received and treated me very kindly. We had several good meetings, and twice I spoke in Bethel Church, when the outpouring of the Spirit was truly great. In company with a good sister, who took a gig and horse, I travelled about three hundred miles, and labored in different places. Went to Denton African Church, and on the first Sabbath gave two sermons. The Church was in a thriving, prosperous condition, and the Lord blessed the word to our comfort. During the week I labored in the court-house before a large concourse of hearers. The Lord was unspeakably good, and one fell to the floor under the power.

By request, I also spoke in the Old Methodist Church in Denton, which was full to overflowing. It was a happy meeting. My tongue was loosened, and my heart warm with the love of God and souls—a season yet sweet to my memory. From there I went to Greensboro'—the elder gave a sermon, after which I exhorted the poor sinner to prepare to meet the Lord in peace, before mercy was clear gone forever. The Old Methodist connexion gave an invitation for me to speak in their house, which I embraced, feeling thankful that the middle wall of partition had, thus far, been broken down. "He that feareth God and worketh righteousness shall be accepted of him"—not he who hath a different skin—not he who belongs to this denomination, or, to that—but "he that feareth God." My Master is no respecter of persons. May the partition walls that divide His sincere followers be broken down by the spirit of love.

In Whitehall Chapel I spoke to a respectable congregation, from Isaiah liii. 1. Though in a slave country, I found the Omnipresent One was with us. Dr. Clarke took us home to dine with his family —for which uncommon attention I felt highly gratified. I believe him a Christian in heart, and one, no doubt, who has read the words of the Saviour: "Whosoever shall give to drink unto one of these little ones a cup of cold water only, shall in no wise lose his reward." And, notwithstanding the doctor was a Presbyterian, Mr. Buly had the privilege of baptizing two of their colored children. * * *

I stopped next at Concord, and in the Old Methodist connexion tried to encourage the Lord's people to persevere. God displayed His power by a general outpouring of the Spirit—sinners cried for mercy, while others shouted for joy. Spoke also to a congregation of colored and white at Stanton Mills; and arrived again at Eastern Shore, where I spoke in Bethel Church during Quarterly Meeting. Attended their love-feast, where several joined society, and many encouraging testimonies were given by young converts that "God hath power on earth to forgive sins." May they be faithful stewards of the manifold gifts of God—and never be ashamed to confess what the Lord had done for them. Many lose the witness out of the heart by withholding their testimony from their friends and neighbors of the power of God to save. They run well for a season, but the tempter whispers "not now"—and by and by the soul becomes barren and unfruitful. May God help the young converts to "watch," and tell around what a dear Saviour they have found.

> "Ashamed of Jesus!—yes, I may,
> When I've no guilt to wash away—
> No tears to wipe—no good to crave—
> No fears to quell—no soul to save."

June 10th, 1824. Left Eastern Shore for a journey to Bath, and went around the circuit with brother J. B , the elder. In the Old Methodist Church, at Fory's Neck, I had the privilege of speaking to a large congregation, which was made the power of God unto salvation. Visited Lewistown, and had a blessed meeting in the Methodist Church. The tears of the penitent flowed sweetly, which always encourages me to persevere in proclaiming the glad tidings of a risen Saviour to my fellow beings. When the heart is thus melted into tenderless, I feel assured the Lord sanctions the feeble effort of His poor servant—it is a good omen to my mind that the mourner is not forsaken of God, and that he yet stands knocking at the door for admittance. Oh! that those who weep for an absent Jesus may be comforted by hearing Him say—"Thy sins, which were many, are all forgiven thee: go in peace and sin no more."

Elder J. B. preached in Greensboro', where I attended, and had a quickening time. Some enmity had existed among the brethren, but the spirit of love got the ascendancy, and the lion became as the lamb. The gospel is the best remedy to subdue the evil passions of men that has ever been discovered. Dear Master, let Thy gospel spread to earth's remotest bounds.

I have travelled, in four years, sixteen hundred miles and of that I walked two hundred and eleven miles, and preached the kingdom of God to the falling sons and daughters of Adam, counting it all joy for the sake of Jesus. Many times cast down but not forsaken; willing to suffer as well as love. I spoke at Harris's Mills, in a dwelling house, to a large concourse of people, from Paul's Epistle to the Ephesians, xviii. 19–20. I felt much drawn out, in the Spirit of God, meanwhile from my feelings. I observed there were some present that never would meet me again. Mr. J. B., the elder, then requested me to lead the class. Much mourning, weeping and rejoicing. Four days afterwards, a man that sat under this sermon, (a shoemaker by occupation) fell dead from his bench without having any testimony of a hope in Christ. How dreadful to relate the wicked shall not live out half their days. In Easton I spoke from the Evan. John, 1 chap. 45 ver., the Lord's time. Then proceeded to Dagsberry, 25 miles, preached in Bethel Church to a multitude of people, it being to them a new thing, but only the old made more manifest. Bless God for what my heart feels, for a good conscience is better than a sacrifice. Two sermons preached in said Church, I spoke from Acts 13 chap., 41 ver.,—the power of God filled the place—some shouted, others mourned, some testified God for Christ's sake had forgiven sin, whilst others were felled to the floor. From thence we went to Sinapuxom, spoke on Sabbath day to a large congregation from Num. 24 chap., 17 ver.—the Lord gave light, life and liberty on that portion of Scripture. Great time. The elder closed the meeting, the memory of which will be sweet in eternity. I intended to take an appointment, but being taken sick the elder filled the appointment, and while preaching, there were 10 or 11 white men came and said they wanted to see the preacher; he sent for them to come into the house, but they seemed afraid or refused ; after he had finished, they came to the door to know by what authority he was preaching—but it was me they were after, but I was fortified, for their laws, by my credentials, having the United States seal upon them,—they tried to get him out of the house, they said, on business. But he told them he would meet them at 9 o'clock in the morning before the magistrate, seven miles distant. Brother J. B. then took my credentials and also showed his own, and, upon examination, the magistrate said, she is highly recommended and I am bound to protect her. An under-officer, anxious to get hold of my papers, very much opposed to our being in the State, tried hard to frighten us out of it, and went to lay his hands on it, but was rebuked by the magistrate; and two days after the magistrate sent word to me to go on and preach, he did not care if I preached till I died. I never met them but told the friends that God would make an example of them before one year. My mind led me to Solsbury and to Snow Hill—the brother, through persuasion, did not go, for fear of some difficulty, under which consideration I declined going for that time, I then returned to Easton, but my mind still led me to pay that religious visit, which was still accomplished by a sister and myself. I called on brother Massey, a preacher, who conducted us to Snow Hill and Solsbury. In the afternoon, the elder and one of the Trustees of the white Methodist Church, called on me to know of my faith and doctrine, and, while conversing, the spirit of the Lord breathed upon us—we had groans and shedding of tears— that evening the Elder gave me an appointment in the colored church to a large congregation, and we had a powerful time, sinners awakened and backsliders reclaimed. So great was the time that the meeting lasted until three or four o'clock in the morning. It was like a Camp meeting, they came seven miles distance from only three or four hours' notice. Next morning we left for Snow Hill, the Elder sent down for the friends to take care of us all, and our board, with the horses, should be paid for, consequently we were treated with great hospitality. I preached in the Old Methodist Church to an immense congregation of both the slaves and the holders, and felt great liberty in word and doctrine; the power of God seemed without intermission. We left there and rode 16 miles, spoke to a small company of people. In the afternoon to a large congregation, chiefly Presbyterians, and at many other places too tedious for me to mention, I preached twenty-seven sermons and then returned to Easton again, where I was informed that the constable who was so enraged against me before was then dying; the other white man who came and set at the end of the table twice while I was laboring, thinking I would say something to implicate myself and wanted me arrested so bad, had been sold and his family broke up; it is thus the Lord fights for Israel.

I then made an appointment at a place called the Hole in the Wall, it was a little settlement of coloured people, but we had no Church, but used a dwelling house, and had a large congregation. I had no help but an old man, one hundred and odd years of age; he prayed, and his prayers made us feel awful, he died in the year 1825, and has gone to reap the reward of his labor; freed from the toils and cares of life, no more to labor under a hard task master, but to rest where the slave is freed from his master. I strove then to fill the appointment at 11 o'clock in the morning, from Daniel 5 chap. 27 ver. the declaration was, there is no other way under heaven that men can be saved only through Jesus Christ; the Lord gave me great light on this subject. At 3 o'clock, in the afternoon, we stood in the open air in the woods, and I spoke from 12 chap. 2—3 ver. I felt greater liberty on this subject than the other; the Lord was with me ; of a truth I felt the force of it now. Glory to God. Who can constrain against the power of God ? We had people of all descriptions, from the true Christian to the Devil, and from slave-holder to slave. We visited Georgetown Jail, saw four men there sentenced to be hung, two white men and two colored ; one of the white men, by the name of Sharp had killed all his family, except his oldest daughter ; she was the most hardened wretch I ever saw ; I read a chapter and conversed with them. Sharp treated it with contempt, but the other answered with a degree of humility ; but they were hung according to the laws of their state.

But O, their end,
Their dreadful end !

I was invited by one of the Trustees of the Old Methodist Church to pay them a visit on the ensuing Sabbath morning. I made the appointment for said day. I left Georgetown on the morning early, half past ten o'clock we arrived in Milford ; Church bell was ringing. We were conducted into the Church ; a local preacher was in the pulpit and had prayed, but was asked to come down by another who invited me there. I spoke for them and afterwards they gave out for another appointment at night, but it caused a controversy among themselves, and they threw it on him to come and see if I would fill it. Previous to this the coloured preachers told me there was controversy about woman preaching. But he came and asked me how long I had been preaching the Gospel. I answered, rising, 5 or 6 years. He said it was something new. I told him it seemed to be supposed so. I referred him to Mrs. Fletcher, of England, an able preacher and wife of Mr. Fletcher, a great and worthy minister of the Parish. He asked why I did not go to the Quakers. I told him I was sent to the Methodists. I asked if he had a sister in the Church, and she witnessed a Christian life, and was called and qualified to preach, do you think you would be justified before God, to stop her ? He has not answered me yet. I found it was prejudice in his mind. He talked as if he had not known what the operation of the Spirit of God was. We may say, with propriety, he had not tarried at Jerusalem long enough. When about to part, he asked me if I would come, but I could not then promise. At night, the people came in their carriages from the country, but were disappointed, for I spoke in a colored Church. The doors and windows were opened on account of the heat, but were crowded with people ; pride and prejudice were buried. We had a powerful time. I was quite taken out of myself —the meeting held till day-break ; but I returned to my home.

They told me that sinners were converted, backsliders reclaimed, mourners comforted, and believers built up in the most holy faith. Then they wished us to stay until next night to preach again ; but I thought it best to leave them hungry. Previous to this I was sent for by a slave-holder to come to his house to preach three funeral sermons, all at one time, two grown persons and one child ; they had been dead about a year, but their graves were only filled up even with the earth. I spoke standing in the door of his dwelling to a great congregation, from the 2 Book of Samuel, 12 chap. 23 ver.—dwelling much on the certainty of the child's happiness, through the redemption of Christ—shewing how men might be saved living in accordance with the truth. When finished we fell in procession and moved to the graves of the departed. Brother Massey rehearsed the funeral ceremony, then the graves were raised and made oval, as usual, a most affecting scene, one of the deceased being the mother of two little girls there present. They were so affected, it seemed they would go in fits ; several persons tried to pacify them, but in vain. It was a solemn time ; many were deeply affected that day at the graves, and mourning of the whites in the house, but they treated us kindly, and we left them, visiting many places too tedious to mention. I met a Camp meeting of the African Methodist Episcopal Church at Denton. The Elder was much encouraged in commencing the Camp. Although in a slave State, we had every thing in order, good preaching, a solemn time, and long to be remembered. Some of the poor slaves came happy in the Lord ; walked from 20 to 30, and from that to seventy miles, to worship God. Although through hardships they counted it all joy for the excellency of Christ ; and, before day, they, or a number of them, had to be at home, ready for work ; but some said they came as sinners before God, but went away as new creatures in Christ; and they could not be disputed. My heart glows with joy while I write; truly God is inscrutable. The Elder, J. B. then appointed a Camp meeting within five miles of Easton, too near the town, but it was done to glorify God. Yet it seemed there was not that general good done like the previous time. He gave me an appointment on Sunday afternoon; to myself I appeared lost ; thought I was doing nothing, but the south wind from the hill of the Lord began to blow upon the spices of his garden. The power of God arrested a person who started to run, but fell in the flight, and begged God for mercy and obtained it. After the sermon, which was the first of my being apprized of it, but no merit to me, but all glory to God, for the good done at Camp meetings, though much persecuted, but they are a glorious meeting to me. I pray God to protect the camp-meetings while I thank him for the invention. Various are the operations of the Spirit of God on the human family. We must believe in the truth of God, and then we can behold the mysteries and enjoy the truth of them with joy and thanks-giving. I went to speak about 10 miles from Centreville at early candle light—warm weather—in a dwelling house, the largest con-gregation being out-of-doors. I felt an open mind, the power of God fell upon the assembly in open air, and I heard an awful cry. A woman had started, jumped over the fence and run, but fell and rose again; that woman contended until she found redemption in Jesus Christ. I went to a place called Beaver Dams and spoke there; left there for Hillsborough, and spoke there to a large congregation; from there to Greensborough, and preached in white Methodist Church. The visit not so prosperous; from there to Boomsborough. We were much favoured and approbated by the people, and blessed with the presence of the Lord in power. I then preached at Cecil Cross roads in an old meeting house, almost down, to a large congregation, and it was warm. I was informed a gentleman rode fourteen miles to attend that meeting. Previous to this the Methodists had almost died away, a very few excepted at that place, but from that time they took a rise as I was informed by two young ladies from there. In about 5 years after I left they built a large Church on that same spot where the old one stood, and had a fine congregation; from there brother J. B. appointed a Quarterly Meeting on Mr. John Peaker's Island, for a society of 60 members, which was composed altogether of the said gentleman's slaves. We were entertained in the best of style, had a powerful meeting, and a great manifestation of the power of God. From there we returned to Easton a second time, and were entertained by the overseer very highly at Mr. John Peakey's Island. Went to Baltimore, from there I visited Hales' Mills, and preached three sermons, much favored of the Lord by his presence, after which I returned to Baltimore. The elder gave me an appointment and collection, and I returned to Philadelphia. And on Sunday morning Bishop Allen gave me an appointment in Bethel Church, and we had a shout in the Camp of Israel.

I had spent six months in Maryland and I only remained in this city three or four weeks, during which time the Lord was with me, and opened my way through opposition, but I felt willing to suffer cheerfully.

Through tribulations deep
The way to glory is.

I also preached in the Union Church, the Lord verified his promise according to what he told Mary, to go, he would meet her, whomso-ever I will put forth I will go before, so there was a shaking among the dry bones. My mind soon became oppressed and craved to travel. In 1825 I left Philadelphia for a journey through Pennsylvania. I spoke first at Weston; we had an elder on West Chester Circuit, named Jacob Richardson. We had buried a young Christian before preaching the sermon, and gave me the sacrament sermon in the afternoon. I spoke from Matt. 26 chap. 26–27 ver. I felt as solemn as death; much weeping in the Church, tears stole down the faces of the people.

Jacob Richardson was a spiritual preacher. God attended the word with power, and blessed his labors much on his circuit. From there a friend carried me to Downingtown, where I took stage and went on to Lancaster; but prospect not so good there; they had a new Church but not paid for; the proprietor took the key in possession and deprived them of worshipping God in it. But I spoke in a dwelling house, and I felt a great zeal for the cause of God to soften that man's heart, or kill him out of the way; one had better die than many. Brother Israel Williams, a few days, called to converse with him on the subject, and he gave him the key; he was then on his death-bed, and died in a short time afterwards, and we must leave him in the hands of God, for he can open and no man can shut. I went on to Columbia and spoke in the Church, and my tongue fails to describe the encouragement I met with. The Lord converted poor mourners, convicted sinners, and strengthened believers in the most holy faith. God's name be glorified for the display of his saving power. I led class, held prayer meetings, and left with a good conscience for little York. The first sermon I preached was in the Church at 10 o'clock in the morning, from Mat. xxvi, 26, 27, to a large congregation. My faith it seemed almost failed me, for when I got in the stand, so hard was the task that I trembled, and my heart beat heavy, but in giving out the hymn I felt strength of mind, and before I got through, I felt so much of life and liberty in the word, I could but wonder, and in the doctrine of Christ it was a sacramental sermon indeed to my soul. I spent some weeks there, and we enjoyed good meetings and powerful outpourings of the Spirit. I truly met with both good and bad; my scenes were many and my feelings various. I bless the Lord that the prayers of the righteous availeth much. After freeing my mind, I passed on to York Haven, and preached in a School-house to a white congregation; I was not left alone, but was treated very well by a white Methodist lady. I took lodgings at her house all night; next afternoon took stage for Harrisburg, and when I stopped at the Hotel a gentleman introduced me to the Steward, who took charge of me and escorted me to Mr. Williams, where I took supper. It was on a New Year's evening; the colored congregation had expected me and made a fire in our Church, but being late when I arrived, they had gone to hear a sermon in a white Methodist Church, and I had retired to rest a while in the evening. When they returned they came after me, taking no excuse, and I had to come down stairs, go to the Church, and preach a sermon for them, then 10 o'clock at night. The text from Acts xv, 36. Hymn 250th, as follows:

And now my soul another year
Of thy short life is past,
I cannot long continue here,
And this may be the last.

The effects of the gospel of Christ was no less than at other great seasons, but was wonderful—backsliders reclaimed and sinners converted—there was mourning, weeping, shouting and praising of God for what he had done. I preached several sermons, and was well treated by all circles of people. We had large congregations of well-behaved people; and feeling my work done in this part, I proceeded to Carlisle, Pa. There was a small body of members; I spoke and led class for them during the time I was there, which was ten days; felt my discharge of God, and took stage to Shippensburg. There was great success at this place; fifteen joined the Church; some of the most hardened sinners became serious and reformed. I was astonished at the wonderful operations of the Spirit, and the immense congregations. At the first sermon the house was crowded, and I had the good attention of the people. A man came into the house intoxicated, and offered to interrupt by speaking, but a gentleman put him out so quietly that it had no effect upon the meeting. When I contemplate the goodness of God to the human family, in putting them in a proper capacity of choosing the way of salvation, I feel sometimes almost lost, to think that God has called such a worm as I to spread the common Saviour's name. But said the Lord, "I will send by whom I will"—praise the Lord who willeth not the death of sinners—"as I live, saith the Lord, I have no pleasure in the death of the wicked, but that they turn and live."

I then proceeded on to Chambersburg by stage, and met with one Rev. Winton, who displayed much of a christian disposition, and conversed freely with me on the most particular points of the God-Head, for my instruction, showing his benevolence. He knew I was a stranger—he had friends to go to at that place, but he offered to pay my bill for a room at the Inn. I never have forgot the goodness of that gentleman, who, I believe, to be a great gospel minister. I stopt at brother Snowden's, who were very kind to me. The Lord continued to pour out His Spirit and clear the way for me, and also continued to convict, convert, and reclaim the backsliders in heart. There were very large congregations, both in and out of doors, and great revivals throughout the circuit. The elders generally treated me well, for which may the Lord bless them and their labors in his vineyard, and add to the Church such as shall be forever saved from the power of sin—may I take heed lest I fall, while I teach others. Saith the Apostle: "Paul may plant and Apollos water, but God must give the increase," for which I feel thankful. I remained in this place for some weeks, but being debilitated in body, I left for Philadelphia about the middle of April. On my return, I met with such a severe trial of opposition, that I thought I never would preach again, but the Apostle says, "ye are not your own but are bought with a price." I feel glad that God is able to keep all that put their trust in him, though the mis-steps of others often interrupt our own way— I always found friends on different parts of Globe. I preached and led classes on my return. Praise God for his delivering grace—"Oh the depth of the riches" of the glory of God, how unsearchable are his ways; they are past finding out—a sea without bottom or shore. One thing is encouraging, "When he who is my life shall appear, I shall be like him." "I know my Redeemer liveth, and shall stand on the latter day upon the earth, and though worms destroy this body, yet in my flesh shall I see God." Lord help me to keep this confidence. Rev. Richard Williams, a gentle and christian-minded man, treated me well. God would not suffer me to be destroyed. It is not by might or by power, but by the Spirit, saith the Lord of hosts. Dear reader, give ear to the truth, for the mouth of the Lord has spoken it.

> If such a worm as I can spread
> The common Saviour's name,
> Let him who raised thee from the dead,
> Quicken my mortal frame.

On my return I stopped at Lancaster; the Church was opened, and I preached to large congregations, and with powerful success; the dead were brought to life by the preaching of the cross of Christ. From there I left for Philadelphia.

In July, 1824, I felt an exercise of mind to take a journey to Reading, Pa., to speak to the fallen sons and daughters of Adam. I left the city and stopped at Norristown on my way to Reading. I spoke in the Academy to a respectable congregation, the same evening I arrived there. I felt a degree of liberty in speaking, though it was a quiet meeting, and I also felt thankful that the Lord would manifest himself through such a worm as me. Next morning I walked four miles and stopped at Littleton Morris's, and preached two sermons on the Sabbath day, and God struck a woman, and she had liked to have fallen to the floor; I spoke in the Dunkard's meeting house. This ended my visit with them at this time. On Tuesday I walked three miles to Schuylkill, to take the Canal boat on Wednesday morning. I met in company with a Presbyterian minister and lady on the boat; they treated me very kindly indeed. We arrived in Reading about 7 o'clock in the evening. I was recommended to a family in that place, the man of which had once confessed religion, but had fallen from grace, and they were very kind to me. The next morning I enquired for other respectable families of color, and an elderly lady of color that belonged to the white connexion, and the only colored Methodist in the place at that time, conveyed me to Mrs. Murray's, where I remainded a while; then the elderly lady, just mentioned, feeling interested for me, went to the proprietors of the Court-house with me, to see if we could get it to preach in, and like Esther the Queen, who fasted and prayed, and commanded the men of Jerusalem and the women of Zion to pray; as she approached the King the sceptre was bowed to her, and her request was answered to the saving of Mordica, and all the Jewish nation. When we approached this gentleman, who was the head Trustee of the Protestant Church, I showed him my recommendation, and he answered me, "Madam, you can have it," and I felt humble to God for the answer. I felt it my duty to preach to the citizens, and accordingly made an appointment for Sunday afternoon at 4 o'clock. Rev. James Ward, a colored Presbyterian, assembled with us, although he was so prejudiced he would not let me in his pulpit to speak; but the Lord made a way where there was no way to be seen; there was no person to intercede until this sister tried to open the way; the men of color, with no spirit of christianity, remained idle in the enterprize, but we got possession and we had a large concourse of people. I spoke with the ability God gave me. I met with a family of color, but very respectable, that formerly had belonged to our Church in Baltimore; they invited me to their house, and it was a home to me, praise God. I held a meeting in their house previous to holding meetings in the Court-house; the white brethren and sisters assembled with us. We called on a minister's lady, and she treated me very kindly, while he, like a Christian, united and helped to go through with the meetings. I visited the Quaker friends (amounting to four only) then in the place, and very pleasant visits they were. A great number of christian friends called on me, among the rest this minister's lady, who left a donation in my hand, consequently the way was made where there was no way, but I left in friendship. Praise God I feel the approbation now. It is to be lamented, that James Ward, colored, with his over-ruling prejudice, which he manifested by saying no woman should stand in his pulpit, and with all the advantages of a liberal education, was in a few weeks after I left there, turned out of the Church.

On returning to Philadelphia, I stopped at Pottsgrove and found a Society of colored persons, christians I believe. We had solemn meetings there; I felt strength of mind. I met kind friends there, and visited a Church about six miles off; preached in the morning; the Lord was with us; of this truth my soul is a witness; in the afternoon I preached to a large congregation. Next morning I left for Philadelphia. I continued to preach, paid some short visits about, and was welcomed home again..

I left Philadelphia again for Lewistown, Del., to attend a camp meeting of the African Methodist Episcopal connexion, of which I was a member, to be held in Gov. Paynter's Woods. There was immense large congregations, and a greater display of God's power I never saw. The people came from all parts, without distinction of sex, size, or color, and the display of God's power commenced from singing; I recollect a brother Camell standing under a tree singing, and the people drew nigh to hear him, and a large number were struck to the ground before preaching began, and signs and wonders followed. There appeared to be a great union with the white friends. James Towson was the Elder holding the camp; he was in the bloom of the gospel of Christ. But poor brother, may the Lord give him a Peter's look by the way of mercy. Right Rev. Bishop Allen was present. The ministry were all for me, and the Elder gave me an appointment, and the Governor with a great concourse came to hear the weak female. My heart beat, my limbs trembled, and my voice was faint, but I spoke from Eccles. xi, 9, 10. After I took my text, it appeared to me as if I had nothing to do but open my mouth, and the Lord filled it, consequently I was much encouraged : it was an immense assembly of people.

> Content with beholding his face,
> I all to his pleasure resigned.

After the camp-meeting was over, the Elder visited another camp-meeting, and left me in liberty to preach around the circuit, which I did, and afterwards returned to Lewistown, and spoke in the old Methodist meeting-house; I had a great time among my colored brethren. I feel thankful to my friends for their kindness to me, especially to brother Peter Lewis, whose house was a home to me. I had much happiness in leading class and prayer meetings; preaching the gospel seemed to be the great task. Brother Lewis conveyed me to Georgetown ; I spoke in our colored people's Church, and we enjoyed ourselves very much; the Lord drew people from all quarters; a wonderful outpouring of the Spirit indeed ; weeping in all directions. It is a good sign to see tears of contrition stealing down the cheeks of the hearers; it makes me believe the word is sanctioned. The last place was at the head of the river; I then returned to Lewistown, and in a few days I left for Philadelphia. I had a very uncomfortable passage ; very sea-sick indeed—the vessel could not come out of the mouth of the creek for a couple of days, in consequence of a severe storm, after which we arrived in the city on Tuesday morning. After a short stay in the city, I took a visit to Trenton, Dec. 25. I spoke as usual, for there we had lively meetings, after which I had no home, but the Lord provides, for sister Roberts and family were my friends and took me in, and we often had sweet counsel together. From there I went to Princeton. The Elder, Joseph Harper, of our connexion, was a friend to me, but I had to withstand a beast at Princeton, in opposition, like the one I had to front on Bucks county circuit; the former named Thomas Voris, a local preacher, and using the language of the Psalmist prophesying in reference to the Saviour, "mine equal, my guide hath lifted up his heel against me." We had preached—he invited me to come to his house to hold meetings the next week, but I was taken sick for a few days, but in the interval, S. R., of Attleborough Circuit, had a Quarterly meeting. They consulted together to stop me from preaching in Princeton ; so his door was shut, but bless the Lord, another was opened, Brother Thomas Vinsant, his sister's husband, a Christian man, opened his house. We had a powerful time. I came in the town on Saturday, the next day I walked two miles and spoke twice It was Thomas' appointment on Sabbath morning, and he had but two persons to meet him in class. An invitation came to me to make an appointment for Wednesday night in the Coloured Presbyterian Church, upon the grant of Rev. Mr. Woodhall, elder of that order in Princeton. Thos. Vorris, though a Methodist, was like a roaring lion—went to Elder Woodhall for him to stop it, as I was informed. But the meeting went on, it was a respectable, and comfortable congregation. I preached and led class and prayer meetings, and read, and explained the Scriptures. We had mourning and rejoicing, and I saw the kingdom of Satan fall. When Brother J. H. came round again, from some cause, he removed Thomas from that class, as they would not meet him, and placed him over one of five or six persons ; also impeached him, taking his license from him, and left him only verbally licenced. Glory to God for his Divine power. I do not rejoice for his downfall, but for God's grace which enables me to stand against the enemies of the Cross. Glory to God, I am not ashamed of the Gospel of Christ, for it is the power of God unto salvation. I spoke from Ephe. 2d chap. 8th ver. I felt life and liberty in word and doctrine. Thank God for the victory, Brother Oakham, one of the Elders of the Coloured Presbyterian Church, invited me to their house, and himself and wife treated me like Christians, which, I believe, they were ; my heart glows toward them. I held a meeting in a dwelling house.

Jan., 1827. Contemplating on the great responsibility I owe to my God for my stewardship, I fain would go round the Cross or shrink beneath the load, but I rest upon the promises of God, which are as firm of the pillars of heaven. My labors here cease a little.

April, 1827. My health having been bad, I have not travelled so largely, and in this, as in some other moment's of reflection, I felt somewhat oppressed, and I resorted to the Hymn Book for something to suit my feelings; the poetry as follows :

1.   Soon as I heard my Father say,
     Ye children seek my grace,

My heart replies, without delay,
　I'll seek my father's face.

2. Let not thy face be hid from me,
　　Nor frown my soul away,
　God of my life I fly to thee
　　In a distressing day.

3. Should friends and kindred, near and dear,
　　Leave me to want and die.
　My God will make my life his care,
　　And all my wants supply.

4. My fainting flesh had died with grief,
　　Had not my soul believed
　To see thy grace prove a relief,
　　Nor was my hope deceived.

5. Wait on the Lord, ye trembling Saints,
　　And keep your courage up,
　He'll raise your spirit when it faints,
　　And far exceed your hope.

However I went to Baltimore in the same month with the Bishop and Elders, and enjoyed myself under great preaching, and preached several sermons. Praise God, and the slain of the Lord appeared to be many. After Conference, my mind led me over to Eastern Shore the second time; spent a few days with the Church. (Peter D. Schuman, Elder of the charge) and then returned to Baltimore, from there to the city of Philadelphia, and then made some short visits from 40 to 60, and from that to 100 miles round about; then down to Lewistown Camp-meeting, the second time; then to a Camp-meeting at Mount Ephraim, N. J. The last of August I left for New York Camp, on arriving there I spoke once or twice. The same as at other places, our camp-meeting was not as great as I have seen before. I spoke in both the Churches. We had a good time together, rejoicing in the Lord. I left then for Albany; had a pleasant passage up the North river, one hundred and sixty miles; the mountains and their stupendous looks preached to me in my journey through. Oh, the wisdom of God, and how marvellous in our eyes; enough to convince the infidel, yea, the Atheist, that there is some first cause. From the effects produced, look at the ingenuity of mankind, which actually comes from God, and is displayed in building steamboats, and other great novelties in mechanism. We accomplished the route the same day we started, and I found myself entirely among strangers. But I made inquiry for Methodist friends, and found brother Streeter, a coloured family, very respectable. They treated me very kind; they were under the white Bishop, and I under the coloured. But the same faith, same doctrine, same Baptism, same spirit. Glory to God. Among the coloured people, the Baptists had the ascendancy. There was a large hall prepared for me, and we had a large congregation of different denominations. I spoke from these words and this Gospel of the kingdom shall be preached unto all the world as for a witness, and then shall the end come. God owned the word, sinners screamed; some fell to the floor, others wept, while Christians rejoiced. A lady of color was present, though she was a member of the Dutch Presbyterian Church; her husband belonged to no Church, but was under an exercise of mind. The Lord reached his heart, he mourned more than three days. They sent for me to come to their house. I paid them a visit, and held prayer meeting at their house. That Sabbath two weeks he joined the Methodist Church. I spoke three times the first Sabbath afternoon; we had a large congregation, at night still larger. Text. Never man spake like this man. God's spirit was poured out in a miraculous manner. On the ensuing third day evening I spoke again, from these words. And came seeking fruit on the tree and found none. To all appearance there was nothing done, but God directed the word to the heart of a little girl, a gentleman's daughter, between eleven and twelve years of age. She joined the Church before I left there. A good old Missionary, by the name of Mitchell, came to the city before I left, and preached three sermons, in which there was a great revival. The Elder appointed prayer meetings, north and south of the city of Albany. I preached two or three sermons in a school house, the last I spoke was in Brother Streeter's house, from St. Matt. Chap. 21 ver. 12th. I thank God for the comfortable visit I had there in the discharge of my duty. This Methodist preacher, Mitchell, had a book with him called the Essence of John Steward, a coloured man, with his miraculous call to the ministry; the first one who succeeded in Christianizing the Methodist Indians in Sandusky and that province, and he sold them in Albany, and it seemed to have its desired effect also with the revival, in encouraging us to hold a fast.

How good to contemplate or to think the heathen has caught the sound of salvation through the name of Jesus, our Lord. I saw a goodly number added to the Church on Sabbath-day. I still continued engaged in my mind with the Lord, in their behalf, when I was informed that they had three and four of an evening at their prayer meetings, then my mind felt at liberty to leave for Schenectady. Sister Streeter rode with me fourteen miles; I stopped eleven days, at which place there was a large upper room that was appropriated for a preaching place, where I spoke to a small number of coloured persons several times. They were under the white elder, he was a friend to me, and appointed a meeting for me in the white Brother's house to speak for them. We had a favourable time. But the people, feeling an uninterested spirit in propagating the religion of Jesus Christ, I left the dust with them. Got on board a Canal boat for Utica, there I met with my own connexion, African Methodist Episcopal Church, we had a prosperous time. I spoke ade had prayer meetings on board of the Canal boat. There was a pasture there notwithstanding the difficulties of this life and the people being hunted like partridges on the mountain. It deprives a man's usefulness among the people, but the work of the Lord went on, and there is no weapon formed by the enemy that can stop the work of God. Therefore we have nothing to fear. We have large and respectable congregations, and I felt strengthened in warning man to flee from the wrath to come. If signs and wonders did not follow sometimes, I must certainly die, but glory to God for refreshing showers. I led class, had prayer meetings, and took my passage on another canal boat for Rochester; had a pleasant passage. I soon found some Methodists, and our local Elder was then a smart preacher. I was there three or four weeks, and he treated me very kindly and opened my way. They erected a new brick church, basement for schools; the corner-stone was laid while I was there. The elder was a man of good repute; people of color of different denominations, but much united together. The elder held the charge from there to Buffalo, he had then a Quarterly Meeting on hand. I left Rochester with him and rode about seventy miles. Next morning I left Lewistown and rode seven miles, crossed the Lakes, on the British side. When we left Rochester the snow was ankle deep, when ten mile from Lewistown, it became dry and hard, and when we crossed the Lakes it was clear and cold, and the air very pure. I told the elder this was the first time I ever breathed pure air. I walked about a mile and the first house I stopped at was sister Holmes'. I felt strange and lonely. I waited to see if the peace of God would abide on the house. Previous to my being introduced, I arose from my chair and the power of God fell upon the people, and, it seemed to me, that God answered me. I was fully convinced that God would make bare his arm, in this part of his moral vineyard. We had a Church in Niagara; the elder made an appointment there, and forty or fifty miles round the circuit, being now about six hundred miles from Philadelphia. I felt the loss of my former companions and friends, the elder and deacon, in two days time left for Buffalo, to hold a quarterly meeting in York state about sevenly miles. I commenced to speak for the people, and God owned the word, and I saw many displays of his power—the people in Niagara seemed to me to be a kind and Christian like people. The white inhabitants united with us, and ladies of great renown. The slaves that came there felt their freedom, began to see the necessity of education, and hired a white man to teach them to read and write among themselves, and have Sabbath schools. I am astonished to see so many there that came from a free state, and not take more interest in instilling the science of education among their fellow beings. The winter was cold—I never had experienced such —but very healthy. I went to a town called Niagara. I spoke in a dwelling house. The next night I spoke in the Old Methodist Church to a large congregation of respectable people. There were three ladies, one the widow of a great Judge, and one daughter and sister of first education; they sympathized with me in this important work of the Gospel of Christ. They assembled with us in our meeting. A little girl about 8 or 9 years of age experienced religion and prayed in public, and attended to their private devotion, so much for early piety. Teach the child the way he should go and when he gets old he will not depart from it. But, it is to be lamented, that so few of our children experience this early piety; the cause we must try to find out and avoid the evil effects, and not bring up our children in so much pride and heathenism. We, as a people, are generally poor and cannot support so many changes of fashion; they grow up and crave it, and oftimes substitute evil practices to support themselves, either girls or boys, and often bring a stigma upon their parents and family connexions, though very respectable. Let us bring up our children in industry, for work is honorable, and it is the way to get riches and to keep them. I travelled back and forward again from Niagara to Buffalo, and had regular appointments in our Churches. We had a great opposition among the coloured people, one trying to excel the other in point of eminence. One of our preachers left us on the promise of forty dollars per year. Poor man, he was like Simon Magus who perished with his money. Our Circuit rider was absent on the Sunday of the split, but the Lord was with us. I spoke three times to the remaining part of the congregation, which was increased much by a large body of bystanders, and great good followed; and we continued to sow and gather for two or three months, and the Lord blessed our labors abundantly. Feeling I had discharged my duty, I left and crossed the Lake from Buffaloe to Fort George, and spoke about eight miles from there, it was cold and snowed very fast—it was four o'clock in the afternoon—the congregation had been there and gone. We were in a sleigh, and the driver got lost; we all brought up in a swamp, among the fallen tree tops, but we turned about and found a house and lodged all night; and spoke next morning at eleven o'clock to a quiet congregation, and the Lord was with us, though composed of all denominations. I appointed another meeting and rode about eight miles on horseback —it snowed and was very sleety—after I spoke to the people I left them for good and made an appointment for the Indians; two of the chiefs called at where I stopped to see me. I asked them to pray for us; they complied, but done it in their own tongue. I felt the power of God in my own heart. Then they held a council about it, and granted my visit at Buffalo village, about three miles from Buffalo city. We rode and got there before their worshipping hour, their school had not dismissed, after a while they dismissed school—of 50 children—and as they gathered to worship I saw an old chief come, he stood and prayed very devoutly, tears running down his cheek. I told them I had not come to worship with them, and wanted to preach for them after their worship ended. They held a council and they agreed I should preach for them, but I could not help admiring the ways as well as gestures of the children. The teachers bring them up in the English language and dress some of them in the English style, but the greatest number are clad in the Indian style; those of the old Indians in their blankets. Some of them met me from seven or eight miles round—they filled the house. It was in the month of March—it rained and snowed—yet they walked in their moccasins, and some bare-headed—they made a large congregation. Their Elder or missionary had gone to teach another tribe that day, and he only taught them very plainly, and read out of pamphlets the experiences of others. I commenced by giving out the hymn in our language, and the interpreter spoke in their tongue. Hymn thus, O for a thousand tongues to sing, &c. They sung it beautiful,—two long benches of them sung by note (their books printed in their own language) a very familiar note tune, such as we use in congregations. I spoke plain and deliberate and very pointed, the interpreter spoke it after me in the Indian tongue, and one of the women cried out Amen. Much weeping among them, dear reader, take notice, notwithstanding they are a nation revolted from Israel, and would not be governed. Yet they can be civilized and christianized. We might call them heathens, but they are endowed with a Christian spirit. I felt happy in my visit; the missionary wished me to speak for them that evening, but I had an appointment that night at Buffalo, after which my mind was calm and serene. I left on Tuesday, 1st of April, on my return for Philadelphia, and arrived home May 18th.

That year I travelled two thousand three hundred and twenty-five miles, and preached one hundred and seventy-eight sermons. Praise God for health and strength, O my soul, and magnify his name for protection through various scenes of life.

> God of my life whose gracious power
> Through various deaths my soul has led,
> Or turned aside the fated hour,
> Or lifted up my sinking head.

While I was in Buffalo, a journey to the West was shewed to me so plain that I could not stop in the city of Philadelphia but five weeks only, then left for the western country. I started in a mail stage, and stopped first at Westtown and spoke in our own connexion Church, and then at West Chester in the old Methodist Episcopal white connexion. We had a large congregation of quiet hearers. I felt liberty but no great displays of God's power. I had several meetings in different places, visiting the sick. Having discharged my duty I left teere and proceeded on to Old Lancaster and spent some days. We have a good Church there, and great meetings—the word of the Lord grew and was multiplied. God poured out his spirit upon us, and we had a shout in the camp. I then started for Columbia, Pa. The people are much divided, and it looked very gloomy, but God directed me and he commanded his disciple to be a sheep among wolves, and harmless as doves, notwithstanding the darkness, God aided me in speaking to the people, and aided them in hearing, and his name was praised. The people united, temptations and clouds were vanished away. Then we sung, prayed, spake, and shouted in the spirit, this is true Methodism. I led class, visited the sick and was much favoured with the presence of the Lord. Our faith was increased, our hopes confirmed. The preachers were kind and treated me well, and by their help I travelled on my journey to Harrisburg. Feeling thankful for the visit I had paid it seemed gloomy here, but I spoke there next day. I took stage and rode to Chambersburg, and spent some days there, and proceeeed on to Fredericktown, Maryland, and spoke there from there to Hagerstown, Macallansburg, and, I must confess, It do not remember of ever seeing such a people, for, it seemed strong drink had been their ruin. The circuit minister was there, and we had some signs and wonders to follow after the preaching of the cross of Christ, and I trust to meet some of them on the banks of deliverance, and help to swell the notes of redeeming love. After the preacher left me I took stage for Pittsburgh, at eight in the evening, rode all night until eight in the morning. I was kindly treated, there were other persons in the stage, four of them gentlemen, as I thought there was one who talked a great deal, wise in his own conceit, about religion, and from that he displayed a quantity of degraded principle, with disgusting language, at which I made several sharp replies, and in my way, reprimanded him and the other gentlemen looked on him with silent contempt, at which he got ashamed, and afterwards treated me with great politeness, and I was comfortable and arrived in Pittsburgh at 5 o'clock in the afternoon. I went to Church that night and heard a sermon from one of my brothers. I met with six or seven ministers, very friendly, and treated me like Christians. I remained in Pittsburgh six weeks, there had been one or two revivals previous to my visit, especially the winter before I arrived, last day of August, 1820. My labors commenced—the field was large—but the Lord was with us—this gave me much encouragement, I was not ashamed of the Gospel—it is the power of God unto salvation, to every one that believes, both Jew or Gentile. We had very good meetings, the Elder and preachers, all received me with one accord— thanks to God for his divine goodness—I felt moved by the Lord to pay Wheeling a visit although we had no society there, I arrived and found but a small class of coloured people with the whites, an old gentleman of color with the elder in charge granted me the Church —the elder being a great preacher of college order. We had a large congregation; I spoke for them once, and gave an exhortation at another time, and felt no difficulty on that head, and after that they could not treat me well enough. And, on the ensuing Sabbath, I helped to lead class; and we all enjoyed ourselves, and on Tuesday I left for Washington, according as I had promised our elder before I left him. On my arrival there I met kind friends, and a large congregation of coloured people. On Lords' day I met the class; the people spoke with humility—it was a melting down time—in the Spirit of God I preached several sermons, visited the sick, and, in this spirit strove to uphold the aged. Feeling a discharge of my duty I left for Steubensville, Ohio, and met a small society—some true Christians there; no Church there; the Baptists granted their Church; we had meetings there, and the Lord was with us—quiet congregations— and the word had effect in the hearts of sinners—and believers were established. I stopped a few days and left in the name of the Lord. I proceeded on to Mt. Pleasant, and arrived on seventh day evening, and the trustee gave me an appointment on Sabbath morning. At 11 o'clock I was feeble in both body and mind, but the Lord was with us according to promise, think not what ye shall say, but open thy mouth and I will fill it saith the Lord, he caused a shaking among the dry bones, that morning. I think if any creature has a right to praise God I have, and that in thankfulness, and I love him because he first loved me. Bless his name. I preached several sermons to large gatherings, but revivals not so manifest as at other places. I had some difficulty in that journey, but only what is common among us; for many times deceitful persons will set the Church on fire but can't burn it up.

Moses saw it as a bush in a flame, yet not consumed. We have to be tried as gold in the fire. After my visit was out a brother (leader in the Church) conveyed me ten miles on my way, I stopped at Sinclairsville; there was an appointment published on the next evening. At 7 o'clock I spoke in the Court house to a large concourse of well behaved and respectable citizens. I felt at liberty and left in peace of mind which makes the work sweet. I was aided on to Cap-teen, a settlement of coloured people; some from the lower counties; but they are industrious, and have a Church of their own, and were about to send their children to school, I held several meetings and there was some very respectable people of colour—and the Lord was with us —I stopped with an aged family, very respectable, they treated me very kind, and between 2 and 3 weeks, I left in peace with God and man, and went to Barnsborough and spoke in the white Methodist Episcopal Church, from thence to Zanesville, at which place I felt much discouraged from the appearance of things. I did not think of tarrying there, but at the first appointment I chose the words " I am not ashamed of the Gospel."—Paul. The room was very small for the number of people, after which an old man well scented with ardent spirits, tried to give an exhortation. I was astonished at the scene, the people laughed, I got up and went out. I tried to labor again at night and exhort the young ladies to the evil consequences of ill-behavior in the Church of God ; after which we had better order, and the old gentleman was discovered to be intoxicated with spiritous liquor, and was disowned from the Church, after which there was a great revival took place among the white Methodists, both rich and poor.

Mrs. Dillin, who once was a Friend, and now a member of the Church, spoke to the Trustees and Ministers, and they opened the Church and I spoke twice in that Church, and after that I spoke in West Zanesville, back of that place, and I still remained among my colored friends, and they seemed much revived; after which they formed a Resolution to build themselves a Meeting House. A Quaker Friend, so called, presented them with a piece of ground to build one on, which they did. Glory to God, for his glory stood over the doors of the Tabernacle. Many were convicted, and converted, and many added to the old Methodist Church. and I left there on New-Years day for for New-Lancaster, where we had a Church, standing on a frame of a house for three or four years, and had not been used to preach in ; but the Lord opened the way, and a great revival took place among the people, and their eyes being opened, they with willing minds commenced and built a new Church, and God blessed their labors. I preached several Sermons and led Class, &c. My common way is to visit the sick and afflicted in whatsoever city I may stop in, that I may get my spiritual strength renewed in the Lord. Although I preached the Gospel through the Commission of my Lord, yet, I have nothing to boast of.

I opened a Love-Feast in the said Church in New Lancaster. We held Prayer Meetings. I spoke in the White's Church also. The people were very friendly. I met them in Class, and after the lapse of eleven days, I left for Columbus. The Preachers generally were very kind to me. Both white and colored. A worthy brother conducted me on further. It snow'd, and I was very cold, but the Lord was with us, and my mind was free'd. But notwithstanding, I met an antagonist, who was ready to destroy my character, and the principles of the Work that God saw good to make me instrumental of doing in his name, which caused me to open the case to the Trustees and Preaches, who were much astonished at him to be preaching four or five years with malice in his heart. I was favored to see him in the morning before he went away, that was the first time he had spoke

:o me anything like a Christian in that time. He knew from the first period I went to him to satisfy his mind. But his heart was bitter. I felt his spirit like a viper. But the word of the Lord was verified at that time also. "When the Tempter raises a flood against you, I will set up a standard against him." He told me he had sent a letter to Pittsburg to stop me, although I had my Licence from the Bishop, with his own signature. I told him he was a worse enemy to me than I was aware of, and I was ashamed of him, professing to be a Preacher in charge, and setting such an example in a strange laud, and begged him to throw away his prejudices, or he would never obtain the Kingdom of Heaven. He left me in a flash, and I saw him no more until Conference. I wrote a letter to Bishop Allen to let him know of my grievances, as I was innocent of any crime. I felt under no obligation to bear the reproaches of progressing Preachers; and I wanted it settled at Conference. But it was looked upon with little effect by the Preachers and Leaders. I laid it before the Conference, and it was settled. But I tarried all winter. Preached, led Class, visited the sick, &c., with great success- I bless God for the witness of a good conscience. Old Sinners were awakened, and constrained to come trembling, and enquiring the way to Zion.

L. W., a respectable brother from Chillicothe, had never heard a woman preach, and was much opposed to it. An appointment was given me, and when I went into the desk and commenced reading the hymn to commence the worship, he looked at me a while, then got up and went out and stood until I had nearly got through the hymn, and then came in, when I asked him to pray for us but he refused. I prayed myself, after which I took my text, and felt much liberty in speaking in the spirit indeed. And after meeting he came and shook hands with me in the spirit of a christian, and next day he came and confessed to me his prejudices had been so great, so much like his father, that he could not unite with me, but now he believed that God was no respecter of persons, and that a woman as well as a man, when called of God, had a right to preach. He afterwards became a licensed preacher, and we parted in peace. I took the stage and left for Chilicothe, but there was but one house that would open for me in the city, although I had my recommendation with me. As soon as that friend heard of me she met me in christian bonds, and her house was my home, her husband being a man of christian qualifications, and I went on my mission doing my Father's will. I spoke once in the week and on Sabbath afternoon, to crowded houses; it was like a camp-meeting, and twenty-one lay under the power of God at one time; after preaching we called them up to be prayed for; some got religion that day and some on the next Sabbath, and the father L. W. became one of my best friends, and a doer of the work. There was large fields of labor open to my view, and I visited both colored and white, and many were concerned about sanctification. I was with them about six weeks, during which time I had an interview with a lady, who informed me she had a call to preach the everlasting gospel of Christ. She was a Presbyterian by profession, and she told me she feared the church government. But the greatest objection was, her husband was a Deist by profession; she also told me of her experience she passed through; it was a broken heart and a contrite spirit. God answers the prayers of such a supplicant, but she could not enjoy that sweet fulness of religion in that situation of life, although very rich as regards this world's goods; also knowing that gold and silver should vanish away, but the word of God should endure forever. And some feel their labors a long time before it comes to perfection. Our Methodist sisters established a prayer meeting, and the people worked in the unity of the spirit, and much good was done in the name of the Holy child. Glory to God for what my heart feels while I use my pen in hand. I felt peace of conscience and left Chilicothe for Hillsborough to meet a quarterly meeting of W. C., he being Elder at that place; the Governor and his family residing there, six in number, were all Methodists, and one son a preacher; they had the spirit of christians. The trustees of the Methodist church opened their doors and gave us liberty to hold our quarterly meeting and love feast in their church, and we had a good time. The friends mostly gave me a small donation, which was very thankful; after which I left there for Cincinnati, where I spoke to a large congregation. I stop't at Williamsport and spoke in the white Methodist church to a respectable congregation. I felt liberty in the spirit of God, and we left there about daybreak in the morning. All nature seemed in silence (except the chirping notes of a little bird.) A few rods from us a Panther screamed very loud and sudden, but we could not see him, it being a dense thicket on either side of the road, but the unseen arm of God sheltered us from harm; one of the gentlemen seemed quite used to hearing them. We arrived safe in Cincinnati about 11 o'clock; the Elder W. C. was very liberal in giving me appointments, and the friends were very affectionate to me, and large congregations attended. I remained there some time, feeling to be blessed in my weak endeavors to a great extent. The next day after I arrived there, one of our sisters fell sick and I had the pleasure of visiting her on her death-bed, and in her last hour she told me in presence of others, her peace was made, and raised her hands toward heaven and told us she was going. This is the end of sister Crosby; who can doubt this faithful saying, by grace ye are saved. A month or more previous, she had buried a daughter, who was a member of our church; before she left the world, she called her young companions and caused them to promise to meet her in heaven, and then closed her eyes triumphing in death. Brother Crosby laid the heavy task on me to preach their funeral sermons, which I did, as feeble a worm as I am, on Sabbath morning. Words of my choice were found in 2d Ephe. 8th v:—"For by grace ye are saved through faith, and that not of yourselves, it is the gift of God," which of itself is a sermon to all that believe—glory to God, Christ has overcome the world. And while laboring many tears were shed both in joy and sorrow. But it's better to be one day in the house of the Lord than a thousand in the tents of the wicked.

Another circumstance worthy of notice, was a young man whose heart was in the world and in worldly affairs, or the pursuits of nature, and diverted much of his time on Sabbath days on the Mississippi River, fighting against all impressions of the Spirit of grace, until God stopped him by the heavy hand of his power, in a death-bed affliction. After some time he began to inquire the way to Zion. His mother was also a stranger to the blood of Jesus, but wished me to come and see her son; being conducted to the house, I found him looking like an anatomy. I asked him if he believed in Christ and his all sufficiency to save; his answer was in the affirmative. We had prayers with him and there was a display of God's power; a white woman screamed and nearly fell to the floor, but strove hard to keep from it. And on that day he acknowledged his Saviour to be reconciled to his poor soul. Praise God! my soul replied. Afterwards he wished me to hold a meeting with as many persons as the room would contain with him, which I accepted; one day and night after, he departed this life, and requested me to preach his funeral sermon at the house before the procession moved to the ground. I spoke from the 14th chap. 13 v., and we had a solemn time; you may anticipate the weight of that important task, but we had joy in the midst of sorrow, and this was the last of James Thompson. I also left his sister in the last stage of consumption, and she confessed to be in favor with the Lord. Having finished my visit, I left in steamboat for Dayton. I spoke three times, and tried to preach the whole salvation, God the Father, God the Son, and God the Holy Ghost. The members of the New-light church deny the divinity of Christ. Once I spoke in a large dwelling of Dr. Esley, after which himself and wife went on a journey to Indiana and wished me to go with them, but I was deprived by a previous engagement, having to attend a camp-meeting at Cap-teen. After my return to Urbanna, Ohio, I took stage for Springfield, and from there to Columbus, and spoke several times. The Elder's class consisted of about twenty; a young man and myself led the class in 1829. The Elder W. C. ordered a camp-meeting for the Cincinnati people, and the brother at Cap-teen and Rev. Bishop Brown, held a conference, and we had a very large camp-meeting, and manifestations of great good, and at the close of the Love-feast, there were thirty-two or three testified that they experienced the love of God. The people of color came out forcibly, and the preachers preached in power. My health was much destroyed by speaking so often and laboring so very hard, having a heavy fever preying upon my system. I was called upon to speak at a camp-meeting, I could scarcely accomplish the task, and I was obliged to take my bed (having also lost my appetite) as soon as my sermon was over. After a while my particular friends conveyed me to Mount Pleasant in a carriage; the day was pleasant, but in the woods at night we were overtaken by a dreadful storm of thunder, wind and rain, but through the will of Providence I escaped the inclemency of the weather and stopped at brother and sister Hance's; after being medically renovated, I fulfilled an appointment, and commenced to visit the sick in that place, but was arrested by a heavy fever. A physician was called, and by daybreak my senses left me, so severe was the disease, which caused the physician to visit me two and three times a day, which proved to be the bilious fever. After my mind returned and became calm, I was convinced that it would not terminate in death at that time. I had faith in the Lord. Eleven days I lived on rice water and chicken tea without salt, at the end of which time I felt an appetite to eat. I had been under a deep sallavation which proved a blessing in effecting a cure. After a lapse of four weeks I was enabled to get out of that house, but very weak; my money was short; I left seven dollars with them hoping the Lord may bless them; then I returned to brother Hance, and was well treated. I commenced preaching, though very weak, and I accepted an appointment on Sabbath in the white Methodist Episcopal church, to a well-behaved congregation, about ten miles distance. I had to be carried to the carriage in a blanket and returned the same way, and was well taken care of by brother and sister Moor and family, for which may the Lord bless them in basket and store. Elder Jones gave me an invitation to go to Pittsburg and try to gather a little strength, which I accepted, and was kindly taken care of by brother Lewis and wife, which I very much profitted by the assistance of his family doctor, which he called in amid the blessings of Providence; this was in May, 1830. I then commenced to labor amid the souls of the people, which are precious. After gaining strength in body and mind in my recovery, I spoke to a good number of colored friends on the Hill, and they were about to build a church for worship as they owned the property. When I was able to travel, one of the preacher's wives and a kind brother conducted me on to Washington, from which I took stage for Mount Pleasant; labored for them, enjoyed a love-feast with them, and in a few days left for St. Clairsville and the next successive place; then took stage for Zanesville, continuing to labor around the circuit, and then went to Columbus. I was invited to attend a quarterly meeting at Urbana; we had quite a profitable waiting upon the Lord; it makes me glad when they say let us go up to the house of the Lord. After trying to rest myself four or five weeks, a brother preacher, in company with brother Steward's widow and myself, visited the Indians, she having lived nine years in Sandusky. We heard them preach in their own language, but I could only understand when he said Jesus Christ or God, and the interpreter had gone to conference. I spoke to them in English, was entertained in an Indian family, and that very kindly, after which I shook the dust off my feet and left them in peace. Thank the Lord for Urbana. The Elder appointed a camp-meeting at Hillsborough; it was nothing to boast off; after which I turned towards Philadelphia. Brother Rains paid my stage fare on to Springfield; there I endeavored to speak to a small and very quiet congregation; from thence to Columbus and paid seven dollars and a half, and left for Wheeling; stopped at a camp-meeting at the request of the Wheeling friends, but it seemed that both the golden wedge and Babalonish garment was there, as the wheel could not turn, for Christ said I could not do many mighty works on account of your unbelief; the Devil was at work, but the Lord was above.

I spoke at Wilkesbarre to both white and colored, Baptists and Methodists, and had an invitation to preach in the afternoon, had good congregations, and tears of contrition were visible in many places. I had life and liberty. I next visited Wheeling, stopped a few days and labored several times, which was much blessed, and the Elder organized a new class of twenty-one young men, brother and [my-self led them the first time, and they seemed very zealous. But in a few months the severity of the Laws stopped their religious privileges, which is an honor to any people; while sin is a reproach to any Nation. I then paid $10 and took passage to Hagerstown. My health was poor. Passengers consisted of three white ladies, members of the Episcopal Church, and one old gentleman, (a Deist) 73 years of age, who would reproach Religion, until I told him that Solomon spoke of a man 70 years of age, and called him a fool,—and exhorted him to get religion; for God's name is worthy to be praised by all inrelligent beings. I have found Him to be a strong hold in the day of trouble. We arrived at Hagerstown in eight or ten days. We had a Meeting House there. I met the Elder, Joseph Harper, Deacon John Cornish. Had good Metings; a visit of the Holy Ghost. The house was crowded, and many hundred sinners struck to the heart,—back-sliders were reclaimed—and believers built up in the most Holy Faith. Praise God for so much. I spoke to a very respectable congregation of white people about eleven miles distant.

> " Go, preach my Gospel saith the Lord,
> Bid the whole world my grace receive;
> He shall be sav'd that trusts my word,
> He shall be damn'd that won't believe."

I then took my passage for Fredericktown. The Society was small, but willing to encourage the Gospel of Christ. We had meeting in a large upper room of a building; the congregation was of both white and colored persons. I felt life and liberty, and an increase of my labors. In about ten days sinners were awakened—backsliders reclaimed—and believers built up in the most Holy Faith. The white Preachers threatened to turn them out of their Church for going to the African Methodist Episcopal Church. I thought when war commenced it was time to run. Oh ! what prejudice and stupidity : for love is the fulfilment of the Law.

We had a remnant of our Connexion from Virginia, years before, but through some contention among themselves, the owner of the Church took it from them, run up a chimney in the centre of the house, and rented it out to different families to live in. He also went into the yard, kick'd over the head and foot boards of the graves, and levelled them down, and made a garden of the grave-yard. But the Lord afflicted him even unto death, and he was buried a day or two before I arrived at Frederick-town.

But God has a people everywhere ; a remnant that never has bowed their knee to Baal. A Lutherian brother, (minister,) interceded in their behalf, (the Church being offered for sale,) and receiving One Hundred Dollars from the Trustees' hands, bought it in for them, and a firm Deed being made for the Trustees, the Elder taking charge of it. So much, for Delivering Grace.

> " God moves in a mysterious way
> His wonders to perform;
> He plants His foot-steps in the sea
> And rides upon the storm."

I next started for Washington City ; took passage in the stage about 1 o'clock in the afternoon, and arrived about 1 o'clock in the morning, and the clerk of the office conveyed me to a very respectable colored family, (Mr. Adam's') who kindly received me, and continued so to do, but I met my antagonist in that place, who strove to stop my Ministerial Mission ; but Right is more than Might. Bishop Allen being a man of renown, and having Grace abounding in his heart, he sent a letter to his son-in-Law who resided in that place, to intercede for me during my stay, which he did- Truly, the way seemed somewhat dark at first. I saw revivals among the members, though the congregation was small, the Lord raised me up plenty of friends among them, for God is all in all. The Elder in charge was not to be seen until the last Sabbath I was there. He preached in the morning, but I was ashamed of his conduct towards me, through prejudice, while he was a leading man for the people. Reader, judge for thyself. But my God gave me a part and lot in this matter, saying, " Behold, I send you as Sheep among Wolves, be not afraid:—Lo ! I am with you always ;— even unto the end of the world." Praise God for his endurable promises. In a few days I left for Baltimore in stage. Some part of the rout was by Rail Road. Pleasant, journey ; arrived safe in Baltimore, engaged a colored man's hack, which conveyed me to Mrs. A. H.'s., to whom I ever shall feel indebted; for herself and family were some of my warmest-hearted friends. Truly, I must say " the Lord remembered me in my lowest state. The Elder and Preachers of Baltimore with one accord, gave me appointments, and we had prosperous Meetings. We had a female speaker there, who seemed very zealous I asked permission to take her into the pulpit, which was granted, and she spoke much in the spirit of God—which was attended with power. she being a woman of God; deportment graceful, and her ideas in Scripture very correct, and they were all very much pleased with her. She was a Teacher in the Sabbath School, at which place she often took occasion to extend her usefulness in speaking for the cause of God, for which she suffered much opposition, even from her husband; although he was a Preacher of the Gospel, she encountered severe trials. Next I left Baltimore for Philadelphia, my home, and found my friends all well; and my only son also, was well, and remained with Rev. Bishop Allen, where I left him before I went away. After being absent for two years and six months, I found Bishop Allen in very ill health, but he ever had continued with unwearied interest in my son's welfare, by sending to school, and otherwise improving him in education; by which he has made considerable improvements therefrom; which give me great reconciliation of mind; one thing lacking, which was a trade. But finally, Rev. Bishop grew nearer and nearer his time of departure,—prior to which he was much interested for the good of my son in getting a trade, but it being the winter of 1830, he concluded to keep him until spring; but the Rev. Bishop coming to the steep of time, departed this life March 26th, 1831, after seeing 72 years in a world of affliction. Immediately afterwards I placed my son with a French gentleman, with whom he stayed and learned the Cabinet-making business in this city. This is the way I have got along after getting my son to a trade. felt myself to be like a poor pilgrim indeed; wandering through this world so wide; having to travel among strangers, and being poor and destitute; I was sorely tempted. My money was gone, my health was gone, and I measurably without a home. But I rested on the promises of God. " They that put their trust in me shall never be confounded." Without having a dollar to help myself, I saw the Lord would verify his promise, bless his name for it.

I stopped a few weeks with my sister and Dr. Burton; boarded with her, and he seeing my debilitation of body, rendered medical assistance, which helped me much; but I was unable to labor and preach for some months. After my business of 1831 had been accomplished, I felt it my duty to visit my aged Parent, whom I had not seen for eleven years. At length I started on my journey for Cape May, West Jersey, in the following way: By Steam Boat to Salem, N. J., and preached in the African M. E. Church to a good congregation, and we had a comfortable waiting upon the Lord. Some signs followed the preaching of the Cross of Christ; the people were very kind. From thence by Stages to Greenwich, and spoke with the Elder to a very humble people; a great display of God's power, six joined the Church, seven were baptized, and others fell to the floor and cried for mercy; thank God for it.

On Monday morning I left for Bridgeton; we having no Society there, I preached in the Court House to a large assembly of different denominations. I felt a degree of liberty in speaking, and I then stopped a few days with them, and was kindly received and entertained. I then proceeded on to Fair-field, and endeavored to labor for them at 11 o'clock, Sabbath morning, and at 3 o'clock, P. M. to crowded houses of respectable and quiet congregations, and the Lord poured out his spirit upon us and we had a solemn waiting in his presence, for which my soul rejoices even now.

I next went on to Port Elizabeth, which was very thinly inhabited, some two or three very respectable families there with only three persons belonging to Church; among them a Sqr., Brick, a man of ability. Through him the Church was opened for me, and I preached two Sermons to large congregations of respectable inhabitants of the place, in which I placed myself as in my Saviour's hand, and staying there as clay in the hands of the Potter. I had liberty, whilst I could hear the humble groans of the people, which caused my breast to swell as with pure Seraphic joy. I bless the Lord, that the Gospel has never been left without a witness. Wisdom is justified of her children saith our Lord; if it was not so, thousands of Christians would have sunk in despair; but now and then I come across a great many whose sins were cancelled, and in whom pride was destroyed, and respecters of persons were not known. Among such, God will prosper the labors of his servants. "God knows the proud afar off, but his Saints are beloved in his sight." I next proceeded to Goshen; there I found my aged mother, who I had not seen for eleven years, well in health and very active. But above all the rest, enjoying Religion, the love of God in the soul; which is more than the Gold of Opher; though poor, making many rich. Truly, she dropped many aged tears on account of my exposures in travelling, but I strove to compose her by the word of God, which tells us " in this world we shall have tribulation, but in him we shall have peace." 'Tis there, the Christian's warfare ends, and sorrow cannot come. We dropped a few tears of gratitude with uplifted hearts to Almighty God for bringing us together once more in the flesh.

But my work soon again commenced. I preached in a dwelling house the next; in Goshen School-house, to both white and colored; and was assisted by the prayers of some humble souls, and felt both life and liberty. My colored brethren held a protracted meeting. Some were Baptists and some Methodists. But all one in Christ. I think I never saw a greater display of God's eternal power; it was somewhat inexpressible : Glory to God for it. Four miles from there I preached in the Court House to a congregation of different denominations, and the house was crowded. Text—28th Chap. of St. Matt. 18th and 19th verses. On the following Sabbath I spoke in a School-house to a white Methodist congregation. We had a weeping time in the afternoon of the same day. Spoke to my own people, and the Lord blessed several souls. It was a time long to be remembered. Truly a sword that is so often whetted, must keep Sharp, but in the midst of difficulties it appeared the word had its more perfect effect. After feeling I had discharged my duty towards God in that part of his vineyard, I returned home and spent the winter in Philadelphia, but very much afflicted. But in the midst of it my peace was like a river.

Some time in February 1832, the Lord sent two friends to take me out of town to visit a part of his vineyard, and they thought it would improve my health. I rode about twenty-two miles,—grew worse again—but medicine was applied which proved effectual. I spent a few weeks, preached in the Free Church in Norristown, three or four times, built by a lady of the Church of England, for all, or any that preach Christ and Him crucified.

Having gained my health, I returned in peace to Philadelphia, where I labored under some difficulties until the middle of May : After which I took a journey with a sister preacher for about two or three weeks, and truly the Lord blessed her labors abundantly, and my heart rejoiced to witness the out-pouring of the Spirit of that Gospel visit with a Hand-Maiden of the Lord. The Scriptures are fulfilled as spoken of by the Prophet Joel, Chap. 27th, 2nd verse. " Ye shall know that I am in the midst of Israel, and that I am the Lord, your God, and none else, and my people shall never be ashamed. And it shall come to pass afterwards, that I will pour out my spirit upon all flesh, and your sons and your daughters shall Prophecy. " Your old men shall dream dreams, and your young men shall see visions." In 1831, a young man who professed to be righteous, says he saw in the sky men, marching like armies, whetherit was with the naked eye, or a Vision by the eye of Faith, I cannot tell. But the wickedness of the people certainly calls for the lowering Judgments of God to be let loose upon the Nation and Slavery, that wretched system that eminated from the bottomless pit, is one of the greatest curses to any Nation.

June 1832, my mind was led to travel towards the east part of New Jersey, through Trenton, N. J., &c., and I preached three or four times, and found considerable consolation; The Elder made me appointments about two or three miles in the country, where there were a class of Methodists. There was a white came next morning to invite me to speak for them the next Sobbath afternoon, and himself proposed to make me a collection. I thus, truly, saw a way made for me I knew not, for I had but three or four cents in my pocket. Yet I had not mentioned it; but according to promise, after I had spoken, their contribution for me amounted to four or five Dollars; which aided me on my journey. So much for trusting in God. I then went to Princeton. Not much success there, the Society being small. Preached three or four times there. Left for New-Brunswick, and had very good meetings; more praying people, and had more life and power among them, and the Word of God had its effect. And the Judgments of God was in the land, the Cholera was taking away the people by scores. An awful day to them that had no God with them in deatn. It carried a sword with two edges, it cut right and left, took Saint and sinner, noble and ignoble, white and colored. It showed equality in my God's Decree ; where he speaks of "all men." I next left for Rahway,—still coming among strangers, but was kindly received by friends, both colored and white, of different orders, without distinction. I saw a large field open before me, and a plenty of labourers wanted in that part of God's moral Vineyard. I commenced to obey the Spirit of God, and had great liberty, both in Word and Doctrine. I stopped six weeks, and the Elder only once preached. The people dying fast: News came into town from New York that great mortality was prevailing,—the people dying at the rate of 120 to 160 a day. It was truly alarming, but we were highly favored in Rahway, there being only about four or five cases; and among thom it clearly shown that God had no respect for persons. One poor colored man, who had used too much ardent spirits, was boasting about 8 o'clock that Cholera could do nothing with him ; but while harnessing the horse for the family to go to church only two hours after, being 10 o'clock, A. M., he was seized with cramps, carried into the barn, and several Doctors sent for who remained with him, he having no friends. But at last, there being no hope for him by 8 o'clock P. M., the Doctors requested some colored Methodist family to let him die in their house, which was cheerfully acceded to, and he died about 12 o'clock, and was buried before day-light the same morning. A very rich man also died who was buried in splendor in day light, but the poor beggar was hurried away at night; yet they both died wicked. A short notice indeed. But Oh! their end, their dreadful end.

I still continued to labor, and witnessed good revivals. When the President's Proclamation went out for a General Fasting throughout the United States on account of the Judgment of God, it was obeyed by all denominations, and of course came under our notice,— and we having no Elder in that place, held it ourselves,—and it fell to my lot to give a Sermon on that occasion, which I did through some embarrassment, from St. Matt. chap. 24th, 21st and 22d vrs. And the Spirit of the Lord was upon me, and the Scriptures opened to my mind. The stammering tongue was loosed, and the feast truly glorious. At night we held Prayer-meetings, and so continued until I felt at liberty to leave them. I then proceeded on to New York. On my arrival I called on the Elder, S. T——, and was kindly received by him, and after a few days he gave me an appointment in Brooklyn Church, it having been near six years since I had spoken to that people. But while filling several successive appointments I saw signs of much good being done in the name of the Holy Child Jesus, which was owned with one accord. When entering the pulpit, the Bible being torn, I was deprived of finding the Text. A young gentleman of the Episcopal Methodist Church being present, took occasion on my next appointment to present the Church with a large new Bible. So much for the principles of Christianity. The Elder also gave me three appointments in the Bethel Church, New York, at Asberry, in Allen st. upper part of the city,—several times in Flushing Church, and attended a Love-Feast, where the people spoke in the Spirit. Praise God for it.

I then returned to New York again, feeling my strength much renewed in the inward man Christ Jesus. I saw a large want of labor there, as the Prophet Ezekiel said : "I saw the river rise to the loins of a man."

After laboring about six weeks and seeing it was not in vain; with the approbation of the Brethren and in answer to a good conscience. Oh! that I had language to express my mind while I hold my pen in hand. But had I the tongue of an Hannah, whilst she spoke to Eli ! I could not express the revelation of Jesus ; but the bodily strength seemed to fail fast. I then returned to Philadelphia, rested four days and was called to Salem, N. J., and after preaching two or three times crossed the Bay for St. Georges, a town in the State of Delaware, and preached twice by invitation of the citizens, and also by request I spoke in Delaware City. Here a horse, gig and driver being provided for me, I rode four or five miles in the evening and preached to a large congregation of white and colored persons. Good behaviour, but no particular display of God's power. I returned the same night to St. Georges, and spent a few days with my sister, whom I had not seen for eleven years previous. I left there a few days before Christmas for Philadelphia, where I remained until January 1, 1833. After which I started, in company with another sister for New Hope, Pa. We held meetings in Frankford, then I proceeded to Ben-Salem ; from thence to Attleboro'. The Elder, P. S., was on that circuit, he cordially gave me appointments, and we were caused to rejoice. The Devil was also at work, setting up difficulties like mountains high, but having a skilful Pilot I steered between the rocks. The Church, having been in a seven years law suit, was gained by the African M. E. Connexion. A brother, L. I——, conveyed us seven miles, and I attended an appointment which was visited by the Spirit of the Holy Ghost. Sister C—— followed in exhortation and the meeting was closed by a brother—a crowded house—and were requested to hold another. But we appointed the next in Holmesburgh, which was alike prosperous. After which I returned to Philadelphia, and there remained until July 2, at which time I left for Canada, being a second visit to my scattered nation, for which I felt a painful impression. For more than six years the first stop was in New York, from there to Albany, where I remained three or four weeks, but the Church was wading through deep waters. I had, long before, felt a great anxiety to publish my religious experience and exercise to a dying world, but, laboring under the disadvantages of education, I thought it a favour to pay $5 to have a portion of it taken from the original of my own registering, and corrected for press. By special request I visited Troy and found a christian spirited minister, Rev. Wm. Bishop, with a lively society, and I spoke for them—the Lord was with us, and gave seed to the sower and bread to the eater, at different times; and, the next Sabbath I preached my Farewell sermon, and on Sunday night I held prayer meeting in the Church, and on the next Saturday I left for Schenectady, preached in the Presbyterian Church twice on Sunday, and was kindly entertained ; after which I left on Monday for Utica, and arrived there next morning about sunrise. I spoke for them on Thursday evening, also on Sunday afternoon to crowded houses of lively Christians, and they administered to my necessities to assist me in travelling. I felt a great liberty in the gospel. From there I proceeded to Rochester, where I arrived, after being two days and a night on the Canal, and found Elder Graham with a prosperous Church, which seemed as though his labors were much blessed. But, alas ! the Devil crept in—he left them—they became scattered, the old trustees died, and the other connexion caught them. But during my stay they added several to the Church. I then left for Little York in Canada, which was one day's sail across the Lakes; the passage was very rough that day. I was directed to Brother Brown's, the preacher, and was kindly received by himself and wife. I preached on Sabbath morning and afternoon, and that day we had a shout in the Camp of Israel. Praise God, the mission was both owned and received. After speaking several times and holding prayer meetings, I left them for Niagara, spoke three times. From there to St. David, and preached to a respectable congregation of whites and colored persons. Six years before this I visited Niagara and there was a large society of the A. M. E. Connexion, but at this time the very Chapel was gone, the minister dead, the people scattered and backslid. I, finding only two or three members at this time and no school, and children coming up in sin, then left for St. Catharine ; spoke three times, but no particular revival, there were some who wished to be lords among God's heritage, and the work seemed stagnated, but they used me well, and I left them with peace of mind, in discharging my duty, fort George, and spoke on Sabbath morning to a white and colored congregation in a school-house—wonderful time indeed—some shouted, some mourned, others sought for mercy, and I felt the Holy Ghost upon me, glory, glory, glory to God. After I helped to lead the class, I was insisted upon specially to preach a child's funeral sermon, before the corps left the house, a curious circumstance, which was caused by the following incident: Seven years before I had preached in the neighborhood, to a great mixed multitude, after which I was invited to dine by this person, on which visit this child was born, or on that day ; after some little hesitation on my part, I accepted the invitation and preached from the 2d Book of Samuel, "I shall go to him, but he shall not return to me." It was a very solemn time—the corps was then taken to the Church of England, and laid before the altar, the clergy spake over it, and very much to the purpose, without partiality, and then committed it to the breathless grave. On Thursday night I filled an appointment at a brother's house, the Lord was there. On the next Sabbath I rode seven miles, preached and helped to lead class, and the next week I left in stage for Little York, but stopped in Niagara, preached several times and paid a visit to a new society of Wesleyan Methodists, also then returned to York again, and preached for a society of Baptists, a very quiet and attentive congregation, with one exception. Text, by grace ye are saved through faith, that's not of yourselves, it's the gift of God. The Devil is always busy in his agency as in the following : a school-teacher was present in the congregation who, after I concluded my subject, arose to contradict my argument, he became very much excited and red in his face, but while he was on his feet I expressed a desire of the congregation not to notice his reply, and they accordingly treated it with contempt, which caused him to desist with all his prejudices against women. The people were very kind. From thence by steamboat, I proceeded to Hambleton, which was 50 miles ; I found no colored society in that place, but the children went to school ; about two miles from there I found a class, and, by permission of the trustees, on Wednesday evening, I spoke in the Methodist Chapel, to a small congregation, from a very short notice, but the Lord owned His Word. After the close of the meeting, an English gentleman and his lady invited me to go home and lodge one night at their house, which I did, and they exhibited a great degree of benevolence towards me; may God reward them for it. On Sabbath morning I spoke to my own people, and afterwards led class and found the same one God owned them in worship also. I saw that seed must be sown accordingly. I spoke in the afternoon, and the Lord made himself manifest by His Spirit in great display; the people, though very poor, were exceedingly kind; one of the brother preachers, conveyed me to Dundas and Flamburg, west. I preached to a large congregation in the white Methodist Chapel. We had an humble waiting upon the Lord. From there I went to Ancaster, there the Lord prepared a friend to take care of me through the winter. I preached several times and met many friends whom I had seen in Cincinnati; some gifted preachers there, but no elder to preside. There were many of our society there, called from place to place, which had been scattered like sheep without a shepherd—it truly was heart-rending to hear them lamenting the loss of their shepherd who was deceased. The brethren kept a watch meeting on Christmas eve. We enjoyed the meeting and spent the night like St. Paul; the next day it fell to my lot to fill an appointment which I did with both life and liberty, (praise God for it) from the 2nd chap. of St. Luke, verses 10, 11. I felt my mind lead me to a village called Ammonsburg, on Lake Ontario, on what was called the Bush side, but I kept it with myself and the Lord, and kept travelling and preaching as the Lord gave ability. Brother S. Lewis was much interested at my anxiety for that people's welfare, and also Brother Wm. Edwards, a gospel preacher, who had been instrumental in civilizing and christianizing many of the natives whom I saw in Brentford, an Indian town on the Mohawk river, where a number of the natives lived along the river side, in the woods formed churches of societies of different denominations, ours excepted, and having no Methodist Church, a gentleman, seeing the necessity of a place of worship for us, gave us the privilege of a large house to worship in several times; truly it was cold, but we had many comfortable meetings, and very many solemn impressions made on a number of the minds of those present; afterwards I left for Buffalo. The road was so rough that it caused me to be quite sick. I could not stand it to ride 200 miles that cold weather, and I continued to preach in and out of town to different denominations through frost and snow. A gentleman came to me after the sermon was over, and wished me God's speed in a very friendly manner, then quietly withdrew with his ladies in company with him, with politeness. My mind was on Buffalo, Brother Edwards had not yet formed any society. I particularly desired him to take my appointment, which he did, and also read the discipline with proper explanations, wishing to know who would be subject to the government of the same, and there were ten persons came forward and consented to be subject as members of our Discipline. I went to Ancaster, stopped at brother Lewis' and wife, and although she was a young married woman, she was very much like a mother to me. My mind was exercised to go to Am-

monsburg, through a gloomy winter; that night, after serious meditation, I fell asleep, and suddenly awoke and received the witness
that I must go. Next morning I informed brother Lewis that I must
go, and, he, feeling interested for me, had me conveyed, in a private
carriage, that I might travel comfortably. In the middle of February
I left for Chatham, and arrived there on the 26th of the same month,
where I found a society scattered, without a shepherd; some living
in the faith of Christ, while others had gone back to the beggarly
elements of the world. Mr. Lightfoot received me very kindly; his
house was open for worship, where I had large gatherings some five
or six times, for a new place. The house being quite commodious,
and Mr. Lightfoot used every endeavor to send me on with the gospel to others. In April I left for Ammonsburg, there the believers
seemed much strengthened; backsliders reclaimed, and sinners converted to God. Among which was a woman that had belonged to
the Methodists by profession, having the form of godliness but was
destitute of the power, until the Spirit of God arrested her at this
time. After which she ceased her carnal amusements; quit dancing and went to praying, at which time she arose on her feet and said
that she never saw that dancing was wrong before now—but she had
resolved to serve God in spirit and truth—praise God for the victory.
For three days in Ammonsburg we could scarcely get any rest,
from the effects of the outpouring of the spirit of God, on both white
and colored. I was still more confirmed in mind that my visit was
accepted of my God, who gave me this mission in Christ Jesus. I
stopped with a brother, Jas. McKenney, and his affectionate wife,
who had suffered much in the fear of Jesus. Brother made an ap
pointment for the next evening for me, which I tried to fill. Text as
follows: 16th chap. of St. Matthew's Gospel, 26th verse. I was in
a strange part of God's vineyard, but his power was manifest even
there; after which another appointment was made for Sunday morning, which was alike prosperous, and I helped to lead class; then
spoke in the afternoon and at night with equal success. My mind
was much exercised, seeing the need of schools. I counted 25 children and some young people whom I loved. I lamented their obscurity, and advised them to get a white man to teach them, and
endeavored to shew them, that, without the advantages of education
they never would be a moral people, and, in the course of time, their
own children could, by proper advancement, become teachers for
themselves. So I continued in all the towns, finally they caught the
spirit and commenced in the following places; in Ancaster they chose
their trustees to build a house for school, and likewise to preach in,
at Brantford, at Chatham, and St. Catharine. Some went to St. David's
and Toronto, to Sabbath Schools, and in the week also; colored
and white, all went together. After the course of two or three

weeks, a colored teacher came to the last named place and established a school of between 30 or 40 scholars (after being examined and found competent) which improved the manners of the people very much, and they worshipped in their own Chapels. Their own preachers, exhorters, and class-leaders (colored.) There was a young sister that wished to travel with me a little way, and brother McKenney furnished us with a driver and conveyance, and the friends received us very kindly, and, to my astonishment, we were given appointments by the trustees of the Church. I spoke from the following text, By grace ye are saved through faith, that is not of yourselves, but it is the gift of God. A Friend, W——, was there, who was ever ready to oppose the Methodists; he was a Baptist preacher, and would invite the Methodists to preach for them, and then get up and contradict them; he wished me to come and preach for them, but I felt no spirit of contention in religion and I declined. Our own people were talking of forming a union with the Canadian Methodists who were a branch of the Old Episcopal Methodists, that was raised by the missionaries from America; this being the time of the split, but some would leave to the Wesleyan Methodists. I preached five or six different times in this village for several Sabbaths two sermons a day, in which the Lord gave ability. We continued our meetings as usual, and invited the old ministers to visit us, which they did; and one of them gave an exhortation after me, and God's power filled the house and the guilty were alarmed, while believers rejoiced in hope of a better resurrection. I left that morning, rode five miles with a friend, and on Wednesday afternoon preached again—signs and wonders followed—after which I continued to visit the sick the remainder of the week; and on Sabbath day I rode five miles again to the Chapel, and filled an appointment in the afternoon for the last time as I thought, but the Lord seen best, and I was retained another week; the next Sabbath I filled an appointment from the following text: Finally, brethren, pray for us that the word of the Lord have free course and be glorified even as it is with you; which was my Farewell Sermon. After which I returned to Ammonsburg in the fear of God; where I preached several times and saw many manifestations of the operations of the Spirit of grace, and, on the following Sabbath, Brother A—— made an appointment for me six miles distant, and one also for 6 o'clock in the evening; we had a very hard ride through the swamp, and met a large gathering both in and out of doors, and sinners were cut to the heart, and cried aloud for mercy, which was a joyful sound to believers in Christ Jesus. The next evening I spoke again from Isaiah, chap. 59 ver. 1; and several of the nobility taking into consideration my necessities, contributed to me the sum of $5. We had a quiet waiting upon the Lord; after which I and a sister that was with me, called on Mr. Gardiner and he collected some subscriptions and added to the for mer sum, for which, I trust, God will reward all the cheerful givers, as they were very generous. I held prayer-meetings, visited the sick, and passed many joyful moments of sweet communion especially in one sister's company, who was a member of the National Church in Ammonsburg.

But in affliction she enjoyed the Spirit's grace, and, in May, 1834, we parted as for eternity, and I trust to meet her where parting will be no more, neither will any of us shake the parting hand, for we have had sweet communion together, in spiritual exercises. Dear reader, think not that I am going to heaven as in golden slippers, for I have various trials to encounter while travelling over this world so wide, but I feel willing to suffer for the cause of God, after which I shall (if faithful) meet many of my friends that have communed with me in the Spirit, where we never, never shall shake the parting hand—these are the consolations in affliction as described in Rev. chap. 12, 11th verse. And they overcame him by the Blood of the Lamb, and by the word of their testimony, and they loved not their lives unto death; and whilst I move my pen my soul rejoices in God my Redeemer. Having filled my mission I parted with my friends in joy. I sailed for Detroit city, 18 miles, then bid adieu to British shores, not knowing that I should ever step on them again. I was kindly received on American possessions by a respectable family from Cincinnati, a Mr. D——. I felt there was a work for me to do in that part of God's vineyard. I arrived on Tuesday and on Thursday evening we had a comfortable meeting at the usual place. I met with much encouragement in laboring for the Lord, and many impressions were made on the minds of the hearers. The evening previous to my landing I saw some of the American affliction towards the people of color, such as mobbing, theft and destruction. Wo unto the inhabitants of the earth and the sea, for the Devil is come down unto you. On the following Sabbath morning, 10 o'clock, I preached again, then lead class —a soul reviving time, indeed—at 7 o'clock, P. M. I preached again, and the house was crowded to overflowing, it not being sufficient to hold the people. Text as follows: And the gospel of the kingdom shall be preached unto all the world for a witness, and then shall the end come. After which we visited a prayer meeting held by the stationed minister in the white Church, which was truly comfortable. On the next Sabbath I had an appointment made for me on the British side in a dwelling house, but, it not being sufficient to hold the people, the Episcopal Methodists opened their session-room which was larger and well crowded with various denominations. Text, 1st chap. St. John; ver. 45. The Lord touched my tongue as with a live coal from his altar, and we had a good time as from the hand of the Lord, and the Amens of the preachers, elders, and leaders, helped to swell the theme of rejoicing. Glory to God, we had all things common. But now feeling my mission ended I waited for the firs opportunity and took passage for Buffalo. Three hundred and sixty miles on Lake Ontaria, and, I must say, the most uncomfortable passage I ever experienced, although the boat was commodious, yet they treated the people of color very indifferently indeed, as regards their accommodation, and yet charged them a high price, I having paid $4.50. After two uncomfortable days' and nights' sail, me arrived at Buffalo wharf about six o'clock, A. M. Six years had elapsed since I had been in Buffalo, which was the first time, but during my absence many changes had taken place, the loss of some of my particular friends by death and other moveable causes. But I found a Mrs. Davis, who was a great friend indeed to the people of God. I felt my mission truly in this part of His vineyard—there were a few of the Episcopal Methodists, but no established society. The Baptist denomination had the majority of the people, they opened their places of worship and I preached and held prayer meetings three or or four times among them, which was attended with considerable success. I also had the pleasure of meeting an anti-slavery society where I heard some very able discussions on the rights of the oppressed, and also clear demonstrations of the cruelty of the slaveholder, which was exposed with all its horror by a young man by the name of L——, but was greatly opposed by the Judge of the city, after which the young man arose to his feet the second time in which it seemed nothing escaped his exposure. I, about this time had written from Buffalo to Philadelphia (as it was shown me by the Spirit that my son had embraced religion) to know the fact of the matter, as I was some hundred miles from home and received the satisfactory answer by letter from his own hand, which explained his conviction —the length of the distress of his mind—the severity of which had caused him to seek opportunity to put an end to his own existence, but in the act he was told to try to pray once more, by the voice of the Spirit, which he consented to do, but concealed his intention from the people, which had been suggested by the Devil, to take his own life, and it would be all over. In this extremity it was God's opportunity by his act of obedience to convert his soul, after bringing him to the ground like a Saul of Tarsus, and now stands as a living witness that God has power on earth to forgive sin.

O Reader, you may only imagine the joy of my heart at such language as this from my only son, whom, it seemed, God had left as a comfort to me in my old age, more especially after not having had any communication from him for eight months, and then he was very ill which made my cross seem very heavy, but I trusted in God, although I expected to hear of his death when I did hear any thing, but, on my knees at a brother and sister L——'s at family prayer was shown these things by revelation of Spirit, which caused me to get up off my knees and I exclaimed aloud, the Lord has converted the soul of my son, for which we had a shout around the room, and then comes the letter as a witness of the same from his own written composition. I scarcely knew how to praise the Lord enough, and for another reason when I thought that God granted what I had prayed for, from the days of his childhood, while I travelled the barren wilds, of lonesome hills, and gloomy vales. But so much for trusting in God who will not let the prayers of his people pass unnoticed, but is bound to hear and answer when they pray aright. Praise the Lord, O my soul, magnify his name.

> With joy let Judah stand
> On Zion's chosen hill,
> Proclaim the wonders of thy hand,
> And councils of thy will.

I now began to feel my mission somewhat complete as regards distance, and therefore concluded to return towards home. A brother and his wife crossed the Lakes with me for company, I then took the cars, and bid them adieu. I remained in Rochester a while after my arrival, but, to my sorrow and surprise, a society that, twelve months previous, was large and seemed every way prosperous, had nearly dwindled away—the preacher gone and the people scattered except a resolute few, who were bound to go through, and that at the risk of their all; and to them I endeavored to fulfil my mission. I also spoke for the Wesleyan Methodists—they treated me with christian fellowship. Our Lord said, they that are for us are not against us, forbid them not—it truly was comfortable. There was seed to the sower and bread to the eater. I also stopped at Palmyra, visited the sick and otherwise endeavored to fill my mission. A little difficulty existed, relative to a slave girl being concealed and taken away, but while we were at worship the Justice of the Peace was in the house and every thing seemed quiet. After service, the congregation quietly withdrew—this was on the 6th of August. On the next day a lady of color paid for a seat for herself and me, and we took passage on to Canondagua, 16 miles; there I found a Church and people prosperous. They received me kindly—my first appointment, 11 o'clock, Sabbath morning; the word had some impressions, in the afternoon still better, at night God was his own interpreter, the hallowed fire began to run to sin's confusion. I had several appointments through the week, which were alike prosperous. Although I felt my inabilty, yet the answer to a good conscience strengthened me, even in a strange land, and, with Paul, I can say I am not ashamed of the Gospel of Christ, for it is the power of God to every one that believes. I then took stage for Geneva, having recommendations to these little towns or villages, I found a few members of the Episcopal Methodists, and also of the Presbyterian denomination; they were very friendly and opened their house to entertain me—the colored gentlemen of the vicinity around were building a house for the Travelling Missionaries to preach in; it was opened for me, and I felt great liberty in endeavoring to labour for the Lord; tears of contrition dropped freely; a sister there shewed great hospitality towards me. After filling three appointments, I left on the third day of the week. I took stage for Ithaca, having had an invitation from the Rev. H. J—— who had the charge. I arrived about 4 o'clock in the afternoon and was taken to Elder H. J——. Before I entered the town I felt, according to the movings of the Spirit, that the Lord would pour out his Spirit upon the people, for which I yet rejoice in hope of a better resurrection. We met in the unity of the Spirit and continued so with humility—the friends were kind indeed to me, in and from the noble edifices of the large conveniences, to the humble cottage of Christian inmates. But an humble heart is better than a sacrifice. The society was young but was composed of some very respectable people, and useful citizens. Congregations large, class lively, and the Spirit of God visited us in abundant measure, which made the people speak with great confidence in the Lord. Though hard toiling, yet duty makes labor light; some backsliders reclaimed, sinners converted, and believers strengthened; while many joined the Church, which was a sign of some good in the name of the holy child Jesus. After which my visit closed in peace with God, peace with all men, and the answer of a good conscience. I was next conveyed by carriage to the steamboat, and took passage for Albany. Crossing the Seneca river or lake, where passengers meet the canal boat for Albany, which was my next stopping place. I was recommended by a gentleman to the captain; took passage; and after a pleasant voyage of two days and nights, we arrived at Schenectady, and the next morning we arrived at Albany. The Rev. Mr. Williams was stationed there; I payed him a visit; the preachers generally professed a Christian Spirit. The task seemed as though laid on a Jonah; I preached twice on Sabbath day; and through the aid of Bro. S. S——, I was able to get to New York. Rev. R. W—— was one of the oldest Elders in the African Methodist Episcopal Church, who has since that fell in the battle-field, declaring war against the power of Darkness, and his bones were buried with all the honors of war. Let me live the lite of the righteous and let my last end be like his. On my arrival at New York, I found the Rev. S. S ——, Elder, stationed there; I spent three weeks in that city; I preached in Bethel; in Allen Church several times; good congregations for that part of the town, but the other was crowded. I only mention a few texts, 1st Sam. 2d chap. 6th ver.; 3d chap Hebrews, 3 first verses. Brother Jacob Matthews gave me an appointment in Zion Church, and I felt the Lord, as before mentioned, to be very close to me. The Rev. T. E—— gave me an appointment in Asbury Church on Sabbath night, text, 3d chap. of St. Matthew, 12th verse, which was a night long to be remembered by all present; the Lord made bare his arm; some were arrested under the power of God, and fell to the floor crying for mercy, while believers were strengthened in the faith of Christ. I also had appointments in Brooklyn, L. I.; there we were much favored with good meetings; a number of Old Methodists, with faithful preachers who kept the flock of Christ alive; and our labors were crowned with success, and additions to the Church. In the midst of life we are in death. Since I had been last at this place, previous to my tour in British America, the young gentleman that manifested such friendship for the Church by presenting it with a Bible for my appointment, had bid adieu to time and had gone to the mansions of bliss. The day previous to my arrival, I stopped at Bro. T———'s, one of the oldest standard families that celebrated the Church of God; his wife, a mother and sister upwards of seventy years of age; whose character was unblemished, faith firm, although afflicted, yet cheerful, with a short illness, in September, 1835, left the world in triumph. I commenced my journey for Canada, in 1832. From the second day of July to the fifteenth day of October, years following, 1833, I had preached 138 sermons, and travelled between 27 and 28 hundred miles. Returned from Brooklyn, and attended a quarterly meeting at Flushing; Bro. J. S———, elder in charge. Saturday evening I gave an exhortation, and preached Sunday afternoon at 3 o'clock, the Lord accompanied the word, and, be it remembered, it will be either a savor of life unto life or of death unto death. Having finished my visit I felt anxious to go to Philadelphia; feeling my labors to come to a close for the present. I arrived safe at home, found my son and friends all well, and then heard the truth of his conversion, for which I yet give glory to God. I was three days in the city and left for Salem, N. J., on business; finding the doors opened to me I preached in the Church; we had a comfortable waiting upon the Lord, but no particular display of his power. After which I crossed the bay to New Castle, Del. and then proceeded to see my long lost sister; this being the second time in forty-two or forty-three years—there I found a large field of labor. Preached in a school-house by permission of Mr. S———, he being a man of authority, and chief owner of a large part of the town. I was also sent for to speak in Delaware —a horse and gig and dinner prepared—I was taken five or six miles, blessed with a full house and I felt the power from the upper world, and the Lord was with me. After two days visit my mind being easy, I rested, and on the third day I left for Philadelphia; finding all well, I remained for a few days, and then left for the Rev. R. R———'s circuit, and found him a Christian and a gentleman. I first hailed Burlington, and met the ministerial order of Brethren, who received me with joy.

The Vineyard of the Lord before the laborer lies.

We had several very good meetings ; I then crossed over to Bristol and spoke once or twice in a dwelling-house, at which time the Lord verified his promises, which are, I will hearken unto. I proceeded on my journey to Trenton, which was Elder Robinson's Circuit. Two or three days after this he arrived in the city. On Sabbath morning he preached and was much favored by the Spirit of the Lord. At night I preached and felt joy in my soul ; from there he gave me other appointments. My mind was cleared and the Scriptures open-ed themselves to my mind and I felt strengthened ; some shouted, others wept. I feel the holy influence of that fire now, while my pen makes record of the same to a dying world. Let the inhabi-tants of the rocks sing, and let them shout as from the top of the mountains. I preached another sermon from the 59th chap. of Isaiah, 12th verse. The fire kindled some where, and the hearty amens that ascended the hill of the Lord seemed to strike guilt to the hearts of sinners. I helped to lead class. O, the worth and value of precious souls which cause me oft to mourn. I preached again from the 22d chap. of Rev. 1st ver. The prayers of God's people helped me, and the power of God, like the dew of heaven, was let down upon us, and the sower and reaper rejoiced together, independent of various opposition. I also spoke from Romans, 1st chap. 16th ver., and spoke three times on Sabbath day ; and I felt more strength at the last ap-pointment than I did at the first, which proves the assertion of Scrip-ture, freely give and freely receive. I also visited the sick, after which they gave me some appointments at Princeton, a hard part of the vineyard. I had my talent and to use it I was not ashamed, although the substance seemed to be lost—full houses. The Presby-terian friends were very kind to me and received me with Christian friendship. The weather cold, and travelling hard, through wintry storms to pass. The first text, Let the dead bury the dead. It seemed a little astonishing, especially to the brethren. I continued, and on different times filling appointments. From thence to Brunswick ; and one of the coldest days, rode sixteen miles; the Lord was with me, and I had great liberty of speech ; a church and a large congrega-tion ; and the power of God was more fully manifest than at Prince-ton ; and the Lord added such to the Church as, I trust, will be eter-nally saved. I remained there to labor for the Lord two or three weeks, and there was a general revival throughout in prayer meetings, both of male and female, and in class meetings ; not my labors, reader, but the merit belongs to God alone.

> Praise the Lord, ye heavens adore him;
> Praise him all ye stars of light;
> Sun and moon rejoice before him,
> Praise him, angels in your heights.

After my return to Philadelphia in December, 1835, I saw a large field open to my view, it being a strong place, and many different spirits to contend with, I endeavored to commend this portion of sacred Writ: Job, 22d chap. 10th ver., But he knoweth the way I take; when he hath tried me I shall come forth as gold; again, Rev. 3d chap., 8th ver., and I seemed much troubled, as being measurably debarred from my own Church as regards this privilege I had been so much used to ; I could scarcely tell where to go or stay in my own house. I said, Lord, where shall I go ? and was directed to brother Murray, Elder then of Little Wesley Church, and when coming to his house he expressed his astonishment at my coming out through the inclemency of such weather, I paused, then told him I was sent to him and knew not for what; he said I know—then he gave me an appointment on Sunday night, and on the following Wednesday evening; from there I received an appointment at Zoar Church, by the elder, and the Lord converted one soul, which caused me still more to rejoice in God my Saviour ; from that the elder of Wesley Church gave me an appointment and I preached to a large congregation, and felt strong in the cause of my God. My call seemed chiefly in Philadelphia. In the year 1835 I travelled 721 miles, and preached 692 sermons. I also spoke in Bethel Church ; some false brethren. They that are not for us are against us, and if they are against God's ministry, whether male or female, they are against God, who says I send by whom I will, for all are one in Christ Jesus. May the Lord pardon their errors, and make them be careful how they handle edged tools. In 1836 I travelled 556 miles, and preached 111 sermons; and felt under much exercise to print a book, and I had some friends to encourage me, such as the Rev. R. R——, and the Bishop, with others; and every circumstance was so favorable that I finally succeeded, and when they were brought home, I sat down in the house and wondered how I should dispose of them ; to sell them appears too much like merchandize. While in this situation it was suggested to my mind, you must pay for them, or it will do more harm to the Gospel than if you had not printed them. But to myself, (if not printed) would be the scourge of a guilty conscience before the Lord. At 4 o'clock, P. M., my mind was directed to a Presbyterian sister, and on my way I met Bishop Allen's widow who bought one, and that afternoon I sold one dollar and fifty cents' worth. The Lord so blessed the offering of that work to the world, that in less than four months I paid sixty dollars through God's assistance, for the expenses which gave me great tranquility of mind, and caused me to feel still more like wearing out in the service of God. Various are the ways through the interposition of Providence that I succeeded in disposing of that little work, viz: camp-meetings, quarterly meetings, in the public streets, &c. Praise God for his mercies as well as his graces.

After this I started for a Camp-meeting, near Baltimore. On my arrival I received two appointments, and after the Bishop came, still
more was given to me, and at one time the power of God arrested an
individual and he cried aloud, fell out of the door and was reclaimed.
I preached three sermons in the African M. E. Church, and God gave
us souls at every meeting, and my heart rejoiced to see sinners coming to God. Notwithstanding I had my opposers I out-live them
through the strength of Him, that yet loves His faithful followers.
After seeing so many displays of the miraculous power of God, I returned to the city of Baltimore, with peace of conscience. After
which my mind was exercised to go to Elicott's Mills to preach in the
African M. E. Church, and was accompanied by a dear sister, previously having had conversation with Bishop Walters he sent a letter
to the preacher in charge, who received me with christian spirit. In
the morning I led class and in the afternoon I had an appointment,
and preached from the 5th Chapter of St. Luke, 18th & 19th verses.
A full house, with attentive hearers,—praise God for a visitation of His
Spirit. An humble groan is better than a sacrifice. At night I spoke
from the .7th Chapter of Hebrews, 12th & 13th verses, and wonderful
to relate, if language could, the power of feeling. And well may it
be said that feeling has no fellow. On Thursday night I spoke from
the 61st Chapter of Isaiah, 1st verse: And truly I was annointed.
And one visible sign of the manifestation of the Spirit of God was, an
aged lady was caused to cry aloud, under the distress of mind, and
many more, too tedious to mention. During the whole week, I continued to visit the sick, &c. One case I here mention as a caution to
those who procrastinate the day of Salvation, which is as follows. By
request, I called to see a Slave-holder of a tyranical turn, said to be
very wicked. But he had received a summons, served by the officer
Death, and I saw it pictured in his face ; previous to which I had
heard of his selling two men from their wives, recently. I asked him
what he thought of dying ; if he was prepared to meet the change.
He told me he was not. He was very ill, could not recover, but wanted religion and could not get it ; but wished me to have prayers with
him. This I did, but it was of no avail, although it was truly solemn.
I then exhorted him to have faith in the merits of the blood of Christ,
and then left him, a repining subject for eternity.

"Don't you see how unexpected in my chariot I do ride,
Convulsion fits, Plagues and Fevers, are the weapons by my side."
                                                           Death.

After this, I returned to Baltimore, and from thence I was conducted to Springtown, and spoke in the morning, Sunday, 11 o'clock.
Text, in Psalms. No extra display in the afternoon. Brother H. U.,
held forth to a very large congregation. At night I preached again.

By this time there was inroads made upon the minds of the people,—they caught the Hallowed Flame, and some shouted, while others were convicted and reclaimed, and I was lifted up in Word and Doctrines of our Lord and Saviour Jesus Christ. On Monday night I held a Prayer-meeting,—next morning I started for Baltimore, quite indisposed, but being once more restored to health, I preached on the following Sabbath night in Bethel Church, Baltimore, appointment by Bishop Walters. Text, Acts 18th Chapter, 9th & 10th verses, with special references, from Chapter 20; 19th, 20th, 21st & 22d verses. On the ensuing Wednesday night I preached again from Prophet Joel, Chapter 1st., & 1st ver. The slain of the Lord truly was many. Again I spoke from Hebrews, Chapter 7th; 12th & 13th verses, at 3 o'clock, P. M.. and God's name was glorified. I had great liberty of speech—bless the Lord. It is a good cause to live in, but better to die in. It is sweeter than life and stronger than death.

The Bishop gave me an appointment on the following Sabbath night. Text, from one of Peters' Epistles, 5th verse. The word preached had its effect. Three persons were arrested under the power of God and felled to the floor at once. The grand-mother and her daughter and grand-daughter cried aloud for mercy. In the meanwhile a gentleman fell on his face and cried for Sanctification; and there was a general rumbling among the dry bones. Praise God, for I feel the unction from on high, while I hold my pen.

I next started for Long Green, a distance of sixteen miles. A sister I——— who had been travelling with me, as also brother Dunn, accompanied us. I spoke from Acts 17, verse 31. Three persons found peace, several under serious impressions. The word still had a lasting effect, and they sent for us again. We complied, accompanied by our Rev. brother; although the morning was very cold, we were blest to get there in time for Church, and by the help of God, I tried to speak to the people from these words. " Although you tread upon scorpions and serpents, they shall not hurt you, having faith." The word went out and did not return void; for two found peace that day, and we left some on the floor mourning for redemption in Christ, while others wore deep symptoms of serious impressions for the welfare of their souls. We left at 4 o'clock in the afternoon, but the meeting continued until night. May God continue to water every plant in Zion. I preached and sold my books, and paid my own way. I returned to Philadelphia in December. After I arrived my health was much impaired, and I had a severe spell of sicknes. So ended 1836.

I commenced travelling March 11th, 1837. Eight miles from Philadelphia, I preached three Sermons. Two at Blaketown, N. J., after which I took Steam-boat for St. Georges, Del., to see my sister; at the request of Doct.———, he being the main proprietor of the town, I accepted an appointment and filled it. I then spent a few days with my sister, and left for Salem, N. J. Preached two Sermons on Sabbath day, two miles from Salem, and we had a good meeting,—for, where the Lord is, there is liberty. On Wednesday I left for Greenwich, preached three times, and the Lord was there in power, and my soul witnessed it. From thence I proceeded to —————— and there truly was a revival among the people, which gave me encouragement to trust in God. From there I proceeded on to Port Elizabeth, and spoke in the Ebenezer Church, to a very large and respectable congregation from seventh chapter, Hebrews, 12th & 13th verses. On Sunday 3 o'clock, P. M., I preached at the same Church, then I proceeded six miles further and preached one Sermon to the Forgemen, and tried to give them the Gospel, but I did not feel that liberty of Spiritual fellowship as I did at many places, to see professing Christians working hard on the Sabbath at the forge, and then walk into Church, to keep the Sabbath Holy is, in my opinion, altogether out of the question. However I returned from that place the same night, and on Monday I left for Goshen, Cape May, to see my aged mother, then 78 years of age. I found her happy in the Lord, and my sister also. I preached three sermons on Cape May and left them as I found them, in the hands of God. I arrived on my return, at Port Elizabeth on the next Sabbath morning, filled an appointment both morning and night. Next morning I took stage for Philadelphia, where I arrived on June 5th, found all well. Our Conference being held in May, I concluded I must have some of the Feast. Three or four days after this I proceeded to New York, from there on to Albany, Elder Williams having charge of the Church. I preached nine sermons. Some revivals, some joined the Church, and members strengthened in the Faith of Christ. I also visited Troy, preached three Sermons there, one for a white congregation. We had a good meeting; and I was well treated by the friends. On my return to Albany I preached two sermons—and truly enjoyed myself in the Lord. I then returned to New York with an appeal to the conscience of every man, as regards my endeavors to do good,—bless the Lord. Duty makes labor light. My visit was to be accomplished in New York and Brooklyn. Rev. Wm. C. ——————, having charge at both places, gave me appointments. Preached four sermons in New York, five in Brooklyn and two in Flushing and one in Williamsburg.

Knowing my religious visits were nearly closed for the present I availed myself of the opportunity of visiting the different Schools, the most impressive was that of Mr. Louis Tappan, which I think exceeded all I had ever seen; the principles in different branches which had been, and in some instances, are yet hid from the people of color, to deprive them of their enjoyments, were here taught them, which greatly helped to elevate them to a position that would command respect through the short voyage of life. These are the proceeds of vital piety. " Do unto all men, as ye would they should do unto you." Love, truly, is the fulfilment of the Law. O! may the day speedily come when the yoke of oppression shall be finally destroyed. Under a striking impulse of gratitude, and at the request of Mr. Tappan, I delivered a short address and then left the School with the answer to a good conscience. Then leaving New York, I arrived at New Brunswick, where I was kindly received. Preached three sermons; truly, the Lord was there in power. Next I proceeded to Rahway, preached four sermons, and some were added to the church. From that to Princeton, and preached four sermons. No particular display of God's power; yet my soul rejoices in hope of the promise. "If Israel is not gathered, Jacob shall not lose his reward." I then left for Trenton, met a Quarterly Meeting, and the Elder gave me two appointments. His labors had been very successful on his circuit. I then left for Philadelphia, and found my friends well. This being the month of November, I remained a-while in the city. I preached in Bethel Church and the Union also. Dec. 2nd I left for New-Hope, with a sister speaker. She and myself attended two churches by the permission of the Elder, R. R. ——— I preached five sermons before Christmas, 1st at brother S's house, 2nd at the Mountain, and 3rd in the new church; praise God for it. " Long expected, seen at last." The 1st text as follows: "Wisdom is justified of her children," &c. it was a time long to be remembered. I preached the Watch-Night sermon Christmas Eve, from Matt. 2nd chap. and 10th verse, and during my stay until New-Years Eve, there was great good done in the name of the Holy Child Jesus. In travelling towards Frankford I stopped at Holmesburg for the purpose of warning some persons of approaching danger, but finding an intimate friend of mine very ill, I paid her a religious visit, which gave me much satisfaction to see her resignation unto death. I purposed leaving next morning for Frankford at 9 o'clock, but she died, and the Elder and preacher being at a far distance from there, by special request I attended the funeral, and after a short sermon at the house I had to commit the body to the earth, as no other person was present to do it. I then left for Frankford, preached four sermons which was profitable through God's grace.

Feb'ry. 16th, I started for Attleboro. I spoke from the following passages : Romans 6th chap. 21st 22d 23d verses. Also from the 8th Chapter, 36th & 37th verses. At first it seemed like seed sown in stony ground, but the deadness began to remove, and life, light and immortality was come to pass through the preaching of the Cross of Christ. I preached one sermon in Ben-Salem, and held a prayer meeting, and the Lord smiled upon us, and truly some had in a measure lost their first love, and others who had not defiled their garments, but contended for the fulfilment of the promise. Now, coming towards

6

Philadelphia, I found my son and my friends all well. After preaching one hundred and forty-six sermons and travelling nine hundred and ninety-nine miles.

In April, I felt impressed to visit Reading, Pa., which I did, and met some that I had met with years before, testifying that God is God, and changes not. I preached five sermons, and truly I must say that the Gospel is prevailing. Some few years previous there was not one member of church, now there is a good church and a large society. I now went to Norristown, spoke five times and led class. A man formerly lived there that played on the violin, but leaving his place of residence went to Philadelphia and embraced religion, and was called to go to the people of that town to preach the gospel to them, and the Lord blessed his labors, and they now live in hope of a better.resurrection.

July 15th, 1838, I left for Westchester, preached two sermons. From there I went to Chichester, from that to the Valley, laboring as I passed along to lively congregations. On the 23d I left for Columbia, calling on Rev. S. S.——, he gave me three appointments. God revived his work in the hearts of his people, and while my pen moves my heart burns with love to God. Next I left for West-town and visited some aged friends, such as could not get to the church, and two remarkable ones in particular, which were regarded as pillars of the church. I was conducted on board the canal boat for Lewistown. I had a pleasant passage, arrived at 1 or 2 o'clock, A. M. and was kindly treated by them. Preached four sermons to a hard people. I was sick during my stay, my system was much debilitated before I reached Pittsburg; however, I pressed on to Huntingdon, found a small society suffering for want of help. I was received by all the brethren, preached five sermons, rode 11 miles and spoke to the Forgemen, but through bad management the congregation was small, but the word had its effect; the souls of the redeemed are precious. I next proceeded to Hollidaysburg. Took passage by stage at night, arrived at 8 o'clock A. M. I was kindly received by a gentleman belonging to Wesley church, and entertained in a friendly manner. Preached two sermons to a comfortable congregation, and then left for Johnstown. After I got out of the car I thought it almost the last end of the world as regards accommodations. I had to stand near one hour before I could get a person to carry my trunk. The Caprain was kind and offered to send me a person, but I got a man at last to take my trunk there. His wife was kind, although I introduced myself to her, knowing her to be the Barber's wife. She sent for him to come in, and then introduced me to her husband. When he sat down he said, " you preach do you ?" I try, said I. " Do you understand the Scriptures?" Some parts of it, was my answer. [He appointed a meeting, and the time arrived, congregation gathered. When I commenced I felt a little confusion in the house, but in a few minutes every thing was still, and we had a solemn waiting upon the Lord; after which the Barber closed the service. So I left them. A brother informed me that the chief Magistrate of the town said we must hold another meeting and he would attend it, but the preacher did not seem to feel interested for the welfare of souls; for this cause I took passage on steam boat for Pittsburg, which was pleasant although crowded. The last day being Sabbath, I sat in serious meditation on the beauties of Creation and the plan of Redemption. There were some lady passengers from Charleston that enjoyed religion would come and sit by me to read. When about to leave, one of them requested me to pray for her husband and daughter. I hope that Elijah's God will prosper her desire for their welfare. We arrived at Pittsburg about 8 o'clock, P. M. I was conducted to the house of a worthy Father in Israel, where I remained awhile, preached four or five sermons in Pittsburg. My mind still urging me on to Brownsville; and the Lord opened the way. The Elder of the circuit coming into Pittsburg, made a way for me, and provided me with a sister to accompany me. The Lord blessed the labors of his servants. In three months time there were one hundred and ten added to his circuit. Some converts, some mourners. Five out of one family fell in love with this Heaven-born plan. I commenced my winter journey the 10th of December. I left Pittsburg for a Quarterly Meeting at Williamsport; it was a tedious journey. We had to walk seven miles, and on entering the town we met a brother coming to meet us with a conveyance. That night the meeting commenced, and truly the battle was the Lord's. Six were slain by his mighty power, and the faith of believers strengthened. I spoke at 11 o'clock from the 12th Chapter of Isaiah, 5th & 6th verses, and at night again, to a crowded house of well-behaved people. Elder Clemens, a successful laborer for the Lord was on this circuit. After preaching, the mourner's bench was erected, and the slain of the Lord were many. This meeting continued two days and nights, after which our Love-feast took place. The Lord was in the midst, and the people were crying for mercy in every direction. The Wesleyan Methodists opened their church and gave me an appointment on Monday at 3 o'clock, P. M., after which the Elder gave us privilege to hold prayer meetings, which continued all night, was very successful, and a revival took place with both white and colored people, and one of the members informed me there were thirty persons added to the church that time. Praise God for the victory.

> The world cannot withstand
> Its ancient conqueror;
> It sure must fall beneath the hand
> That arms us for the war :

We then rested a few days and started for Uniontown, a female travelling with me; and we were received very kindly by Bro. Jackson and wife, and the friends generally. I preached out at the forge to an attentive people and felt both life and liberty. The Elder returning from his circuit, preached again, and five united with us in the Church, after which the Elder formed a new Society, fourteen miles distant. I then preached in the white M. E. Church to a very attentive congregation, whose groans ascended the hill of the Lord, and I felt his presence in a powerful manner—text, Isaiah lix. 1 v. On 24th of December the Elder held a watch-night, and on the 25th we started for Ridge Port again. I received the morning appointment and the Elder preached at night, and the Lord continued to pour out his Spirit upon the people, which caused a general revival. Ten joined the Church on trial. Some we left mourning for the redemption in Christ, while others seemed to be in full stretch for the Kingdom of God. I had a previous invitation to a church five miles distant on the turnpike, and I spoke in the morning at 11 o'clock, and just closed the sermon, when a gentleman came with a swift horse and vehicle on express for me to come and fill an appointment for them at 3 o'clock P. M., and accordingly went. We arrived between 2 and 3 o'clock. I met a large congregation of very respectable people, and preached from these words: "The Spirit of the Lord God is upon me," &c. The next Wednesday I attended an appointment in Greenfield in the old M. E. church; it was a very stormy night, and I thought from the inclemency of the weather there would be no person out; but through the perseverance of the Brother and his wife that came for me, there was quite a large congregation gathered, after which he handed me up in the pulpit, and I endeavored to preach from these words: "We have found him of whom Moses and the Prophets did write," and I must say that the christian groans that were uttered, and the hearty Amens that ascended the hill of Zion, were answered seemingly as with coals of fire from God's holy altar, which warmed every heart. Pray God to carry on the work.

> Thy banner unfurl,
> Bid the nation surrender ;
> And own Thee their God,
> Their King, and Defender.

Some hundreds were added to that circuit that year, ending February, 1839. In a few days I left for Williamsport, where I remained a few days at Bro. C's., and attended several very good meetings at Washington, Pa. I had an appointment given me by the Elder of the white M. E. Church, which I accepted. By special request, I visited a white young lady in the last stage of consumption, and after conversing with her about the salvation of her soul, I received great satisfaction, who I trust now rests in Abraham's bosom. I attended a quarterly meeting at Washington, and I heard some powerful exhortations—God owned the word and by his infinite power arrested a woman who formerly kept a dance house, and with her, her family also, (saving her husband who had lately died,) and they, five in number, cried aloud for mercy at the hand of God, and afterwards joined the church; the old lady appeared very serious, and they all spoke well in Love-feast.

I had a special invitation, by letter, to go to Waynesburg, which I received, and spoke in the old Methodist church, after being conveyed there by a brother that was sent for me expressly. On Wednesday evening I spoke in the Court house; it was in the month of February, and the walking was very difficult; the friends were very kind; but few colored persons, only two members of the church, and six joined. I spoke for them five times—after discharging my duty I left in peace with God and man. On my return to Washington, I spent a week or ten days, and preached on Sabbath day, and at night three sermons. The Mayor of the city declared his intention to impose a heavy punishment upon any person or persons disturbing any church, and it had the effect to make some of the wildest of the rabble behave themselves in the church with respect, while I endeavored to declare the oracles of truth. After which I left for Meconnoburg, and preached eleven sermons.

In March I left for Pittsburg, and we met in joy; and at my first appointment I spoke from Isaiah c. 50, v. 31. I then rested three or four weeks, during which time my mind become much exercised to go to Cincinnati—it was difficult to travel, but God always makes a way for his people. A friend both to God and me, got a passage for me on board of a Steamboat, with a preacher and his family, and on my arrival, I was recommended to friends there, Elder King and wife, and I found them. I told them it was my business to preach. An appointment was given me. I spoke several times, and the Lord approbated the efforts of the feeble worm, and believers were built up in the most holy faith. My visit was joyous. My pamphlets went off as by a wind, the Elder recommending them very highly, and also encouraged me to have the 2d edition printed, which I had done—there being then one thousand more for sale, in which I was successful. Five joined the church after the last sermon.

I then left for Dayton, Ohio, and found a large church and building. The colored population there was very large—there I preached six sermons, and one in the other church. I was aided by both churches. I then took steamboat for Hambleton, a well situated place, and preached two sermons; had a good visit, much favored of the Lord, although the members were much scattered abroad. But a worthy brother, a man of God, had settled there and formed a Society of some twenty persons, which was still prosperous. After preaching two sermons, I took passage in steamboat for Cincinnati; remained there awhile until I had some new direction opened to my mind, where I might call the people to the arms of Christ. The recent printing of my tracts, had caused me to be very scarce of money, (price of print ing 1000 copies, $38.) There were individuals who helped me in a way for travelling. The Elder being absent that Sabbath morning, there was some disorder prevailed among some who seemed double-minded, yet they were officers. But God can make a way where there appears to be no way. Mrs. E. J., her husband and children, made me a present of seven dollars, and another friend interceded for me in getting a good cabin passage in a comfortable boat, and no distinction—captain was a gentleman. I enjoyed sweet communion with the spirit of the Lord. But a painful circumstance took place near our journey's end, which seemed to me awful in the extreme. There was a woman on board of the boat who was called insane. I thought she was laboring under a despair of mind. She had seen herself a dreadful sinner, and set in a melancholy position; at times only she would seemingly arouse and ask us not to let them hurt her. On one occasion I asked her how she felt. She answered, "I hear some persons talking; they will hurt me—I would drown myself, but it is such a sin." A lady and myself strove to comfort her, after which the lady read to her respecting the storms. She set very quiet, then she suddenly arose to her feet, and said she must pray. I told her to kneel down by my side, which she did very orderly; she first prayed in Dutch; I could not understand her only as she said God or Jesus, and then she prayed in English very feeling, then clapped her hands and said he has taken a load off me—this was about 10 or 11 o'clock, A. M. She arose, washed her face and hands, combed her hair, and then put on a cap and looked like another person, and thus remained until candle-light, she and the young lady walking and talking. I was reading and felt greatly relieved from the care of her. Suddenly the chambermaid came in and asked me for her, and it seemed only five minutes since I missed her. The captain made search, went down on the deck and there found her, but she begged so hard to stay there that he left her. The boat arrived at Portsmouth next morning at sunrise, and that morning at 8 o'clock, she was seen to jump overboard. They lowered a boat and tried to save her, but before they reached her she sank to rise no more; and on the authority of God's word, I say, no self-murderer hath eternal life. Reader, be careful, exceedingly careful, how you trifle with the spirit of God, lest it should take its flight and leave thee to undergo eternal punishment.

Take the warning, turn and live,
And God will his Spirit give.

After landing, I felt to be a stranger in a strange land, but the Lord ever provides in time of need. Accordingly I was conducted by a gentleman and introduced to a friend who received me and treated me kindly, and in a few days introduced me to one of the Trustees, who welcomed me to the Church. Now I began to feel the spirit of my station. On Thursday night I filled an appointment. It was altogether a strange thing to hear a woman preach there, so it made quite an excitement, which made my labor very heavy, as the people were all eyes and prayed none. But on Sabbath day we had a crowded house, and an old backslider fell to the floor like Dagon before the Ark. Six joined the church on probation. On next Sabbath, Elder Peters' quarterly meeting took place, which was greatly enjoyed by all present. I met many of my friends from Pittsburg and other places, and we rejoiced together. One day in the house of the Lord is more than a thousand in the courts of the wicked. The first Sabbath I spoke to the class, five fell to the floor under the influence of God's power. Two days afterward we left for Gallopeler quarterly meeting; took passage on board of steamboat, which was very pleasant, without distinction. When we arrived, it being night, a gentleman conducted us to our lodgings and introduced us, where we were kindly received. I preached one sermon to a small society that seemed almost without a shepherd to look to their welfare. I was astonished at the situation of the church—after which time the Elder came. A Baptist society occupied the house in the morning, and in the afternoon the Elder preached—it was a dull time indeed, none joined. At night I tried to preach, but could not tell what the Lord had done for them people, for they seemed both barren and unfruitful.

I felt an anxiety to go to Chilicothe, for which place I took passage and arrived on Wednesday; found a large field of labor open. I preached on the next night (Thursday) to a very large and well informed congregation. I then took passage via canal, and my mind was much exercised, indeed, somewhat uncommon. Text 1st, Thessalonions: "Because iniquity abounds the love of many waxed cold, but they that endure to the end the same shall be saved." Text 2d: "For Christ sent me not to baptize, but to preach the gospel lest the cause of Christ should be made of non effect." Text 3d. Prov. 5th c. 6th v., I preached again from these words: "All flesh is as grass." Fifth and last: "I am the true Vine," &c. My visit being out, I left for Williamsport in peace with God, likewise the brethren, as the friends had used me very kind. After the quarterly meeting, we all took passage with the Elder for Pittsburg, to meet the conference. I there met the Rt. Rev. Bishop, and others I was glad to see. I remained there two or three weeks, and preached four sermons. Both preachers and people used me like christians. The conference was largely attended with ministers from every direction. The Bishop granted an open house for persons to visit and hear the arrangements and appointments on the circuits. The preaching was very good, and it seemed as if the word fell heavy upon the hearts of the King's enemies; a general revival took place. The Bishop gave me an appointment during the conference. After my visit came to a close, I was exercised to leave for Philadelphia. A lady, named Mrs. Dorsey, being acquainted with one of the captains of the boats, succeeded in procuring a comfortable passage for me for $15, and $3 for board, making $18 in all, when it was $48 from Philadelphia to Pittsburg. I felt grateful towards God for his mindfulness of me. The captain was a gentleman, and the passengers of the first circle, and I enjoyed their company. When we changed boats at Hollidaysburg, the captoin put me on the fast line that I might arrive at Philadelphia in the day. There was a white lady on the boat with me, bound to Philadelphia, who had travelled from New Orleans. A gentleman who was coming to the city, seeing her lonely situation and also mine, he never left the cars until he saw each of our baggages in the omnibus and starting for our doors—a gentleman indeed. Thus ended this journey, Sept. 1839.

After my arrival, my first inquiry was after the state of health of my son and his family, and to my great disappointment I found that my little grandson had died. This was startling news to me, you may think, but the Lord removed him for some wise purpose of his providence, and in this I felt perfectly resigned to his will, with a heart of gratitude for my protection and safe arrival at home. I remained in the city about three months, and received appointments in our churches on Thursday nights, although in years past I always had them at any time, Sunday afternoons not excepted. In Philadelphia, N. York, Baltimore, and all the principal cities, from 100 to 1000 miles distant, as I travelled under the reign of the first Bishop Rt. Rev. Richard Allen, I have been instrumental in the hands of God of gaining many hundreds of dollars for the connexion, by raising societies where there never had been any, since which time they have grown to such a mass as to build large churches, and that in different places, and likewise have spent hundreds, but don't regret it, as I was about the work of Him that sent me, for which my reward is promised if I but hold out faithful.

Now, pray for me,
That while on earth I roam ;
That with the joyful Jubilee,
I may arrive at home.

I again was impressed upon to go into the western part of the State of Pennsylvania and labor for the Lord, as the field appeared large before me. About this time sister Elaw, a speaker belonging under the jurisdiction of the E. Methodist connexion, coming to this place, she received an appointment which had been given to me, and I closed the meeting after her, and we enjoyed good seasons together. The greatest display of God's power seemed visible in a Protestant congregation; sister preached, and I gave an exhortation and closed, in which there was a great shout for victory. I was informed by those that were in the spirit, that they saw the glory of God like a sun over the pulpit, and a face shone after it, thus the battle was the Lord's.

My sister leaving for England to visit the world's convention, I started alone. My first appointment was over Schuylkill—then I was conveyed nine miles farther, preached three sermons, and then returned to the city; on the following week I left again for Lancaster, Pa., but meeting friends going to Columbia I went with them. The meetings were attended by the spirit of God, and the speakers felt the spirit of their station, and the feast was glorious; over thirty were added to the church in less than a week, and many of them found peace with God. From thence I went to Marietta, preached two sermons, and then left for Lancaster. The Lord owned the word spoken, and after preaching, ten joined the church. "Praise the Lord, for He only doeth great wonders."—Psalms. I then proceeded on to Carlisle. Seemingly the wolf had got in among the fold and had scattered some clear away. But God's word will have its effect where it is promulgated in its purity. The consequence was, we had a great rejoicing. I preached six sermons, including one for the Protestant Methodists. I employed my time, as usual, endeavoring to explain the effects of the everlasting gospel of the kingdom, even in common conversation. The happy seasons I have seen are ever memorable to me, and my prayer is, that all Israel may be saved, not only from the trials of life, but from the power of hell. I then proceeded to Harrisburg, preached one sermon to a good congregation, and felt considerable liberty in speaking. I left next morning for Marietta; it was a very cold day; sometimes I rode in a slay and sometimes in a carriage. I preached one sermon on Sabbath, and next day took passage in a slay for Columbia. I stopped a few days, preached one sermon, then left for Penningtonville. I preached there on Sabbath day to a good congregation of different denominations—it was a glorious day to my soul. Upon the authority of God's word, there need be no doubt about religion, for they that have it carry the witness within themselves. Thus, having finished my visit with a peace of conscience, I returned to Philadelphia, March 1st, and found all my friends well. I waited in the temple of the Lord and preached several times. I felt anxious to go to Baltimore on a visit to the general conference, being the first of that kind held there for many years. After mentioning it to the Bishop, he said I should be paid for it if I wished to go, for which I felt very grateful. After making the necessary preparations by arranging my clothes, &c., the morning came for to start; the boat was to leave Philadelphia at 6 o'clock, A. M. My mind had been somewhat divided about going to N. York, as I wanted to see the convention of the American Anti-Slavery Society. But on my way to the Baltimore boat, in company with a young sister, my mind was suddenly arrested by a strange sensation, which proceeded from some supernatural cause, followed by a voice which seemingly spake thus: "a watery grave !

a watery grave!!" I told the sister what had been revealed to me, yet not half a square from the house. She believed as I did, and I consequently turned back with an impression I should be drowned if I went, as I seemingly saw the water. "How unsearchable are God's judgments, and his ways are past finding out."

The same month, April, I was sent for in great haste to visit Cape May, to see my aged mother, as it was thought for the last time, as she was very ill, at the advanced age of 82 years. I went and remained with her several weeks, when she nearly recovered. I then filled several appointments unexpectedly. But my way was I know not where. During my stay there I lost a nephew 12 years of age, whom I trust rests. But I should have mentioned, the day I returned from the Baltimore boat, I took passage at 2 o'clock, P. M., for Burlington, and preached for them on Sabbath day at a quarterly meeting, and second day after I left for New York and arrived the first day the convention sat, which I attended in company with Mrs. H. Lane, who was ever zealous in the good cause of liberty and the rights of all, and I heard some very eloquent speeches which pleased me very much, and my heart responded with this instruction: "Do unto all men as you would they should do unto you;" and as we are all children of one parent, no one is justified in holding slaves. I felt that the spirit of God was in the work, and also felt it my duty to unite with this Society. Doubtless the cause is good, and I pray God to forward on the work of abolition until it fills the world, and then the gospel will have free course to every nation, und in every clime.— After the convention was over I returned to Philadelphia, and prepared for a long journey. But previously I visited a part of Rev. Turner's circuit—Jersey, viz. of Burlington, Trenton, &c. His charge was extensive and laborers were much wanted. I endeavored to preach two sermons in Burlington, and in other places nine more, and then visited Allentown and preached three sermons. I visited a camp meeting and never saw a greater display of God's power, for truly signs and wonders followed the preaching of the cross of Christ, while the voice of prayer made sinners stare and filled them with awe and wonder. I also preached to a small society five miles farther, called Lawrenceville, after which I returned to Trenton, Princeton, &c., and in a few days I left for Brunswick. I left for this journey in 1843, in one of the brother's own conveyance, for which I felt very thankful. I filled several appointments, and then left for New York, where I remained several weeks, and proposed the holding of a protracted meeting to the Elder Boggs, in charge, and he thought well of it, and appointed one, and it seemed that the people truly had a mind to work, and the Lord blessed our labors. I preached on two Sabbath nights and once in the middle of the week. A revival broke out and twenty-one were added to the church, and it concluded with a victorious Love-feast, glory to God. During my absence my son was taken very ill with a severe disease, and I felt very anxious to see him after an absence of several months; consequently in December I left N. York on my return, and I found him much better than I expected, which greatly relieved my mind. I preached once in the Bethel, once in the Wesley church, which came in the connexion, Hurst St., and other places, but soon finished my work in this city, and notwithstanding the severity of the winter, I returned to Rahway, and found the friends very kind to me. I thank the Lord for giving them hearts to be so, as the winter was trying. I preached ten sermons during my stay, in which time a great revival took place in the church, and many were added, amongst whom was a Rev. father E——, who had left our church but at this time returned, and truly we made use of that very appropriate phrase: "The dead is alive and the lost is found," and the brother rejoiced much, seeing the Providence of God. Now I began fo feel my labors nearly completed in that part. I returned to N. York (as my visit was not accomplished in that city) on the 1st of March, 1841, and tarried some time, after which I took passage on steamboat for New Haven and arrived there at 1 o'clock, P. M. I was conducted by carriage to Mr. B's. and his family was kind; on next Wednesday I was taken to a brother's house, near the meeting house, which they commenced in January, and I preached in it in March. Being a people there whose minds were much cultivated, I felt at liberty to speak, believing God would own his word, which he did, and we had a revival. But Lucifer had prepared an engine to play upon it and put it out. But we had some firm members that turned neither to the right or left, as the scripture saith "the righteous shall hold on their way." Ah! reader, many scenes I have passed through, but I yet live by faith in the Son of God. I preached twenty-one sermons, and made my home at brother White's, near the church; this saved me from a great deal of exposure in going to and returning from the church. I perceived their slothfulness in coming out to Sabbath morning services. My first text was Rev. i, 10. God was with us truly, for signs and wonders followed, and we commenced a protracted meeting, and on the fifth night there were fourteen mourning souls at the anxious bench. After a stay of seven weeks, I felt at liberty to leave them, which I did, and arrived in New York on the 24th of April. Elder B. gave me an appointment the ensuing Sabbath morning in Bethel church. After that I went over to Brooklyn and spoke three or four times, but my heart mourned to see such a great falling off that had taken place in a few months past. But the conference sit there, and they had good preaching, and the congregation soon began to increase. The brothers were kind to me and gave me appointments at different places. I continued to travel round about, and spoke a number of times in Flushing, eight sermons in

Jamaica, three in Flatbush, three in Huntingdon south, three in Glen-cove, and then returned to Brooklyn again, and remained awhile with a sister who was ever kind to me, for which I hope God will reward her, with others. There was a camp-meeting to commence that week of my return, to be held by Rev. Boggs, near Harvest Straw, and I through invitation went in company—it was a very rainy time, but we had a great meeting, and I received two appointments. We caught no cold, and the christians rejoiced in the victories of the Cross, for we believed the Lord would shelter us even in the midst of storm.

Having a great desire to go to Massachusetts, I paid my way to Harvest Straw to take the boat, but was disappointed, not being in time, after which I had to pay a gentleman to convey me ten miles and conduct me safe on board of the boat for Albany. I had a plea-sant cabin passage for $1 50. On my arrival I employed a person to convey me and my baggage to a friend's house, and when I got there, they being absent, I did not stop even for breakfast, but returned to a N. York boat that stopped at Hudson, and there to take passage by Railroad. On my arrival, I found the cars did not start until 4 o'clock, P. M. It then occurred to my mind that I was in Hudson unexpect-edly, and truly the hand of the Lord must be in it, as I wanted to visit that place some time before. I then went out in search of some of my own people of color, trying to find out if I could get a place to preach in on my return, as I felt anxious to call the fallen sons and daughters of Adam. When about to start in the cars for Stockbridge, one of the brothers of the church went in company with me to the camp. By 7 o'clock we were safely landed and found the meeting prosperous, and I felt warm for the battle, as though I must press through fire or water. We had one mile to walk or pay 25 cents—after walking the distance, we found the tent that the Albany friends were accommodated at; soon after which the Elder heard of it and called upon me, which seemed to approbate my coming to his camp. I felt a great degree of liberty, believing myself to be in the right place. After several other strangers had labored in their turn, the Elder gave me another appointment on Saturday night. I endeavored to speak as God gave ability, and a brother closed meeting after me. On Sabbath morning at 10 o'clock, I tried to speak again to a large congregation. It rained very heavy, but they gave the best atten-tion and withstood the storm in all quietness; I felt free, the tongue was loosed, the lip was touched, and the heart was warm, which seemed to operate with the language of the text, in Rev.: "I was in the spirit on the Lord's day." The Lord owned the word, and the hearty Amens that went up, caused the woods to echo. A white Methodist gentleman was present, who had become almost choked to death with the glutted cares of this world; while sitting, God through his mercy, sent his awakening power to his heart, and he rejoiced louder than others, telling me he was glad the Lord had sent me, that his mind had been overcharged with the cares of this life truly, and all of this while Irael shouted for the battle. The wicked were somewhat rude on Sunday night, and the Elder gave a very appropriate address to the gentlemen of the State of Massachusetts, showing how our rights were invaded, after which the gentlemen took it on themselves to guard the camp ground, and we had good order. The breaking up was a time long to be remembered, and on that day at 12 o'clock I left for Hudson. I there preached one or two sermons, visited the sick, &c., and was then taken to Pittsfield, preached one sermon, and then proceeded by stage to Hudson city, where I remained a while with a kind sister and her daughter. I attended the church on Sabbath morning and enjoyed a good sermon delivered by the Elder.

At 2 o'clock, P. M., I tried to preach in the same church to a full congregation. Text from the general epistle of James, 1st Chapter & 25th verse. At night I spoke in the old Methodist church for the first time, from these words; "We have found him of whom Moses and the Prophet's did write, Jesus of Nazereth, the son of Joseph." My mind was much exercised on the subject; receiving light from Heaven. I preached one sermon in the School-House at Catskill from these words; "I will give you power to tread on serpents and scorpions, and they shall not harm you." The Lord was there of a truth. After this, by request, I spoke in the white Methodist church from these words: "Therefore, cast not away your confidence, which has great recompense of reward." The Lord was there, and assisted the clay to speak in his name. On Monday night I spoke from these words of Paul to the Hebrews: "If the words spoken by Angels, are steadfast," &c., which had its desired effect. On Saturday I left for Albany, taking with me a good report for the Elder of our connection; after which, we wrote for him to come and form a Society, which he did sometime afterwards. The Elder was kind, and gave me appointments frequently. He held a Protracted Meeting, at which all of our laborers were successful. I preached seven sermons in Albany and one in Troy; after which I felt moved upon to visit Binghampton, and sister Tilghman was on her way to the same place to visit her father and mother, from whom she had been absent for some time, preaching the Everlasting Gospel of the Kingdom. But we were detained on the canal some time; but the Captain was kind and treated us well. After five days sail we arrived safe, and found our friends well; but not well in the Lord.

As soon as I enter a city I can feel the spirit that I may have to contend with; but by the permission of the Elder I filled appointments for a week or two, and then left for Montrose Quarterly Meeting. Preached five sermons, and passed through many things that were not agreeable, but duty makes labor light. I also spoke to a white congregation. After riding five or six miles and back the same night, and preaching two sermons in the town, I returned again to Binghampton, and held the Christmas Watch-Night meeting, as I found it was about to be omitted, and feeling interested, made application to the Trustees the Elder being absent, and thus gained permission. It was a task for me, as sister Tilghman was sick ; but the Lord was with us, while we rejoiced in the light that had come into the world. Glory to God for the gift of his Son. In the morning three of us attended the Episcopal church, and associated with them in receiving the Lord's Supper. At night I preached again, and I felt zealous in the cause of God, who was, and is ever faithful to his promise ; " Lo! I am with you alway, even to the end of the world."

The Elder then returned and urged me to stay, but I saw my way was onward. After preaching once more, I was aided on my way to Owego, where I found the enemies were many, standing in opposition to female preaching, or preachers of any kind ; but God always clears the way for his people. While they were preparing to have a dance rather than come to hear preaching, and boasting that they would invite the Elder to come to it, God laid his heavy hand upon the man that was to play the fiddle for them ; he fell sick on the floor; but he was determined to carry it out, and sent for another man, and he refused, and at last this Goliah-like man was glad to send for the Elder to come and pray for him. "O! sinner, thou cans't not measure arms with Jehovah ! He is a man of war, and the Lord is his name." In this very place, God worked miracles among them. I preached on Friday night, Sabbath morning, afternoon and night—and God worked wonders ; cnverting some of the most wicked among them.

After this, I left for Smithboro ; it seemed truly a hard place, and my labors were attended with but little success. There were a few scattering Methodists that assembled to worship, and seemed profited thereby. After I delivered my message I left for Towanda ; and there we had very comfortable meetings. I then proceeded ten miles further and preached ; there were eight persons, there one being an exhorter. They met us in the spirit of the gospel. After doing my duty I returned to Towanda, and on Wednesday I left for Athens; remained two days, preaching two sermons in the Academy. Next morning I rode about two miles, but we had to wait until the next Tuesday, in consequence of the flood being so great. I now was among strangers, with very little money; but finding the lady was a christian, I ventured to open my mind to her, telling her the nature of my mission. She told her husband, who said he would charge me only six shillings. I sewed three spreads together for her to quilt. She then informed me of a lady preacher in the neighborhood, one mile distant. I was kindly received by her, and met another person there also that seemed greatly wrought upon. After a seasonable word of exhortation, I took tea with them. In three days time I left for Towanda again, and met with great success by preaching in private houses. There was a gentlemen that seemed as if he never thought of God in all his life, but was arrested by the conviction of God's spirit, and sent for me to come and pray for him and his family. In this my soul greatly rejoiced, leaving him with a promise to call again, which I did. After inquiring my manner of travelling, and what I depended upon for support. I replied by giving him a statement of how I travelled, when he kindly aided me by a donation, and wished me success, requesting me to pray for him and his family before I left them, and I believe I saw him then fast ripening for eternal blessedness.

I was then sent for to return again to Owego, a distance of 38 miles, and they would pay my way on to Montrose, on my way to Philadelphia. I obeyed the request and found things very prosperous indeed. At night we had prayer meetings, and the Lord continued to pour out his spirit upon the people, and we had a meeting every night. Mr. J. H., formerly of Columbia, whose lot was cast as in a strange land, where there were only a few people that were members of the M. E. church; several husbands, strangers to God until now, and their wives, servants of the most High God, and two daughters of Mr. J. H., were justified through faith—three joined the church previously. I was selected to make a class book, and did so, as I wanted to see how many were for us. The Baptists had held an anxious meeting, after which five joined them. I made the trial by special invitation, and thirteen joined us. I had preached on Sabbath morning and night, and then held prayer meetings every night afterwards that week, except Saturday night; a man and his wife fell to the floor and cried for mercy, and both arose in the same hour soundly converted, giving God the glory. I preached on the next Sabbath morning and then led class, and at night again—text, Judges iv. 25, 26. They all marvelled at a woman taking such a deep subject, but the Lord assisted the organ of clay, and we had the victory, as there were twenty-one persons joined from that revival, and nearly all of them evinced justifying grace. On 3d day night we wound up, as I was to start on my journey on next day, which I did—brother paid my passage. I rode 28 miles in good company with a lady and gentleman who were going to New York. She said she was sorry to part; we had a heavy thunder storm with rain, and it was very dark, but we had a very careful driver, and we arrived safe at Montrose and took supper—between 12 and 1 o'clock at night I took stage for Wilkesbarre and arrived there at 8 next morning, and there I crossed the Susquehanna; I was very hungry, and having a little time I went to the house and asked the lady for breakfast and I would pay her. She said she had nothing, but would try and get me a good breakfast and take no pay, which she did. I truly feel thankful to God that he has proved himself a table in the wilderness. About 4 o'clock in the afternoon I arrived safe and was kindly received, and preached on Sabbath morning and night. Between the two appointments I rode two miles and preached in the afternoon. That day the Lord was in the house in power. Tuesday evening we had a glorious prayer meeting. I rode all night around the mountain, and some walked and appeared to be a quarter of a mile off. But the Lord preserved me in the mail stage alone. I adore his name now and I shall for evermore. The preacher in charge arrived the next day after I did, and spent his labors of love among the people. On the Wednesday following he went away and left me in charge of the class, (eight persons) to regulate them, and by the permission of the elder I addressed them. After I had relieved my mind and taken my seat the preacher formed them into a class and appointed a leader, who but three months before, was unconverted; but being so interested for the prosperity of Zion, seemed worthy of the appointment. After this I endeavored to hold prayer meetings through the week; preached twice on Sabbath day and helped to lead class, as the brother was young,—but they were all willing people, and truly it seemed to be the day of God's power among them, and " Peace abided at our House."

At the expiration of three weeks and four days l left them fifteen names on their class book. I then rode a distance of sixty miles over a hard road, hills and mountains, (there being no turn-pike or rail-road on that rout from Wilksbarre to Easton ;)—some part of the way there was good sleighing. Through the help of Providence we arrived at Easton about 8'clock, P. M. I took supper and lodging in the Hotel, where I was well accommodated; after which I found a small number of colored friends. We had a meeting, and " it was good for us to be there." After this I called at New Hope, thirty-two miles I think from Philadelphia ; visited the family I was brought up in, stopped and rested myself, as I felt much exhausted from travelling, so much winter and summer. I preached two or three times. Brother J. B. ———— was holding a protracted meeting. I gained strength; thank the Lord, and then left for home, and arrived in the city the last day of March 1842, having been two years, wanting a few days, almost incessantly travelling. I found my son, together with the rest of my family connections quite well; yet I could hear of the ravages of death, the relentless murderer, who never takes denials ; my little grand-daughter, a promising child indeed, was taken with the rest. O ! how soon delights may perish, and my heart responds—" The Lord's will be done."

My health being very much impaired, I knew not but that I should be the next one called away, but the Lord spared me for some other purpose, and upon my recovery I commenced travelling again, feeling it better to wear out than to rust out—and so expect to do until death ends the struggle—knowing, if I lose my life for Christ's sake, I shall find it again.

I now conclude—by requesting the prayers of God's people every-where, who worship in His holy fear, to pray for me, that I ever may endeavor to keep a conscience void of offence, either towards God or man—for I feel as anxious to blow the Trumpet in Zion, and sound the alarm in God's Holy Mount, as ever;—

> Though Nature's strength decay,
> And earth and hell withstand—
> To Canaan's land I'l urge my way,
> At HIS Divine command.

But here I feel constrained to give over, as from the smallness of this pamphlet I cannot go through with the whole of my journal, as it would probably make a volume of two hundred pages; which, if the Lord be willing, may at some future day be published. But for the satisfaction of such as may follow after me, when I am no more, I have recorded how the Lord called me to his work, and how he has kept me from falling from grace, as I feared I should. In all things he has proved himself a God of truth to me; and in his service I am now as much determined to spend and be spent, as at the very first. My ardour for the progress of his cause abates not a whit, so far as I am able to judge, though I am now something more than fifty years of age.

As to the nature of uncommon impressions, which the reader can-not but have noticed, and possibly sneered at in the course of these pages, they may be accounted for in this way : It is known that the blind have the sense of hearing in a manner much more acute than those who can see : also their sense of feeling is exceedingly fine, and is found to detect any roughness on the smoothest surface, where those who can see find none. So it may be with such as I am, who has never had more than three months schooling ; and wishing to know much of the way and law of God, have therefore watched the more closely, the operations of the Spirit, and have in consequence been led thereby. But let it be remarked that I have never found that Spirit lead me contrary to the Scriptures of truth, as I understand them. "For as many as are led by tha *Spirit* of God are the sons of God."—Rom. viii. 14.

I have now only to say, May the blessing of the Father, and of the Son, and of the Holy Ghost, accompany the reading of this poor effort to speak well of his name, wherever it may be read. AMEN.

P. S. Please to pardon errors, and excuse all imperfections, as I have been deprived of the advantages of education (which I hope all will appreciate) as I am measurably a self-taught person. I hope the contents of this work may be instrumental in leaving a lasting impression upon the minds of the impenitent ; may it prove to be encouraging to the justified soul, and a comfort to the sanctified

Though much opposed, it is certainly essential in life, as Mr. Wesley wisely observes. Thus ends the Narrative of Jarena Lee, the first female preacher of the First African Methodist Episcopal Church.

Bethel at Philadelphia, Penn., United States of America.

FINIS.

A BRAND

PLUCKED FROM THE FIRE.

AN AUTOBIOGRAPHICAL SKETCH

PY

MRS. JULIA A. J. FOOTE.

"*Is not this a brand plucked out of the fire?*"— ZECH. III. 2.

CLEVELAND, OHIO.

PRINTED FOR THE AUTHOR BY LAUER & YOST.

1886.

PREFACE.

I HAVE written this little book after many prayers to ascertain the will of God—having long had an impression to do it. I have a consciousness of obedience to the will of my dear Lord and Master.

My object has been to testify more extensively to the sufficiency of the blood of Jesus Christ to save from all sin. Many have not the means of-purchasing.large and expensive works on this important Bible theme.

Those who are fully in the truth cannot possess a prejudiced or sectarian spirit. As they hold fellowship with Christ, they cannot reject those whom he has received, nor receive those whom he rejects, but all are brought into a blessed harmony with God and each other.

3

The Christian who does not believe in salvation from all sin in this life, cannot have a
constant, complete peace. The evil of the
heart will rise up and give trouble. But let
all such remember the words of Paul: "I am
crucified with Christ; nevertheless, I live; yet
not I, but Christ liveth in me; and the life
which I now live in the flesh, I live by faith
of the Son of God, who loved me, and gave
himself for me." "Ask, and ye shall receive."
The blood of Jesus will not only purge your
conscience from the guilt of sin, and from dead
works, but it will destroy the very root of sin
that is in the heart, by faith, so that you may
serve the living God in the beauty of holiness.

My earnest desire is that many—especially
of my own race—may be led to believe and
enter into rest, "For we which have believed
do enter into rest"—sweet soul rest.

INTRODUCTION.

The author of this sketch is well known in many parts of Ohio, and in other days was known in several States, as an Evangelist. The purity of her life and the success of her labors are acknowledged. After severe mental and spiritual conflicts, she obeyed God, in public labor for his cause, and still continues in this, although, with many, she is thereby guilty of three great crimes.

1. The first is, that of Color. For, though not now the slaves of individual men, our brethren continue to be under the bondage of society. But if there be crime in color, it lies at the door of Him who "hath made of one blood all nations of men for to dwell on all the face of the earth," and who declares himself to be "no respecter of persons." Holiness takes

the prejudice of color out of both the white
and the black, and declares that "The [heart's]
the standard of the man."

2. In the next place, we see the crime of
Womanhood. As though any one, with heart
and lips of love, may not speak forth the
praises of Him who hath called us out of
darkness into light! The "anointing which
abideth" unseals all lips, so that in Christ
"there is neither male nor female." Praise
God forever!

3. In the last place, our sister, as stated, is
an Evangelist. We respect the pastoral office
highly, for we know the heart of a pastor; but
while the regular field-hands are reaping,
pray, let Ruth glean, even if "her hap is to
light on a part of the field belonging to Boaz."

> "If you cannot, in the harvest,
> 　　Garner up the richest sheaves,
> Many a grain, both ripe and golden,
> 　　Will the careless reapers leave;
> Go and glean among the briers,
> 　　Growing rank against the wall;
> For it may be that their shadow
> 　　Hides the heaviest wheat of all."

Our dear sister is not a genius. She is simply strong in common sense, and strong in the Lord. Those of us who heard her preach, last year, at Lodi, where she held the almost breathless attention of five thousand people, by the eloquence of the Holy Ghost, know well where is the hiding of her power.

This is a simple narrative of a life of incidents, many of them stirring and strange. We commend it to all; and with it, the soundness of the doctrine and exhortation with which Sister Foote enforces the sublime cause of Holiness.

THOS. K. DOTY.

Christian Harvester Office,
  Cleveland, June, 1879.

CONTENTS.

8

Plucked from the Fire.

CHAPTER I.

Birth and Parentage.

I was born in 1823, in Schenectady, N. Y. I was my mother's fourth child. My father was born free, but was stolen, when a child, and enslaved. My mother was born a slave, in the State of New York. She had one very cruel master and mistress. This man, whom she was obliged to call master, tied her up and whipped her because she refused to submit herself to him, and reported his conduct to her mistress. After the whipping, he himself washed her quivering back with strong salt water. At the expiration of a week she was sent to change her clothing, which stuck fast to her back. Her mistress, seeing that she could not remove it, took hold of the rough tow-linen under-garment and pulled it off over

9

her head with a jerk, which took the skin with it, leaving her back all raw and sore.

This cruel master soon sold my mother, and she passed from one person's hands to another's, until she found a comparatively kind master and mistress in Mr. and Mrs. Cheeseman, who kept a public house.

My father endured many hardships in slavery, the worst of which was his constant exposure to all sorts of weather. There being no railroads at that time, all goods and merchandise were moved from place to place with teams, one of which my father drove.

My father bought himself, and then his wife and their first child, at that time an infant. That infant is now a woman, more than seventy years old, and an invalid, dependent upon the bounty of her poor relatives.

I remember hearing my parents tell what first led them to think seriously of their sinful course. One night, as they were on their way home from a dance, they came to a stream of water, which, owing to rain the night previous, had risen and carried away the log crossing. In their endeavor to ford the stream, my mother made a misstep, and came very nearly being drowned, with her babe in her arms. This nearly fatal accident made such

an impression upon their minds that they
said, "We'll go to no more dances;" and they
kept their word. Soon after, they made a
public profession of religion and united with
the M. E. Church. They were not treated as
Christian believers, but as poor lepers. They
were obliged to occupy certain seats in one
corner of the gallery, and dared not come down
to partake of the Holy Communion until the
last white communicant had left the table.

One day my mother and another colored sister waited until all the white people had, as
they thought, been served, when they started
for the communion table. Just as they reached
the lower door, two of the poorer class of white
folks arose to go to the table. At this, a mother
in Israel caught hold of my mother's dress and
said to her, "Don't you know better than to go
to the table when white folks are there?" Ah!
she did know better than to do such a thing
purposely. This was one of the fruits of slavery. Although professing to love the same
God, members of the same church, and expecting to find the same heaven at last, they could
not partake of the Lord's Supper until the
lowest of the whites had been served. Were
they led by the Holy Spirit? Who shall say?
The Spirit of Truth can never be mistaken,
nor can he inspire anything unholy. How

many at the present day profess great spirituality, and even holiness, and yet are deluded
by a spirit of error, which leads them to say to
the poor and the colored ones among them,
"Stand back a little—I am holier than thou."

My parents continued to attend to the ordinances of God as instructed, but knew little of
the power of Christ to save; for their spiritual
guides were as blind as those they led.

It was the custom, at that time, for all to
drink freely of wine, brandy and gin. I can
remember when it was customary at funerals,
as well as at weddings, to pass around the
decanter and glasses, and sometimes it happened that the pall-bearers could scarcely
move out with the coffin. When not handed
round, one after another would go to the closet
and drink as much as they chose of the liquors
they were sure to find there. The officiating
clergyman would imbibe as freely as any one.
My parents kept liquor in the house constantly, and every morning sling was made,
and the children were given the bottom of the
cup, where the sugar and a little of the liquor
was left, on purpose for them. It is no wonder, is it, that every one of my mother's children loved the taste of liquor?

One day, when I was but five years of age, I
found the blue chest, where the black bottle

was kept, unlocked—an unusual thing. Raising the lid, I took the bottle, put it to my
mouth, and drained it to the bottom. Soon
after, the rest of the children becoming frightened at my actions, ran and told aunt Giney—
an old colored lady living in a part of our
house—who sent at once for my mother, who
was away working. She came in great haste,
and at once pronounced me DRUNK. And so I
was—stupidly drunk. They walked with me,
and blew tobacco smoke into my face, to bring
me to. Sickness almost unto death followed,
but my life was spared. I was like a "brand
plucked from the burning."

Dear reader, have you innocent children,
given you from the hand of God? Children,
whose purity rouses all that is holy and good
in your nature? Do not, I pray, give to these
little ones of God the accursed cup which will
send them down to misery and death. Listen
to the voice of conscience, the woes of the
drunkard, the wailing of poverty-stricken
women and children, and touch not the
accursed cup. From Sinai come the awful
words of Jehovah, " No drunkard shall inherit
the kingdom of heaven."

CHAPTER II.

Religious Impressions---Learning the Alphabet.

I DO not remember having any distinct religious impression until I was about eight years old. At this time there was a "big meeting," as it was called, held in the church to which my parents belonged. Two of the ministers called at our house: one had long gray hair and beard, such as I had never seen before. He came to me, placed his hand on my head, and asked me if I prayed. I said, "Yes, sir," but was so frightened that I fell down on my knees before him and began to say the only prayer I knew, "Now I lay me down to sleep." He lifted me up, saying, "You must be a good girl and pray." He prayed for me long and loud. I trembled with fear, and cried as though my heart would break, for I thought he was the Lord, and I must die. After they had gone, my mother talked with me about my soul more than she ever had before, and told me that this preacher was a good man, but not the Lord; and that, if I were a good girl, and said my prayers, I would go to heaven. This gave me great comfort. I stopped crying, but continued to say, "Now I lay me." A white woman, who came to our house to sew, taught me the Lord's prayer. No tongue can tell the joy that filled my poor heart when I could repeat, "Our Father, which art in heaven." It has always seemed to me that I was converted at this time.

When my father had family worship, which was every Sunday morning, he used to sing,

"Lord, in the morning thou shalt hear
My voice ascending high."

I took great delight in this worship, and began to have a desire to learn to read the Bible. There were none of our family able to read except my father, who had picked up a little here and there, and who could, by carefully spelling out the words, read a little in the New Testament, which was a great pleasure to him. My father would very gladly have educated his children, but there were no schools where colored children were allowed. One day, when he was reading, I asked him to teach me the letters. He replied, "Child, I hardly know them myself." Nevertheless, he commenced with "A," and taught me the alphabet. Imagine, if you can, my childish glee over this, my first lesson. The children of the present time, taught at five years of age, can not realize my joy at being able to say the entire alphabet when I was nine years old.

I still continued to repeat the Lord's prayer and " Now I lay me," &c., but not so often as I had done months before. Perhaps I had begun to backslide, for I was but a child, surrounded by children, and deprived of the proper kind of teaching. This is my only excuse for not proving as faithful to God as I should have done.

Dear children, with enlightened Christian parents to teach you, how thankful you should be that "from a child you are able to say that you have known the Holy Scriptures, which are able to make you wise unto salvation, through faith which is in Christ Jesus." I hope all my young readers will heed the admonition, "Remember now thy Creator in the days of thy youth," etc. It will save you from a thousand snares to mind religion young. God says: "I love those that love me, and those that seek me early shall find me." Oh! I am glad that we are never too young to pray, or too ignorant or too sinful. The younger, the more welcome. You have nothing to fear, dear children; come right to Jesus.

Why was Adam afraid of the voice of God in the garden? It was not a strange voice; it was a voice he had always loved. Why did he flee away, and hide himself among the trees? It was because he had disobeyed God. Sin makes us afraid of God, who is holy; nothing but sin makes us fear One so good and so kind. It is a sin for children to disobey their parents. The Bible says: "Honor thy father and thy mother." Dear children, honor your parents by loving and obeying them. If Jesus, the Lord of glory, was subject and obedient to his earthly parents, will you not try to follow his example? Lift up your hearts to the dear, loving Jesus, who, when on earth, took little children in his arms, and blessed them. He will help you, if you pray, "Our Father, which art in heaven, thy dear Son, Jesus Christ, my Saviour, did say, 'Suffer little children to come unto me.' I am a little child, and I come to thee. Draw near to me, I pray thee. Hear me, and forgive the many wicked things I have done, and accept my thanks for the many good gifts thou hast given me. Most of all, I thank thee, dear Father, for the gift of thy dear Son, Jesus Christ, who died for me, and for whose sake I pray thee hear my prayer. Amen."

[2]

CHAPTER III.

𝕿𝖍𝖊 𝕻𝖗𝖎𝖒𝖊𝖘---𝕲𝖔𝖎𝖓𝖌 𝖙𝖔 𝕾𝖈𝖍𝖔𝖔𝖑.

When I was ten years of age I was sent to
live in the country with a family by the name
of Prime. They had no children, and soon
became quite fond of me. I really think Mrs.
Prime loved me. She had a brother who was
dying with consumption, and she herself was
a cripple. For some time after I went there,
Mr. John, the brother, was able to walk from
his father's house, which was quite near, to
ours, and I used to stand, with tears in my
eyes, and watch him as he slowly moved across
the fields, leaning against the fence to rest
himself by the way. I heard them say he
could not live much longer, and that worried
me dreadfully; and then I used to wonder if
he said his prayers. He always treated me
kindly, and often stopped to talk with me.

One day, as he started for home, I stepped
up to him and said, "Mr. John, do you say
your prayers?" and then I began to cry. He
looked at me for a moment, then took my hand

in his and said: "Sometimes I pray; do you?"
I answered, "Yes, sir." Then said he, "You
must pray for me"—and turned and left me.
I ran to the barn, fell down on my knees, and
said: "Our Father, who art in heaven, send
that good man to put his hand on Mr. John's
head." I repeated this many times a day as
long as he lived. After his death I heard
them say he died very happy, and had gone to
heaven. Oh, how my little heart leaped for
joy when 1 heard that Mr. John had gone to
heaven; I was sure the good man had been
there and laid his hand on his head. "Bless
the Lord, O my soul, and all that is within
me praise his holy name," for good men and
good women, who are not afraid to teach dear
children to pray.

The Primes being an old and influential
family, they were able to send me to a country
school, where I was well treated by both teacher
and scholars.

Children were trained very differently in
those days from what they are now. We were
taught to treat those older than ourselves with
great respect. Boys were required to make a
bow, and girls to drop a courtesy, to any person whom they might chance to meet in the
street. Now, many of us dread to meet children almost as much as we do the half-drunken

men coming out of the saloons. Who is to
blame for this? Parents, are you training
your children in the way they should go?
Are you teaching them obedience and respect?
Are you bringing your little ones to Jesus?
Are they found at your side in the house of
God, on Sunday, or are they roving the streets
or fields? Or, what is worse, are they at home
reading books or newspapers that corrupt the
heart, bewilder the mind, and lead down to
the bottomless pit? Father, mother, look on
this picture, and then on the dear children God
has given you to train up for lives of usefulness that will fit them for heaven. May the
dear Father reign in and rule over you, is the
prayer of one who desires to meet you all in
heaven.

CHAPTER IV.

My Teacher Hung for Crime.

My great anxiety to read the Testament caused me to learn to spell quite rapidly, and I was just commencing to read when a great calamity came upon us. Our teacher's name was John Van Paten. He was keeping company with a young lady, who repeated to him a remark made by a lady friend of hers, to the effect that John Van Paten was not very smart, and she didn't see why this young lady should wish to marry him. He became very angry, and, armed with a shotgun, proceeded to the lady's house, and shot her dead. She fell, surrounded by her five weeping children. He then started for town, to give himself up to the authorities. On the way he met the woman's husband and told him what he had done. The poor husband found, on reaching home, that John's words were but too true; his wife had died almost instantly.

After the funeral, the bereaved man went to the prison and talked with John and prayed for his conversion until his prayers were answered, and John Van Paten, the murderer, professed faith in Christ.

Finally the day came for the condemned to be publicly hung (they did not plead emotional insanity in those days). Everybody went to the execution, and I with the rest. Such a sight! Never shall I forget the execution of my first school-teacher. On the scaffold he made a speech, which I cannot remember, only that he said he was happy, and ready to die. He sang a hymn, the chorus of which was,

 "I am bound for the kingdom ;
    Will you go to glory with me?"

clasping his hands, and rejoicing all the while.

The remembrance of this scene left such an impression upon my mind that I could not sleep for many a night. As soon as I fell into a doze, I could see my teacher's head tumbling about the room as fast as it could go; I would waken with a scream, and could not be quieted until some one came and staid with me.

Never since that day have I heard of a person being hung, but a shudder runs through my whole frame, and a trembling seizes me. Oh, what a barbarous thing is the taking of human life, even though it be "a life for a life," as many believe God commands. That was the old dispensation. Jesus said: "A new commandment I give unto you, that ye love one another." Again: "Resist not evil; but whosoever shall smite thee on thy right cheek, turn to him the other also." Living as we do in the Gospel dispensation, may God help us to follow the precepts and example of Him, who, when he was reviled, reviled not again, and in the agony of death prayed: "Father, forgive them, for they know not what they do." Christian men, vote as you pray, that the legalized traffic in ardent spirits may be abolished, and God grant that capital punishment may be banished from our land.

CHAPTER V.

An Undeserved Whipping.

ALL this time the Primes had treated me as
though I were their own child. Now my feelings underwent a great change toward them;
my dislike for them was greater than my love
had been, and this was the reason. One day,
Mrs. Prime, having company, sent me to the
cellar to bring up some little pound cakes,
which she had made a few days previously.
There were but two or three left; these I
brought to her. She asked me where the rest
were. I told her "I didn't know." At this
she grew very angry, and said, "I'll make you
know, when the company is gone." She, who
had always been so kind and motherly, frightened me so by her looks and action that I
trembled so violently I could not speak. This
was taken as an evidence of my guilt. The
dear Lord alone knows how my little heart
ached, for I was entirely innocent of the crime
laid to my charge. I had no need to steal
anything, for I had a plenty of everything
there was.

There was a boy working for Mr. Prime that I always thought took the cakes, for I had seen him put his hand into his pocket hastily, and wipe his mouth carefully, if he met any one on his way from the cellar. But what could I do? I could not prove it, and his stout denial was believed as against my unsupported word.

That night I wished over and over again that I could be hung as John Van Paten had been. In the darkness and silence, Satan came to me and told me to go to the barn and hang myself. In the morning I was fully determined to do so. I went to the barn for that purpose, but that boy, whom I disliked very much, was there, and he laughed at me as hard as he could. All at once my weak feelings left me, and I sprang at him in a great rage, such as I had never known before; but he eluded my grasp, and ran away, laughing. Thus was I a second time saved from a dreadful sin.

That day, Mr. and Mrs. Prime, on their return from town, brought a rawhide. This Mrs. Prime applied to my back until she was tired, all the time insisting that I should confess that I took the cakes. This, of course, I could not do. She then put the rawhide up, saying, "I'll use it again to-morrow; I am determined to make you tell the truth."

That afternoon Mrs. Prime went away, leaving me alone in the house. I carried the rawhide out to the wood pile, took the axe, and cut it up into small pieces, which I threw away, determined not to be whipped with that thing again. The next morning I rose very early, before any one else was up in the house, and started for home. It was a long, lonely road, through the woods; every sound frightened me, and made me run for fear some one was after me. When I reached home, I told my mother all that had happened, but she did not say very much about it. In the afternoon Mr. and Mrs. Prime came to the house, and had a long talk with us about the affair. My mother did not believe I had told a falsehood, though she did not say much before me. She told me in after years that she talked very sharply to the Primes when I was not by. They promised not to whip me again, and my mother sent me back with them, very much against my will.

They were as kind to me as ever, after my return, though I did not think so at the time. I was not contented to stay there, and left when I was about twelve years old. The experience of that last year made me quite a

hardened sinner. I did not pray very often,
and, when I did, something seemed to say to
me, "That good man, with the white hair,
don't like you any more."

CHAPTER VI.

Varied Experiences—First and Last Dancing.

I HAD grown to be quite a large girl by this
time, so that my mother arranged for me to
stay at home, do the work, and attend the
younger children while she went out to days'
work. My older sister went to service, and
the entire care of four youngsters devolved
upon me—a thing which I did not at all relish.

About this time my parents moved to
Albany, where there was an African Methodist Church. My father and mother both joined
the church, and went regularly to all the services, taking all the children with them. This
was the first time in my life that I was able to
understand, with any degree of intelligence,

what religion was. The minister frequently visited our house, singing, praying, and talking with us all. I was very much wrought upon by these visits, and began to see such a beauty in religion that I resolved to serve God whatever might happen. But this resolution was soon broken, having been made in my own strength.

The pomps and vanities of this world began to engross my attention as they never had before. I was at just the right age to be led away by improper acquaintances. I would gain my mother's consent to visit some of the girls, and then would go off to a party, and once went to the theater, the only time I ever went in my life. My mother found this out, and punished me so severely that I never had any desire to go again. Thus I bartered the things of the kingdom for the fooleries of the world.

All this time conviction followed me, and there were times when I felt a faint desire to serve the Lord; but I had had a taste of the world, and thought I could not part with its idle pleasures. The Holy Spirit seemed not to strive with me; I was apparently left to take my fill of the world and its pleasures. Yet I did not entirely forget God. I went to church, and said my prayers, though not so

often as I had done. I thank my heavenly
Father that he did not quite leave me to my
own self-destruction, but followed me, sometimes embittering my pleasures and thwarting
my schemes of worldly happiness, and most
graciously preserving me from following the
full bent of my inclination.

My parents had at this time a great deal of
trouble with my eldest sister, who would run
away from home and go to dances — a place
forbidden to us all. The first time I ever
attempted to dance was at a quilting, where
the boys came in the evening, and brought
with them an old man to fiddle. I refused
several invitations, fearing my mother might
come or send for me; but, as she did not, I
yielded to the persuasions of the old fiddler,
and went on to the floor with him, to dance.

The last time I made a public effort at
dancing I seemed to feel a heavy hand upon
my arm pulling me from the floor. I was so
frightened that I fell; the people all crowded
around me, asking what was the matter, thinking I was ill. I told them I was not sick, but
that it was wrong for me to dance. Such loud,
mocking laughter as greeted my answer,
methinks is not often heard this side the gates
of torment, and only then when they are
opened to admit a false-hearted professor of

Christianity. They called me a "little Methodist fool," and urged me to try it again. Being
shamed into it, I did try it again, but I had
taken only a few steps, when I was seized with
a smothering sensation, and felt the same
heavy grasp upon my arm, and in my ears a
voice kept saying, "Repent! repent!" I
immediately left the floor and sank into a seat.
The company gathered around me, but not
with mocking laughter as before; an invisible
presence seemed to fill the place. The dance
broke up—all leaving very quietly. Thus was
I again "plucked as a brand from the burning."

Had I persisted in dancing, I believe God
would have smitten me dead on the spot.
Dear reader, do you engage in this ensnaring
folly of dancing? Reflect a moment; ask
yourself, What good is all this dissipation of
body and mind? You are ruining your
health, squandering your money, and losing
all relish for spiritual things. What good does
it do you? Does dancing help to make you a
better Christian? Does it brighten your hopes
of happiness beyond the grave? The Holy
Spirit whispers to your inmost soul, to come
out from among the wicked and be separate.

I am often told that the Bible does not
condemn dancing — that David danced. Yes,
David did dance, but he danced to express his

pious joy to the Lord. So Miriam danced, but it was an act of worship, accompanied by a hymn of praise. Herod's daughter, who was a heathen, danced, and her dancing caused the beheading of one of God's servants. Do you find anything in these examples to countenance dancing? No, no; a thousand times, no Put away your idols, and give God the whole heart.

After the dance to which I have alluded, I spent several days and nights in an agony of prayer, asking God to have mercy on me; but the veil was still upon my heart. Soon after this, there was a large party given, to which our whole family were invited. I did not care to go, but my mother insisted that I should, saying that it would do me good, for I had been moping for several days. So I went to the party. There I laughed and sang, and engaged in all the sports of the evening, and soon my conviction for sin wore away, and foolish amusements took its place.

Mothers, you know not what you do when you urge your daughter to go to parties to make her more cheerful. You may even be causing the eternal destruction of that daughter. God help you, mothers, to do right.

CHAPTER VII.

My Conversion.

I was converted when fifteen years old. It
was on a Sunday evening at a quarterly meeting. The minister preached from the text:
"And they sung as it were a new song before
the throne, and before the four beasts and the
elders, and no man could learn that song but
the hundred and forty and four thousand which
were redeemed from the earth." Rev. xiv. 3.

As the minister dwelt with great force and
power on the first clause of the text, I beheld
my lost condition as I never had done before.
Something within me kept saying, "Such a
sinner as you are can never sing that new
song." No tongue can tell the agony I suffered. I fell to the floor, unconscious, and was
carried home. Several remained with me all
night, singing and praying. I did not recognize any one, but seemed to be walking in the
dark, followed by some one who kept saying,
"Such a sinner as you are can never sing that
new song." Every converted man and woman

can imagine what my feelings were. I thought
God was driving me on to hell. In great terror I cried : "Lord, have mercy on me, a poor
sinner!" The voice which had been crying
in my ears ceased at once, and a ray of light
flashed across my eyes, accompanied by a sound
of far distant singing; the light grew brighter
and brighter, and the singing more distinct,
and soon I caught the words: "This is the new
song—redeemed, redeemed!" I at once sprang
from the bed where I had been lying for twenty
hours, without meat or drink, and commenced
singing: "Redeemed! redeemed! glory! glory!"
Such joy and peace as filled my heart, when I
felt that I was redeemed and could sing the
new song. Thus was I wonderfully saved from
eternal burning.

I hastened to take down the Bible, that I
might read of the new song, and the first words
that caught my eye were: "But now, thus saith
the Lord that created thee, O Jacob, and he
that formed thee, O Israel, fear not, for I have
redeemed thee; I have called thee by thy
name; thou art mine. When thou passest
through the waters, I will be with thee, and
through the rivers they shall not overflow
thee; when thou walkest through the fire,
thou shalt not be burned, neither shall the
flame kindle upon thee." Isaiah xliii. 1, 2.

[3]

My soul cried, "Glory! glory!" and I was filled with rapture too deep for words. Was I not indeed a brand plucked from the burning? I went from house to house, telling my young friends what a dear Saviour I had found, and that he had taught me the new song. Oh! how memory goes back to those childish days of innocence and joy.

Some of my friends laughed at me, and said: "We have seen you serious before, but it didn't last long." I said: "Yes, I have been serious before, but I could never sing the new song until now."

One week from the time of my conversion, Satan tempted me dreadfully, telling me I was deceived; people didn't get religion in that way, but went to the altar, and were prayed for by the minister. This seemed so very reasonable that I began to doubt if I had religion. But, in the first hour of this doubting, God sent our minister in to talk with me. I told him how I was feeling, and that I feared I was not converted. He replied: "My child, it is not the altar nor the minister that saves souls, but faith in the Lord Jesus Christ, who died for all men." Taking down the Bible, he read: "By grace are ye saved, through faith, and that not of yourselves; it is the gift of God." He asked me then if I believed my

sins had all been forgiven, and that the
Saviour loved me. I replied that I believed it
with all my heart. No tongue can express the
joy that came to me at that moment. There
is great peace in believing. Glory to the
Lamb!

CHAPTER VIII.

A Desire for Knowledge—Inward Foes.

I STUDIED the Bible at every spare moment,
that I might be able to read it with a better
understanding. I used to read at night by
the light of the dying fire, after the rest of the
family had gone to bed. One night I dropped
the tongs, which made such a noise that my
mother came to see what was the matter.
When she found that I had been in the habit
of reading at night, she was very much displeased, and took the Bible away from me, and
would not allow me to have it at such times
any more.

Soon after this, my minister made me a
present of a new Bible and Testament. Had
he given me a thousand dollars, I should not

have cared for it as I did for this Bible. I
cherished it tenderly, but did not read in it at
night, for I dared not disobey my mother.

I now felt the need of an education more
than ever. I was a poor reader and a poor
writer; but the dear Holy Spirit helped me by
quickening my mental faculties. O Lord, I
will praise thee, for great is thy goodness! Oh,
that everything that hath a being would praise
the Lord! From this time, Satan never had
power to make me doubt my conversion. Bless
God! I knew in whom I believed.

For six months I had uninterrupted peace
and joy in Jesus, my love. At the end of that
time an accident befell me, which aroused a
spirit within me such as I had not known that
I possessed. One day, as I was sitting at work,
my younger brother, who was playing with
the other small children, accidentally hit me
in the eye, causing the most intense suffering.
The eye was so impaired that I lost the sight
of it. I was very angry; and soon pride, impa-
tience, and other signs of carnality, gave me a
great deal of trouble. Satan said: "There!
you see you never were converted." But he
could not make me believe that, though I did
not know the cause of these repinings within.

I went to God with my troubles, and felt
relieved for a while; but they returned again

and again. Again I went to the Lord, earnestly striving to find what was the matter. I
knew what was right, and tried to do right,
but when I would do good, evil was present
with me. Like Gad, I was weak and feeble,
having neither might, wisdom nor ability to
overcome my enemies or maintain my ground
without many a foil. Yet, never being entirely
defeated, disabled or vanquished, I would gather
fresh courage, and renew the fight. Oh, that
I had then had some one to lead me into the
light of full salvation!

But instead of getting light, my preacher,
class-leader, and parents, told me that all
Christians had these inward troubles to contend with, and were never free from them until
death; that this was my work here, and I must
keep fighting and that, when I died, God
would give me a bright crown. What delu-
sion! However, I believed my minister was
too good and too wise not to know what was
right; so I kept on struggling and fighting
with this inbeing monster, hoping all the
time I should soon die and be at rest—never
for a moment supposing I could be cleansed
from all sin, and live.

I had heard of the doctrine of Holiness, but
in such a way as to give me no light, nor to
beget a power in me to strive after the expe-

rience. How frivolous and fruitless is that preaching which describes the mere history of the work and has not the power of the Holy Ghost. My observation has shown me that there are many, ah! too many shepherds now, who live under the dreadful woe pronounced by the Lord upon the shepherds of Israel (Ezekiel xxxiv.).

CHAPTER IX.

Various Hopes Blasted.

THE more my besetting sin troubled me, the more anxious I became for an education. I believed that, if I were educated, God could make me understand what I needed; for, in spite of what others said, it would come to me, now and then, that I needed something more than what I had, but what that something was I could not tell.

About this time Mrs. Phileos and Miss Crandall met with great indignity from a pro-slavery mob in Canterbury, Conn., because they dared to teach colored children to read. If they went out to walk, they were followed by a rabble of men and boys, who hooted at

them, and threw rotten eggs and other mis-
siles at them, endangering their lives and
frightening them terribly.

One scholar, with whom I was acquainted,
was so frightened that she went into spasms,
which resulted in a derangement from which
she never recovered. We were a despised and
oppressed people; we had no refuge but God.
He heard our cries, saw our tears, and wonderfully delivered us.

Bless the Lord that he is "a man of war!"
"I am that I am" is his name. Mr. and Mrs.
Phileos and their daughter opened a school in
Albany for colored children of both sexes.
This was joyful news to me. I had saved a
little money from my earnings, and my father
promised to help me; so I started with hopes,
expecting in a short time to be able to understand the Bible, and read and write well.
Again was I doomed to disappointment: for
some inexplicable reason, the family left the
place in a few weeks after beginning the
school. My poor heart sank within me. I
could scarcely speak for constant weeping.
That was my last schooling. Being quite a
young woman, I was obliged to work, and
study the Bible as best I could. The dear
Holy Spirit helped me wonderfully to understand the precious Word.

Through temptation I was brought into great distress of mind; the enemy of souls thrust sore at me; but I was saved from falling into his snares—saved in the hour of trial from my impetuous spirit, by the angel of the Lord standing in the gap, staying me in my course.

"Oh, bless the name of Jesus! he maketh the rebel a
       priest and king;
He hath bought me and taught me the new song to sing."

I continued to live in an up-and-down way for more than a year, when there came to our church an old man and his wife, who, when speaking in meeting, told of the trouble they once had had in trying to overcome their temper, subdue their pride, etc. But they took all to Jesus, believing his blood could wash them clean and sanctify them wholly to himself; and, oh! the peace, the sweet peace, they had enjoyed ever since. Their words thrilled me through and through.

I at once understood what I needed. Though I had read in my Bible many things they told me, I had never understood what I read. I needed a Philip to teach me.

I told my parents, my minister, and my leader that I wanted to be sanctified. They told me sanctification was for the aged and persons about to die, and not for one like me.

All they said did me no good. I had wandered
in the wilderness a long time, and now that I
could see a ray of the light for which I had so
long sought, I could not rest day nor night
until I was free.

I wanted to go and visit these old people
who had been sanctified, but my mother said:
" No, you can't go; you are half crazy now, and
these people don't know what they are talking
about." To have my mother refuse my request
so peremptorily made me very sorrowful for
many days. Darkness came upon me, and my
listress was greater than before, for, instead of
following the true light, I was turned away
from it.

CHAPTER X.

Disobedience, but Happy Results.

FINALLY, I did something I never had done before : I deliberately disobeyed my mother. I visited these old saints, weeping as though my heart would break. When I grew calm, I told them all my troubles, and asked them what I must do to get rid of them. They told me that sanctification was for the young believer, as well as the old. These words were a portion in due season. After talking a long time, and they had prayed with me, I returned home, though not yet satisfied.

I remained in this condition more than a week, going many times to my secret place of prayer, which was behind the chimney in the garret of our house. None but those who have passed up this way know how wretched every moment of my life was. I thought I must die. But truly, God does make his little ones ministering angels — sending them forth on missions of love and mercy. So he sent that dear old mother in Israel to me one fine morning in May. At the sight of her my heart seemed to

melt within me, so unexpected, and yet so
much desired was her visit. Oh, bless the
Lord for sanctified men and women!

There was no one at home except the
younger children, so our coming together was
uninterrupted. She read and explained many
passages of Scripture to me, such as, John
xvii; 1 Thess. iv. 3; v. 23; 1 Cor. vi. 9–12;
Heb. ii. 11; and many others—carefully mark-
ing them in my Bible. All this had been as a
sealed book to me until now. Glory to Jesus!
the seals were broken and light began to shine
upon the blessed Word of God as I had never
seen it before.

The second day after that pilgrim's visit,
while waiting on the Lord, my large desire
was granted, through faith in my precious
Saviour. The glory of God seemed almost to
prostrate me to the floor. There was, indeed,
a weight of glory resting upon me. I sang
with all my heart,

"This is the way I long have sought,
And mourned because I found it not."

Glory to the Father! glory to the Son! and
glory to the Holy Ghost! who hath plucked
me as a brand from the burning, and sealed
me unto eternal life. I no longer hoped for
glory, but I had the full assurance of it. Praise

the Lord for Paul-like faith! "I am crucified with Christ: nevertheless, I live; yet not I, but Christ liveth in me." This, my constant prayer, was answered, that I might be strengthened with might by his Spirit in the inner man; that being rooted and grounded in love, I might be able to comprehend with all saints what is the length, and breadth, and heighth, and depth, and to know the love of Christ which passeth knowledge, and be filled with all the fullness of God.

I had been afraid to tell my mother I was praying for sanctification, but when the "old man" was cast out of my heart, and perfect love took possession, I lost all fear. I went straight to my mother and told her I was sanctified. She was astonished, and called my father and told him what I had said. He was amazed as well, but said not a word. I at once began to read to them out of my Bible, and to many others, thinking, in my simplicity, that they would believe and receive the same blessing at once. To the glory of God, some did believe and were saved, but many were too wise to be taught by a child—too good to be made better.

From this time, many, who had been my warmest friends, and seemed to think me a Christian, turned against me, saying I did not

know what I was talking about – that there
was no such thing as sanctification and holiness in this life — and that the devil had
deluded me into self-righteousness. Many of
them fought holiness with more zeal and vigor
than they did sin. Amid all this, I had that
sweet peace that passeth all understanding
springing up within my soul like a perennial
fountain—glory to the precious blood of Jesus!

"The King of heaven and earth
Deigns to dwell with mortals here."

CHAPTER XI.

A Religion as Old as the Bible.

THE pastor of our church visited me one day, to talk about my "new religion," as he called it. I took my Bible and read many of my choice passages to him, such as — "Come and hear, all ye that fear God, and I will declare what he hath done for my soul." (Psa. lxvi. 16) "Blessed is he whose transgression is forgiven, whose sin is covered." (Psa. xxxii. 1.) While reading this verse, my whole being was so filled with the glory of God that I exclaimed: "Glory to Jesus! he has freed me from the guilt of sin, and sin hath no longer dominion over me; Christ makes me holy as well as happy."

I also read these words from Ezekiel xxxvi.: "Then will I sprinkle clean water upon you, and ye shall be clean; from all your filthiness and from all your idols will I cleanse you; a new heart also will I give you, and a new spirit will I put within you, and I will take away

the stony heart out of your flesh, and I will
give you a heart of flesh. And I will put my
Spirit within you, and cause you to walk in
my statutes, and ye shall keep my judgments,
and do them."

I stopped reading, and asked the preacher
to explain these last verses to me. He replied:
"They are all well enough; but you must
remember that you are too young to read and
dictate to persons older than yourself, and
many in the church are dissatisfied with the
way you are talking and acting." As he
answered me, the Lord spoke to my heart and
glory filled my soul. I said : " My dear minister, I wish they would all go to Jesus, in prayer
and faith, and he will teach them as he has
taught me." As the minister left me, I involuntarily burst forth into praises :

"My soul is full of glory inspiring my tongue,
　Could I meet with angels I would sing them a song."

Though my gifts were but small, I could not
be shaken by what man might think or say.

I continued day by day, month after month,
to walk in the light as He is in the light,
having fellowship with the Trinity and those
aged saints. The blood of Jesus Christ cleansed
me from all sin, and enabled me to rejoice in
persecution.

Bless the Lord, O my soul, for this wonderful
salvation, that snatched me as a brand from
the burning, even me, a poor, ignorant girl!

And will he not do for all what he did for
me? Yes, yes; God is no respecter of persons.
Jesus' blood will wash away all your sin and
make you whiter than snow.

CHAPTER XII.

My Marriage.

Soon after my conversion, a young man,
who had accompanied me to places of amusement, and for whom I had formed quite an
attachment, professed faith in Christ and
united with the same church to which I
belonged. A few months after, he made me
an offer of marriage. I struggled not a little
to banish the thought from my mind, chiefly
because he was not sanctified. But my feelings were so strongly enlisted that I felt sure
he would some day be my husband. I read to
him and talked to him on the subject of a
cleansed heart. He assented to all my argu-

ments, saying he believed and would seek for it.

The few weeks that he remained with us I labored hard with him for his deliverance, but he left us to go to Boston, Mass. We cor-responded regularly, he telling me of his relig-ious enjoyment, but that he did not hear any-thing about sanctification. Great was my anx-iety lest the devil should steal away the good seed out of his heart. The Lord, and he only, knows how many times I besought him to let the clear light of holiness shine into that man's heart. Through all this my mind was stayed upon God; I rested in the will of the Lord.

One night, about a month after his depart-ure, I could not sleep, the tempter being unu-sually busy with me. Rising, I prostrated myself before the Lord. While thus upon my face, these words of God came to me: "For we have not an high priest which cannot be touched with the feeling of our infirmities; but was in all points tempted like as we are, yet without sin." (Heb. iv. 15.) I at once rose up, thanking God for his precious words: I took my Bible and read them over and over again; also the eighteenth verse of the second chapter of Hebrews. I was not conscious of having committed sin, and I cried out: " Leave

[4]

me, Satan; I am the Lord's." At that the
tempter left, and I surrendered myself and all
my interests into the hands of God. Glory to
his holy name! "For it pleased the Father
that in him should all fullness dwell," and of
his fullness have I received, and grace for
grace.

> "Praise God from whom all blessings flow,
> Praise him all creatures here below."

The day following this night of temptation
was one of great peace — peace flowing as a
river, even to overflowing its banks, and such
glory of the Lord appeared as to almost deprive
me of bodily powers. I forgot all toil and care.

This was just a year after my heart was
emptied of sin. Through faith I received the
Saviour, and in the same have continued ever
since and proved him able to keep from sin.
Bless God! all my desires are satisfied in him.
He is indeed my reconciled God, the Christ
Jesus whose precious blood is all my righteous-
ness.

> "Nought of good that I have done,
> Nothing but the blood of Jesus."

Glory to the blood that hath bought me!
glory to the blood that hath cleansed me!
glory to the blood that keeps me clean!—me, a
brand plucked from the fire.

George returned in about a year to claim me as his bride. He still gave evidence of being a Christian, but had not been cleansed from the carnal mind. I still continued to pray for his sanctification, and desired that it should take place before our union, but I was so much attached to him that I could not . resist his pleadings; so, at the appointed time, we were married, in the church, in the presence of a large number of people, many of whom followed us to my father's house to offer their congratulations.

We staid at home but one day after the ceremony. This day I spent in preparing for our departure and in taking leave of my friends. Tenderly as I loved my parents, much as I loved the church, yet I found myself quite willing to leave them all in the divine appointment.

The day following, accompanied by several friends, we started for Boston, in an old-fashioned stage-coach, there being no railroads at that time. As I rode along I admired the goodness of God, and my heart overflowed with gratitude to him, who had blessed me with power to choose his will and make me able to say with truth, " I gladly forsake all to follow thee."

Once, the thought of leaving my father's

house, to go among strangers, would have been terrible, but now I rejoiced in being so favored as to be called to make this little sacrifice, and evince my love to him who saith : "He that loveth father or mother more than me is not worthy of me."

CHAPTER XIII.

Removal to Boston—The Work of Full Salvation.

ON our arrival in Boston, after a long, wearisome journey, we went at once to the house of Mrs. Burrows, where my husband had made arrangements for me to board while he was away at work during the week. He worked in Chelsea, and could not come to look after my welfare but once a week. The boarders in this house were mostly gentlemen, nearly all of whom were out of Christ. Mrs. Burrows was a church-member, but knew nothing of the full joys of salvation.

I went to church the first Sabbath I was there, remained at class-meeting, gave my letter of membership to the minister, and was received into the church. In giving my first testimony, I told of my thorough and happy conversion, and of my sanctification as a second, distinct work of the Holy Ghost.

After class-meeting, a good many came to me, asking questions about sanctification; others stood off in groups, talking, while a few followed me to my boarding-house. They all seemed very much excited over what I had told them. I began to see that it was not the voice of man that had bidden me go out from the land of my nativity and from my kindred, but the voice of my dear Lord I was completely prepared for all that followed, knowing that "All things work together for good to them that love God." Change of people, places and circumstances, weighed nothing with me, for I had a safe abiding place with my Father. Some people had been to me in such an unchristianlike spirit that I had spoken to and about them in rather an incautious manner. I now more and more saw the great need of ordering all my words as in the immediate presence of God, that I might be able to maintain that purity of lips and life which the Gospel required. God is holy, and if I would enjoy constant communion with him I must guard every avenue of my soul, and watch

every thought of my heart and word of my
tongue, that I may be blameless before him in
love. The Lord help me evermore to be upon
my guard, and having done all, to stand.
Amen and amen.

In a few months my husband rented a house
just across the road from my boarding-house,
and I went to housekeeping. "Mam" Riley,
a most excellent Christian, became as a mother
to me in this strange land, far from my own
dear mother. Bless the Lord! He supplied
all my needs. "Mam" Riley had two grown
daughters, one about my own age, married,
who had two children. They were dear Christian women, and like sisters to me. The
mother thought she once enjoyed the blessing
of heart purity, but the girls had not heard of
such a thing as being sanctified and permitted
to live. The elder girl, who was a consump-
tive and in delicate health, soon became deeply
interested in the subject. She began to hun-
ger and thirst after righteousness, and did not
rest until she was washed and made clean in
the blood of Jesus. Her clear, definite testimony had a great effect upon the church, as
her family was one of the first in point of
wealth and standing in the community.

God wonderfully honored the faith of this
young saint in her ceaseless labor for others.

We attended meetings and visited from house
to house, together, almost constantly, when she
was able to go out. Glory to God! the church
became much aroused; some plunged into the
ocean of perfect love, and came forth testifying
to the power of the blood. Others disbelieved
and ridiculed this "foolish doctrine," as they
called it, saying it was just as impossible to
live without committing sin as it was to live
without eating, and brought disjointed passages of Scripture to bear them out.

CHAPTER XIV.

Early Fruit Gathered Home.

AFTER I went to Boston I was much drawn
out in prayer for the sanctification of believers.
Notwithstanding the enemy labored by various
means to hinder the work of grace, yet the
Lord wrought a wonderful change in many.

The mother of my friend received a fresh
baptism, and came back into the light, praising the Lord. That the Holy Spirit might
keep my dear "Mam" Riley pure until death,
was my prayer.

The health of my dear friend, Mrs. Simpson,
began rapidly to fail. One morning, in reply
to my question as to her health, she said:
"Dear sister, I have been in great pain through
the night, but you know Jesus said, 'I will
never leave thee nor forsake thee.' Praise God,
who has been with me in great mercy through
the darkness of the night." I remained with
her the following night, and such calmness,
patience and resignation through suffering, I
never had witnessed. Toward morning she
was more easy, and asked for her husband.

When he came, she embraced him, repeated passages of Scripture to him, and exhorted him, as she had many times before, to receive God in all his fullness.

There, in that death-chamber, in the still-ness of night, we prayed for that pious and exemplary man, that he might present his body a living sacrifice. He was deeply moved upon by the Holy Spirit, so that he cried aloud for deliverance; but almost on the instant began to doubt, and left the room. His wife requested me to read and talk to her about Jesus, which I did, and she was filled with heavenly joy and shouted aloud: "Oh, the blood, the precious blood of Jesus cleanses me now!"

Her mother, who was sleeping in an adjoin-ing room, was awakened by the noise and came in, saying, as she did so: "This room is filled with the glory of God. Hallelujah! Amen."

As the morning dawned, Mrs. Simpson sank into a quiet slumber, which lasted several hours. She awoke singing:

"How happy are they who their Saviour obey,
And have laid up their treasure above."

She was comparatively free from pain for several days, though very weak. She talked to all who came to see her of salvation free and

full. Her last morning on earth came. She
was peaceful and serene, with a heavenly smile
upon her countenance. She asked me to pray,
which I did with streaming eyes and quivering voice. She then asked us to sing the
hymn,

> "Oh, for a thousand tongues to sing
> My great Redeemer's praise."

She sang with us in a much stronger voice
than she had used for many days. As we sang
the last verse, she raised herself up in bed,
clapped her hands and cried: "He sets the
prisoner free! Glory! glory! I am free! They
have come for me!" She pointed toward the
east. Her mother asked her who had come.

She said: "Don't you see the chariot and
horses? Glory! glory to the blood!"

She dropped back upon her pillow, and was
gone. She had stepped aboard the chariot,
which we could not see, but we felt the fire.

While many in the room were weeping, her
mother shed not a tear, but shouted, "Glory to
God!" Then, with her own hands, she assisted
in arranging and preparing the remains for
burial. Thus did another sanctified saint
enter into eternal life. Though her period of
sanctification was short, it was full of precious
fruit.

CHAPTER XV.

New and Unpleasant Revelations.

My husband had always treated the subject
of heart purity with favor, but now he began
to speak against it. He said I was getting
more crazy every day, and getting others in
the same way, and that if I did not stop he
would send me back home or to the crazy-
house. I questioned him closely respecting
the state of his mind, feeling that he had been
prejudiced. I did not attempt to contend with
him on the danger and fallacy of his notions,
but simply asked what his state of grace was,
if God should require his soul of him then.
He gave me no answer until I insisted upon
one. Then he said: "Julia, I don't think I
can ever believe myself as holy as you think
you are."

I then urged him to believe in Christ's holiness, if he had no faith in the power of the
blood of Christ to cleanse from all sin. He

that hath this hope purifies himself as God is pure. We knelt in prayer together, my husband leading, and he seemed much affected while praying. To me it was à precious season, though there was an indescribable something between us—something dark and high. As I looked at it, these words of the poet came to me:

> "God moves in a mysterious way,
> His wonders to perform."

From that time I never beheld my husband's face clear and distinct, as before, the dark shadow being ever present. This caused me not a little anxiety and many prayers. Soon after, he accepted an offer to go to sea for six months, leaving me to draw half of his wages. To this arrangement I reluctantly consented, fully realizing how lonely I should be among strangers. Had it not been for dear "Mam" Riley, I could hardly have endured it. Her precept and example taught me to lean more heavily on Christ for support. God gave me these precious words: "Be careful for nothing, but in everything, by prayer and supplication, with thanksgiving, let your requests be made known unto God." Truly, God is the great Arbiter of all events, and "because he lives, I shall live also."

The day my husband went on ship-board was one of close trial and great inward conflicts. It was difficult for me to mark the exact line between disapprobation and Christian forbearance and patient love. How I longed for wisdom to meet everything in a spirit of meekness and fear, that I might not be surprised into evil or hindered from improving all things to the glory of God.

While under this apparent cloud, I took the Bible to my closet, asking Divine aid. As I opened the book, my eyes fell on these words: "For thy Maker is thine husband." I then read the fifty-fourth chapter of Isaiah over and over again. It seemed to me that I had never seen it before. I went forth glorifying God.

CHAPTER XVI.

A Long-Lost Brother Found.

Having no children, I had a good deal of leisure after my husband's departure, so I visited many of the poor and forsaken ones, reading and talking to them of Jesus, the Saviour. One day I was directed by the Spirit to visit the Marine Hospital. In passing through one of the wards I heard myself called by my maiden name. Going to the cot from whence the voice came, I beheld what seemed to me a human skeleton. As I looked I began to see our family likeness, and recognized my eldest brother, who left home many years before, when I was quite young. Not hearing from him, we had mourned him as dead. With a feeble voice, he told me of his roving and seafaring life; "and now, sister," he said, "I am dying."

I asked him if he was willing to die—if he was ready to stand before God. "No, oh, no!" he said. I entreated him to pray. He shook his head, saying, "I can't pray; my heart is too hard, and my mind dark and bewildered," and then cried out, in the agony of his soul, "Oh, that dreadful, burning hell! how can I escape it?"

I urged him to pray, and to believe that Jesus died for all. I prayed for him, and staid with him as much as possible. One morning, when I went to see him, I was shown his life-less remains in the dead-house. This was indeed, a solemn time for me.

I had very little hope in my brother's death. But there is an High Priest who ever liveth to make intercession for all, and I trust that he prevailed. The Lord is the Judge of all the earth, and all souls are in his hands, and he will in no wise clear the guilty, though merciful and wise. Willful unbelief is a crying sin, and will not be passed by without punishment. God judges righteously, and is the avenger of all sin. Justice is meted out to all, either here or in eternity. Praise the Lord! My whole soul joins in saying, Praise the Lord!

God, in great mercy, returned my husband to me in safety, for which I bowed in great thankfulness. George told me that the ship was a poor place to serve the Lord, and that the most he heard was oaths. He said that sometimes he would slip away and pray, and that, upon one occasion, the captain came upon him unawares, and called him "a fool," and told him to get up and go to work. Notwith- standing all this, my husband shipped for a second voyage. Praise the Lord! he saved me from a painful feeling at parting. With joy could I say, "Thou everywhere-present God! thy will be done."

During the year I had been from home, let- ters from my parents and friends had come to me quite often, filling me with gladness and thanksgiving for the many blessings and cheering words they contained. But now a letter came bringing the intelligence that my family were about to move to Silver Lake, which was much farther from me. I trem- blingly went to my heavenly Father, who gave me grace and strength at once.

CHAPTER XVII.

My Call to Preach the Gospel.

For months I had been moved upon to exhort and pray with the people, in my visits from house to house; and in meetings my whole soul seemed drawn out for the salvation of souls. The love of Christ in me was not limited. Some of my mistaken friends said I was too forward, but a desire to work for the Master, and to promote the glory of his kingdom in the salvation of souls, was food to my poor soul.

When called of God, on a particular occasion, to a definite work, I said, "No, Lord, not me." Day by day I was more impressed that God would have me work in his vineyard. I thought it could not be that I was called to preach—I, so weak and ignorant. Still, I knew all things were possible with God, even to confounding the wise by the foolish things of this earth. Yet in me there was a shrinking.

[5]

I took all my doubts and fears to the Lord in prayer, when, what seemed to be an angel, made his appearance. In his hand was a scroll, on which were these words: "Thee have I chosen to preach my Gospel without delay." The moment my eyes saw it, it appeared to be printed on my heart. The angel was gone in an instant, and I, in agony, cried out, "Lord, I cannot do it!" It was eleven o'clock in the morning, yet everything grew dark as night. The darkness was so great that I feared to stir.

At last "Mam" Riley entered. As she did so, the room grew lighter, and I arose from my knees. My heart was so heavy I scarce could speak. Dear "Mam" Riley saw my distress, and soon left·me.

From that day my appetite failed me and sleep fled from my eyes. I seemed as one tormented. I prayed, but felt no better. I belonged to a band of sisters whom I loved dearly, and to them I partially opened my mind. One of them seemed to understand my case at once, and advised me to do as God had bid me, or I would never be happy here or here-after. But it seemed too hard—I could not give up and obey.

One night, as I lay weeping and beseeching the dear Lord to remove this burden from me, there appeared the same angel that came to me before, and on his breast were these words: " You are lost unless you obey God's righteous commands." I saw the writing, and that was enough. I covered my head and awoke my husband, who had returned a few days before. He asked me why I trembled so, but I had not power to answer him. I remained in that condition until morning, when I tried to arise and go about my usual duties, but was too ill. Then my husband called a physician, who prescribed medicine, but it did me no good.

I had always been opposed to the preaching of women, and had spoken against it, though, I acknowledge, without foundation. This rose before me like a mountain, and when I thought of the difficulties they had to encounter, both from professors and non-professors, I shrank back and cried, " Lord, I cannot go!"

The trouble my heavenly Father has had to keep me out of the fire that is never quenched, he alone knoweth. My husband and friends said I would die or go crazy if something favorable did not take place soon. I expected to die and be lost, knowing I had been enlightened and had tasted the heavenly gift. I read again and again the sixth chapter of Hebrews.

CHAPTER XVIII.

Heavenly Visitations Again.

Nearly two months from the time I first
saw the angel, I said that I would do anything
or go anywhere for God, if it were made plain
to me. He took me at my word, and sent the
angel again with this message: "You have I
chosen to go in my name and warn the people
of their sins." I bowed my head and said, "I
will go, Lord."

That moment I felt a joy and peace I had
not known for months. But strange as it may
appear, it is not the less true, that, ere one
hour had passed, I began to reason thus :"I am
elected to preach the Gospel without the requisite qualifications, and, besides, my parents
and friends will forsake me and turn against
me; and I regret that I made a promise." At
that instant all the joy and peace I had felt
left me, and I thought I was standing on the
brink of hell, and heard the devil say: "Let
her go! let her go! I will catch her." Reader,

can you imagine how I felt? If you were ever snatched from the mouth of hell, you can, in part, realize my feelings.

I continued in this state for some time, when, on a Sabbath evening—ah! that memorable Sabbath evening—while engaged in fervent prayer, the same supernatural presence came to me once more and took me by the hand. At that moment I became lost to everything of this world. The angel led me to a place where there was a large tree, the branches of which seemed to extend either way beyond sight. Beneath it sat, as I thought, God the Father, the Son, and the Holy Spirit, besides many others, whom I thought were angels. I was led before them: they looked me over from head to foot, but said nothing. Finally, the Father said to me : " Before these people make your choice, whether you will obey me or go from this place to eternal misery and pain." I answered not a word. He then took me by the hand to lead me, as I thought, to hell, when I cried out, " I will obey thee, Lord!" He then pointed my hand in different directions, and asked if I would go there. I replied, " Yes, Lord." He then led me, all the others following, till we came to a place where there was a great quantity of water, which looked like silver, where we made a halt. My hand was given to Christ, who led me into the water and stripped me of my clothing, which at once vanished from sight. Christ then appeared to wash me, the water feeling quite warm.

During this operation, all the others stood on the bank, looking on in profound silence. When the washing was ended, the sweetest music I had ever heard greeted my ears. We walked to the shore, where an angel stood with a clean, white robe, which the Father at once put on me. In an instant I appeared to be changed into an angel. The whole company looked at me with delight, and began to make a noise which I called shouting. We all marched back with music. When we reached the tree to which the angel first led me, it hung full of fruit, which I had not seen before. The Holy Ghost plucked some and gave me, and the rest helped themselves. We sat down and ate of the fruit, which had a taste like nothing I had ever tasted before. When we had finished, we all arose and gave another shout. Then God the Father said to me: " You are now prepared, and must go where I have commanded you." I replied, "If I go, they will not believe me." Christ then appeared to write something with a golden pen and golden ink, upon golden paper. Then he rolled it up, and said to me : " Put this in your bosom, and, wherever you go, show it, and they will know that I have sent you to proclaim salvation to all." He then put it into my bosom, and they all went with me to a bright, shining gate, singing and shouting. Here they embraced me, and I found myself once more on earth.

When I came to myself, I found that several friends had been with me all night, and my husband had called a physician, but he had not been able to do anything for me. He ordered those around me to keep very quiet, or to go home. He returned in the morning, when I told him, in part, my story. He seemed amazed, but made no answer, and left me.

Several friends were in, during the day. While talking to them, I would, without thinking, put my hand into my bosom, to show them my letter of authority. But I soon found, as my friends told me, it was in my heart, and was to be shown in my life, instead of in my hand. Among others, my minister, Jehial C. Beman, came to see me. He looked very coldly upon me and said: " I guess you will find out your mistake before you are many months older." He was a scholar, and a fine speaker; and the sneering, indifferent way in which he addressed me, said most plainly:

"You don't know anything." I replied: "My gifts are very small, I know, but I can no longer be shaken by what you or any one else may think or say."

⚜

CHAPTER XIX.

Public Effort—Excommunication.

From this time the opposition to my life-work commenced, instigated by the minister, Mr. Beman. Many in the church were anxious to have me preach in the hall, where our meetings were held at that time, and were not a little astonished at the minister's cool treatment of me. At length two of the trustees got some of the elder sisters to call on the minister and ask him to let me preach. His answer was: "No; she can't preach her holiness stuff here, and I am astonished that you should ask it of me." The sisters said he seemed to be in quite a rage, although he said he was not angry.

There being no meeting of the society on Monday evening, a brother in the church 'opened his house to me, that I might preach, which displeased Mr. Beman very much. He appointed a committee to wait upon the brother and sister who had opened their doors to me, to tell them they must not allow any more meetings of that kind, and that they must abide by the rules of the church, making them believe they would be excommunicated if they disobeyed him. I happened to be present at this interview, and the committee remonstrated with me for the course I had taken. I told them my business was with the Lord, and wherever I found a door opened I intended to go in and work for my Master.

There was another meeting appointed at the same place, which I, of course, attended; after which the meetings were stopped for that time, though I held many more there after these people had withdrawn from Mr. Beman's church.

I then held meetings in my own house; whereat the minister told the members that if they attended them he would deal with them, for they were breaking the rules of the church. When he found that I continued the meetings, and that the Lord was blessing my feeble efforts, he sent a committee of two to ask me if I considered myself a member of his church. I told them I did, and should con-

tinue to do so until I had done something
worthy of dismembership.

At this, Mr. Beman sent another committee
with a note, asking me to meet him with the
committee, which I did. He asked me a number of questions, nearly all of which I have
forgotten. One, however, I do remember: he
asked if I was willing to comply with the
rules of the discipline. To this I answered:
"Not if the discipline prohibits me from doing
what God has bidden me to do; I fear God
more than man." Similar questions were
asked and answered in the same manner.
The committee said what they wished to say,
and then told me I could go home. When I
reached the door, I turned and said: "I now
shake off the dust of my feet as a witness
against you. See to it that this meeting does
not rise in judgment against you."

The next evening, one of the committee
came to me and told me that I was no longer a
member of the church, because I had violated
the rules of the discipline by preaching.

When this action became known, the people
wondered how any one could be excommunicated for trying to do good. I did not say
much, and my friends simply said I had done
nothing but hold meetings. Others, anxious
to know the particulars, asked the minister

what the trouble was. He told them he had
given me the privilege of speaking or preaching as long as I chose, but that he could not
give me the right to use the pulpit, and that I
was not satisfied with any other place. Also,
that I had appointed meeting on the evening
of his meetings, which was a thing no member
had a right to do. For these reasons he said
he had turned me out of the church.

Now, if the people who repeated this to me
told the truth—and I have no doubt but they
did—Mr. Beman told an actual falsehood. I
had never asked for his pulpit, but had told
him and others, repeatedly, that I did not care
where I stood—any corner of the hall would
do. To which Mr. Beman had answered:
"You cannot have any place in the hall."
Then I said: "I'll preach in a private house."
He answered me: "No, not in this place; I
am stationed over all Boston." He was determined I should not preach in the city of Boston. To cover up his deceptive, unrighteous
course toward me, he told the above false-
hoods.

From his statements, many erroneous stories
concerning me gained credence with a large
number of people. At that time, I thought it
my duty as well as privilege to address a letter
to the Conference, which I took to them in

person, stating all the facts. At the same
time I told them it was not in the power of
Mr. Beman, or any one else, to truthfully bring
anything against my moral or religious character—that my only offence was in trying to
preach the Gospel of Christ—and that I cherished no ill feelings toward Mr. Beman or any
one else, but that I desired the Conference to
give the case an impartial hearing, and then
give me a written statement expressive of
their opinion. I also said I considered myself
a member of the Conference, and should do so
until they said I was not, and gave me their
reasons, that I might let the world know what
my offence had been.

My letter was slightingly noticed, and then
thrown under the table. Why should they
notice it? It was only the grievance of a
woman, and there was no justice meted out to
women in those days. Even ministers of
Christ did not feel that women had any rights
which they were bound to respect.

CHAPTER XX.

Women in the Gospel.

THIRTY years ago there could scarcely a person be found, in the churches, to sympathize with any one who talked of Holiness. But, in my simplicity, I did think that a body of Christian ministers would understand my case and judge righteously. I was, however, disappointed.

It is no little thing to feel that every man's hand is against us, and ours against every man, as seemed to be the case with me at this time; yet how precious, if Jesus but be with us. In this severe trial I had constant access to God, and a clear consciousness that he heard me; yet I did not seem to have that plenitude of the Spirit that I had before. I realized most keenly that the closer the communion that may have existed, the keener the suffering of the slightest departure from God. Unbroken communion can only be retained by a constant application of the blood which cleanseth.

Though I did not wish to pain any one, neither could I please any one only as I was led
by the Holy Spirit. I saw, as never before,
that the best men were liable to err, and that
the only safe way was to fall on Christ, even
though censure and reproach fell upon me for
obeying his voice. Man's opinion weighed
nothing with me, for my commission was from
heaven, and my reward was with the Most
High.

I could not believe that it was a short-lived
impulse or spasmodic influence that impelled
me to preach. I read that on the day of Pentecost was the Scripture fulfilled as found in
Joel ii. 28, 29; and it certainly will not be
denied that women as well as men were at
that time filled with the Holy Ghost, because
it is expressly stated that women were among
those who continued in prayer and supplication, waiting for the fulfillment of the promise.
Women and men are classed together, and if
the power to preach the Gospel is short-lived
and spasmodic in the case of women, it must
be equally so in that of men; and if women
have lost the gift of prophecy, so have men.

We are sometimes told that if a woman pre-
tends to a Divine call, and thereon grounds the
right to plead the cause of a crucified Redeemer
in public, she will be believed when she shows

credentials from heaven; that is, when she works a miracle. If it be necessary to prove one's right to preach the Gospel, I ask of my brethren to show me their credentials, or I can not believe in the propriety of their ministry.

But the Bible puts an end to this strife when it says: " There is neither male nor female in Christ Jesus." Philip had four daughters that prophesied, or preached. Paul called Priscilla, as well as Aquila, his " helper," or, as in the Greek, his "fellow-laborer." Rom. xv. 3; 2 Cor. viii. 23; Phil. ii. 5; 1 Thess. iii. 2. The same word, which, in our common translation, is now rendered a "servant of the church," in speaking of Phebe (Rom. xix. 1.), is rendered "minister" when applied to Tychicus. Eph. vi. 21. When Paul said, "Help those women who labor with me in the Gospel," he certainly meant that they did more than to pour out tea. In the eleventh chapter of First Corinthians Paul gives directions, to men and women, how they should appear when they prophesy or pray in public assemblies; and he defines prophesying to be speaking to edification, exhortation and comfort.

I may further remark that the conduct of holy women is recorded in Scripture as an example to others of their sex. And in the early ages of Christianity many women were happy and glorious in martyrdom. How nobly, how heroically, too, in later ages, have women suffered persecution and death for the name of the Lord Jesus.

In looking over these facts, I could see no miracle wrought for those women more than in myself.

Though opposed, I went forth laboring for God, and he owned and blessed my labors, and has done so wherever I have been until this day. And while I walk obediently, I know he will, though hell may rage and vent its spite.

CHAPTER XXI.

The Lord Leadeth—Labor in Philadelphia.

As I left the Conference, God wonderfully filled my heart with his love, so that, as I passed from place to place, meeting one and another of the ministers, my heart went out in love to each of them as though he had been my father; and the language of 1 Pet. i. 7, came forcibly to my mind: "The trial of our faith is much more precious than of gold that perisheth, though it be tried by fire." Fiery trials are not strange things to the Lord's anointed. The rejoicing in them is born only of the Holy Spirit. Oh, praise his holy name for a circumcised heart, teaching us that each trial of our faith hath its commission from the Father of spirits. Each wave of trial bears the Galilean Pilot on its crest. Listen: his voice is in the storm, and winds and waves obey that voice: "It is I; be not afraid." He has promised us help and safety in the fires, and not escape from them.

(6)

"And hereby we know that he abideth in us, by the Spirit which he hath given us." 1 John iii. 24. Giory to the Lamb for the witness of the Holy Spirit! He knoweth that every step I have taken has been for the glory of God and the good of souls. How‑ver much I may have erred in judgment, it has been the fault of my head and not of my heart. I sleep, but my heart waketh; bless the Lord.

Had this opposition come from the world, it would have seemed as nothing. But coming, as it did, from those who had been much blessed—blessed with me—and who had once been friends of mine, it touched a tender spot; and had it not been for the precious blood of Jesus, I should have been lost.

While in Philadelphia, attending the Conference, I became acquainted with three sisters who believed they were called to public labors in their Master's vineyard. But they had been so opposed, they were very much distressed and shrank from their duty. One of them professed sanctification. They had met with more opposition from ministers than from any one else.

After the Conference had adjourned, I proposed to these sisters to procure a place and hold a series of meetings. They were pleased with the idea, and were willing to help if I would take charge of the meetings. They apprehended some difficulty, as there had never been a meeting there under the sole charge of women. The language of my heart was:

"Only Thou my Leader be
And I still will follow Thee."

Trusting in my Leader, I went on with the work. I hired a large place in Canal street, and there we opened our meetings, which continued eleven nights, and over one Sabbath. The room was crowded every night—some coming to receive good, others to criticise, sneer, and say hard things against us.

One of the sisters left us after a day or two, fearing that the Church to which she belonged would disown her if she continued to assist us. We regretted this very much, but could only say, "An enemy hath done this."

These meetings were a time of refreshing from the presence of the Lord. Many were converted, and a few stepped into the fountain of cleansing.

Some of the ministers, who remained in the city after the Conference, attended our meetings, and occasionally asked us if we were organizing a new Conference, with a view of drawing out from the churches. This was simply to ridicule our meeting.

We closed with a love-feast, which caused such a stir among the ministers and many of the church-members, that we could not imagine what the end would be. They seemed to think we had well nigh committed the unpardonable sin.

CHAPTER XXII.

A Visit to my Parents—Further Labors.

Some of the dear sisters accompanied me to Flatbush, where I assisted in a bush meeting. The Lord met the people in great power, and I doubt not there are many souls in glory to-day praising God for that meeting.

From that place I went home to my father's house in Binghamton, N. Y. They were filled with joy to have me with them once more, after an absence of six years. As my mother embraced me, she exclaimed: "So you are a preacher, are you?" I replied: "So they say." "Well, Julia," said she, "when I first heard that you were a preacher, I said that I would rather hear you were dead." These words, coming so unexpectedly from my mother, filled me with anguish. Was I to meet opposition here, too? But my mother, with streaming eyes, continued: " My dear daughter, it is all past now. I have heard from those who have attended your meetings what the Lord has done for you, and I am satisfied."

My stay in Binghamton was protracted several months. I held meetings in and around the town, to the acceptance of the people, and, I trust, to the glory of God. I felt perfectly satisfied, when the time came for me to leave, that my work was all for the Lord, and my soul was filled with joy and thankfulness for salvation. Before leaving, my parents decided to move to Boston, which they did soon after.

I left Binghamton the first of February, 1855, in company with the Rev. Henry Johnson and his wife, for Ithaca, N. Y., where I labored a short time. I met with some opposition from one of the A. M. E. Church trustees. He said a woman should not preach in the church. Beloved, the God we serve fights all our battles, and before I left the place that trustee was one of the most faithful at my meetings, and was very kind to assist me on my journey when I left Ithaca. I stopped one night at Owego, at Brother Loyd's, and I also stopped for a short time at Onondaga, returned to Ithaca on the 14th of February, and staid until the 7th of March, during which time the work of grace was greatly revived. Some believed and entered into the rest of full salvation, many were converted, and a number of backsliders were reclaimed. I held prayer-meetings from house to house. The sisters formed a woman's prayer-meeting, and the whole church seemed to be working in unison for Christ.

March 7th I took the stage for Geneva, and, arriving late at night, went to a hotel. In the morning Brother Rosel Jeffrey took me to his house and left me with his wife. He was a zealous Christian, but she scoffed at religion, and laughed and made sport during family worship. I do not know, but hope that long ere this she has ceased to ridicule the cause or the followers of Christ. In the latter part of the day Brother Condell came and invited me to his house. I found his wife a pleasant Christian woman. Sabbath afternoon I held a meeting in Brother Condell's house. The colored people had a church which the whites had given them. It was a union church, to be occupied on alternate Sundays by the Methodists and Baptists.

According to arrangement, this Sunday evening was the time for the Methodists to

occupy the church. The Rev. Dawsey, of Can-
andaigua, came to fill his appointment, but,
when we arrived at the church, the Baptist
minister, William Monroe, objected to our
holding a meeting in the house that evening,
and his members joined with him in his
unchristian course. Rather than have any
trouble, we returned to Brother Condell's
house. The minister preached and I followed
with a short exhortation. The Lord was present to bless. They made an appointment for
me to preach at the union meeting-house on
the following Tuesday evening.

Monday evening I went with some of the
sisters to the church, where there was a meeting for the purpose of forming a moral reform
society.

After the meeting, Brother Condell asked
the trustees if they had any objection to having me speak in the church the next evening.
To this, Minister Monroe and another man—I
had almost said a fiend in human shape —
answered that they did not believe in women's
preaching, and would not admit one in the
church, striving hard to justify themselves
from the Bible, which one of them held in his
unholy hands.

I arose to speak, when Mr. Monroe inter-
rupted me. After a few words I left the house.

The next afternoon, while taking tea at the house of one of the sisters, Minister Monroe came in to tell me he heard that our brethren had said they would have the church for me if they had to "shed blood." He asked me if I wanted to have anything to do with a fight of that kind. I replied: "The weapons with which I fight are not carnal, and, if I go to a place and am invited to use the weapons God has given me, I must use them to his glory."

"Well," said he, "I shall be in the pulpit at an early hour, and will not leave it though they break my head."

"Mr. Monroe," said I, "God can take you from the pulpit without breaking your head." At this he became very much excited, and raved as if he were a madman. For two hours he walked the floor, talking and reading all the time. I made him no reply and tried not to notice him, and finally he left me.

At the proper time we went to the church. It was full, but everything was in confusion. Mr. Monroe was in the pulpit. I saw at once that God could not be glorified in the midst of such a pandemonium; so I withdrew at once. I was told they kept up the contention until after ten o'clock. Mr. Monroe tried hard to get our trustees to say I should not preach in the place, but they would give him no such promise.

As I was obliged to leave in a few days, to meet other appointments, our men procured a large house, where I held a meeting the next evening. All that attended were quiet and orderly; one man arose for prayers.

Dear sisters, who are in the evangelistic work now, you may think you have hard times; but let me tell you, I feel that the lion and lamb are lying down together, as compared with the state of things twenty-five or thirty years ago. Yes, yes; our God is marching on. Glory to his name!

CHAPTER XXIII.

Indignities on Account of Color—General Conference.

I REACHED Rochester on the 16th of March, where I remained three weeks, laboring constantly for my Master, who rewarded me in the salvation of souls. Here God visited me after the same manner he did Elijah, when Elijah prayed to die. He strengthened me and bid me go forward with the promises recorded in the first chapter of Joshua.

April 21st I bade good-bye to Brother John H. Bishop's people, who had entertained me while in Rochester, and went to Binghamton to visit my parents again. I found them all well, and labored constantly for the Lord while I was there. I remained at home until the 8th of May, when I once more started out on my travels for the Lord. There was but one passenger in the stage besides myself. He gave his name as White, seemed very uneasy, and, at each stopping place, he would say : "I am afraid the public will take me for an aboli-

tionist to-day;" thus showing his dark, slave-
holding principles.

I staid one night in Oxford, at Mr. Jackson's. At six o'clock the next morning I took
passage on the canal packet "Governor Sew-
ard," with Captain George Keeler. That night,
at a late hour, I made my way into the ladies'
cabin, and, finding an empty berth, retired.
In a short time a man came into the cabin,
saying that the berths in the gentlemen's
cabin were all occupied, and he was going to
sleep in the ladies' cabin. Then he pointed
to me and said: "That nigger has no business
here. My family are coming on board the
boat at Utica, and they shall not come where a
nigger is." They called the captain, and he
ordered me to get up; but I did not stir, thinking it best not to leave the bed except by force.
Finally they left me, and the man found lodging among the seamen, swearing vengeance on
the "niggers."

The next night the boat stopped at a village, and the captain procured lodging for me
at an inn. Thus I escaped further abuse from
that ungodly man.

The second night we reached Utica, where I
staid over Sunday. Then I went to Schenectady, where I remained a few days, working for
my Master. Then I went to Albany, my old

home. Sunday afternoon I preached in Troy, and that Sunday evening in Albany, to a crowded house. There were many of my old friends and acquaintances in the audience. This was the most solemn and interesting meeting I ever held. The entire audience seemed moved to prayer and tears by the power of the Holy Ghost.

On May 21st I went to New York. During the year that followed I visited too large a number of places to mention in this little work.

I went from Philadelphia in company with thirty ministers and Bishop Brown, to attend the General Conference, which was held in Pittsburgh, Pa. The ministers chartered the conveyance, and we had a very pleasant and interesting journey. The discussions during the day and meetings at night, on the canal boat, were instructive and entertaining. A very dear sister, Ann M. Johnson, accompanied me. The grand, romantic scenery, which I beheld while crossing the Alleghany mountains, filled me with adoration and praise to the great Creator of all things. We reached Pittsburgh on the 4th of June, and the General Conference of the A. M. E. Church convened on the 6th of June. The Conference lasted two weeks, and was held with open doors.

The business common to such meetings was transacted with spirit and harmony, with few exceptions. One was, a motion to prevent Free Masons from ministering in the churches. Another, to allow all the women preachers to become members of the conferences. This caused quite a sensation, bringing many members to their feet at once. They all talked and screamed to the bishop, who could scarcely keep order. The Conference was so incensed at the brother who offered the petition that they threatened to take action against him.

I remained several weeks, laboring among the people, much to the comfort of my own soul, and, I humbly trust, to the upbuilding of my dear Master's kingdom. I found the people very kind and benevolent.

CHAPTER XXIV.

Continued Labors—Death of my Husband and Father.

From Pittsburgh I went to Cincinnati, where I found a large number of colored people of different denominations. The Methodists had a very good meeting-house on Sixth street, below Broad street. The members appeared to enjoy religion, but were very much like the world in their external appearance and cold indifference toward each other.

The station and circuit joined in holding a camp-meeting. The minister urged me very strongly to attend, which I did. Several souls professed faith in Christ at this meeting, but only one was willing to receive him in all his fullness.

After this meeting I labored in quite a number of places in Ohio. At some places I was kindly received, at others I was not allowed to labor publicly.

While thus laboring far from home, the sad intelligence of my husband's death came to me

so suddenly as to almost cause me to sink
beneath the blow. But the arm of my dear,
loving, heavenly Father sustained me, and I
was enabled to say: "Though he slay me, yet
will I trust in him." I immediately hastened
home to Boston, where I learned the particulars of my husband's death, which occurred on
ship-board several months before. None but
the dear Lord knew what my feelings were. I
dared not complain, and thus cast contempt on
my blessed Saviour, for I knew he would not
lay more upon me than I could bear. He
knows how to deliver the godly out of temptation and affliction; all events belong to him.
All we have to be careful for is, to know of a
truth that Christ is formed in our hearts the
hope of glory, and hath set up his kingdom
there, to reign over every affection and desire.
Glory to the Lamb, who giveth me power thus
to live!

After arranging my affairs at home, I went
to Albany, where my sister lived, staid a short
time with her, and held some meetings there.
Then I went to Bethlehem, where I held several meetings, one in the M. E. Church, which
was arranged only after there had been considerable controversy about letting a woman
preach in their house. From there I went to
Troy, where I also held meetings. In each of

these places this "brand plucked from the
burning" was used of God to his glory in
saving precious souls. To his name be all the
glory!

I spent one Sunday in Poughkeepsie, working for Jesus. I then went to New York,
where I took the boat for Boston. We were
detained some hours by one of the shafts
breaking. I took a very severe cold by being
compelled to sit on deck all night, in the cold,
damp air—prejudice not permitting one of my
color to enter the cabin except in the capacity
of a servant. O Prejudice! thou cruel monster! wilt thou ever cease to exist? Not until
all shall know the Lord, and holiness shall be
written upon the bells of the horses—upon all
things in earth as well as in heaven. Glory
to the Lamb, whose right it is to reign!

Upon my arrival home I found my father
quite ill. He was sick for several months, and
I remained at home until after his death, which
event took place in May, 1849. He bore his
long, painful illness with Christian patience
and resignation. Just before leaving us for
the better world, he called each of his children
that were present to his bedside, exhorting
them to live here in such a manner that they
might meet him in heaven. To me he said:
"My dear daughter, be faithful to your heav-

enly calling, and fear not to preach full salvation." After some precious words to his weeping wife, my dear father was taken to his eternal rest. Bless the Lord, O my soul, for an
earnest, Christian father! Reader, I trust it is
your lot to have faithful, believing parents.

~~~~~~~~~~

CHAPTER XXV.

Work in Various Places.

June 18th, 1849, I bade my mother and family
farewell, and started out on my mission again.
I stopped in New York, where I was joined by
Sister Ann M. Johnson, who became my traveling companion. We went to Philadelphia,
where we were entertained by Brother and
Sister Lee. The dear, kind friends welcomed
us warmly. Sister Johnson did not feel moved
to labor in public, except to sing, pray, and
recount her experience. I labored constantly
while in this city, going from church to
church.

On the 28th we went to Snow Hill, where
we spent one Sunday. We visited Fethers-

(7)

ville, Bordentown, Westchester and Westtown, all to the glory of God. I must say, the dear Holy Spirit wonderfully visited the people in all these places. Many were converted, and, now and then, one would step into the fountain of cleansing.

July 20th we left for New York, stopping at Burlington, Trenton, Princeton, Rahway, Brunswick and Newark. In each of these places we spent several days, much to our comfort and the apparent good of the churches. We arrived in New York city August 3d, and went to Bridgeport (Conn.) by boat. We found the church there in a very unsettled condition because of unbelief. We next went to New Haven, where we had some precious meetings. In Providence, R. I., we also received God's blessing on our labors.

At this time I received a pressing invitation from Rev. Daniel A. Paine, who is now bishop of the A. M. E. Church, to visit Baltimore, which I accepted. Upon our arrival there we were closely questioned as to our freedom, and carefully examined for marks on our persons by which to identify us if we should prove to be runaways. While there, a daughter of the lady with whom we boarded ran away from her self-styled master. He came, with others, to her mother's house at midnight, burst in

the door without ceremony, and swore the girl
was hid in the house, and that he would have
her, dead or alive. They repeated this for
several nights. They often came to our bed
and held their light in our faces, to see if the
one for whom they were looking was not with
us. The mother was, of course, in great distress. I believe they never recovered the girl.
Thank the dear Lord we do not have to suffer
such indignities now, though the monster,
Slavery, is not yet dead in all its forms.

We remained some time in Baltimore, laboring mostly in Brother Paine's charge. We
then went to Washington, D. C., where our
Conference was in session. The meetings were
excellent, and great good was being done,
when an incident occurred which cast a gloom
over the whole Conference. One day, when a
number of the ministers, Sister Johnson and
myself, were dining at the house of one of the
brethren, a slaveholder came and searched the
house for a runaway. We realized more and
more what a terrible thing it was for one
human being to have absolute control over
another.

We remained in Washington a few weeks,
laboring for Christ. Although, at the time, it
seemed as though Satan ruled there supreme,
God gave us to know that his righteousness

was being set up in many hearts. Glory to his excellent name.

The larger portion of the past year had been a time of close trial, yet I do not recollect ever closing a year more fully in Christ than I did that one. On taking a retrospective view of it, I found great cause for humiliation as well as thankfulness. I was satisfied with the Lord's dealings with me; my mind was kept in peace, while many had declined on the right hand and on the left; I was thankful that any were spared to bear the standard of the Redeemer.

Since I first entered the vineyard of my divine Master, I have seen many a star fall, and many a shining light go out and sink into darkness. Many, who have been singularly owned and blessed of God, have deserted his standard in the day of trial; yet, through his abounding grace, have I been kept. Glory be to the keeping power of the blood that cleanseth me, even me, from all sin!

CHAPTER XXVI.

Further Labors—A "Threshing" Sermon.

In June, 1850, I crossed the Alleghany mountains the second time. I was very sick on the journey, and on arriving in Pittsburgh, was not able to sit up. Finding me in a raging fever, my friends called in a physician, and, as I continued to grow worse, another one. For three weeks my life was despaired of; and finally, on beginning to recover, it was many months before I felt quite well. In this severe affliction grace wonderfully sustained me. Bless the Lord!

I was advised to go down the Ohio river for the benefit of my health. Therefore, as soon as I was able to do so, I started for Cincinnati. I staid there several weeks with some friends by the name of Jones. The Lord so strengthened me, that, in a few months, I was able to resume my labors.

In October we went to Columbus. We labored there and in that vicinity for some time, content that in our protracted effort quite a number were converted. There were three persons there who said they had once enjoyed the blessing of sanctification, but were not then clear in the experience. Oh, how few are advocates for full salvation! Some will hold the whole truth in profession when and where it is not opposed, but, if they must become fools for the truth's sake, they compromise with error. Such have not and will not come to the perfect rest and inheritance of the saints on earth.

In April, 1851, we visited Chillicothe, and had some glorious meetings there. Great crowds attended every night, and the altar was crowded with anxious inquirers. Some of the deacons of the white people's Baptist church invited me to preach in their church, but I declined to do so, on account of the opposition of the pastor, who was very much set against women's preaching. He said so much against it, and against the members who wished me to preach, that they called a church meeting, and I heard that they finally dismissed him.

The white Methodists invited me to speak for them, but did not want the colored people to attend the meeting. I would not agree to any such arrangement, and, therefore, I did

not speak for them. Prejudice had closed the
door of their sanctuary against the colored
people of the place, virtually saying: "The
Gospel shall not be free to all." Our benign
Master and Saviour said: "Go, preach my Gospel to all."

We visited Zanesville, Ohio, laboring for
white and colored people. The white Methodists opened their house for the admission of
colored people for the first time. Hundreds
were turned away at each meeting, unable to
get in; and, although the house was so crowded,
perfect order prevailed. We also held meetings on the other side of the river. God the
Holy Ghost was powerfully manifest in all
these meetings. I was the recipient of many
mercies, and passed through various exercises.
In all of them I could trace the hand of God
and claim divine assistance whenever I most
needed it. Whatever I needed, by faith I had.
Glory! glory!! While God lives, and Jesus
sits on his right hand, nothing shall be impossible unto me, if I hold fast faith with a pure
conscience.

On the 27th we went to Detroit, Mich. On
the way, Sister Johnson had a very severe
attack of ague, which lasted for several weeks.
My soul had great liberty for God while laboring in this place.

One day, quite an influential man in the community, though a sinner, called on me and appeared deeply concerned about his soul's welfare. He urged me to speak from Micah iv. 13: "Arise and thresh, O daughter of Zion," etc. I took his desire to the Lord, and was permitted to speak from that passage after this manner: 710 B. C. corn was threshed among the Orientals by means of oxen or horses, which were driven round an area filled with loose sheaves. By their continued tramping the corn was separated from the straw. That this might be done the more effectually, the text promised an addition to the natural horny substance on the feet of these animals, by making the horn iron and the hoof brass.

Corn is not threshed in this manner by us, but by means of flails, so that I feel I am doing no injury to the sentiment of the text by changing a few of the terms into those which are the most familiar to us now. The passage portrays the Gospel times, though in a more restricted sense it applies to the preachers of the word. Yet it has a direct reference to all God's people, who were and are commanded to arise and thresh. Glory to Jesus! now is this prophecy fulfilled—Joel ii. 28 and 29. They are also commanded to go to God, who alone is able to qualify them for their labors by making their horns iron and their hoofs brass. The Lord was desirous of imparting stability and perpetuity to his own divine work, by granting supernatural aid to the faithful that they might perform for him those services for which their own feeble and unassisted powers were totally inadequate. More than this, it is encouraging to the saints to know that they are provided with weapons both offensive and defensive.

The threshing instrument is of the former description. It is of the same quality as that which is quick and powerful and sharper than any two-edged sword. "For this purpose the Son of God was manifested, that he might destroy the works of the devil," and this is one of the weapons which he employs in the hands of his people to carry his gracious designs into execution, together with the promise that they shall beat in pieces many people. Isa. xxiii. 18; lx. 6–9.

There are many instances of the successful application of the Gospel flail, by which means the devil is threshed out of sinners. With the help of God, I am resolved, O sinner, to try what effect the smart strokes of this threshing instrument will produce on thy unhumbled soul. This is called the sword of the Spirit, and is in reality the word of God.

Such a weapon may seem contemptible in the eyes of the natural man; yet, when it is powerfully wielded, the consequences are invariably potent and salutary. Bless God! the Revelator says: "They overcame by the blood of the Lamb and by the word of their testimony; and they loved not their lives unto the death." The atonement is the greatest weapon. In making trial of its efficacy, little children have caused the parent to cry aloud for mercy; but, in every case, much of its heavenly charm and virtue depends upon the mode in which it is applied.

This Gospel flail should be lifted up in a kind and loving spirit. Many shrink at sight of the flail, and some of us know, by blessed experience, that when its smart strokes are applied in the power and demonstration of the Holy Spirit, it causes the very heart to feel sore and painful. Penitent soul, receive the castigation, and you will feel, after it, like saying: "Now let me be crucified, and this work of the devil, inbred sin, put to death, that Christ may live and reign in me without a rival."

To the glory of God I wish to say, that the unconverted man, who gave me the text for the above discourse, gave his heart to God, together with many others, before we left

Detroit. In after years I was informed of his happy death. Praise the Lord for full and free salvation! Reader, have you this salvation—an ever-flowing fountain—in your soul? God grant it. Amen!

CHAPTER XXVII.

My Cleveland Home—Later Labors.

In June, 1851, we went to Canada, where we were kindly received. We labored in different churches with great success. We found many living Christians there — some holding high the light of full salvation, and others willing to be cleansed. After spending a few weeks there, we crossed to Buffalo, but did not make any stay there at that time.

The places visited during that year are too numerous to mention here. Suffice it to say, the great Head of the Church went before us, clearing the way and giving us unmistakable evidence of his presence in every battle. Hallelujah!

We returned to Columbus to fill an appointment which was awaiting us. After this, we made arrangements to go to Cleveland. One of the brethren engaged our passage and paid the fare, but we were not permitted to leave until four days afterward. At that time a colored person was not allowed to ride in the stage if any white passenger objected to it. There were objections made for three mornings, but, on the fourth, the stage called for us, and we had a safe journey to Cleveland. We expected to make a visit only, as in other cities; but the All-Father intended otherwise, and, more than twenty years ago, Cleveland became my home. After settling down, we still continued to visit neighboring cities and labor for Christ.

It was about this time that I became afflicted with the throat difficulty, of which I shall speak later. Beloved, the dear Lord only knows how sorely I was tried and tempted over this affliction.

St. James speaks of temptations as being common to the most holy of men, and also as a matter of joy and rejoicing to such as are exercised thereby, if so be they are not overcome by them. I think all temptation has a tendency to sin, but all temptation is not sin. There is a diversity of temptations, and a diversity of causes from which temptations proceed. Some come immediately from our corrupt nature, and are in themselves sinful. Others arise from the infirmity of our nature, and these every Christian has to contend with so long as he sojourns in a tabernacle of clay. There are also temptations which come directly from the enemy of souls. These our blessed Lord severely labored under, and so do the majority of his children. " Blessed is the man that endureth temptation"!

During the years that I rested from my labors and tried to recover my health, God permitted me to pass through the furnace of trial, heated seven times hotter than usual. Had not the three-one God been with me, I surely must have gone beneath the waves. God permits afflictions and persecutions to come upon his chosen people to answer various ends. Sometimes for the trial of their faith, and the exercise of their patience and resignation to his will, and sometimes to draw them off from all human dependence, and to teach them to trust in Him alone. Sometimes he suffers the wicked to go a great way, and the ungodly to triumph over us, that he may prove our steadfastness and make manifest his power in upholding us. Thus it was with me. I had trusted too much in human wisdom, and

God suffered all these things to come upon me.
He upheld me by his grace, freeing me from
all care or concern about my health or what
man could do. He taught me to sit patiently,
and wait to hear my Shepherd's voice; for I
was resolved to follow no stranger, however
plausibly he might plead.

I shall praise God through all eternity for
sending me to Cleveland, even though I have
been called to suffer.

In 1856, Sister Johnson, who had been my
companion during all these years of travel,
left me for her heavenly home. She bore her
short illness without a murmur, resting on
Jesus. As she had lived, so she died, in the
full assurance of faith, happy and collected to
the last, maintaining her standing in the way
of holiness without swerving either to the
right or to the left. Glory to the blood that
keeps us!

My now sainted mother, who was then in
feeble health, lived with me in Cleveland for a
few years. As the time for her departure drew
near, she very much desired to visit her two
daughters—one in Albany, the other in Boston. I feared she was not able to endure the
journey, but her desire was so strong, and her
confidence in God so great that he would spare
her to see her girls again, that I finally con-

sented that she should undertake the journey
I put her in charge of friends who were going
east, and she reached my sister's house in
safety. She had been with them but a few
weeks, when she bade them a long farewell
and passed peacefully to heaven. I shall see
her again where parting is unknown.

The glorious wave of holiness, which has
been rolling through Ohio during the past few
years, has swept every hindrance out of my
way, and sent me to sea once more with chart
and compass.

"The Bible is my chart; it is a chart and compass too,
  Whose needle points forever true."

When I drop anchor again, it will be in
heaven's broad bay.

Glory to Jesus for putting into my hand
that precious, living light, "*The Christian Harvester.*" May it and its self-sacrificing editor
live many years, reflecting holy light as they
go.

If any one arise from the perusal of this
book, scoffing at the word of truth which he
has read, I charge him to prepare to answer
for the profanation at the peril of his soul.

CHAPTER XXVIII.

A Word to my Christian Sisters.

Dear Sisters: I would that I could tell you a hundredth part of what God has revealed to me of his glory, especially on that never-to-be-forgotten night when I received my high and holy calling. The songs I heard I think were those which Job, David and Isaiah speak of hearing at night upon their beds, or the one of which the Revelator says "no man could learn." Certain it is, I have not been able to sing it since, though at times I have seemed to hear the distant echo of the music. When I tried to repeat it, it vanished in the dim distance. Glory! glory! glory to the Most High!

Sisters, shall not you and I unite with the heavenly host in the grand chorus? If so, you will not let what man may say or do, keep you from doing the will of the Lord or using the gifts you have for the good of others. How much easier to bear the reproach of men than to live at a distance from God. Be not kept in bondage by those who say, "We suffer not a woman to teach," thus quoting Paul's words, but not rightly applying them. What though we are called to pass through deep waters, so our anchor is cast within the veil, both sure and steadfast? Blessed experience! I have had to weep because this was not my constant experience. At times, a cloud of heaviness has covered my mind, and disobedience has caused me to lose the clear witness of perfect love.

One time I allowed my mind to dwell too much on my physical condition. I was suffering severely from throat difficulty, and took the advice of friends, and sought a cure from earthly physicians, instead of applying to the Great Physician. For this reason my joy was checked, and I was obliged to cease my public labors for several years. During all this time I was less spiritual, less zealous, yet I was not willing to accept the suggestion of Satan, that I had forfeited the blessing of holiness. But alas! the witness was not clear, and God suffered me to pass through close trials, tossed by the billows of temptation.

Losing my loving husband just at this time, I had much of the world to struggle with and against.

(8)

Those who are wholly sanctified need not fear that God will hide his face, if they continue to walk in the light even as Christ is in the light. Then they have fellowship with the Father and the Son, and become of one spirit with the Lord. I do not believe God ever withdraws himself from a soul which does not first withdraw itself from him, though such may abide under a cloud for a season, and have to cry: "My God! my God! why hast thou forsaken me?"

Glory to God, who giveth us the victory through our Lord Jesus Christ! His blood meets all the demands of the law against us. It is the blood of Christ that sues for the fulfillment of his last will and testament, and brings down every blessing into the soul.

When I had well nigh despaired of a cure from my bodily infirmities, I cried from the depths of my soul for the blood of Jesus to be applied to my throat. My faith laid hold of the precious promises—John xiv. 14; Mark ii. 23; xi. 24. At once I ceased trying to join the iron and the clay—the truth of God with the sayings and advice of men. I looked to my God for a fresh act of his sanctifying power. Bless his name! deliverance did come, with the balm, and my throat has troubled me but little since. This was ten years ago. Praise

the Lord for that holy fire which many waters
of trial and temptation cannot quench.

Dear sisters in Christ, are any of you also
without understanding and slow of heart to
believe, as were the disciples? Although they
had seen their Master do many mighty works,
yet, with change of place or circumstances,
they would go back upon the old ground of
carnal reasoning and unbelieving fears. The
darkness and ignorance of our natures are
such, that, even after we have embraced the
Saviour and received his teaching, we are
ready to stumble at the plainest truths!
Blind unbelief is always sure to err; it càn
neither trace God nor trust him. Unbelief is
ever alive to distrust and fear. So long as
this evil root has a place in us, our fears can
not be removed nor our hopes confirmed.

Not till the day of Pentecost did Christ's
chosen ones see clearly, or have their under-
standings opened; and nothing short of a full
baptism of the Spirit will dispel our unbelief.
Without this, we are but babes—all our lives
are often carried away by our carnal natures
and kept in bondage; whereas, if we are
wholly saved and live under the full sanctifying influence of the Holy Ghost, we cannot be
tossed about with every wind, but, like an iron
pillar or a house built upon a rock, prove

immovable. Our minds will then be fully illuminated, our hearts purified, and our souls filled with the pure love of God, bringing forth fruit to his glory.

<hr />

CHAPTER XXIX.

Love not the World.

"If any man love the world, the love of the Father is not in him." 1 John ii. 15. The spirit which is in the world is widely different from the Spirit which is of God; yet many vainly imagine they can unite the two. But as we read in Luke x. 26, so it is between the spirit of the world and the Spirit which is of God. There is a great gulf fixed between them—a gulf which cuts off all union and intercourse; and this gulf will eternally prevent the least degree of fellowship in spirit.

If we be of God and have the love of the Father in our hearts, we are not of the world, because whatsoever is of the world is not of God. We must be one or the other. We can not unite heaven and hell—light and dark-

ness. Worldly honor, worldly pleasure, worldly
grandeur, worldly designs and worldly pursuits are all incompatible with the love of the
Father and with that kingdom of righteousness, peace and joy in the Holy Ghost, which
is not of the world, but of God. Therefore,
God says: "Be not conformed to the world, but
be ye transformed by the renewing of your
mind, that ye may prove what is that good,
and acceptable. and perfect will of God."
Rom. xii. 2.

As we look at the professing Christians of
to-day, the question arises, Are they not all
conformed to the maxims and fashions of this
world, even many of those who profess to have
been sanctified? But they say the transforming and renewing here spoken of means, as it
says, the mind, not the clothing. But, if the
mind be renewed, it must affect the clothing.
It is by the Word of God we are to be judged,
not by our opinion of the Word; hence, to the
law and the testimony. In a like manner the
Word also says: "That women adorn themselves in modest apparel, with shamefacedness
and sobriety, not with broidered hair, or gold,
or pearls, or costly array, but which becometh
a woman professing godliness, with good
works." 1 Tim. ii. 9, 10; 1 Pet. iii. 3–5. I
might quote many passages to the same effect,

if I had time or room. Will you not hunt them up, and read carefully and prayerfully for yourselves?

Dear Christians, is not the low state of pure religion among all the churches the result of this worldly-mindedness? There is much outward show; and doth not this outward show portend the sore judgments of God to be executed upon the ministers and members? Malachi ii. 7, says: "The priest's lips should keep knowledge," etc. But it is a lamentable fact that too many priests' lips speak vanity. Many profess to teach, but few are able to feed the lambs, while the sheep are dying for lack of nourishment and the true knowledge of salvation.

The priests' office being to stand between God and the people, they ought to know the mind of God toward his people — what the acceptable and perfect will of God is. Under the law, it was required that the priests should be without blemish—having the whole of the inward and outward man as complete, uniform and consistent as it was possible to be under that dispensation; thereby showing the great purity that is required by God in all those who approach near unto him. "Speak unto Aaron and his sons that they separate themselves," etc. The Lord here gives a charge to

the priests, under a severe penalty, that in all
their approaches they shall sanctify themselves. Thus God would teach his ministers,
and people that he is a holy God, and will be
worshiped in the beauty of holiness by all
those who come into his presence.

Man may fill his office in the church out-
wardly, and God may in much mercy draw
nigh to the people when devoutly assembled
to worship him; but, if the minister has not
had previous recourse to the fountain which is
opened for sin and uncleanness, and felt the
sanctifying and renewing influences of the
Holy Ghost, he will feel himself shut out from
these divine communications. Oh, that God
may baptize the ministry and church with the
Holy Ghost and with fire.

By the baptism of fire the church must be
purged from its dead forms and notions respecting the inbeing of sin in all believers till
death. The Master said: "Now ye are clean
through the word which I have spoken unto
you; abide in me," etc. Oh! blessed union.
Christian, God wants to establish your heart
unblamable in holiness. 1 Thess. i. 13; iv. 7;
Heb. xii. 14; Rom. vi. 19. Will you let him
do it, by putting away all filthiness of the flesh
as well as of the spirit? "Know ye not that
ye are the temple of God?" etc. 1 Cor. iii. 16,

17; 2 Cor. vi. 16, 17. Thus we will continue to search and find what the will of God is concerning his children. 1 Thess. iv. 3, 4. Bless God! we may all have that inward, instantaneous sanctification, whereby the root, the inbeing of sin, is destroyed.

Do not misunderstand me. I am not teaching absolute perfection, for that belongs to God alone. Nor do I mean a state of angelic or Adamic perfection, but Christian perfection— an extinction of every temper contrary to love.

"Now, the God of peace sanctify you wholly— your whole spirit, soul and body. 2 Thess. v. 23. Glory to the blood!" " Faithful is he that calleth you, who also will do it." Paul says: He is able to do exceeding abundantly, above all that we ask or think. Eph. iii. 20.

Beloved reader, remember that you cannot commit sin and be a Christian, for "He that committeth sin is of the devil." If you are regenerated, sin does not reign in your mortal body; but if you are sanctified, sin does not exist in you. The sole ground of our perfect peace from all the carnal mind is by the blood of Jesus, for he is our peace, whom God hath set forth to be a propiation, through faith in his blood. " By whom also we have access by faith into this grace wherein we stand"—having entered into the holiest by the blood of Jesus.

Let the blood be the sentinel, keeping the tempter without, that you may have constant peace within; for Satan cannot swim in still, waters. Isa. xxx. 7.

CHAPTER XXX.

How to Obtain Sanctification.

How is sanctification to be obtained? An important question. I answer, by faith. Faith is the only condition of sanctification. By this I mean a faith that dies out to the world and every form of sin; that gives up the sin of the heart; and that believes, according to God's promise, he is able to perform, and will do it now—doeth it now.

Why not yield, believe, and be sanctified now—now, while reading? "Now is the day of salvation." Say: "Here, Lord, I will, I do believe; thou hast said now—now let it be— now apply the blood of Jesus to my waiting, longing soul."

> "Hallelujah! 'tis done!
> I believe on the Son;
> I am saved by the blood
> Of the crucified One."

HOLY IS THE LAMB.

Mrs. J. A. J. Foote.　　　　　　　　　　E. A. Hoffman.

1. Mixture of joy and sor-row Daily do I pass through;
2. Sometimes I am ex-alt-ed, On eagle's wings I fly;
3. Sometimes I am in doubting, And think I have no grace;

Sometimes I'm in the valley, Then sinking down with woe.
Ris-ing above Mount Pisgah, I almost reach the sky.
Sometimes I am a-shouting, And camp-meeting is the place.

CHORUS.

Holy, holy, holy is the Lamb, Who saves me from all sin, from all [my sin!

Holy, holy, holy is the Lamb, Whose blood doth make me clean!

4. Sometimes, when I am praying,
It almost seems a task;
Sometimes I get a blessing,
The greatest I can ask.

5. Sometimes I read my Bible,
It seems a sealed book;
Sometimes I find a blessing
Wherever I do look.

6. O, why am I thus tossed—
Thus tossed to and fro?
Because the blood of Jesus
Hasn't washed me white as snow.

7. Oh, come to Christ, the Savior,
Drink of that living stream;
Your thirst he'll quench forever
And cleanse you from all sin.

Now, dear reader, I conclude by praying that this little work may be blessed of God to your spiritual and everlasting good. I trust also that it will promote the cause of holiness in the Church.

Now, unto Him who is able to do exceeding abundantly, above all that we ask or think, according to the power that worketh in us; unto Him be glory in the church by Christ Jesus throughout all ages, world without end. Amen.

Twenty Year's Experience
of
A Missionary

CHICAGO
THE PONY PRESS, PUBLISHERS
2351 STATE STREET
MXCVII

PREFACE.

This booklet has been written upon the earnest request of friends who desired the people generally to know something of the experiences we have enjoyed during the past twenty years as a Christian missionary. Hoping our experiences may encourage others to dedicate their lives to the Master's service, we send forth this booklet as our contribution to the history of a race, whose true story must yet be told by members of the race would we give our young people the needed encouragement to make their lives what they should be. Respectfully,

Y. W. Broughton, Authoress.

CONTENTS.

CONTENTS—Continued

CHAPTER X.
Sanctification.

CHAPTER XI.
Fireside School Work.

CHAPTER XII.
Virginia's Work Extended.

CHAPTER XIII.
Places or special Interest Visited.

CHAPTER XIV.
The John C. Martin Bible Movement.

CHAPTER XV.
One Year's Work in A. and M. College, Normal, Ala.

CHAPTER XVI.
Songs and Texts of Special Significance.

DEDICATED

To the memories of my sainted mother and beloved
brother and sister.

CHAPTER I.

Call to Service.

In a certain city of the fair South Land of the United States of America there was born a wee little girl baby, whom her father named Virginia, in honor of the state of his nativity, which he never ceased to praise. This Negro child had the godly heritage of being well born of honorable parents who had secured their freedom at great cost.

Virginia's father was an industrious, intelligent man, who, early in life, hired his time from his master and thereby was enabled to purchase his own freedom and also that of his wife.

As freedmen they began to build up a home and rear children who could enjoy the privileges of education that only very few of our race could enjoy at that time. Before the late Civil War Virginia attended a private school, taught by Professor Daniel Watkins, and was reading in the fourth reader when the new day of freedom dawned upon the race and brought with it the glorious light of education for all who would receive it.

Fisk University was one of the first institutions of learning established for the Freedmen. Virginia was enrolled among its first pupils and classified with the most advanced. After ten consecutive years of faithful study she graduated from the College Department of Fisk University, May, 1875.

Virginia has the distinction of being the first college graduate of womankind south of Mason and Dixon line. The prevailing custom in the South at that time regarding the education of woman made it possible for this Negro girl to have such a distinction.

Immediately after her graduation, in answer to a telegram, she went to Memphis and there passed a creditable examination for a position in the public schools of that city. So brilliant was her success in the examination, her friends insisted that she take the principal's examination. This, however, she declined to do, as she did not wish to be a rival of her male classmate who was aspiring for that position.

For twelve years she taught in the public schools of Memphis, being promoted from time to time, until she became principal of the North Memphis school, and later assistant principal of the Kortrecht grammar school, the most advanced public school in that city for colored youth.

While teaching in the last position mentioned a stranger introduced as Miss J. P. Moore, accompanied by Miss E. B. King, called to see Virginia, and invited her to attend a missionary meeting appointed for women only. As this was an entirely new thing under the sun twenty years ago, curiosity prompted Virginia to go and ascertain what such a meeting would be. Miss J. P. Moore, the good woman who called the meeting, stated the object and opened the service with an appropriate devotional exercise. She at once enlisted the sympathy and promised coöperation of the women in attendance. We organized what was then called a Bible Band. The principal object of the organization was the daily study of the Bible. This organization grew and increased in numbers, influence, and spiritual strength. The work began in one of our intelligent progressive churches, in which the pastor was a strong, intellectual, devout man, well prepared to encourage and defend this new feature in the church life of our people. Soon Bible Bands were organized throughout the city of Memphis and the women of our churches took on new life. Every Monday afternoon women could be seen in all sections of the city with Bibles in their hands, going to their Bible Band meetings.

The interest became so general in this Bible Band work that Miss J. P. Moore advised the women to petition the W. B. H. M. S. for a Stationary Missionary. This was done. Miss Burdette, corresponding secretary W. B. H. M. S., came to Memphis and after thorough investigation Memphis was selected as a regular mis-

sion station, and beloved Mrs. M. Ehlers was sent as
our first missionary to train our women and children
to do their Lord's work more perfectly.

This Bible Band work being fairly established in
Memphis, as a means of greater development, God
opened a way through that fearless pastor, Rev. R. N.
Countee, for the establishment of a Christian school,
known as ''The Bible and Normal Institute.'' Ere this
school was completed a heartless assassin slew the phi-
lanthropist who was providing the means for erecting and furnishing the building.

Alas! Alas! Imagine the dilemma this blow placed
our work in; school building and furnishings incomplete and a debt of several thousand dollars upon us.
We can say with the song writer at this point,

''God moves in a mysterious way
His wonders to perform;
He plants his footsteps in the sea,
And rides upon the storm.''

This crisis was God's way of opening the doors for
women to speak in many of our churches in that section that were interested in the new Bible School.
Hitherto Paul's statement, ''Let your women keep silence in the churches, for it is not permitted unto them
to speak,'' had locked and barred the doors of our
churches against women speaking.

In the meantime, while God was providing the way

to enter churches, He was also preparing His female
servants to enter them with an effectual message from
His Word, even as He prepared Peter while on the
house top for meeting the committee that came to
greet him in behalf of Cornelius, the Gentile, with
whom he had had no dealings. Although Virginia
was interested in Bible Band 'work she had no dream
of doing missionary work, for she was teaching at a
lucrative salary, and fully engaged in her home and
school duties. About this time Virginia's beloved
mother, the joy of her heart, was called to her home
beyond the skies. This blow came like a clap of thunder in a clear sky—the deepest sorrow Virginia had
ever known up to that time. The whole world seemed
lone and drear to Virginia, and her greatest comfort
came from the hope of soon departing this life and
joining her mother in the blessed home-land of the
soul. Virginia's health was poor at that time, and
she felt so confident she would soon die, she resigned
her position in the school and moved off to another
city, where she hoped her children would be cared for,
should she die. Conditions and circumstances were so
unsatisfactory she did not remain long in her adopted
city, but soon returned to her former home. In the
spring of 1887 Virginia had a very serious illness; her
life was despaired of; she had selected her burial robes,
and made such other preparations as she deemed necessary, and with intense longing to depart she lay on

her bed waiting on the Lord for the expected summons.

Husband, children and all other earthly ties and possessions were given up. By and by the Lord manifestly came, but not as she expected, to bear her ran-
somed spirit home, but she was overshadowed with
the veritable presence of God, and made to understand
thoroughly and clearly in language spoken to the soul,
that God was not ready for her then, but He had a
work for her to do. That marvelous experience was
accompanied with renewed strength of body that
continued to increase from that moment until she was able to leave her bed. Virginia's physical
weakness, at that time, prohibited her from witnessing
a great baptizing that she desired greatly to see, but
she was given another rich spiritual blessing that more
than compensated her for failing to see the baptizing.
She was privileged to hear sweet heavenly music that
is unlawful for man to utter, and she quietly rested,
sweetly rejoicing in the Lord, as a babe lulled to rest
in its mother's arms. In time her strength increased
and she came to her normal condition of health. The
following song was at once given her, suggestive of
many of her experiences, and also as one of the ways
God would direct her in her work.

SONG.

"How firm a foundation, ye saints of the Lord,
Is·laid for your faith in His excellent Word;
What more can He say, than to you He hath said,
You, who with Jesus, for refuge hath fled?"

This song, through all these twenty years, has not only been an inspiration for service, but its truths have been verified in the varied experiences we herein relate.

Virginia gladly began her work again in the Bible class taught by Mrs. M. Ehlers, the stationed missionary in her home city. The first meeting she attended after her recovery was one of great joy to her; she was so full of joy she spoke twice in that meeting, and then and there won friends to the Lord's cause that have ever since proved faithful allies of hers in the great work of missions whereunto God had called her. Among those friends we would mention the two devoted sisters, Peggie and Hannah.

Mrs. Ehlers, and the other white missionaries who visited us in those early days, were not slow in discerning Virginia's adaptability and ability to help in advancing the work. They began at once to encourage her and develop her gifts by assigning her special duties to perform in the meetings. Virginia's increased zeal was also manifest in her church, and she was used in various official capacities in the local Bible Band of her church and the Sunday-school work.

Bible Band meetings were held throughout the city, and Virginia was seen going here and there to these meetings whenever an opportunity was given her to encourage the work. Because of her readiness to speak and her Bible knowledge she soon came to be an important factor to help conduct the devotional services.

This great Bible Band work among our women was soon noised abroad and invitations came to us from the regions around to send out a worker that the people generally might learn of the work and share in its blessings. A certain district association met in Memphis, and Rev. Copeland, another staunch friend to the woman's work, presented our Bible Band work to his associate brethren. Many of them were favorably impressed and requested that we send one of our Bible women to their churches to tell them more about the work, and organize the women of their churches. Thus, in due season, being approved by the church, Virginia was sent on her first missionary journey to the regions beyond her home city.

CHAPTER II.

Virginia's First Missionary Journey.

Upon invitation of a certain pastor, Virginia started on her first missionary journey up the Mississippi river. She was naturally afraid to travel on water and needed special encouragement as well as preparation for that first trip. Accordingly after much hesitation on her part amidst doubts and fears, she was assured that God was on the water as well as on the land, and with the following song ringing within her soul she began the journey:

> "Oh, for a closer walk with God,
>   A calm and heavenly frame;
> A light to shine upon the road
>   That leads me to the Lamb."

On this first trip she visited Hales Point, Tenn., Cooter, Mo., Hickman Bend and Osceola, Ark., and a few other points in that immediate vicinity. Perils on land and water were experienced. She crossed the Mississippi river twice in a skiff. The first time some

one was obliged to constantly bail out the water that-
came in through a leak to keep from going under,
while only one other man remained to perform the
strenuous task of rowing the skiff across the stream.
Having crossed the river, she pursued her journey that
same winter's night in an open ox wagon. Although a
small fire had been kindled in an ill-provised heater
in the wagon, the smoke made the journey quite as uncomfortable as the cold would have been. Finally,
about midnight, she reached her destination and was
cozily tucked to bed in one of the old-time typical
high soft beds that prosperous farmers have on our
southern plantations. The house was a clean one-room
log cabin, with its one door, large fireplace, and no
window at all, but sufficient crevices for air and sun-
light. Monday Virginia visited all the neighbors and
encouraged them to live the beautiful Christian life.
After dinner, in company with the minister, she took
a trip through the country on horseback to Cooter, Mo.,
a place where few Negro men dared to go to preach,
and a woman missionary of no race had ever gone.
The road lay through a low, flat, marshy country near
the Mississippi river, much of it being under water at
the time of this trip. The preacher would ride on
ahead through the water and bid Virginia to follow
him, which she did with much fear and trembling, the
water often coming up to her saddle skirts. Virginia,

being an inexperienced rider and unaccustomed to
such hardships, heaved a sigh of relief when once again
dry ground appeared. It was cotton-picking time and
the people were having a merry time weighing their
cotton when Virginia rode up to the settlement. The
news of a woman missionary being in town soon
spread, and the small church house was filled to overflowing; both white and colored people came out. Evidently God used the missionary to give the right message, from the many expressions of joy and God bless
you, heard from all sides. The white and colored people
stood on the roadside to bid us farewell, as we began
our return trip the next morning. Throughout this section Virginia was received warmly and the messages
she bore were heard gladly. When she planned to make
her next point it was difficult to get any kind of conveyance. Finally a good brother said that he had one
mule, and if the missionary could ride behind him, he
would carry her. Bears and wildcats were common
through that river bottom and it was quite dangerous
to travel through it unprotected. God protected our
missionary and her escort, and Virginia made that
journey safely riding, as she did, behind the brother
on his mule. The people were awaiting her. She held
a meeting with the people which all seemed to enjoy.
While she was singing the closing song, ''Steal Away
to Jesus,'' all at once a whistle blew that announced

the near approach of a boat, and Virginia did steal
away from those happy people, went aboard the vessel
and pursued her journey. Much of her fear of water
was now gone; the experiences of the trip had greatly
increased her courage and zeal. Rev. Aaron Ware, one
of the fathers of the gospel in West Tennessee, was a
great leader in this Mississippi river district, and it is
just to say that he was friendly to the woman's missionary work in those early days when few ministers
were.

Virginia had a warm reception at Osceola, Ark. She
spoke acceptably to Rev. J. Owen's congregation.
Tangible expression of their appreciation was given
in a liberal contribution to our missionary. All expenses were covered on this first trip, and Virginia returned home rejoicing, with the assurance that God
was on the water, as well as on the land, and that He
would provide for his servants according to his riches
in glory, through Christ Jesus.

For several years Virginia taught five days of the
week in the school room and gave the other two to
missionary work in the rural districts as far as fifty
miles away. She often returned to the school room
Monday morning directly from the railroad station,
often without having slept Sunday night or break-
fasted Monday morning. Those were days when great

sacrifice was necessary to establish the woman's missionary work, but no service for Christ seems so wondrously blessed as that which requires great sacrifice, so the rich spiritual blessings that came to Virginia in those days nerved and energized her to suffer and endure all things that came to her without murmuring or complaining.

CHAPTER III.

Commissioned by the Board of Directors of "The Bible and Normal Institute."

In the spring of 1888 the Board of Directors of "The Bible and Normal Institute" decided to send out two of our Bible women to visit the churches and organize the women and children to come to the relief of the school that was then suffering under the great embarrassment occasioned by the death of Mr. Peter Howe, its benefactor, who was murdered as we have mentioned.

The blessed results that were manifest from the labors of the white missionaries sent to us by the W. B. H. M. S. with headquarters in Chicago, Ill., encouraged this school board to undertake a similar work throughout the surrounding country, which should be organized and fostered by women of the race. Thus God opened a great and effectual door for the women of the Baptist churches throughout West Tennessee. Miss E. B. King and Virginia were the two women appointed. These two consecrated women with Bibles in hand went forth, going in different directions in order to convass the entire district in a specified time, organize the women and children locally, and arrange for a general district organization. Everywhere these women went the people were aroused, some for them and many against them. Bible Bands were organized throughout the district. Exciting days were those! Bibles were being searched as never before by that people to find out if there was any divine authority for such work; women were rising up and striving to get to the meetings to hear what new doctrine those women missionaries were teaching, and men were discussing and opposing.

September, 1888, was the date fixed for the general organization of the district. **Great Interest** prevailed everywhere. People came from all directions and in every conceivable way. This first associational meeting was held in Mt. Zion Baptist Church, Stanton, Tenn. All the roads leading to Stanton were crowded, people going and coming continually during the four days' sessions. The presence of God was unmistakably manifest. Christians rejoiced, testified, prayed, sung and preached until one dear woman just stood up in front of the vast audience and exemplified what many had been saying (viz., that they were speechless), for she was unable to say a word, being so completely overcome with the joy of the moment. Eternity alone will reveal the glorious results that have come from that meeting. In this beginning of organized missionary effort among Negro women in Tennessee the following fundamental principles were emphasized as necessary to our Christian development as women: First, simplicity, cleanliness and neatness in dress and in our home furnishings. Second, wholesome, well prepared food. Third, the temperate use of all good things and total abstinence from poisons, tobacco and liquors being specified. Fourth, the education of heart, head and hand. Fifth, above all things, loyalty to Christ as we should be taught of Him through the daily prayerful study of His Word.

Dr. McVicar at that time was superintendent of education for A. B. H. M. S. When he visited the school at Memphis Dr. H. R. Traver, president of the Bible and Normal Institute at that time, told him the story of the unprecedented success of this mission work as conducted by Virginia and her associate workers. Dr. McVicar became thoroughly aroused to this fact, that after all the salvation and education of the Negro depended largely upon himself, and men and women of the race should be helped and trained for leadership along all lines of religious and educational work as well as industrial pursuits. He then decided with Dr. Traver to make a special effort for the missionary training of our women. Accordingly, through Dr. McVicar's counsel and influence, missionary departments for women were established at Spelman Seminary, Atlanta, Ga.; Bible and Normal Institute, Memphis, Tenn.; Shaw University, Raleigh, N. C., and Bishop College, Texas. Thus provision was made for the missionary training of our women for work, either on the home or foreign field. Miss E. B. Delaney, who has spent several years of hard service in Blantyre, East Africa, is one of the representative missionaries from Spelman Seminary; also Mrs. G. Patton, Washington, D. C., who did faithful service on the foreign field, and then returned to America where she did faithful service as a successful medical practitioner ere the dear Lord called her to her home beyond the skies. Missionaries from the other schools are scattered throughout this country doing good service, some under commission of W. B. H. M. S., Chicago, others under the coöperative plan of the Southern Baptist Convention and the N. B. Convention and still others under national, state and district religious organizations. These missionary training schools for Negro women owe their birth largely to the success that attended the first year's labors of our heroine when serving under the commission of the Board of Directors of the Bible and Normal Institute, Memphis, Tenn. Members of that memorable board who have ever stood by Virginia to encourage her work, still live to rejoice in the glorious culmination, now manifest, of what they then believed, which is the general recognition of woman as man's helpmeet in the church as well as in the school and home.

The following are the names of those good men who still live: Revs. R. N. Countee, Wm. Brinkley, Hardin Smith, H. C. Owen, Wm. J. McMichael, T. J. Searcy. To these worthy Christian gentlemen our women owe the deepest gratitude. Our prayers shall ever be for them a blessed life here and an abundant entrance into life eternal.

CHAPTER IV.

Ten Great District Meetings.

Ten women's district associations in as many years were held in West Tennessee. Stanton, Woodlawn, Memphis, Trenton, Paris, Martin, Humboldt, Stanton, Durhamville and Woodlawn were the places where the meetings were held. The first meeting held at Stanton has been referred to. The second annual meeting was held at Woodlawn, a country church, seven miles distant from the nearest railroad station. A wagon train, however, was waiting for the arrival of our delegation which carried the women to the place of meeting free of charge. This kindness was the result of the efforts of the good pastor, Rev. H. Smith, who was a member of that notable school board who had given Virginia her first commission. The interest in our work had grown in that part of the district. Marked development was apparent in the women of our local Bible Bands. A goodly number of ministers and laymen had been converted to this work. Conspicuous among these new friends were men whom God had given visions to make clear to them his approval of this woman's work. Wise plans for operating a girl's dormitory in connection with ''The Bible and Normal Institute'' were perfected at this meeting. Virginia executed the plan and through it the women of the district helped the school greatly by furnishing board and bedding for quite a number of the girls during the next school year. The Memphis meeting gave the country women the privilege of seeing the school they were working for, which greatly strengthened our work throughout the district. The women returned home with renewed zeal to continue their efforts and raise more money to carry on the school that was destined to do so much for our people.

The Trenton District Association will never be forgotten by those privileged to attend it from the special Providence that interposed for the entertainment of the delegation. After the meeting had been in session one day, the delegation being so much larger than was expected, provisions gave out. Virginia stated conditions of affairs to the sisters of the association and asked them to pray that God would provide food for the delegates if they wished the meeting to continue through the time appointed.

Praise God! The windows of Heaven were opened and God poured out such a blessing upon us we were scarcely able to contain it. God touched the hearts of the good white people of Trenton and they bade the entertainment committee come to their groceries, bakeries and meat market and get all supplies needed without money or price as long as the convention lasted. This was a marvelous Providence, and this Trenton meeting was one continuous round of praise and rejoicings. Miss J. P. Moore was present to rejoice with us; also a white gentleman who had recently returned to America from a foreign mission journey. He said many helpful and encouraging things to us and bade us a hearty God-speed. Large numbers of the white citizens attended this meeting and expressed themselves as pleased with our effort. Sister Mattie B., who then lived at Trenton, and was beautifully situated in a cozy little home of her own, had been opposed to this woman's work up to this time, but this meeting convinced her of her folly. She was converted to the work, joined in heartily to care for the delegation after her conversion, and in time became a faithful, zealous worker throughout her district. This dear sister had a beautiful flower garden of plants rich and rare. She expressed her love for the sisterhood and the joy of her new experience by placing a buttonhole bouquet of flowers, culled from her own garden and arranged by her own hands, upon every one of the more than a hundred delegates as they stood in line in the aisles of the church.

Beautiful sight was this! Women all agreeing and harmoniously laboring together so that both men and women alike, of both races, were convinced that our work was truly heaven ordained, and we should be substantially encouraged to carry it forward. Many friends joined our organization and liberal contributions were donated to the work. Virginia and Miss E. B. King were both sent as delegates to the N. B. Convention. God used Virginia to sway that noble band of Christian women as with a magic wand.

The Paris meeting was rendered glorious by the activity of our mothers in Israel, who hitherto had been suppressed and discouraged in every effort they had made to exercise their spiritual gifts. Dear sister Kitty N., of blessed memory, actually led in a song as she walked the floor and praised God for the liberty of speech she then enjoyed. All believers rejoiced as she told the story of Jesus' love. Several persons in Paris who had refused to entertain delegates before they came were so thoroughly changed during the exercises of the meetings that they came and begged to have some share in providing for the comfort of the delegation.

The Martin meeting was noted for the unusual encouragement given the work by' ministers of the gospel. One of them preached a sermon for us from this text,

"Let Her Alone!"

This message was very opportune in that early day of our women's work, for the large majority of men really believed the work unlawful and forbidden by the Scriptures, as they had been taught to believe a special message of the Apostle Paul on this subject. In this same town at one time Virginia had been so frowned upon and criticised by a certain churchman that God came to her rescue by rebuking the man and showing him if he would sweep around his own door he would have no time to interfere with those who were doing his bidding. That accuser went to Rev. Hurt, who was then pastoring in Trenton, confessed his fault and sent Virginia a word of cheer. Her oppressions and discouragements weighed heavily upon her and she longed to go home and rest from her labors. As ever, the dear Lord comforted his servant by giving her this sweet message from His Word, "I must work the work of Him that sent me while it is day, for the night cometh when no man can work." That message was all sufficient. Virginia saw she need not worry about the carelessness of others, she was only required to do the work assigned her and leave the results with God. Ever since she has striven to heed that message as clear guidance has been given her. Another incident in connection with the Martin meeting should be mentioned. Virginia discovered a certain embarrassment was likely to come to the sisterhood unless God interposed in their behalf, as He had done in Trenton, so she again entreated the women to pray for God's help to overcome the difficulty. The prayer was answered and the women passed safely through the threatening difficulty. The weight of the burden fell so heavily upon Virginia she took seriously ill with fever and was compelled to remain at Milan for treatment ere she could continue her journey home.

The Humboldt meeting evidenced great growth in the workers. Several of the sisters from the rural districts had attended the Missionary Training School in Memphis and were giving valuable services toward building up and extending the work. Sisters Julia S., Mary B., Mattie B., Mattie P., Amy S., Nancy T., Sarah B., Bell C., Nealy R., Lizzie S., Hannah J. and Maggie C. were very helpful in their respective neighborhoods. Several of these sisters were able to conduct services in the other churches of Humboldt on the Sunday our association was in session there. With the increase of work and workers, jealousy, rivalry and other evils began to be manifest in the ranks of the Bible women. Miss Fanny K. was for several years recording secretary of the Woman's West Tennessee District Association. Being an ambitious young woman the sisters all seemed pleased to encourage her.

The second Stanton meeting was well attended and blessed of the Lord. The spirit of position and power was manifestly growing, hence the same sweet peace and harmony did not prevail so generally in this meeting as hitherto. The interests of the school were well defended and a host of pupils came to us from the Stanton district.

The Durhamville meeting was attended with more powerful spiritual manifestations than any previous annual meeting. Virginia's sister, Mrs. Selena J. G., was used mightily of God to encourage women to live pure, virtuous lives and train up a consecrated, intelligent ministry from the youth of the race to lead the race forward as God directed in His Word. This dear woman, somehow, missed her trunk, but so determined was she to attend this meeting she gathered a few necessary garments together, dropped them in a pillow case, and came on in time to join the wagon train that conveyed the women from the railroad station to the place of meeting. Several sisters came with revelations, visions and prophecies that made indelible impressions upon the large gatherings assembled day after day. Sister Hart had a song of her own composition about ''The Bible Band.'' Sister Broadnax was conspicuous for her deep spiritual testimonies. Sisters B. Crowder and Lizzie S. taught Bible lessons with telling effect. Such a cruel warfare followed this meeting it is fitting to say that contrary to any previous custom we wore red badges that year, significant of the fight that followed, of which we knew nothing when the color was selected. Satan was intensely enraged over our victories for righteousness, and he turned out all his artillery against us ere we met again in our final separate women's district association at Woodlawn.

As God hath declared in Is. 54: 17, ''No weapon that is formed against thee shall prosper, and every tongue that shall rise against thee in judgment thou shalt condemn.'' We found it true; glory be to God! Virginia was tried to the uttermost, and persecuted with cruel hatred for no other cause than her contention for holiness of heart and uprightness of daily deportment. A general awakening in the study of the Bible followed these great meetings. Bible texts were repeated around the firesides and at the dining-room tables as well as in Sunday school and other religious meetings. A general reform was evidently going on toward the development of the women and the betterment of the home and church life of the people. Women were giving up the vile habits of beer drinking and snuff-dipping, and using their little mites thus saved in getting our Christian literature and contributing to our missionary and educational work. Besides ''Hope,'' Miss J. P, Moore's paper that was generally used by our women for Bible study, Virginia published at different times ''The Women's Messenger'' and ''The Missionary Helper'' to assist in the development of our women's work.

The last Woodlawn district association meeting was greatly hindered because of the opposition that was then raging, hence comparatively few attended, but a sufficient number to justify Virginia in her contention for Bible righteousness and encourage her to continue contending for the faith once delivered to the saints. This opposition that came so heavily upon us only gave wings to our speed. In the course of time the work grew more rapidly and more surely after it passed victoriously through the fiery trials of affliction.

Today women's Christian organizations belt the globe, and the Negro woman is doing a noble part to forward every righteous movement that makes for the peace and uplift of humanity and the glory of God.

CHAPTER V.

A Period of Stern Opposition.

The Lord permitted a few of our Bible women to grow strong under this special ministry of grace known as the Bible Band work. This strength led the women to contend for the Bible plan of church government in the discipline of members, in supporting churches, and in preaching and teaching the gospel. The common evil practices of intemperance in beer drinking, tobacco using, excessive eating and dressing, and the desecrating custom of using church houses for fairs, festivals and other worldly amusements were all strongly condemned by our Bible women, while righteousness, holiness, purity and all the kindred graces of Christianity were upheld and emphasized. Ministers and laymen, who looked with disdain upon a criticism that came from a woman, and all those who were jealous of the growing popularity of the woman's work, as if there was some cause of alarm for the safety of their own positions of power and honor, all rose up in their churches, with all the influence and power of speech they could summon to oppose the woman's work and break it up if possible. The work had taken root too deeply in the hearts of our women ever to be uprooted, but we were given a good shaking and thrashing, and for a season the work seemed to stand still. The separate associational meeting was broken up, many local Bible Bands disbanded, and the good women patiently waited in silence, praying for God's will to be done. Virginia continued to hold meetings where she could find an opportunity. As God has always provided some way of escape for his servants, He provided for Virginia, for there were some preachers who never closed their churches against our work, and hence an opportunity was given for self-defense in the thickest of the fight. Brethren would come to our meetings to catch every word spoken, if thereby they might have some just cause to condemn our teaching, as being false doctrine. One minister was so desirous to destroy the work like Saul of Tarsus, he desired letters of authority that he might follow in the wake of our missionaries and destroy whatever good they might have accomplished. We praise God that just as He arrested Paul in his wild career and caused him to repent, He also stopped that minister, turned him around completely and made him one

of the strongest friends to our work we have in all
the land.

While in his rage, desiring to destroy our work, he
came to hear Virginia speak for the expressed purpose
of getting a just case against her. Virginia was totally ignorant of this scheme, but she did notice the
reverend gentleman sat with his back toward her while
she spoke, as if warming himself near the stove. She
spoke in her usual earnest, impressive manner, and
from the sequel that we will now relate, it is quite
evident she spoke more wisely than she knew. When
she concluded her remarks and asked those who wished
to speak to express themselves, this Rev. H. arose and
made a marvelous confession. He told of his purpose
in coming to that meeting, as already stated, and then
said that he was regarded by his church as a fluent
speaker, but he was then unable to speak and only rose
to make a confession. The following are his words:

"I have been washed, rinsed, starched, hung up,
dried, sprinkled and ironed, and am now ready for
service; not to destroy, but to do all in my power to
forward this branch of God's work as zealously as I
had determined to oppose it."

He has kept his word and today our woman's work
has no better friend among the able ministers of the
race than that brother. This minister had a brother,
Frank, who lived in the town where we met him. The

brother was so opposed to our work when Miss King and Virginia called to see his wife, who was specially interested in their work, he left his own house, refusing even to meet the missionary women. He went to his work, and from his own testimony, he became so troubled he could not work, but was compelled to come down to the church and hear what those women said. Suffice it to say, just as his brother was so wondrously transformed during Virginia's discourse, so was he. Great joy came to all our sisters in that place, for those two men's friendship meant much to the existence of our work there.

Another brother who opposed our work said, on a certain occasion, "I would rather take a rail and flail the life out of a woman than to hear her speak in the church." As he spoke, not knowing what he said, God forgave him, brought him to the light, and he made an open confession of his fault.

There was another brother in the Durhamville district who took special delight in harassing the weaker women in the absence of their teacher. Upon a certain occasion, when Virginia was visiting that section, the sisters reported that brother and asked Virginia to speak to him. As usual an opportunity was given the missionary to present her work to the church. All believers rejoiced as she spoke, and the enemies were silenced for the time being. In concluding her address she said: ''If any one present is not convinced of the Divine authority of the woman's work, ask any question and a far as I am able I'll gladly give the Bible teaching relating to it.'' No one asked a single question, although the brother was present that had given the sisters of that church so much annoyance. When the service closed, however, we met the brother and rejoiced to learn that he had been won over to the cause of missions and he joined heart and hand with the Bible women to push the Lord's work on to victory. He never faltered after that day, but ever defended and supported our cause to the day of his death.

When the opposition raged fiercely, a certain minister, Bob T. by name, came to one of our churches with the expressed intention to throw Virginia out of the window. God was manifestly present that night, and raised up friends to protect her and maintain the cause she represented, that she had never known before, and no hand was raised against her. Glory be to God for his great power of deliverance, as shown on that special occasion.

In some places church houses were locked against our Bible women, and violent hands even laid upon some. Dear Sister Nancy C. said had not Sister Susan S. come to her rescue she would have been badly beaten for attempting to hold a woman's meeting in her own church.

In another vicinity Brother F. P. became so enraged he drew a gun on his wife after she had gotten in a wagon to go to one of our Bible Band meetings, and threatened to take her life if she went a step farther. Of course she was obliged to stop that time and stay home, but that man soon died; he was not permitted to live long enough to prohibit that good woman a second time from going when her missionary sisters called a meeting. This incident did much to allay the persecution throughout that section. While men opposed and Satan strove our progress to retard, God was with us and was only permitting those trials our dross to consume and our gold to refine. Those oppositions proved to be stepping stones to nobler and more extended endeavors. Virginia was soon appointed missionary by the W. B. H. M. S. Thus strengthened, she was better prepared to work than ever. She made two missionary tours through the North and East, This was a source of great strength and pleasure to her.

After such a season of conflict she needed the rest and desirable change the northern tours provided. In the great Saratoga meetings of the Northern Baptists' Anniversary Virginia spoke twice and seemed to please the great audiences. The press complimented her addresses as being among the best delivered. All the other lady speakers were of the Caucasian race. God used her in the North to touch many hearts by singing the plantation melodies.

In the great state meeting in Rochester, N. Y., Virginia was given a place on the program. The vast audience heard her gladly, and the reception committee gave her a queenly entertainment, several young women vying with each other to see that she was well supplied with the delicacies of the feast. The same hearty welcome was given her wherever she went as missionary of the W. B. H. M. S. in the states of New York, New Jersey, Ohio, Pennsylvania and Illinois. These northern meetings referred to were like oases in the desert to our heroic missionary. Such gracious words of cheer, such hospitable entertainment, such applause, such substantial endorsement Virginia had never before experienced.

One day, after canvassing until eventide in Saratoga, N. Y., in the interest of the B. & N. I. with no apparent success, she finally came to a wealthy man, Mr. A. Trask, that gave her a promise of one hundred dollars on a certain condition. She did not succeed in meeting the condition but the gentleman paid her $50 of the promised sum. You can imagine her joy from that experience. She was also quite highly favored by others in Saratoga and Troy, N. Y., when traveling in the interest of the school.

Returning south to her field of labor she came with new zeal and began afresh to develop the work she had so nobly begun.

New effort was put forth in the industrial feature of our work. Many beautiful quilts were made whereby our treasuries were considerably increased. A beautiful silk crazy patch quilt handsomely worked throughout with various designs and fancy stitches was made by the Memphis Bible women and sent to the W. B. H. M. S. as a donation to missions.

As Virginia traveled through the rural districts during the period of opposition it was difficult at times to get any conveyance. She was never particular, riding in anything that could be secured, from a wheelbarrow to a top buggy, and often walking when nothing could be secured. About this time God moved one of her country friends to dedicate his buggy and two horses to the work of missions. So whenever this friend, whom we will call Brother Jas. T., knew Virginia was expected, conveyance was always provided. The home of that dear brother and his beloved wife ever kept its doors open to God's traveling heralds, and was accordingly blessed both temporarily and spiritually. A certain meeting was appointed in that neighborhood and these good people, Brother J. T. and his wife, expected to meet Virginia there and convey her on her journey through the country. Virginia was

somewhat delayed and came to the place of meeting
after the women had all gathered while they waited.
Rev. Elias A., the pastor, was criticising our work
very severely, counting it a waste of time and even
less than child's play. In the midst of the controversy the women observed a dust in the road which
announced the near approach of some vehicle. All
eyes were turned in that direction and soon the buggy
that brought the missionary came in sight. With
great joy the women arose, clapped their hands, and
cried out in joyous exclamations. They believed that
their cause would be well defended.

The work was fully explained and God used Virginia, little woman as she was, so gently, so sweetly,
and so quietly that the good minister was soon led into
the light of the gospel teaching regarding our work,
and he quieted down as a shorn lamb, bade us go forward and assured us that he would encourage the
work in his church.

Not one of all our opposers would ever enter into
single combat with Virginia.

We'll conclude this chapter on opposition with the
following convincing and pathetic story. While the
church and world were opposing, there were relatives
of Virginia in sympathy with the opposition party
and they would suggest that it was entirely out of
place, unreasonable and unlike God to call a woman

of family so frequently from her home duties.

Of course this family talk soon reached Virginia's ears, so she became very serious about her position, and began to think it did seem unreasonable that God would give her any work that called her so often from her home. Accordingly, while in this mood, she went to Stanton to hold a meeting. After the service one of the good women approacheu her and said, ''God surely sent you to us at this time; our hindrances are so great and so numerous that we could not possibly carry on our Bible Band work without an occasional visit from you.'' Virginia replied, ''I don't know when I'll come again, for it seems that I ought to be at home with my children.'' Immediately there on the spot, this revelation was made to Virginia's inmost soul, ''What if God should take all the children away.'' So great was the change in Virginia's countenance as she quietly sat down the sisters desired to know what had happened to her.

Virginia returned to her home with the understanding she would come back to a neighboring town the following Saturday, if the weather was fair. (Should it rain the place could scarcely be reached, as a low, swampy territory intervened between the railroad station and that country village.) During that week one of her children, dear little Selena, her third daughter, was taken ill. On Saturday morning, the date appointed to go to that meeting, provided the weather was fair, her little girl arose from her breakfast sick and was observed to be unsusually quiet; the weather also was cloudy, whereupon Virginia decided to remain home. She called in a physician to see Selena, who began at once to treat her for tonsilitis. The little one continued to grow worse, until it soon became evident the Lord was going to take her to himself. Through this affliction Virginia was made to see plainly that she could stay home and sit by the bedside of her children and have all the assistance that medical skill could render, and yet God could take her children to himself if he so willed it. After the dear Lord had fully convinced his child that the watchman watched, but in vain, unless God kept the city, He then made Virginia reconciled to his will relative to Selena's recovery or death. He showed Virginia so plainly that He would take the darling little one away that she sat by her bedside the night before she died and prepared her burial clothing. The next day, as the end drew near, the sweet child asked her mama to take her in the parlor. Mama satisfied her by taking her in her arms, with her bed covering about her, to the parlor. After the child looked about all she wished she then expresed a wish to lie on mama's bed. She was granted that wish also, and her mama talked to her of going to Heaven,

as though she was going to school. Virginia sent
messages of love to her mother and sister in Heaven
and told the little darling she would come by and ₋y.
In a little while the child prayed, saying: "Lord
Jesus, help me," and then patting her mama on the
cheeks she said lastly, "Poor little mama," and
sweetly fell asleep in Jesus, without a struggle, after
bidding her papa also to meet her in Heaven.

The home going of our darling little Selena is one
of the most blessed experiences in the life of Virginia.
Heaven has ever since seemed nearer; and what we
call death only a transition, only a gateway into the
Paradise of God. This darling child was laid to rest
Friday afternoon. Virginia went on her mission Saturday morning. So mightily did God use her on that
occasion that her bitterest opposers said: "Let that
woman alone, God is truly with her." She has ever
since been enabled to trust God for the care of her
home and her children; nothing has been allowed to
hinder her from doing her Master's bidding when sufficient light has been given her to direct her course.
We praise God for afflictions; for in mercy they are
all sent to bring us near to God.

CHAPTER VI.

Virginia's Private Life.

I'm sure all would like to know something of the home life of our missionary, and our story would be incomplete did we not at least introduce you to Virginia's dear ones at home. At the beginning of her missionary work she was comfortably situated in her own home, with other possessions that brought her a small income. Her husband was not a professor of religion at the beginning of her missionary career, and naturally was greatly opposed to her frequently going from home. One day he asked her, ''When is this business going to stop?'' She replied, ''I don't know; but I belong to God first, and you next; so you two must settle it.'' Truly God inspired that answer. She took herself absolutely out of the management of the affair and accepted the humble position of an obedient servant. God verily did settle the question. He convinced the husband fully that He had called his wife to a special service and to hinder her would mean death to him. Of course there was no alternative; the husband, after a desperate struggle with the world, the flesh and the devil, yielded to God, and made an open profession of faith in Jesus and joined the church militant. This husband has ever since been helpful in attending to much of the business connected with Virginia's missionary work these twenty years.

Two of Virginia's daughters, Emma and Elizabeth, were converted before their father, but had not been baptized. Twenty years ago there was as little faith among colored people in children's conversions as there was in women's work. The Lord gave Virginia a beautiful experience relative to Emma's and Elizabeth's baptism by using one of his accustomed ways of revealing his will to her through song. On this ocasion this song,

"Go wash in that beautiful pool,"

came ringing in her soul, then through her voice, without cessation, until an investigation was forced upon her. While she meditated God revealed to her that she should give her consent to her children's baptism. This being done, the song had spent its force and gently passed away. Glory be to God! The two girls and their father were all baptized at the same time by Rev. H. Smith, a scene never to be forgotten in the family's history. These two girls developed beautifully into pure, noble womanhood, the joy, the comfort and keepers of the home, together with the good women secured from time to time to assist them; notably among whom were Sisters Kitty, Brinkley and Johnson. Little Selena's death made a deep impression upon all the children; even the two younger ones were made to think seriously of heavenly things. The baby boy said, as he looked in the open grave where his little sister's body was deposited: "Mama, I thought heaven was up (pointing thither as he spoke), where you say sister has gone; why do you place her in the ground?" Soon after this sorrow these two younger children, Virginia and Julius, professed to love Jesus and were baptized into the fellowship of the church.

Emma exhibited special talent for music from a small child, and besides graduating from the Normal course of Howe Institute she was given special musical advantages in the Musical Conservatory of Chicago, Ill., and is now the music teacher in her alma mater. Emma married at an early age; she has a good devoted husband and three bright, intelligent little children. Emma has a merry, cheerful, happy disposition, is naturally musical, careful, economical and contented, never worrying however time or tide go. She and her husband live happily together, even as did Isaac and Rebecca, each sharing the joys and sorrows of life together. Their three children are veritably the re-production of father and mother, all three musical, loving and kind to each other; the baby at three years of age repeats his alphabet and sings several little songs. They all delight to sit in Grandma Virginia's lap and listen to her tell them Bible stories, as well as "Mother Goose's Tales" and "Aesop's Fables." What would home be without the dear innocent little children? May we all praise God for children, and like the good women of Bible times count ourselves blessed of God to be the mothers of many children, that we might train them up for the Master's kingdom, even as did Hannah, Sarah, Rachel, Elizabeth and the Virgin Mary.

Elizabeth, when a little girl, would say to her mother when she returned home, tired and weary from school or a missionary trip, "Sit down, mama, and rest yourself, I'll bring your tea to you.' Elizabeth won laurels as a faithful, capable student at Howe Institute, and thereby, through Dr. H. R. Traver, secured a scholarship in Moody's School for Girls in Northfield, Mass. She spent two sucessful and profitable years there, but her great desire to see the loved ones at home caused her return south, and she graduated from the academic course of Roger Williams University. She has suceeded as a teacher and had the short experience of five years' married life. She was left a widow without children. On her return to her old home she commenced life's work again by pursuing her long cherished hope of studying medicine, a study she has shown special adaptability for from a child. It was due to her excellence in the study of physiology she secured the scholarship in Northfield. Emma and Elizabeth both make excellent housewives.

Virginia herself was brought up under the first idea given the freedmen of education which was to educate the head to the neglect of the hand, and she learned from the hard school of experience the grave mistake of that course and was determined her girls should not suffer the inconveniences she had from so great a misfortune. So all her children were early taught the every day domestic duties of life. As has been stated, Elizabeth was always solicitous about her mother's comfort at home; and while Emma, who was absorbed in her music, might forget and be slow in preparing the supper on time, Elizabeth had her time fixed for her household duties and would see to it that mama had her supper on time. As she grew older, and even during her married life, when she had her husband to please and her own home to care for, she was ever mindful of mother, father, sisters and brother at home; often expressing her love in substantial, generous contributions to the family's necessities. Virginia, the youngest daughter, her

mama's namesake, has just graduated with honor
from Fisk University in the Normal class of 1907.
She is well prepared for any service the Lord may
call her to. She is more than ordinarily prepared to
grace any home as its queen, beintg able to do well
any domestic service required in the home. She is
also prepared to do good work in the school room, having given general satisfaction as practice teacher during her year's experience under the training teacher
of her alma mater. This daughter also has skill in
the dressmaking art, having already made quite a
number of beautiful garments for self and friends.
Our missionary has only one boy; he is named, of
course, for his father, Julius A. O. B., Jr. This child
cared little for books, but early gave evidence of
mechanical skill. He began to repair shoes when
quite a boy, making a shoe shop of one end of his
mama's back porch. After nearing the completion of
the English course at Fisk he was sent to an industrial school, and there improved his natural talent for
shoemaking. He is destined to succeed as a shoemaker when he reaches maturity and the responsibilities of life rest upon him. His employers are delighted with his work and think it quite strange for
one so young as he to have a trade so well in hand.
Virginia is especially anxious about her boy; she took
him with her on many a missionary journey. He
would pass the Bibles and hymn books around, help

her sing, open gates when traveling through country
districts and take general interest in all he thought
his mama was interested in. In his childhood he
would often be seen holding a service, he standing
up preaching with one person (his little sister Virgie)
for his audience. His mother believes God's word,
that says, ''Train up a child in the way he should
go and when he is old he will not depart from it.''
Thus while she is not pleased with her boy's present
deportment in every particular she is praying and
hoping to have her heart's desire realized in her only
son as in her three daughters. Virginia's husband
and children have the utmost confidence in her work,
and give her their devotion and encouragement, in
every effort she puts forth to advance the Master s
work. This little glimpse into the private life of our
missionary may help some other burdened mother to
see that God is able to use all his children, whether
married or single, to do whatever work He has given
them talent to do. Virginia's home was often used
as the home of the missionary women from the country who would attend the training school; hence all
the early workers became interested in Virginia's children, and the children spent many of their summers
visiting these friends, to the mutual enjoyment of the
children and the friends. Virginia's sister Selena
came to visit her at a certain time, and while there
their brother John took quite sick. This caused a

temporary removal of that sister, who had come to visit, as it was deemed necessary for her to stay and help nurse the brother back to health again, if the Lord willed he should recover. This change for Sister Selena proved to be God's plan to lead her into a higher and fuller exprience of grace, which has added much to her usefulness as a Christian worker and enabled her to be of inestimable value to her husband, Rev. William G., in carrying on a sucessful pastorate and managing a mission station. It was during her visit to the south that she was so manifestly used of God in that Durhamville meeting. The two sisters nursed their brother John back to health through the mighty help of God. As we have more to say relative to God's power to heal, we'll conclude this chapter and say more of this illness later.

Virginia's other brothers, William Henry, Robert and Rufus, were not neglected in her ministries of grace; she often visited Robert and Rufus in their homes, prayed with and for them and endeavored by example and precept to show them the beauty and power of the Christian life. They have both professed to love Jesus. We hope their sister's life will inspire them to follow her worthy example. Her sister Annie and family are all active workers in the church. The three sisters, Virginia, Selena and Annie, appear to vie with each other in their earnest endeavors to promote the cause of missions. Rev. William G. and Mr. P., Virginia's brothers-in-law, are loyal supporters of their sister's efforts. Rev. William G. is a most ardent admirer of his sister's devotion to Bible study and her zeal for Christian endeavor, and often makes her blush whene'er she is in his church by the many encomiums of praise he showers upon her. Well, I guess it's all right to scatter a few flowers o'er our friends before they die.

CHAPTER VII.

Missionary Journeys With Associate Workers.

As the Apostle Paul was comforted and helped by the coming of his fellow laborers, Virginia was greatly strengthened as other sisters consecrated themselves to the Lord's work and accompanied her through their respective districts. In the Stanton district Sister J. S. was an indispensable factor. God has given Sister Julia a good, kind husband who loved our work and could be depended upon for any help he was able to render. The train never came too late or too early for Brother S. to meet Virginia at the Stanton depot. He would care for the home and children and arrange for his wife and Virginia to make their missionary tours throughout the district to hold local and quarterly Bible Band meetings. Sister Julia is one of the sweet singers in Israel; many a person has been aroused, waked up and started on a career of usefulness in God's army through the strains of Sister Julia's sweet music. This dear woman soon grew strong enough to direct and foster the Bible Band work of the Stanton district, and Virginia needed to go there only to hold quarterly meetings, at which time the Bible Band of the entire district would come together in some one church of the district. At these stated quarterly meetings the local Bible Band was expected to make reports of the mission work of the quarter, and contribute to the Institute for which they were all laboring. During one of Virginia's tours in this district she and Sister Julia went far away in the country to a church pastored by Rev. J. D. O. There they met a dear old sister who was recognized as the mother of the church. She was deeply moved by the messages delivered by her visiting sisters. In the service they sang

"Is my name written down."

Virginia and Julia had gone to this church to invite the women to the general quarterly meeting to be held in Stanton the next day. No one thought it possible to come because the horses were all in use on the farm and it was too far to walk, but this mother in Israel, referred to above, had been so deeply impressed by the missionaries that she feared her name would be "sitting down" instead of written down if she did not come to our meeting. So she made a great effort and God helped her to get to the meeting. She was running over with joy and she testified to the joy of all present; even Dr. H. R. Traver, who was then president of the Memphis school and had come to this meeting to inspect and encourage the work, was made to rejoice and preach with such power that the common people heard him gladly. Stanton district was very fruitful. Many young people from this district were sent to our school, women gave up snuff dipping, learned to read their Bibles and care for their homes as they had never done before. Indeed, a general reform in the home life of our women was truly begun. Our Bible women of this district were very faithful in administering to the sick of their communities. About this time one of our slanderers was taken seriously ill. Being without means to secure the necessary comforts our Bible women went to her relief; the sick woman was compelled to confess her faults; she begged the good women to forgive her, and promised, if God ever permitted her health to be restored, that she would come to the church and join the Bible Band if she didn't have a hat to wear on her head. Praise God! We can testify that she fulfilled her promise, for Virginia was present when she came to the meeting with a shawl over her head, because she had no hat and no money with which to buy one.

"Great is the mystery of godliness!" God has many ways to lead people to the acknowledgment of the truth; thus sickness often proves to be a blessing in disguise. The Lord blessed Sister Julia through her affiliation with Virginia to educate her oldest daughter and encourage all her children to live noble, useful lives. The oldest daughter married one of our most successful physicians, both of whom love and cherish our missionary for the help she has been to them in directing their lives in the King's highway. Another young man from this Stanton district, Dr. S. G. M., was induced to go to school through our Missionary V., whom he regards as his foster mother, and he has now risen to wealth and renown as a successful medical practitioner in the state of Mississippi. He married an intelligent, strong young woman, who is also a physician; they work beautifully together. Virginia has enjoyed the privilege of visiting their home. The home was one continuous scene of joy, plenty and pleasure during her visit. The young couple seemed never to tire of doing kindnesses to show their love and gratitude to our Virginia. Sister Julia continues to labor zealously in the great work of missions. She enjoys in the home of her nativity

the confidence and respect of the entire community.
Sister Martha P. entered zealously into our Bible
Band work. Starting out she used what she had, a
gray mule and a little dog that went regularly each
week with her to her Bible Band meeting, four miles
from her home, the mule to carry her and the dog to
protect her. This faithful effort, in due season, was
richly rewarded. Sister Martha was apt and soon
learned to give Bible lessons effectively; thus she was
very helpful in our meetings. Her children were all
converted at an early age and joined heartily with
their mother as she labored in our children's meetings in her neighborhood. Her progress was rapid
and she became a helpful ally to our missionary force
in her vicinity. When bitter opposition arose Sister
Martha felt it keenly and she finally decided she could
do more effective service to join with those who were
less opposed to woman's work and were also in sympathy with the doctrine of sanctification. So she
ceased her affiliation with our organized work. There
were other strong Bible women in the Woodlawn district to which Sister Martha first belonged, namely,
Sisters Bell C., Nealy R., Nancy T. and Sarah B. These
have all continued steadfast in the faith and can ever
be relied upon to stand up for the Master's cause as
advocated by the Christian women of this age. Sister
Amanda C. was a power with the children. She had a

host of them in Chelsea, N. Memphis, and God used
her effectively to teach those children the beautiful
story of Jesus and his love. Our children's Sunshine
Bands and sewing schools are very helpful agencies
in the Christian training of our children. Much attention is given to our children's department.

Sisters Amanda C. and Hannah J. of Memphis often
went with Virginia on her mission tours through the
country and took great delight in helping to lead·their
less fortunate sisters and brothers to the highway of
consistent Christian living. Sister Amanda C. was a
devout Christian woman, but she had been deprived of
all educational advantages; so among the first things
she did when awakened to her duty as a Christian
woman she went to our Institute, and soon learned to
read her Bible. Never was a soul happier than she
when she could read her Bible for herself.

After Virginia had made a number of visits to Sister Hannah's home sufficient to provoke the evil
minded to warn Hannah's husband against his wife's
associating with that mannish woman (which many
called Virginia), one night Virginia called again to
have Sister Hannah accompany her to a meeting in
her neighborhood. After the women had gone Hannah's husband concluded he would go and see what
mischief those women were doing. As usual God
directed his words as Virginia spoke them to that

husband's heart; that husband was completely turned around and went home a new man, no longer suspicious of our women's work, but one of its best friends and remained true to us until death. He soon joined the church and lived a faithful, devoted member, always ready to defend and help the women in their special lines of missionary work. Brother Johnson even built a tabernacle on his own ground and argely at his own expense, that the women might have one place where they would be free to worship the Lord according to the dictates of their own consciences, with no preacher or deacon to molest them or make them afraid. The last public service on the last day of this good man's life on earth was the arranging of that tabernacle for a meeting. Virginia and several other sisters had gone to his home to attend the appointed meeting when the summons came that called his wife and children to the bedside to which he had been carried after his fall while in the act of getting upon his wagon to return home after his day's work was done. He was stricken with a paralytic stroke. He was taken to a friend's house near by, where in spite of all the medical aid that could be given he departed this life ere the morning light of the next day. He was conscious when his wife and children reached him and assured them that it was well with his soul. Thus triumphantly, like a warrior fresh from the victory of a battlefield (for only the previous Sunday he had vowed his allegiance to God and to the further success of our missionary work, which God had used to his soul's salvation), he wrapped the drapery of his couch about him and lay down to pleasant dreams. Since Brother Johnson's death Sister H. J. has had many sorrows, but through them all God has been gracious and she has been able to realize to the fullness of God's promise to be a husband to the widow and a father to the fatherless.

Sister Nancy T. entered heartily into our mission work and was very helpful in the Durhamville district. She made one extended trip with Virginia and another district worker, Sister Mattie B. of Trenton. This trip was made through the country partly in a wagon and partly on horseback, up hill, down hill, through creeks, valleys and swamps. One of these hills was so steep all the missionaries save Sister Mattie B. felt obliged to dismount and walk down the rugged slope. When in the saddles again the company traveled on and on until eventide brought them to their journey's end for that day. So weary and worn were our poor missionaries when they reached their destination they slid down from their horses and required help to escort them into the house of the dear sister who awaited them. A hearty welcome was extended and every comfort provided that the hostess could afford.

Our missionaries spent Sunday with Rev. Williams' people and had several blessed services. Usually after great suffering or sacrifice a rich spiritual feast awaited our heroine. That Sunday meeting in that town on the Mississippi river was not an exception to the rule. The missionaries were sufficiently refreshed and edified to begin their return trip Monday morning. In seeking some way to pursue their journey they learned that a person was going to move to the hills that very day, and they could secure passage in that wagon on top of the household goods, for a small fee. The arrangement was made and so we began our travel; the day was cold and stormy, rain and snow striving with each other for the mastery. Patiently the missionaries made that journey, traveling all day, exposed to the inclemency of the weather, with no protection save their ordinary winter wraps, which were so hard frozen when they reached town at nightfall it took all night to thaw out and dry their clothing for the next day's journey. The hardships of this trip was too great for Sister Nancy T., and like Mark of old, she returned home from this point, the town of R. Although Sister Nancy gave up extended missionary work throughout the district she remained faithful to her local Bible Band work until her death. One of the best enlarged pictures of Virginia we have ever seen is the one Sister Nancy T. had made and hung upon the wall of the guest chamber of her neat cottage home.

The other sister, Mattie B., who was accompanying Virginia at this point in our story, was courageous and faithful, so she continued on and went with Virginia throughout the bounds of the Mississippi and Tennessee central district, and also throughout the western Tennessee central district. Sister M. B. on this trip proved that she was able to endure hardness as a good soldier of Jesus Christ. She grew in favor with the people among whom she labored and she worked for several years under the appointment of the Western Tennessee Central District Association. After a time, because of her husband's business, she found it necessary to move to the state of Illinois. However, she continues to labor in Sunday school work and the Woman's Missionary Society of her church. Her persistency and courage make her one of the best agents for circulating our religious literature we have ever had. God has blessed this sister with a kind, indulgent husband who makes her comfortable, well furnished home the happiest place on earth to her, but he himself lacks the one thing needful, the religion of the Lord Jesus, and we kindly ask that all God's people who read this booklet join with us in prayer for his salvation. "For what will it profit a man to gain the whole world, and lose his own soul?" Like

Cornelius of old, Mr. B. has been and is exceedingly kind to the traveling people of God, being ever ready to entertain and administer to their temporal necessities.

Virginia gradually induced her friend Florence P. C. to go with her and learn something of the great work the Master was doing through our women, for our women and children. Through a few missionary trips, visits and meetings this dear woman saw that God had a great work for his female servants to do. Step by step she took hold and God has gently yet surely led her forward until now Sister Florence is one of our most efficient and faithful Christian workers in all lines of church work. She did excellent work last year as corresponding secretary of the woman's Tennessee state convention. She is especially interested in our youth; has been a teacher many years and still teaches; does mission work, and leads a band of Christian women in a noble effort to establish and foster a home for orphans and the aged poor. How like our Lord Jesus, who taught his disciples, was our missionary who taught and then accompanied all these dear women in the beginning of their missionary careers, thus helping to establish them in the great work of Christian missions! Virginia believed that God called all his servants to work, and if she could direct them how to use the varied gifts God had given them her joy was full, thus to serve and see the blessed work of Christ's kingdom grow and multiply through the increase of laborers in the vineyard. Blessed thought is this:

> "Jesus shall reign, where'er the sun,
> Doth his successive journeys run,
> His kingdom stretch from shore to shore,
> Till moons shall wax and wane no more."

Ere this glorious triumph is realized the servants of God are privileged to labor in the Master's vineyard according to their several abilities. Thus laboring, who'll be able to rejoice with our Lord when he comes to make up his jewels and divide the spoils with the strong. Isa. 53: 1, 12.

CHAPTER VIII.

Divine Healing.

Humbly and reverently do we pen the following experiences that increased Virginia's faith in Christ's power to heal our bodily infirmities in this age as when He was here in person. The more we study the Bible the more the Holy Spirit enlightens us in its teachings. Virginia had often read Mark 16: 17, 18, and hoped to see those truths fulfilled in the experiences of her own life. This hope was verily realized. Her own recovery from a serious illness that was considered hopeless was her first experience of the Master's power to heal. Glory be to God! The brother, John, of whom we've written, had two special attacks of sickness in which God's healing power was manifest in his recovery. At one time he had had a bone taken from his arm, he became very despondent and was ill at ease because he feared he could never use that hand again. One morning Virginia was led of the Lord to give him a certain Scripture to read, namely, Jas. 5:

13, 17, while she went off to school, and it its close
brought two of her believing Bible women, Sisters
Celia J. and Amanda C., to her home to pray with her
for her brother's recovery. Every act was performed
from the clear guidance of the Holy Spirit. At the
close of the sister's prayers that brother arose from
his bed kneeled down and prayed, then sang praises to
God in the lines or the following song:

"None but the righteous shall see God."

The next morning he arose, dressed himself and went
to town, using for the first time since the operation
that hand on his afflicted arm. It was a strange incident that this brother went to his friend Smith's
home, who also was expecting to have a serious operation performed the next day (Sunday). Because
Brother John was a medical doctor his friend Smith
urged him to stay with him and see him through his
operation. His case makes us think of these suggestive lines of the song writer:

"He'll make your great commission known,
  And ye shall prove his gospel true,
By all the works that He has done,
  By all the wonders ye shall do."

The following remarkable incident did occur. That
Saturday night Mr. Smith dreamed that Virginia
came to see him and read her Bible to him. He was
so impressed with his dream that he narrated it to
her brother John, who immediately wrote a letter to

his sister, explaining the cause of his failure to return home, telling her also of his friend's dream and urging her to come down at once in company with Sister Celia J. and pray for Mr. Smith as they did for him. The two women went, read the Word, touching God's power to heal, and prayed that God would direct the physicians and in his own way give the needed relief to the sick man. The women then left and went to church. The doctors who expected to perform the operation came according to their appointment. God had preceded the physicians, and brought about such a change in the affected part of the man's body that the physicians decided to defer the operation a week later. In the meantime Virginia made another visit and again prayed for God's power to be manifest in the healing of the sick man. As the effectual fervent prayers of the righteous avail much God healed Mr. Smith without the operation ever being performed, which in the physicians' opinion would have caused the man's death, so serious was the nature of his case. Mr. Smith still lives to testify to what appeared to him a miraculous cure. Simply the fulfillment of God's word and, nothing more. Jas. 5: 14, 15.

The special illness of her brother John, referred to in a previous chapter, when his sister Selena tarried in Memphis to wait upon him, was another case in

which God's healing power was evident. Brother
John had again been operated upon and came to the
verge of the grave; physicians and loved ones all
gave him up, save Virginia, who had been assured he
would escape death, as it were, by the skin of his teeth;
accordingly that Sunday of blessed memory when this
dear brother lay semi-conscious, apparently in the
throes of death, Virginia sat at his bedside watching
and waiting for the manifestation of God's power.
Praise the Lord! Her waiting was not in vain. At
the close of that day of awful suspense and sore distress God's power was manifest. A change for the
better came, the sick man came to himself, as one
awakened from a deep sleep. Soon he began to talk.
About the first thing he said: ''I'm not going now,
I have seen that my way is clear, but God will not
take me now for He has more work for me to do.''
His recovery to health began from that moment. With
much tender care and gentle nursing he was restored
to health. In his extreme weakness it was very painful to move his body in the least, often causing him to
faint. One day when God had brought special comfort and joy to Virginia with this sweet message ringing in her soul: ''Every wedding guest must be
richly dressed, when the King, when the King comes
in.'' She went to her brother's bedside and looking
steadfastly upon him, her soul lifted in prayer to God

for his strength, was enabled finally to say to her sister Selena: "I say with authority you can move him now and he will not faint." Glory be to God! Strength was given him, he was moved and his clothing changed with blessed results. To God be all the glory! And may his Word be magnified through these testimonies. This dear brother was fully restored to health and lived a beautiful Christian life of service about three years longer. He was a successful physician and had a large practice, but he would ever fill his place in church Sunday morning if he had to leave before the service closed. He made a faithful member of the church and contributed largely to every need presented. He took delight in entertaining the missionary workers, both men and women, feeling that he could not do enough for those who were sacrificing their lives for his Master's cause.

On one occasion Virginia was impressed to call and see her friend, Mrs. G. R., who was reported very ill. She talked freely with this friend concerning her affliction and learned that her physician had decided there was no hope of her recovery without an operation, but because of the extreme heat, as it was midsummer, he hoped to give some remedy that would enable her to linger on until fall, when the weather would be more favorable for the operation. After hearing the patient's story Virginia asked her if she would like to have her pray for her. Mrs. G. R. readily responded "Yes." A prayer of faith was offered and Virginia, in company with her friend, F. P. C., bade their sick friend adieu. Mrs. G. R. testified that she was enabled to sit up that very afternoon. She continued to improve and was finally restored to health without an operation. She gave God the praise that was justly his. This experience of Mrs. G. R. did much to establish faith in the Bible teaching of Divine Healing.

Another of Virginia's friends, Mrs. V. M., was sorely afflicted with rheumatism. Virginia happened to call in to see her just at a time she could honor her Master and impress that aristocratic family with the reality of the religion of Jesus Christ and the effectiveness of the mission work that they had so lighty regarded. Mrs. V. M. was lying in bed and other members of the family seated around the bright, cheerful fire. After exchanging a few pleasant friendly greetings Virginia offered to pray, which offer was kindly accepted. The family all seemed greatly moved and the dear sick friend was greatly relieved, sufficiently to get up and expresse herself that she believed God had heard the prayer in her behalf.

Other illustrations might be given, but the above are sufficient to establish the truth that Jesus is the Great Physician, as well as the Great Savior, and it is the lack of faith, wisdom and consecration on the part of God's children that we do not have more evidences of God's healing power.

Notwithstanding we believe in God's power to heal, we would say that does not discard the use of means, and hence we believe also in the, science and practice of medicine as one of the divinely appointed means to man's physical healing. Sometimes in Christ's ministry he used means, as in the case of the man born blind, thus justifying the use of means by his children. In either instance, with or without the use of means, our life and health are dependent upon God's great power. ''In him we live and move and have our continual being.'' What privileges are ours to enjoy, as children of the King!

> ''When we walk with the Lord
> In the light of His Word,
>   What a glory he sheds on our way,
> When we do His good will,
> He abides with us still,
>   And with all who will trust and obey.''

CHAPTER IX.

Revival Meetings.

In our missionary's journeys she often visited churches when engaged in revival meetings. She entered as heartily into those services as any others. She ever realized that the chief object of all Christian work was the salvation of the souls of men.

The Durhamville revival of 1890 was one in which the Lord used Virginia very effectively. At that meeting she was blessed to see several members of her own family baptized into the fellowship of the Baptist church. In the Woodlawn revival much interest prevailed and our missionary labored earnestly and persuaded many to accept Jesus through her clear and simple presentation of God's plan of salvation and through her fervent prayers. Another time a revival meeting was in progress in the First Baptist church, Memphis, and Virginia was privileged to labor in it. Several years after one of the young men who was converted in that meeting told her that she would

never know how God used her to help him in his
struggle to cease from sin and accept Jesus. While
the spiritual part of the church as a whole labor together in our revival meetings for the salvation of
sinners, we would lay no special stress upon our missionary's labors in this particular, and only refer to
these special cases to emphasize the importance of
individual effort in the great work of winning souls to
Christ.

A great revival was in progress in the First Baptist
church, Nashville. There was one gentleman among
those desiring salvation who had attended every revival and heard the gospel preached by some of the
ablest gospel ministers of this day for more than
twenty years, all that time expressing a desire to be
saved. Rev. N. H. Pius was helping the good pastor
conduct the revival; the church members were truly
awake and taking an active part in the services. One
night after every plea had been made that seemed
necessary this anxious friend seemed still in darkness and doubt, when all at once Virginia was moved
of the Holy Spirit to go forward, kneel beside the
man and pray for his conversion. The power of the
Holy Spirit was manifestly present and the man's
heart was so melted under this glowing fire of the
Holy Spirit that he soon made a bright profession of
religion. In telling his experience of conversion he
said: ''I felt if I went to hell after such a prayer

was made for my escape it would be warm, indeed, for me."

A dear young woman at one time was greatly concerned about her salvation and though Satan tried hard to hold her she broke away from his pleadings and impelled by an irresistible force she came to our missionary for prayer and conference. Another consecrated Christian worker, Miss H. K. P., came in about the same time, and she and Virginia labored in prayer, song and in conference concerning God's plan of salvation until the dear girl was happily converted and went out rejoicing to tell the joyous news of her salvation.

A children's meeting, held at Woodlawn, was another special occasion when our missionary had the privilege of leading a number of children to the Savior's loving arms. We praise God that the church now encourages the conversion of children. Youth is the time, above all others, to come to Jesus for salvation.

"Remember now thy creator, in the days of thy youth, when the evil days come not, nor the years draw nigh when thou shalt say, I have no pleasure in them." This quotation is Solomon's injunction to young people, and we would emphasize it with all the power of our being. Those who wait late in life to come to Jesus waste many precious days in sin and folly, are less inclined to obey God's laws, and hence often find the Christian life more burdensome than joyous. ''Seek ye first the Kingdom of God and his righteousness, and all these things shall be added unto you.'' This quotation is the direct message of Jesus. Virginia gives her testimony as one who heeded that command and sayeth, ''Verily, verily God hath provided all things for her highest development as a Christian.'' Glory to God! for the blessed assurance of being an heir of God, an heir to a mansion, a robe and a crown, reserved in Heaven, for all who love Jesus and look for his appearing. These revival seasons have been times of special refreshing and spiritual edification to our churches. We thank God for any part the dear Lord permitted our missionary to share in them. We would not close this chapter without reference to the happy conversion of Brother Sumner. He became deeply convicted of sin, so much so he could not attend to his daily labor; thus burdened, he came into one of our missionary prayer meetings. The sisters were all glad to see him in their meeting and they all entered heartily into the service, making Brother Sumner's conversion the principal object of their prayers. God was present and the burdened soul was relieved and his sorrow changed to joy in his acknowledging Jesus as his personal Savior. We praise God and give him all the glory for the dear ones herein referred to as being saved in these revival meetings.

From the testimonies of the converts we have been emboldened to say what we have as to our missionary's labors in this great work of winning souls to Christ. Daniel sayeth: ''And they that be wise shall shine as the brightness of the firmament, and they that turn many to righteousness as the stars forever.''

Whatever we can do in turning men to righteousness let us ever strive to do, for it is God's will that in Christ's stead his children on earth should strive to reconcile man to God.

CHAPTER X.

Sanctification.

About ten years after the beginning of Virginia's career as missionary the doctrine of sanctification began to agitate the Christian church greatly, and our missionary encouraged the agitation as her own experience, and her conception of the Bible teaching of that truth led her to see the grave need of greater consecration and loyalty to Christ's cause on the part of both ministers and laity. A fresh anointing or filling of the Holy Spirit was given Virginia to give her the needed courage, wisdom and strength to contend for this truth and endure the persecutions that were sure to follow so aggressive a movement. The leading advocates of sanctification in some sections were so radical in their views on this subject that a wave of persecution spread far and wide, in some places churches were torn asunder and new churches were formed under the name of Holiness churches. Virginia bore up bravely under her persecution and providentially was removed from the scene of the conflict and brought in touch with more advanced Christians, who aided her in getting a clearer idea of the Bible teaching of sanctification. Thus she was enabled to adjust much of the growing confusion in the ranks of our Bible women, who like herself desired to follow the Lord wholly and at the same time retain their membership in their respective churches. We praise God for his presence in this special time of need, and for his wonderful deliverance of our missionary from the bitterest persecution of all her experiences, which at one time seemed a direct aim at her earthly existence. Among those who prayed for her special mention should be made of the Woodlawn Bible women, who called a special meeting at their church to pray for their leader. God heard their prayers and then and there assured them that they would see their sister again standing as usual in their church to tell the blessed story of Jesus and his love. Virginia could and did rejoice as one persecuted for righteousness' sake. That experience was a source of great spiritual strength, and although while passing through it to depart this life and be with Christ was far more preferable than life, she has lived to see God's power and wisdom in her deliverance and in prolonging her life on earth for further conflict. All glory and praise be given to the mighty God! whose might was manifestly shown in Virginia's deliverance and restoration. Many have been led into a closer walk with God, and many more have been led to see that God does call his children to a higher plane of consecrated Christian living than the nominal church member lives. God not only calls, but has promised power and assurance of victory o'er temptation to all believers who love him and keep his commandments. God wills that his children represent Him on earth, in their daily lives of useful service. To do this they must have the power and wisdom from above, that God will freely give to those who ask for them. If we know how to give good gifts to our children how much more will God give the Holy Spirit to those who ask for Him. The various helpful agencies God has provided in preachers, teachers, apostles, prophets and evangelists are all sent forth to edify and perfect his people, that they may grow unto the measure of his stature of the fullness of Christ unto a perfect man, and be no longer tossed about as children by every wind of doctrine. Eph. 4: 11, 12, 13.

May we all see the importance of the constant use of the appointed means of grace, the daily study of God's word, humble, faithful prayers, songs of praise and labors of love that our spiritual development may continue to be manifestly increased. In time may we all attain unto the perfect man in Christ Jesus, who of God, is made unto us, wisdom, and righteousness, and sanctification, and redemption. I Cor. 1: 30. Yes, in Christ Jesus all believers are sanctified, and according to their faith they become partakers of that grace that enables them to stand and testify to his power to save his people from their sins.

CHAPTER XI.

Virginia's Experience in Miss Moore's Fireside School.

As has been stated, it seemed to be God's plan for Virginia to move her headquarters. Accordingly she and her family moved to the city of her nativity December, 1899. She found congenial associates in "Sunshine Home," the headquarters of the Fireside School. We'll call this home "The Saints' Retreat," for it served as a resting, edifying and comforting resort for our missionary after her great conflict in contending for the great doctrines of Divine Healing and Sanctification.

For three years she labored in this school as one of Miss Moore's secretaries, assistant editor of Hope, and six months as supervisor of the work. For six months Miss Moore had a colored board of directors to direct her Fireside School. At that time she planned to transfer the management of her work to the colored people, as her own physical strength was failing. At her suggestion that board appointed Virginia as super-visor.

The experience of that six months was altogether satisfactory; the directors held regular monthly meet-ings, heard the various reports of the workers as to condition of work and gave the supervisor and secre-taries wise counsel and substantial encouragement whenever they came to present the work to their churches. The supervisor not only visited local churches of all denominations but the ministers' con-ferences and such other general bodies, either state or national, that met during those six months. Every-where she went the work was endorsed and the litera-ture circulated. The C. M. E. general conference met that spring in Nashville. Virginia, as supervisor of the Fireside School, was given a patient hearing. After her address many congratulations were extended her and the Fireside School recommended in most gracious terms.

Miss Moore's life was so thoroughly absorbed in her Fireside School that she was ill at ease all the while she was testing her new plan (as her letters clearly indicate). After six months she returned and made a new proposition to her board of directors relative toward their assuming the financial responsibility of the work, which responsibility she still carried per agreement. The ministers constituting her board, most of whom were carrying the great burden of church edifice building debt, decided that they could not assume other financial burdens; hence they all withdrew from the board and the Fireside School was again under the sole management of Miss J. P. Moore.

Virginia's experience in this work was very helpful; she regards it as her post course in Bible study for missionary activity in all its phases. The inmates of Sunshine Home at this time were earnest, devout, intelligent Christian women, whose lives were a benediction to every church in the city of Nashville in which they labored. Missionary meetings, children's meetings, Sunday school work, and house to house visiting were weekly services in which all these good women were expected to engage. Besides this the daily routine of work consisted in letter writing, mailing Hope and other literature, bookkeeping and housekeeping. The Wednesday afternoon consecration meeting was looked forward to as the special service of the week to meditate upon the deep things of God as the Holy Spirit revealed them to us in our daily Bible study; it was also a service when special prayers were offered for those making special requests. We praise God for those blessed meetings, of sweet communions and fellowship with those of kindred minds.

Several of God's chosen and tried children, both white and colored, came to the Wednesday afternoon consecration services. We would have you know the three other dear young women who served as secretaries at that time; their names are Henrietta K. Patrick, Mary G. Gibson and Joanna Greenlee. Sister M. H. Flowers was then the city missionary. We never knew a controversy to disturb the love and beautiful companionship of those dear women, whom God used to do a very gracious and acceptable service in promoting the Fireside School work. Before concluding this brief report of Virginia's special experience in the Fireside School, for indirectly she has been laboring in it and for it since her first meeting Miss Moore in January, 1886, we must say the Fireside School stands for Daily Bible study and Christian living consistent with the teachings of that blessed book of God. Then of course it stands for holiness of heart and purity and cleanliness of bodily actions; as a result of surrender and obedience to God's directions given by the indwelling Holy Spirit.

God has provided the power of the Holy Spirit to keep us, and He assures us if we walk in the Spirit we will not fulfill the lusts of the flesh. Gal. 5: 16. Acts 1: 8. I Pet. 1: 5. So wisely and righteously has this Fireside School work been managed that it has stemmed the tide of every wave of opposition. The founder ever urged her constituents to stand by their churches and not desert them when the spirit of dissolution and separation ran high, because of the misunderstandings and misinterpretations of the Bible teaching of holiness.

The principles of this Bible school have been thoroughly tested by the fires of cruel criticism and oppression, but they were founded upon God's sure word of the truth, and today they stand forth ''as clear as the sun and as terrible as an army with banners.''

We praise God, with Miss Moore, the great founder of the Fireside School, the most efficient agency God has given us, to develop the home life of our people, that the day has dawned when thoughtful Christians see the necessity of magnifying God's Word in its entirety, and are pleading with men everywhere to accept the Bible, God's blessed book of truth, for it verily is the power of God unto salvation to all who believe it.

CHAPTER XII.

Virginia's Work Extended.

From the fireside school work Virginia was called to state mission work. A new field of operations was at once entered upon, and other good men and women were reached who gladly embraced the opportunity to engage in our organized mission work. In the East Fork District Sister Crocker was found possessed of great zeal to work and has striven hard to do what she could, but had been greatly hindered. Virginia was enabled to help her specially and all the Christian women of that district generally by instructing them as to the Bible idea of woman's work. Thus the way was opened in the East Fork District for those women who were impelled by the Holy Spirit to do our Lord's blessed work. Sisters Crocker and Bell, who had been spiritually awakened, praised God that he opened the way for them to exercise their Spiritual gifts ere they died. A great work was begun in Clarksville through

Virginia and her associate worker, M. H. Flowers. This work has grown to such proportions that a stationed missionary has been located there through the kindness of the W. B. H. M. Society. Mrs. M. H. Flowers was permitted by this society to foster that work for a short while, then Miss R. J. Carter, of New York, was sent there. She has enlarged and strengthened the mission work in that city and vicinity until its helpfulness is acknowledged by the surrounding country. The following lines of work are successfully engaged in at our mission station in Clarksville: A woman's Bible class is taught; a missionary society does effective local district and state work; an art class and nurse training class are taught for special benefit of our young women; domestic science is taught to all the women; children's kindergarten, industrial school, temperance band and mission Sunday school are all operated under the management of our most efficient missionary, Miss R. J. Carter. This mission also sustains three workers who travel far and near, building up and enlarging the work of this mission. Steps are being taken to purchase ground and establish the mission on a permanent location. We ask our readers' prayers for the continued success of this noble endeavor. As Virginia traveled on toward the East several towns were visited, missionary societies organized, and our women encouraged to join our great organized effort for evangelizing the world.

Sister D. Furgerson of M. has developed into an efficient helper. Another sister of that town has shown much courage and perseverance. We hope success may crown her efforts.

Further on Virginia found a faithful little woman in Wartrace just waiting for some encouragement to go forward in her Lord's work, even as Simeon waited to see the Lord Jesus. A great meeting was held at that point, the good pastor joining heartily with our missionary in conducting a series of meetings that proved a blessing to the church. Quite a number of children were happily converted. The missionary society was organized, and it began at once to improve the dilapidated condition of everything about the church. This new life soon spread throughout the church, and the church edifice was soon changed, the improvements being so great one would scarcely recognize it as the same house only for its location. At S., another wideawake Sister Bell was found. She took hold of our woman's work earnestly from the very first. As we expected, she has developed into a strong worker and is now traveling throughout the Elk River District strengthening and enlarging our mission work. Virginia continued her journey eastward encouraging and enlisting volunteers into the Master's service. T. is the next town she visited. Though a small town a more active and faithful band

of Christian women would be hard to find than those
who enlisted in our work in T. God blessed that society with a good president, Mrs. J. Simmons, to begin with, which means so much to any new organization. The work grew steadily upward under her management. The women have developed beautifully;
they have done good work in their own town reliev-
ing the sick and needy; they have contributed to our
woman's work in the district, state and national organizations, and sent representatives to all these general conventions. Too much cannot be said in praise
of this useful, influential society of Christian women.
They were ever careful regarding the entertainment of
their missionary, at one time even giving her a special
reception as a mark of their high appreciation of her
services in their behalf.

Virginia made her next stop at D. While this place
has been slow in taking hold of our work it has finally
fallen in line and we all rejoice to see the fruit that
now appears after years of toil and care in that Mrs.
Wm. S. has become so interested in missions as to be
made president of the district and then attended our
National Convention as its representative. Truly "He
that goeth forth and weepeth, bearing precious seed,
shall doubtless come again with rejoicing, bringing his
sheaves with him." Ps. 126: 6. We found a strong
young woman in W. God has used her for several

years to hold our work intact in that town and do some excellent work. This society has ever expressed its gratitude to our missionary in such tangible form that she could not doubt for a moment that they hold her in loving remembrance. The district missionary, Mrs. J. S., accompanied Virginia as far as C., another small town, where she held several meetings, organized the women and left them rejoicing that God had given women something they could do to advance his kingdom.

S. P. is a little rugged mountainous town, beautiful for situation, with the lofty picturesque mountains on the north and the peaceful flowing river on the south. Here Virginia stopped again. She had on overflow meeting at this place. A most graceful introduction was made by a friend who had known her for years, and thus every preliminary for a helpful interesting meeting was provided. The Lord blessed Virginia's effort and a strong missionary society was organized; the work has grown steadily all these years, and is now one of the strongest societies of the Elk River District. Further on the historic city of C. was reached. Here our missionary work and the good women of C. were well prepared for the splendid work they are now doing under the efficient management of the stationed missionaries, whom the W. B. H. M. society has located there. Our missionary has only felt it necessary for her to stop occasionally here, say a word of cheer, and get new inspiration from the reports these dear women are ever ready to render. The W. C. T. U. work of that town demands a part of Virginia's service, and she is always welcome, and will stop as she journeys through the state if only a few hours to meet the sisters associated in this great reformatory work.

Another little town farther east has accepted our work, but little progress has been made from lack of some capable woman to lead. London is a town that must be mentioned because of one faithful woman there who, like the Shunamite woman of old, had a room of her house set apart for God's traveling servants, where they could go at any time and be heartily welcomed. Frequent changes of pastors have kept the church of L. so unsettled that our work has been greatly retarded. The next stop was made in the great city of K. Our churches there accepted the woman's work from its incipiency. Strong workers have been developed. Great results of work done are annually reported by the representatives of our two largest and most progressive churches of that city. These two societies minister largely to the upbuilding of their own churches, to our school in East Tennessee, and to the general organized mission work throughout the district, state and nation. Virginia has so many homes in K. she can rarely ever stay there long enough to satisfy the wishes of those who wish to entertain her. Dear Sister Hamilton, who is a tower of strength for our work throughout the state and nation, is specially noted for her hospitality. The people of God are ever welcome at her home; also at Sister Dobson's. These sisters' kind husbands join heartily with them in caring for God's servants in their lovely houses. The W. C. T. U. of this town is also a power for good and never fails to come at the call of the president to hear any message Virginia may have for them on her annual visits as the president of Tennessee W. C. T. U. No. 2. From the delights and encouragements enjoyed in K., where our work is flourishing, the missionary journeys on to the less favored regions beyond. She only stopped where invitations or instructions warranted a stop. The school at Johnson City is of special interest, accordingly a missionary society and children's band were organized there. The school has already been greatly blessed through these auxiliary bodies. Three mining towns were visited in this section. The missionary found the people attentive and appreciative while she delivered her message to them. They readily accepted our work and gave us substantial encouragement by contributing liberally to our missionary's expenses and taking her literature. At Raven C. the miners entered heartily into the services and sang such sweet songs that our missionary would gladly have tarried long with them. In this trip Virginia learned much of the miners' lives and realized more fully the dangers to which the miners are exposed that we might have the fuel and light necessary to our bodily comfort. God has abundantly provided coal and given man the needed skill to secure it. Let us praise God for this bountiful provision, and pray for the protection of those wno go down into the deep mines to secure it. Truly God is good and his love is beyond our understanding. "He that spared not his only begotten Son, how shall He not with Him also freely give us all things?"

From J. C., in company with Rev. H., the superintendent of state missions, and others, Virginia went to a district association at Flat Woods. A long, tedious journey of many hours' ride through the country, brought us to the place of meeting at eventide. Virginia was a stranger in this section and all were anxious to see her and hear her speech, since she had been so highly recommended to this association by the superintendent. of missions. Accordingly an opportunity was soon given her to speak. She was introduced by Rev. H., whose knowledge of her work enabled him to speak so full and free that every obstacle was removed and greater freedom of speech was never given our missionary before. The Lord used her most

effectively while she gave the Bible authority for
women's mission work. The vast congregation was
held spellbound throughout her discourse. The pastor
of that church was one of the leaders of that district.
Until that time he confessed that he had been a
doubting Thomas with many others of his brethren as
to woman's ability to deliver a Bible message, but he
was then thoroughly convinced and has proven to be
a faithful supporter of our cause throughout that section of country ever since. Virginia made many
staunch friends for our cause and her labors did much
to cement the work of union and coöperation between
the associations of East and West that had been effected by Superintendent H. Rev. Breedlove, a young
man dearly beloved by his brethren for his Christian
zeal and piety, pastored more than a hundred miles
further in the mountains, and he became so interested
in the woman's work as presented by Virginia that
he urged her to come to his church as early as possible.
Consequently a tour of that whole section was planned
for the month of December to be made in company
with the superintendent of missions who had visited
that section before and knew its dearth and hardships.
As the superintendent expected our deprivations began as soon as we left M. One day we had only a few
cents above our railroad fare and that was used to
purchase a little fruit, the superintendent saying, ''We

need some refreshment and what we have will not carry us to another point.'' That often occurs in the missionary's life. Virginia remembers even going to the depot without having enough money to buy her ticket, but the Lord ever provided, ''For man's extremity is God's opportunity.'' Superintendent H. and Virginia arrived in Johnson City late in the evening, and found no one awaiting them, and beside, the church was in a most confused condition, wrangling over the call or discharge of the pastor. After considerable stir and parleying a lodging place was given the missionaries for that night. Virginia attended the services next day and according to her custom took an active part, beginning in the Sunday school at 9 a. m. The unfavorable condition of affairs made this first visit somewhat discouraging, but the missionary society was organized and from subsequent visits and reports that work has grown and developed into one of the strongest societies in the state of Tennessee. God has some female servants in Johnson City, who are truly awakened to their duties as Christians. Their interest and development have been frequently manifest in the substantial support of all the objects of organization. Our missionaries journeyed on to Elizabethton, where Moderator Breedlove resided. He gave them a warm, hearty welcome and although his church edifice had been swept away by a terrific flood, our missionaries held a blessed service in the school house, wnich was packed to its uttermost capacity. God blessed the service with showers of blessings. All rejoiced, sang and praised God, in testimonies, praise, prayer and contributions to the cause. One aged man who lived several miles in the country remained over night and called early next morning to have our missionary pray for him. She was glad God had awakened the dear man, and she prayed and reasoned with him from God's Word as best she could, and then left him with the fond hope that a man who had such faith as was evidenced by that aged brother would be duly rewarded. From this point our missionaries began their return trip. They stopped again at Johnson City where they had been so badly disappointed. The friends made every apology for the coolness of Saturday night's reception, and perfect satisfaction was given. The next stop was made at White Pine, where Rev. Thomas has charge of a flourishing congregation. Rev. T. had failed to make the appointment and only a few persons came out the first night of the meeting, hence the pastor prevailed on the superintendent to tarry a night longer, as our missionaries were so impoverished a good meeting was absolutely necessary unless the pastor could provide some other way for their expenses.

Superintendent H. and the neighbors' children gathered cedar and holly bushes ,the day they tarried in White Pine, and our missionaries made beautiful Christmas wreaths, desiring to carry something to gladden the dear ones at home. Conditions in that section were such that our missionaries counted it a special Providence to get railroad fare to their homes. Superintendent H. made a touching plea for missions in his sermon, and Virginia sang a suggestive hymn and then emphasized the points that were calculated to stir the audience to do their full duty as far as they were able on that special occasion. Pastor Thompson was especially helpful; other help came to the missionaries in their homeward journey. One brother even came to the railroad station and brought a contribu tion he had collected from the Morristown church. These valiant heralds of the cross reached their homes in due season, rejoicing that God counted them worthy to suffer some for his dear Name's sake.

CHAPTER XIII.

Places of Special Interest Visited.

In the last National Baptist Convention that Dr.
Wm. J. Simmons attended in Louisville, Ky., Virginia
spoke on the subject, "The Ideal Woman." Prov.
31: 10-3. With other Bible women she contended for
a woman's separate and distinctive organization in
1890. Dr. Simmons, however, did not approve that
idea because he thought the men and women working
together would do more effectual work. Because of
Dr. Simmons' objection the Kentucky women, who
were then doing a successful educational work, did not
encourage a woman's auxiliary convention, hence the
idea was suspended for that time. A few years later
the idea was again advanced in Atlanta, Ga., in the
historic Baptist church once pastored by Rev. Quarls
(the same place that Spelman Seminary began its
splendid work for girls under the management of
Misses Packard and Giles). There the women agreed
they could do better work through a woman's general

organization, whereupon the Baptist women organized a national woman's convention. The next year when the N. B. convention met in St. Louis, Mo., by the counsel of the brethren, the woman's auxiliary national convention was disbanded and women were placed on the various boards of N. B. C.

In the meantime our faithful missionary with many other good women continued to attend the great annual gatherings of N. B. convention, going to Savannah, Ga., Washington, D. C., and Montgomery, Ala., ever making a plea in defense of woman's work, and seeking encouragement toward a woman's national organization. Finally sufficient encouragement was given through Rev. L. G. Jordan, secretary of Foreign Mission Board of N. B. convention, for a few women to come together in Richmond, Va., in 1900, and effect a woman's convention auxiliary to N. B. convention.

The following officers were then elected:

Mrs. S. W. Layton, Philadelphia, Pa., president.

Mrs. P. J. Bryant, Atlanta, Ga., vice-president.

Mrs. V. W. Broughton, Nashville, Tenn., recording secretary.

Miss N. H. Burroughs, Louisville, Ky., corresponding secretary.

Miss S. C. V. Foster, Montgomery, Ala., treasurer.

These officers have all, except the treasurer, served in their respective offices for the past six years continuously, thus showing the wisdom of the good women constituting our N. B. convention, and also the fitness of the officers for their positions.

An effort was again made in Cincinnati the next year after this organization was effected in Richmond to disband it, but the women took a decided stand to hold their organization intact, and they began earnestly to plan, pray and work to prove the wisdom of their decision. Every year since has brought stronger proof through the unprecedented success attained that we made a wise decision. The Birmingham meeting is memorable, not only for the sad disaster that occurred through the false alarm of fire, but also from the determined and successful effort of our women to build a brick house in Africa for their beloved representative, Miss E. B. Delaney, who had suffered so intensely from two attacks of the fearful

African fever that so many foreigners succumb under. The Birmingham meeting also marked the beginning of a regular course of Bible lessons to be developed by Virginia, who was made educational secretary of the Woman's Auxiliary Convention at that meeting for that special purpose. The course was to be taught by circulation of lesson outlines on topic cards and their exposition in ''The Union,'' the organ of the N. B. convention.

The next annual convention met in Philadelphia, Pa. This meeting was attended with increased interest, marked progress had been made along all lines, unholy ambitions and jealousies also appeared that marred the harmony and peace to some extent. The meeting in Austin, Tex., made a goodly number of friends for the race. One white gentleman, who had resided in the South for a number of years as teacher in one of our institutions, remarked: ''This woman's convention gives me more hope for the race than anything I have witnessed since I came South.'' Even the street car conductors, who are generally uncouth and unkind toward our race in the South, reversed their usual methods and sang the praises of our delegation by saying they had never carried more orderly crowds on their lines. The crowds were truly immense, yet no disturbances of any kind occurred during the five days of our meetings. The great western metropolis, Chicago, Ill., was the next place of meeting for the N. B. convention. This meeting was specially memorable because of the presence of our returned missionary, Miss E. B. Delaney, and the glowing report she brought of her experiences in that dark land. All were touched by her pathetic story and a liberal contribution was given her. Her native boy, Daniel, who had walked several hundred miles through the jungle of Africa to reach the coast and accompany his teacher to America to learn more of her Jesus, also greeted us in Chicago, and added greatly to the interest of our foreign mission work. An industrial exhibit to show the skill of our women in plain and fancy needle work was another special feature of the Chicago meeting, which brought considerable revenue to our treasury. Virginia had the added pleasure of visiting her beloved sisters, Gray and Peyton, in their lovely homes while in the Windy City. Her brother-in-law, Rev. Gray, of whom we have spoken as being so devoted to his sister Virginia, took unusual delight in administering to her comfort and encouraging her interests, both in and out of the convention. Virginia often praises God for the many lovely remembrances and kindly actions of that courageous brother-in-law she delights to call brother William. Her sister Annie's little daughter Lucile was among the first to shake her hand and extend congratulations after her election again as recording secretary. Such little things are among the joys of life that cheer the weary pilgrims on their heavenly way.

The last of these annual gatherings we will refer to convened in Memphis, Tenn. This was the overflow meeting. A large cotton shed was the only available place large enough to accommodate the vast crowds that gathered from day to day. The woman's convention, however, convened in the new spacious audience room of the St. John Baptist Church. The message of cheer and good will extended by Miss M. G. Burdette, representative of W. B. H. M. S., was a special feature of the Memphis meeting. She paid a high tribute to the character of our women in that she said of all the sixty odd women of our race that had served under the commission of W. B. H. M. S. not one had betrayed her trust.

The African exhibit, arranged by Miss Delaney, and the Star Musical Concert, illustrative of native African and American Negroes, were also pleasing features of the Memphis convention. Mrs. J. P. Moore's motherly talk was heartily received, and her testimony to the faithfulness and purity of Negro womanhood, as she knew it from forty years personal contact, as perhaps no other white woman in the world had had, made us feel like taking up the struggle of life anew, and though every outlook be dark and drear we would take the uplook and press onward to the goal.

Virginia has not only served her people as teacher, editor, missionary and officer in benevolent and religious institutions; she has also enjoyed the rare privilege of representing. them in the great Northern Baptist Anniversary meeting in Saratoga, N. Y., and other northern meetings of which mention has been made. Besides these meetings she also had the privilege to represent her sisters and keep the record of a meeting held by the Woman's Missionary Union of the Southern Baptist Convention when it met in Nashville, Tenn., May, 1904. Regarding this meeting, in justice to Virginia, we must say when the press reporter came to take a minute of the proceedings Miss Annie Armstrong, corresponding secretary of the M. U., said to the reporter, "If Mrs. B. (our Virginia) will take the record it can't be improved upon, for she takes the best minutes I ever heard."

The reporter committed his work to Virginia upon the suggestion of Miss A. A. We are pleased to say he reported her record "verbatim, et literatim et punctuation."

Virginia's visits to Tibee Beach, on the Atlantic near Savannah, Ga., and to Atlantic City, N. J., were moments of unusual delight, as those were her first opportunities to contemplate God's glory and might, as seen in the dashing spray of the mighty deep, which the great waves, rolling up and down, dash against the shore and sprinkle those who chance to stand near by. No wonder the Psalmist says: "They that go down to the sea in ships, that do business in great waters, these see the works of the Lord, and his wonders in the deep." The many experiences of travel, though often trying and discouraging to the heralds of the cross are excellent means in God's hands for Christian development. Our sister gained much needed wisdom, courage and faith through these many missionary journeys she has been privileged to make. Time and space forbid us telling any of these experiences in detail and indeed many journeys and incidents as interesting as any herein related are not mentioned at all. God has the record in full, and will give just reward to all who in any way have helped or been helped during these twenty years of Virginia's active missionary life, of which we are giving only a brief sketch.

CHAPTER XIV.

The John C. Martin Bible Movement.

While making a missionary tour through Clarksville and vicinity Virginia met Dr. S. G. Miller, the representative of ''The John C. Martin Educational Fund,'' a new movement that had for its specific object the development of the moral and religious life of our people through the systematic study of the Bible. We do not wonder that Virginia was delighted to learn that God had raised up a man to prosecute the work that she had so long endeavored to encourage as outlined by Miss J. P. Moore's Fireside school plan.

Dr. S. G. Miller, noting Virginia's interest upon a lengthy interview concerning her work and that Mr. Martin was endeavoring to establish, solicited her coöperation and expressed a wish to have her services as lecturer and organizer. When the woman's department was inaugurated, Virginia began to use the

"Bulletin," the organ of this movement in her institute work. From her first month's report which consisted of outlines of sermons, and answers to questions on the month's Bible study, Dr. Miller was so
agreeably surprised to find any Negro woman so well
versed in Bible history, that he wrote her that she
should have the first consideration in appointments
for the woman's department of the Bible institute
work. Accordingly in May, 1905, while attending the
Alabama State Bible Institute, Virginia was appointed lecturer for woman's department of ''The
J. C. Martin Educational Fund.'' Her work was
highly complimented and approved by both the management and the people among whom she labored.
She traveled, lectured and organized women's unions
throughout the states of Tennessee, Arkansas, Alabama, Georgia, Mississippi, North Carolina, South
Carolina, Kentucky and Illinois. These unions were
expected to meet regularly and discuss the Bible lessons of the month as outlined in the Bulletin, and report their work monthly to headquarters.

Our people en masse are so unaccustomed to such
work, lacking the needed training to succeed without
some teacher or leader to constantly stimulate and instruct them that they failed to report as desired, both
the men in their local institutes and the women in
their unions. Hence Mr. Martin decided to transfer

his efforts to our Christian institutions of learning altogether and thus help in the religious development
of the youth of the race upon whom the future of the
race so largely depends. This work added much to
Virginia's experience from the great opportunity given
to visit the schools of people. She is naturally op-
timistic, being often heard to say in meetings, ''Praise
the Lord!'' Her hope for the future of her people
was brightened as she saw the great army of Negro
youth gathered in our schools and colleges throughout this country, under the best instructors, using the
most improved methods of education ever known to
mankind. What may we not expect? Educators have
all realized that they must develop the whole man;
his threefold nature must be developed and so the new
education proposes to help the youth find out all his
possibilities and to prepare him to assert them. The
fact that the Bible is being magnified and made a part
of the regular curriculum of our institutions of learning is chief cause of Virginia's hope for better things.
Any nation is blessed whose God is the Lord, and
those who honor God will be honored of God. The
Psalmist says: ''Thou hast magnified thy word above
all thy name.'' Ps. 138; 2. Surely when the people
of God magnify his word by studying, teaching and
obeying it God's favor will rest upon them. ''No
weapon that is formed against them will prosper. This

is the heritage of the servants of the Lord, and their righteousness is of me, saith the Lord.'' Is. 54: 17.

During Virginia's visits to the schools in the interest of the John C. Martin Bible movement, she visited the A. & M. College, Normal, Ala., of which the distinguished Prof. W. H. Councill is president, a man who has been foremost in contending for the education of his people along intellectual, industrial and religious lines, and for their peaceful and friendly coöperation with the white people of the Southland, among whom they dwell, to make this country bloom and blossom as a rose by developing its rich resources of mineral and agricultural wealth. During her visit to this institution President Councill and his faculty were greatly impressed with Virginia as a most capable and effective Bible teacher. So ere she departed the president asked her to consider the wisdom of returning to Normal should she take up the Bible work as outlined for schools and colleges. Thus the Lord provided for the next step in our missionary's career.

CHAPTER XV.

One Year's Work in the Agricultural and Mechanical

College, Normal, Ala.

In September, 1906, Virginia found herself again engaged in the regular work of the school room in the
A. & M. College, Normal, Ala. She met a friendly,
sociable corps of teachers, all apparently deeply interested and ready for the service as outlined by the
management of the institution and its honorable board
of directors.

The president's zealous labors of more than thirty
years to make the A. & M. College the grand school
it now is have been well rewarded in the success attained and he now lives to enjoy some of the rich
fruits of his early seed sowing. For natural beauty
Normal can scarcely be surpassed. It is situated in
North Alabama upon the south side of one of the
spurs of the Cumberland mountains, which greatly
protect the school buildings from the full force of

the northern winds in winter. The campus is so elevated, situated as it is on the mountain side, that one from this point can view all the surrounding country for miles away. The lights in the city of Huntsville, four miles distant, can be easily seen at night. Beautiful green grass covers the mountain side upon which the buildings are erected as with a carpet of green. Evergreen, shade and fruit trees of various kinds adorn the grounds, and beds of flowers and potted plants appear here and there, adding much to the natural picturesque scenery of Normal. The most careless observer that passes is attracted by this scene or beauty. Two railroad stations are adjacent to the grounds and furnish ample accommodations for the ingress and egress of students. There are fourteen buildings for the work of the institution besides the president's home and four cottages for teachers' families. Much emphasis is placed upon industrial education and all students are given opportunity to learn two or more trades. The literary school furnishes three courses, preparatory, normal and college, and all students are required to take two or more studies for their intellectual training.

Bible study is also emphasized and made a special department of the institution's work. The state, however, makes no appropriation for Bible department. For the lack of some definite support the department is crippled to some extent, as sufficient time cannot be given to fully develop it.

Virginia has found the young people even more interested in their Bible study than she expected, as so few young people have been shown the importance of Bible study as a part of their educational training. Bible class work is somewhat new in many of our schools. "The Students' Bible Course" of "The John C. Martin Educational Fund" has been pursued with blessed results.

Books were secured in November, 1906, and the students entered heartily into the systematic study of "The Life of Christ," as recorded in the Gospels. With this perfect threefold system of education carried on in the A. & M. College, Normal, Ala., under the management of that excellent leader of men, President W. H. Councill, and his able corps of teachers, our youth are compelled to be prepared for the arduous duties of life that await them.

Virginia entered into the inner life of the school at once; she was made superintendent of the Sunday school at the beginning of the school year, supervisor of the Y. W. C. A. and Bible teacher in the Normal and College Departments, while Rev. Dr. Brooks gave Bible lessons two days of each week to the entire school. In November Virginia was given the entire class work of Bible study throughout the school. She was thus enabled to come in close touch with all the young people and help them in their religous life. Blessed privilege! She believes many have been led to appreciate the beauty and loveliness of the true Christian life; several have accepted Jesus as their personal Savior and have begun to testify of his love and join heartily in the work of the public religious services. Many can be depended upon to present a creditable exercise for a religious service whenever requested. Special Bible instructions have been given to those aspiring for the ministry and missionary work, thus enabling our young ministers to give the school several practical, theoretical and acceptable ser- mons at the Sunday morning services, the principal church service of the day. Much attention is also given to elocution and music as complements to the more solid and arduous work of the Institution. Every class in its respective order presents a weekly rhe- torical program. Honorable rivalry exists that causes the classes to vie with each other for excellence in these weekly exercises. There are also four literary societies, the Peabody, Douglas, Adelphic and Phyllis Wheatly. Each Friday evening one of these literary societies entertains the school with an excellent pro- gram of a literary and musical character. The social side of life is also given its share of consideration. Occasionally a social is tendered the student body.

One of special interest was given in November as a reward to the students for faithful service in aiding the farm manager to gather the cotton from the fields, when help could not be secured for love nor money. The students volunteered their services and went to the fields in large numbers and soon had all the cotton gathered. The teachers or Normal have a "Round Table," a social and literary meeting, every two weeks, and thus every one is kept busily engaged in art and science, both theoretical and applied; in literature, profane and sacred, ancient and modern, and music, both vocal and instrumental, according to their respective adaptabilities and capabilities. The Bran Band, under the efficient direction of Prof. L. W. Hammond, was a great success this year. In short, Normal A. & M. College is a regular beehive of humanity, and the king bee is sure to drive out all drones if for no other reason that self-defense.

Thanksgiving Day, Christmas, Emancipation Day, Washington's birthday and Easter were all appropriately celebrated at Normal, with helpful instructive and inspiring exercises.

Prof. W. S. Peyton introduced several healthful amusements in the line of sports on Thanksgiving Day. As interest grows in this feature of college life, it is hoped the baseball team of Normal will be prepared to contest successfully with the teams of any of our southern colleges.

A standing committee, representing the various colleges from which the teachers graduated, namely, Dr. Annie B. Marsh, A. & M. College; Mrs. V. W. Broughton, Fisk University; Prof. W. S. Peyton, Lake Forest; Miss M. G. Gibson, Tongaloo; Mrs. C. B. Hamilton, Wilberforce; Miss F. T. Johnson, Walden; Mrs. H. M. F. Archer, Niagara Falls, was appointed to arrange programs for all special occasions. Hence much praise is due said committee for the excellence and suggestiveness of the programs for each of the special occasions referred to. Vice-President Hopkins, who largely had the management of the school in hand this year, owing to the impaired health of President Councill, was found to be most genial and courteous, ever ready to relieve and assist the teachers in their arduous duties, being made arduous because of the small teaching force provided for the work to be done. Prof. Hopkins' years of experience in the school room enabled him to do the work in the class room whenever necessary, as well as do the more responsible work of directing the entire work of the institution.

Virgina counted herself favored to be associated with such a corps of faithful teachers in this particular school year of 1906 and 1907 for many reasons, one especially she would mention, namely: Led by

President Councill with a liberal donation these associated teachers and students of A. & M. College donated a large per cent of the expense of her trip abroad, whither she was delegated by the Woman's Convention Auxiliary to N. B. Convention to attend the World's International Sunday-school Convention. This trip prevents her closing the year's report in full. She will leave her unexpired term to be filled by her daughter, Mrs. E. B. Sykes, if she is required to supply a substitute. The commencement alone remains unreported.

CHAPTER XVI.

Songs and Texts of Special Significance in Virginia's Twenty Years' Experience.

Virginia says she has no special gift to sing, but she does have the spirit of praise, and God has taught her many lessons through songs. A few of which we will record in part, giving their special significance to her:

"How firm a foundation, ye saints of the Lord,
Is laid for your faith in his excellent word;
What more can he say than to you he hath said,
You who unto Jesus for refuge have fled?"

All of this beautiful song, of which we quote one verse, was given Virginia in her call to mission work, hence her devotion to God's Word. As the years have passed by she has been able to see every phase of that song realized in her many experiences, and today her faith mounts up, as if on eagle wings, and causes her to rejoice, whenever that song is sung.

"O, for a closer walk with God,
   A calm and heavenly frame;
A light to shine upon the road
   That leads me to the Lamb."

This song was given as a spur to urge her on her first missionary trip from her home city. She verily needed help, for the trip must be made up the Mississippi river by boat, and Virginia was fearful to take it and would have doubtless given it up had not the dear Lord cheered and urged her forward through the above song and the following message:

"God is on the water as well as on the land."

She clearly saw her need of a closer walk with God would she do the work committed her! On a certain occasion a request was sent to the missionary training class of the Bible and Normal Institute by a very sick man that the Bible women come pray for him. Virginia made known the request to the class and secured a promise from five of the sisters to accompany her to the sick man's home. The following song of triumph was given her the morning of that day the visit was planned. The song thrilled and

filled Virginia's soul so that she was humming it all
the day and thus prepared for effective service:

"O, thou God of my salvation,
My redeemer from all sin,
While the angel choirs are singing,
Glory to the Great I Am,
I with them will still be vying,
Glory, glory to the Lamb!
Soul and body, soul and body,
Shall thy glorious image bear."

The visit was made in the afternoon. The sisters
all prayed, God's word was explained and God's presence was manifest to the edification of all present,
and the conversion of the sick man. Ere the sisters
could make a second visit, as they planned to do,
death had borne him to the world beyond, but he left
us the glorious message that he was going to live with
Jesus and ever be with his Lord.

On another occasion when the opposition was high
and enemies were raging and plotting against us
Virginia had an appointment in the country. Before
leaving her home a heavy rain storm came up, which
she was considering sufficient excuse to defer the appointment. Then the Lord gave her this suggestive
song:

"Ye Christian heralds go proclaim,
Salvation in Emanuel's name;
To distant climes the tidings bear,
And plant the rose of Sharon there.
He'll shield you with a wall of fire,
With holy zeal your heart's inspire,
Bid raging waves their fury cease
And calm the savage breast to peace."

This was enough. Virginia well knew at this time
her Master's voice when he spoke to her in song. So
she arose and took her journey. She passed safely
o'er rough, muddy country roads, through one
place particularly that evoked exclamations of praise
because in that mud hole a mule had recently mired
and died before he could be extricated. This trip was
especially blessed of the Lord; the enemies were
silenced, God protected his servant and enabled her
to strengthen the dear women of that section for the
fight that was then upon them.

The following is another song of special significance:

"A charge to keep I have,
　A God to glorify,
A never dying soul to save,
　And fit it for the skies.

"And can I yet delay,
　My little all to give?
Oh, may it all my powers engage,
　To do my Master's will."

Early in Virginia's missionary career she had much of the Jonah spirit and was loath to break away from her many society and home ties and make the sacrifices necessary to sucess of her work. At a certain time she went out to Stanton to hold a meeting and then purposed to go on to a point far removed from the railroad station. When Brother S. came to town for her he informed her the church was expecting a distinguished brother, Rev. M. Vann, to preach at the time of her appointment. She, desirous of returning home, said: "Very well, I can't afford to lose the time and if Brother Vann comes I'll return home." When the train came Rev. Vann did not appear, so there was no alternative. Virginia was obliged to go. She had scarcely begun her tedious journey through county, in the regular road wagon, with its plain board seat without springs, when this song, "A charge to keep I have," came ringing in her soul; it was with her all the way, then in the family prayer service that Saturday night she sang that song twice and not until Sunday, when she began the church service, was its significance made clear to her, which was this: God had given her a charge and that special service was hers to conduct and no other could do her work; so the expected brother, who was then superintendent of Tennessee state missions, was providentially hindered that Virginia might get the lesson she needed and become settled as to the fact that God had really given her a work to do that could be done by no other.

As the mission work grew and it became necessary for Virginia to give up her school work at a lucrative salary and give herself wholly to developing the missionary work of our women it was somewhat of a struggle to give up a substantial, sure support to engage in a work of faith, with no visible means of support.

Finally the struggle ended and Virginia sweetly surrendered. About this time one afternoon when she had just completed the reading of her Bible through, which she has made a custom for many years, and was rejoicing o'er the blessedness of that study the following song came rushing upon her:

"Jesus paid it all,
Yes, all the debt I owe,
Jesus died and paid it all,
Yes, all the debt I owe.

Jesus paid it all,
All to him I owe,
Jesus died for all mankind,
Jesus died for me."

With the song the following text was given: "He that spared not his own Son, but delivered him up for us all, how shall he not with him also freely give us all things?" Rom. 8: 32. This message could not be mistaken; she knew it meant that she give up the school room for the sacrificial life of the mission- ary; whereupon she surrendered and trusting Him who called her she went forth to do his will as best she could, as revealed to her from time to time by the Holy Spirit, in song or word.

Soon Virginia found herself in Texarkana, Ark., whither she had gone to assist Miss J. P. Moore establish the Bible Band work in connection with the Baptist Women's State Missionary and Educational work. The brethren of that state did not accord Virginia a cordial welcome at that time, but rather opposed and criticised her aggressive movements in church work. As a special comfort and encouragement to her, also significant of the fact that it was her business as well as privilege to praise the Lord all the day long, since she had given up every other vocation for the special work whereunto God had called her, the following song was given:

"Blessed assurance, Jesus is mine,
Oh, what a foretaste of glory divine,
Heir of salvation, purchase of God,
Born of his Spirit, washed in his blood,
This is my story, this is my song,
Praising my Savior all the day long."

To her agreeable surprise, through the influence of Mrs. H. R. Traver, Virginia found on her return home a commission from the W. B. H. M. S. of Chicago, Ill., appointing her as missionary for western Tennessee with headquarters at her home in Memphis.

Thus God provided for the temporal support of his servant, who went out at his command, relying upon his sure word of promise.

Virginia was lost in Washington, D. C., one time. She had misplaced her sister's directions and was a considerable time locating her. While in this dilemma the following song brought a thrill of joy to her soul and enabled her to continue her search courageously until the desired residence was reached:

"Amid the trials which I meet,
Amid the thorns that pierce my feet,
One thought remains supremely sweet,
Thou thinkest, Lord, of me,
Thou thinkest, Lord, of me, of me.
What need I fear when thou art near,
And thinkest, Lord, of me!"

The jubilee melodies

"Steal away to Jesus,"

"Swing low, sweet chariot,"

"Keep inching along, like a poor inch worm,"

were often sung by Virginia with healthful effect.

The following song was given as means of triumphing o'er assurance of victory:

"I have precious news to tell,

Hallelujah!

Christ has come with me to dwell.

Hallelujah!

By his power and love divine
He has cleansed this soul of mine,
And he whispers, I am thine.

Hallelujah!

Hallelujah, I'm redeemed,
Oh, so wondrously redeemed.
I'm rejoicing night and day,
As I walk the narrow way,
For He's washed my sins away.

Hallelujah!

The 150th Psalm was her battle song in her great conflict, when persecuted for her faith in the Bible doctrine of sanctification.

Virginia was strengthened and prepared to receive the sad intelligence of her brother John's departure from this life by the following hymns:

"I would not live always,
I ask not to stay.
The few lurid moments that dawn on us here
Are enough for life's sorrows, full enough for its
  cheer."

"Death has been here and borne away a brother
  from our side."

We might continue this narrative of suggestive sacred songs that God has used so lovingly and effectively to cheer, inspire and direct our missionary as she labored in his cause these twenty years. Those given are sufficient evidence of the powerful influence of song in this eventful life of our missionary.

We shall now give a few texts and outlines that God has enabled Virginia to use effectively:

Bible authority for women's work. Text, Gen. 2: 18.

(1) Woman's creation.

    (a) Made of refined material.

    (b) Man's helpmeet.

    (c) Man incomplete without woman.

(2) Marriage ordained of God.

    (a) Woman, mother of all being.

    (b) Hope of man's restoration. Gen. 3: 15.

    (c) Woman's help indispensable in the home, as man's comforter and the trainer of children.

(3) Woman as helpmeet in business. Illustrations: Deborah, Esther, Ruth, Lydia.

(4) Woman as helpmeet in church.

    (a) As teacher. 2 Kings 22: 14. Acts 18: 26.

    (b) As hostess to care for God's servants. II Kings 4: 10. I Kings 17: 15.

    (c) As missionaries. Acts 9: 39. Rom. 16: 1.

(5) Called of God to service.   Eph. 2: 1-10

    (a) All believers one in Christ. Gal. 3: 28.

    (b) All required to work according to respective gifts. I Cor. 12: 7. Matt. 25: 14, 15.

(6) Appeal to women to develop themselves and prepare for service.

    (a) Bought by blood of Jesus to serve. I Cor. 6: 20.

    (b) Rewarded according to works. Rev. 22: 12.

    (c) Developed through excess of gifts. I Tim. 4: 13-15.

    (d) Growth commanded of God. 2 Pet. 3: 18.

Christian Work.   Text, John 9: 4.

(1) Jesus' declaration.

    (a) What his work was.

    (b) Took delight in his work.

    (c) Finished his work.

(2) Individual work required.

(a) No discharge from service.

(b) All supplies furnished, strength, wisdom, grace. Jas. 1: 5. Phil. 4: 19.

(c) Work indicated by one's natural gifts and adaptability. Illustrations: Peter, Paul, Mary, Dorcas, Lydia.

(3) Time to work specified.

(a) Delay dangerous.

(b) Night of death sure.

(c) Joy comes when work is finished.

(4) Rewarded according to work. Rev. 22: 12.

(a) Faithfulness rewarded. Matt 25: 21, 23.

(b) Love to Christ should be constraining force.

Christian Growth. Text, II Pet. 3: 18.

(1) Why should I grow?

(a) God commands it.

(b) Growth essential to law of spiritual life as well as physical.

(c) To have strength for service.

(2) How can I grow?

(a) By feeding upon God's word, spiritual songs and prayer.

(b) By living in a healthful atmosphere (having proper associates).

(c) By active service.

(3) For what purpose should I grow?

(a) God's glory.

(b) Good of humanity.

(c) Personal edification and usefulness.

"Call to Service." Text, John 11: 28.

(1) Jesus calls a woman.

(a) A prepared woman. Lu. 10: 39.

(b) She loved Jesus supremely. Mark 14: 3.

(c) She anointed Jesus for his burial.

(2) An imperative need.

(a) Women in trouble. John 11: 1.

(b) Send for Jesus.

(c) Required to move stones. John 11: 39.

(d) Divnie power manifest to do what man could not do. John 11: 42-44.

(3) Effect upon Mary and Martha.

   (a) Martha served without complaining.

   (b) Mary expressed her love by her precious gift.

   (c) Many Jews believed.

(4) Application to women of this age.

   (a) Troubled about many things.

   (b) Opportunities of service. Jesus' means of help.

   (c) Women should seize every opportunity given for their development.

   (d) Results already obtained from efforts of awakened womanhood.

Victory of the Cross. Texts, Rev. 11: 15. Heb. 1: 13.

(1) All power given to Jesus.

   (a) Conquest assured. Ps. 2: 8.

   (b) Everything already subject to Jesus. Heb. 2: 8. Illustrations from mineral kingdom. Is. 14: 16. Vegetable kingdom. Mark 11: 20.

In animal kingdom Bible gives illustrations from tiniest insects to king of beasts, showing all things created are subject to God.

(2) Gospel dispensation.

(a) Man's opportunity to share in the glory here after to be manifest.

(b) Christ's service man's highest privilege.

(c) Man called to put on the whole armor of God for the conflict. Eph. 6: 10-19.

(3) Soldiers of Christ fight with assurance of victory. I Cor. 9: 26.

(a) Our captain a victor. John 16: 33.

(b) Through faith we too shall conquer. ,

(c) Faith the victory that overcomes the world. I John 5: 4.

(4) They that overcome will reign with Jesus. Rev. 2: 26; 3: 21.

"Power of Holy Spirit." Text, Acts 1: 8.

(1) Promised to all believers. Acts 2: 4.

(a) Sent on day of Pentecost. Acts 2: 4.

(b) Disciples waited for evidence of Holy Spirit before they began their work after the resurrection. Acts 1: 14.

(c) Not alone for Apostles but for all believers. Acts 2: 39.

(2) Holy Spirit given on condition.

(a) Surrender of self. Gal. 2: 20.

(b) Willingness to serve. John 7: 17.

(c) Obeuience to commandments. John 14: 15, 16.

(3) Holy Spirit manifest.

(a) In consecrated living. Gal. 2: 20.

(b) In effective service. Is. 6: 6-8.

(c) In developing Christian character. Acts 3: 8-13.

(d) In producing fruits of the Spi..*. ꝯal. 5: 22, 23.

(4) Christian life a failure without the nuiy Spirit.

(a) Man unable to overcome temptation without aid of Holy Spirit. I Cor. 10: 13.

(b) Salt without savor good for nothing. Matt. 5: 13.

(c) God's will revealed by Holy Spirit. I Cor. 2: 10.

(5) Plea to Christians to seek the Holy Spirit's power.

(a) God willing to give. Lu. 11: 13.

(b) Can't please God without Holy Spirit's power. Rom. 8: 8.

(c) Carnal mind not subject to God's law. Rom. 8: 7.

(d) Walk in Spirit and you will not fulfill the lust of the flesh. Gal. 5: 16.

An Open Door. Text, I Cor. 16: 9.

(1) Paul's opportunity.

(a) To preach to Gentiles. Acts 14: 27.

(b) He entered heartily upon his work.

(c) Opposition met and overcome. Acts 14: 19, 26.

(2) Applied to Negro women.

(a) Opportunities **or** open doors to serve great. Race to uplift. Beginning in the home.

(b) Professions and schools of all kinds open to women.

(c) Responsibilities **in** proportion to opportunities.

(d) Woman's Christian organizations great means of development.

(3) Appeal to use given opportunities.

(a) Present results spurs to greater effort.

(b) Some results mentioned. Rescue homes, orphanages, homes for aged, reforms in home life, kindergartens, temperance societies, and charitable organizations of all kinds have begun to be established and fostered since women have begun to enter the doors of usefulness open to them.

(c) The gospel is being encouraged and sent to the ends of the earth through the generous support of good women.

(d) Negro women have evidently come to the kingdom for such a time as this. Esther 4: 14. Negro men's hearts are failing before the ruthless hand of oppression and persecution of all kinds and if our nation is encouraged and saved from the fiery furnace through which it now passes Negro women like Esther of old must take the case to the King of kings and by her prayers and tears plead for their deliverance.

(e) In the encouragement given these sisters in black by their more favored white Christian sisters the light begins to dawn and we are nerved for the fray.

(f) Enter the open doors for the judge of all the earth will do right.

Praise. Text, Ps. 150: 6.

(1) God is a jealous God.

(a) He desires manifest expressions of love. Illustration, Lu. 19: 40.

(b) Praise evidence of a conscience void of offense. Ps. 51: 12, 13.

(c) A sad countenance not a good inducement to lead sinners to Christ.

(2) Praise is comely for the upright. Ps. 33: 1 147: 1.

(a) God has done so much for them. Ps. 138: 8.

(b) Hope for future so bright. I Cor. 15: 57.

(c) God is pleased to have his people praise him. Ex. 20: 3.

(d) Praise Him, for his mighty acts; his excellent

greatness; his boundless love; his tender mercies.
Ps. 136.

(3) How shall we praise Him?

(a) With a life of cheerful service.

(b) In songs of praise, words of testimony and
fervent prayers of thanksgiving.

(c) With stringed instruments and all other kinds
of musical instruments. Ps. 150.

Then shall the earth yield her increase and God,
even our God, shall bless us.

O praise the Lord, all ye nations, praise him all ye
people.

For his merciful kindness is great toward us and the
truth of the Lord endureth forever. Praise ye the
Lord. Ps. 117.